"This radiant treatise is an absolutely essential contribution to contemporary foundational literature on psychotherapy unification and to significant directions of evolution that are taking shape in psychotherapy integration. Marquis's unifying system of psychotherapy is sophisticatedly comprehensive in conceptual composition and scope, boundless in implications for psychotherapeutic practice, and liberatingly potent in ramifications for clinical research. His unifying formulations have the potential to be transformative. Whether you are a psychotherapy theorist, practitioner, researcher, and/or trainer, you will find much to chew on in this remarkable volume; enjoy the feast—it is a cornucopia of riches."

—**Jack Anchin, PhD,** clinical associate professor, Department of Counseling and Clinical Psychology, Medaille College and University at Buffalo, State University of New York

"It is time for a paradigm shift in counseling and psychotherapy. Andre Marquis has more than met the challenge with his brilliant *Integral Psychotherapy*. He does a fine job with traditional theory and shows us how to integrate this with modern work in developmental theory and neuroscience. I commend this book as we move to a new era in the helping professions."

—**Allen E. Ivey, EdD, ABPP,** distinguished university professor (emeritus), University of Massachusetts, Amherst

"Andre Marquis's latest volume, *Integral Psychotherapy*, provides a pivot point for psychotherapeutics and clinical science. Introducing the reader to a new paradigm based on integral psychotherapy, Marquis systematically walks readers through the evolution of psychotherapy toward his unifying framework for conceptualizing and treating psychological disorders. Marquis convincingly draws from converging sources to portray a metatheoretical framework that is conceptually clear and offers unparalleled clinical utility for practicing clinicians. This volume is a must read for all mental health professionals."

—**Jeffrey Magnavita, PhD, ABPP,** CEO and founder of Strategic Psychotherapeutics™, LLC, past president of The Society for the Advancement of Psychotherapy (2010)

"This is a book that will stimulate even readers who may, like me, have questions about the sharp distinction drawn between integrative and unified approaches or the level of abstraction at which the metatheoretical project pitches its efforts. Marquis offers us a comprehensive and scholarly exploration of the issues, with relevance for research, theory, and clinical practice. This book is an important contribution to the literature of unified psychotherapy."

—**Paul L. Wachtel, PhD,** distinguished professor, City College of New York and CUNY Graduate Center

"Marquis's distinctive integral psychotherapy creatively and coherently integrates many approaches that span the gamut from empirically supported and time honored to postmodern, from experiential psychodynamic and cognitive behavioral to existential and developmental constructivist. However, at the core of his approach are person-centered empathy, genuineness, positive regard, and compassion. The principles Marquis elaborates—for example, the importance of balancing support and challenge—are immensely practical, not only to beginning mental health professionals but also to seasoned therapists."

—**Howard Kirschenbaum, EdD,** professor emeritus and former chair, Department of Counseling and Human Development, Warner Graduate School, University of Rochester, author of *The Life and Work of Carl Rogers*

"Andre Marquis's *Integral Psychotherapy* clearly evidences a prodigious amount of work undertaken to move the field of psychotherapy closer toward a comprehensive, if not yet unified, perspective. Dr. Marquis's use of the AQAL model is a unique advance in assessment with its emphasis on internal and external views of both individual and systems dimensions. *Integral Psychotherapy* builds another promising rung on the ladder toward a unified perspective on psychotherapy."

—**Barry E. Wolfe, PhD,** founding member of the Society for the Exploration of Psychotherapy Integration (SEPI), Sarasota, Florida

Integral Psychotherapy

Integral Psychotherapy lays out a conceptual framework for understanding and applying the wide range of psychotherapeutic approaches. The unifying model presented here addresses the dynamics of healthy human development, the assessment process, techniques and processes of therapeutic change, and much, much more. Beginning as well as experienced mental health practitioners will find the integral approach to be an exquisitely parsimonious model, one that allows practitioners and researchers to retain their own style and preferences, while simultaneously organizing ideas within a more comprehensive framework for understanding human beings and the psychotherapeutic process.

Andre Marquis, PhD, is associate professor of counseling and human development at the Warner Graduate School, University of Rochester. He is a licensed mental health counselor in New York with a small private practice. Marquis has authored/co-authored *The Integral Intake, Theoretical Models of Counseling and Psychotherapy,* and *Understanding Psychopathology.* He serves in editorial roles for the *Journal of Psychotherapy Integration,* the *Journal of Unified Psychotherapy and Clinical Practice,* and the *Journal of Integral Theory and Practice,* and is on the advisory board of the Unified Psychotherapy Project.

Integral Psychotherapy

A Unifying Approach

Andre Marquis

Routledge
Taylor & Francis Group
NEW YORK AND LONDON

First published 2018
by Routledge
711 Third Avenue, New York, NY 10017

and by Routledge
2 Park Square, Milton Park, Abingdon, Oxon, OX14 4RN

Routledge is an imprint of the Taylor & Francis Group, an informa business

© 2018 Andre Marquis

The right of Andre Marquis to be identified as author of this work has been asserted by him in accordance with sections 77 and 78 of the Copyright, Designs and Patents Act 1988.

All rights reserved. No part of this book may be reprinted or reproduced or utilised in any form or by any electronic, mechanical, or other means, now known or hereafter invented, including photocopying and recording, or in any information storage or retrieval system, without permission in writing from the publishers.

Trademark notice: Product or corporate names may be trademarks or registered trademarks, and are used only for identification and explanation without intent to infringe.

Library of Congress Cataloging-in-Publication Data
A catalog record for this book has been requested

ISBN: 978-1-138-96151-7 (hbk)
ISBN: 978-1-138-96152-4 (pbk)
ISBN: 978-1-315-65092-0 (ebk)

Typeset in Minion
by Keystroke, Neville Lodge, Tettenhall, Wolverhampton

Dedication

I dedicate this book to Ro.

I could not be more grateful for the loving brother, best friend, and ecstatic companion in life that he is. Deeply spirited, enthusiastic, loving, compassionate, generous, understanding, and hilarious, he amplifies the meaning and enjoyment of my life.

Contents

Foreword by Jack Anchin	xi
Preface	xix
Acknowledgments	xxv

Part I. Unifying Psychotherapy: Context and Theory

1	Setting the Context: From Single Schools, Eclecticism, and Integration to Unification	3
2	Integral Metatheory and Integral Psychotherapy: A Model of Interrelationships	19
3	Developmental Dynamics and States of Consciousness	39
4	The Development of Psychopathology: An Integral Perspective on the Etiology of Anxiety Disorders	74

Part II. Treatment

5	Assessment in Integral Psychotherapy: The Integral Intake	109
6	An Integral Taxonomy of Therapeutic Interventions: The Role of Interventions in Integral Psychotherapy	131
7	Principles of Treatment in Integral Psychotherapy	155
8	An Integral Perspective on the Treatment of Anxiety Disorders: An Example of Integral Psychotherapy Treatment	184

Part III. The Role of Research and Conclusion

9 The Methodological Tower of Babel: Integral Methodological
   Pluralism in Psychotherapy Research   **209**

10 **Conclusion**   **228**

Appendix: Integral Culture, Spirituality, and a Category Error   232
References   237
Index   257

Foreword
Jack Anchin

I begin the writing of this Foreword with full disclosure: time spent thinking about "What does it *mean* to unify approaches to psychotherapy?" has inevitably led to my developing a working formulation in response to this question. I think it important that I share this conception with you, since, from the word "go," it has influenced my reading of and reactions to the volume that you hold in your hands. As stated elsewhere (Anchin, 2008),

> to my way of thinking, unification in psychotherapy means the development of a *singular* paradigm that pulls together and interrelates, in one organizing theoretical framework, all of the major accumulating elements of knowledge pertaining to personality, psychopathology, and psychotherapy. Moreover, such a framework, operating as a unifying paradigm, would fundamentally guide how we think about and conceptualize the wealth of phenomena pertinent to psychotherapy, how we scientifically study those phenomena, and how, in the domain of practice, we apply the products of those efforts and synthesize them with the principles, procedures, and processes of psychotherapy. (p. 312, italics in original)

Very much to the good, developments in unified thinking over the past decade have brought forth a variety of conceptions as to the essential conceptual structure and composition of an effective unifying paradigm for psychotherapy (e.g., Critchfield, 2017; Harris & Ingram, 2017; Henriques, 2011; Magnavita & Anchin, 2014; Millon & Grossman, 2008; Smith, 2017). By the same token, there is no shortage of irony in the fact that a diversity of views about how to unify therapeutic approaches is emerging, a circumstance that speaks the truth to Mahoney's (2008) wise entreaty to avoid premature foreclosure in any area of study. Clearly, we are a long way from establishing a consensually agreed upon unifying paradigm—the desirability of which is itself open to vigorous debate.

Stepping into this context of healthy ferment is the radiant treatise you hold in your hands. Succinctly stated, *Integral Psychotherapy: A Unifying Approach* constitutes an absolutely essential contribution to contemporary foundational literature on psychotherapy unification, and thus inseparably to conversations on significant directions of evolution taking shape in the field of psychotherapy integration.

The system of psychotherapy Marquis articulately details is rooted in Ken Wilber's integral theory (Marquis & Wilber, 2008), a wide-ranging, intricate, and consequential (see Esbjörn-Hargens, 2010) biopsychosocial-developmental-spiritual theory about human being, and becoming, across the entirety of the lifespan. As crucially underscored by Marquis, integral theory is more accurately characterized as *metatheory*, a point to which I return momentarily. In ways that illuminate and educate, Marquis details integral concepts and propositions essential to his distinct unifying formulations, while throughout injecting core integral theory with clinically and empirically based elaborations, revisions, and extensions. The upshot is a unifying system of psychotherapy that at one and the same time is sophisticatedly comprehensive in conceptual composition and scope, boundless in implications for psychotherapeutic practice, and liberatingly potent in ramifications for clinical research.

Understanding the metatheoretical character of Marquis' integral approach to treatment is pivotal to appreciating its fertile ontological, epistemological, and practical implications. That which is meta—for example, metacognition or metacommunication—transcends itself by reflecting on and constructing meanings about itself. Thus, metacognition is cognition about cognition—a process illustrated by a patient stepping back and critically assessing the accuracy of a specific belief she holds about herself. Metacommunication is communication about communication—as when co-interactants openly share and discuss their perceptions, thoughts, and feelings about what is going on between them. Correspondingly, metatheory is theory about theory, a category jump implicitly founded on the claim that, relative to a given phenomenon, there exist enough theories and associated bodies of knowledge about this phenomenon, in enough areas that compose its territory, to justify formulation of a broader theory—one that incorporates but transcends these different specific theories and knowledge bases by knitting them together into a unifying narrative.

Marquis' integral metatheory bursts forth as exquisitely suited to serve these purposes vis-à-vis the mind-boggling plurality of knowledge elements generated by the theory, research, and practice of the major contemporary psychotherapy paradigms. At the epicenter of integral metatheory lies the AQAL ("All-Quadrants, All-Levels") model, an illuminating ontological and epistemological framework with striking capacities to systematically bring together, in a shared framework of understanding, multiple domains of thick knowledge pertaining to personality, psychopathology, and psychotherapy.

The quadrant model is constructed from the intersection of two dimensions ineluctably woven into the fabric of what it means to be human—the individual–collective and interior–exterior dimensions of existence. Each of these dimensions has scholarly bona fides. The individual–collective dialectic has been captured by a number of different conceptual vocabularies, for example agency and communion (Pincus, Lukowitsky, & Wright, 2010), self-definition and relatedness (Blatt, 2008), attachment, separation, and exploration (Bowlby, 1988), and the relational matrix (Mitchell, 1988). All of these speak to the centrality of a person's dual existence as both an individual and a member of social/interpersonal collectives, as well as to the inextricable interconnectedness between these two complex worlds. The interior–exterior dimension rests securely on an epistemic foundation that claims the legitimacy of both internal-qualitative-phenomenological and external-quantitative-observable types of knowledge and ways of knowing (e.g., Creswell, 2013; Polkinghorne, 1983).

The interpenetration of the interior–exterior dimension and the individual–collective dimension creates a 2 × 2 matrix, yielding four quadrants—essentially, perspectives—that can be brought to bear in one's psychotherapeutic work: fundamentally, knowing and understanding an individual and her social systems from the inside and from the outside. Taking only a minute here to look over Figure 2.1 (p. 22) will provide you with a sense of this quadratic framework's ontological and epistemological richness, amplified by the proposition that in real time the four quadrants are mutually constitutive and continuously interactive in reciprocal and multidirectional fashion. Developmental stages, levels, and dynamics also figure prominently in integral metatheory's account of personality, psychopathology, and mental health, as do a number of specific constructs—for example, lines, types, states, and the self-system. I leave it to Marquis to guide you through the conceptual and clinical meanings of these differentiating dimensions and the nature of their relationships to the quadratic model; there is much to learn, and Marquis teaches well. Suffice it to say, the integral metatheory he fashions provides a coherent, holistic scaffold for identifying, organizing, and interrelating the enormous array of individual and social/collective internal and external structures and processes that compose human ontological complexity. The framework's descriptive and explanatory power is amplified when one considers that the disordered human biopsychosociality we treat, and the health we seek to promote, are fostered and maintained through webs of interaction among these quadratically defined structures and processes, transpiring over variable time-spans.

Applied to the psychotherapeutic arena, integral metatheory translates into an incredibly nuanced, individually tailored approach to treating psychological disorder and its associated pain and suffering. Importantly, you will not find in Marquis' integral psychotherapy (iPT) new therapeutic interventions and techniques, nor will you be provided with highly operationalized stepwise prescriptions for "how to do" iPT. Rather, as Marquis makes clear, iPT is foremost a *sensibility*—in Marquis' words, a guiding "attitude that fundamentally keeps one open to numerous perspectives ('listening on many channels') rather than explicitly dictating specific interventions."

A sensibility may seem ineffable, but in the present case this is not so. Marquis crystallizes key elements of an integral sensibility in the form of principles designed to help therapists orient, in integral fashion, to the patient and the therapeutic work. I offer here some examples to impart something of their flavor: Be attuned to and nurture the multiple levels of the patient's being—body, mind, and spirit, understanding that "spirit" is definable in religious, spiritual, and/or secular ways. As a therapist, bring not only your mind but also your *heart* to the process of healing. In accord with the AQAL model, be mindful of the patient's complexity, and throughout assessment and treatment translate this awareness into attunement to clinical data pertaining to all quadratic dimensions and developmental dynamics and to their dynamic interplay, all in the service of forging understandings of breadth and depth faithful to this complexity. In a similar vein, be prepared to shift among quadrants as you and the patient collaboratively work on the distinct distressogenic issues and problems in living that have led him to seek psychotherapy. Further, given their determinative and continuously interactive influence on the patient's well-being, seek to cultivate healthy processes within and across all four quadrants. And crucially, contextualize, contextualize, contextualize. These and other principles discussed by Marquis provide not only pathways for bringing an integral sensibility to treatment but also edifying pearls of clinical wisdom.

None of this is to suggest that therapeutic interventions and techniques are unimportant in iPT. Indeed, a *fundamental raison d'être* for unified therapeutic approaches is to bring conceptually coherent order to the plurality of interventions developed by the major therapeutic paradigms to facilitate therapists' access to, and utilization of, the full armamentarium of clinical methods available for fostering enduring therapeutic change. In synch with this essential unifying objective, Marquis deploys the quadratic framework to establish and elucidate a comprehensive taxonomy of therapeutic interventions, classifying each of 200 interventions, at the broadest level, within the particular quadrant each most prominently targets. He attains still greater specificity, however, by nesting the selected interventions in each quadrant within the three different levels of body, mind, and spirit, creating a four-quadrant, three-level scheme for classifying therapeutic interventions.

Marquis' taxonomy is brimming with practical and heuristic value. Clinically, it presents to therapists the eye-opening diversity of techniques and interventions available for promoting different dimensions of therapeutic change. In so doing, it also provides a tool that can facilitate intervention selection processes as a function of the patient's particular needs, issues, defenses, developmental level, treatment goals, and so forth. On a different score, therapeutic interventions are applied expressions of a given psychotherapy theory's key concepts about maladjustment and psychopathology—and though often more implicit, they also speak to the theory's conceptions about the nature of psychological health. Consequently, inquisitively reading through and reflecting on different interventions in each quadrant can build and advance descriptive and explanatory knowledge about the granular, structural, and processual composition—and by implication multicausality—of psychological disorder and health.

Marquis' provision and elaboration of recommendations for how to use the taxonomy with a given psychotherapy patient further enhances its clinical utility. Complementing these recommendations, principles of treatment in iPT, alluded to above, in conjunction with principles of human change processes, provide further guidance for understanding the infrastructural rationale of an "integrally informed" psychotherapy and for its real-time clinical actualization. In the context of this material, the reader gains insight into key conceptual and procedural components of Marquis' personal approach to iPT, a creative integration of psychodynamic, existential-experiential, and developmental-constructivist perspectives whose conceptual and clinical emphases include the patient's in-session moment-to-moment states, the importance of emotion, the consequent prominence of affective "state work," and the vital role of mindfulness and centering exercises. By the same token, reflecting the concept of balance that is fundamental to the ethos of integral metatheory and iPT, Marquis offers a thoughtful caution against the idolatry of techniques, and in this context voices a relational theme that reverberates throughout the volume: of *paramount* importance, develop a genuine, deeply caring connection with your patient; prize empathy, compassion, and emotional safety. Marquis thus brings home the now broadly recognized "therapeutic truth" that, while techniques and the therapeutic relationship can be conceptually and linguistically disentangled, in real time they are "inter" (interconnected, interactive, and intertwined) in every sense.

The conceptual and clinical breadth and depth brought to the therapeutic enterprise by integral metatheory and Marquis' distinctive iPT is unequalled among contemporary unifying approaches to psychotherapy. Still and all, it faces an immense challenge shared by all such approaches: How does one go about empirically investigating the processes and outcomes of a therapeutic approach that knits together all the major psychotherapy paradigms in an overarching framework composed of metatheoretical constructs and propositions? Marquis intrepidly tackles this question in his keenly scholarly chapter "The Methodological Tower of Babel: Integral Methodological Pluralism in Psychotherapy Research." Recognition of the desirability of bringing multiple epistemologies and their methodological translations to the arena of psychotherapy research is becoming increasingly mainstream (see, e.g., American Psychological Association, 2006; Castonguay et al., 2015).

However, given the multiperspectival nature of integral and other unified approaches to psychotherapy, methodological pluralism in studying unification is an irrefutable must. Marquis advances this effort by shining a high resolution light on specific epistemic and methodological issues involved in systematically studying unified psychotherapies, in the process defining and dialectically bridging dichotomies that, historically viewed in "either–or" terms, have impeded both the maximal pursuit of knowledge and the richness of understanding that can derive from synthesizing bodies of knowledge. Marquis' integral methodological pluralism uniquely contributes to the unificationist research agenda by elucidating the manner in which the quadratic model, in its individual–collective and internal–external perspectives, systematically organizes and interrelates diverse epistemologies and research methodologies.

It is critical to point out here that Marquis has also significantly forwarded unified psychotherapy research by putting the rubber to the road. His Integral Psychotherapy in Practice project includes an innovative series of mixed-methods single-case studies (Marquis & Elliot, 2015; Marquis et al., 2015) investigating how a group of therapists experienced in applying integral metatheory actually implemented integral constructs and principles over a full course of therapy with a given patient. In each case, the therapist under study practiced in accord with her or his distinct integration of two or more of the traditional theoretical orientations (e.g., psychodynamic, cognitive-behavioral, and so forth). At the broadest level, the findings revealed that the therapists' respective integrative theoretical orientations were essential to how they worked with their patient, and that throughout treatment integral metatheory facilitatively guided significant clinical processes in identifiable ways (e.g., evolving conceptualizations, treatment foci, and interventions selected as treatment unfolded). This finding and its specifics are meaningful in their own right, but as the first systematic investigations demonstrating that a unifying metatheoretical approach to psychotherapy is researchable, these are also landmark studies. The Integral Psychotherapy in Practice project also provides a prototypic exemplar of the scientist–practitioner interplay fluidly in action: placing (meta)theoretical concepts and propositions of a specific therapeutic approach under the microscope of systematic empirical scrutiny, deriving specific findings, and, as Marquis details in material to come, revising substantive elements of his clinical theory and methods on the basis of those findings. Two questions also pose themselves: Are we looking here at evidence-based practice or practice-based evidence? Or perhaps some of both?

In concluding, I share with you that, in the richness of its content and in its capacity to stretch the mind, *Integral Psychotherapy: A Unifying Approach* reminds me of Gregory Bateson's (1972) timeless *Steps to an Ecology of Mind*. The metalevel thinking required to understand Bateson's concepts and, inseparably related, the continuous exposure to and hence cultivation of systemic forms of thinking as one reads Bateson's work can foster a depth and breadth of thinking that endures. I believe that Marquis' unifying formulations have the potential to be similarly transformative in their impact on how you think about and go about your psychotherapeutically related activities. Whether you are a psychotherapy theorist, practitioner, researcher, and/or trainer, you will find much to chew on in this remarkable volume; enjoy the feast—it is a cornucopia of riches.

References

American Psychological Association Presidential Task Force on Evidence-Based Practice (2006). Evidence-based practice in psychology. *American Psychologist, 61*, 271–285.

Anchin, J. C. (2008). Pursuing a unifying paradigm for psychotherapy: Tasks, dialectical considerations, and biopsychosocial systems metatheory. *Journal of Psychotherapy Integration, 18*, 310–349.

Bateson, G. (1972). *Steps to an ecology of mind*. New York: Ballantine Books.

Blatt, S. J. (2008). *Polarities of experience: Relatedness and self-definition in personality development, psychopathology, and the therapeutic process*. Washington, DC: American Psychological Association.

Bowlby, J. (1988). *A secure base: Parent–child attachment and healthy human development.* New York: Basic Books.
Castonguay, L. G., Eubanks, C. F., Goldfried, M. R., Muran, J. C., & Lutz, W. (2015) Research on psychotherapy integration: Building on the past, looking to the future. *Psychotherapy Research, 25,* 365–382.
Creswell, J. W. (2013). *Research design: Qualitative, quantitative, and mixed methods approaches.* Thousand Oaks, CA: Sage Publications.
Critchfield, K. L. (2017, June). An Interpersonal Reconstructive Therapy lens on teaching the conceptual skills needed for integrative decision-making in unified psychotherapy. In A. Marquis (Chair), *Applying unified metatheories of psychotherapy to training integrative decision-making skills.* Symposium conducted at the 33rd Annual Meeting of the Society for the Exploration of Psychotherapy Integration, Denver, CO.
Esbjörn-Hargens, S. (2010). Introduction: Integral theory in action. In S. Esbjörn-Hargens (Ed.), *Integral theory in action* (pp. 1–22). Albany, NY: SUNY Press.
Harris, J. E. & Ingram, B. L. (2017, June). *Using a unified psychotherapy framework to guide clinical decision-making through case formulation and treatment planning.* Mini-workshop conducted at the 33rd Annual Meeting of the Society for the Exploration of Psychotherapy Integration, Denver, CO.
Henriques, G. (2011). *A new unified theory of psychology.* New York: Springer.
Magnavita, J. J. & Anchin, J. C. (2014). *Unifying psychotherapy: Principles, methods, and evidence from clinical science.* New York: Springer Publishing.
Mahoney, M. J. (2008). Power, politics, and psychotherapy: A constructive caution on unification. *Journal of Psychotherapy Integration, 18,* 367–376.
Marquis, A. & Elliot, A. (2015). Integral Psychotherapy in Practice Part 2: Revisions to the metatheory of integral psychotherapy based on therapeutic practice. *Journal of Unified Psychotherapy and Clinical Science, 3,* 1–40.
Marquis, A., Short, B., Lewis, J., & Hubbard, S. (2015). Integral Psychotherapy in Practice Part 3: Three case studies illustrating the differential use of metatheory in informing unified treatment. *Journal of Unified Psychotherapy and Clinical Science, 3,* 41–79.
Marquis, A. & Wilber, K. (2008). Unification beyond eclecticism: Integral psychotherapy. *Journal of Psychotherapy Integration, 18,* 350–358.
Millon, T. & Grossman, S. D. (2008). Psychotherapy unification. *Journal of Psychotherapy Integration, 18,* 359–372.
Mitchell, S. A. (1988). *Relational concepts in psychoanalysis: An integration.* Cambridge, MA: Harvard University Press.
Pincus, A. L., Lukowitsky, M. R., & Wright, A. G. C. (2010). The interpersonal nexus of personality and psychopathology. In T. Millon, R. Kreuger, & E. Simonsen (Eds.), *Contemporary directions in psychopathology: Scientific foundations for DSM-V and ICD-11* (pp. 523–552). New York: Guilford.
Polkinghorne, D. (1983). *Methodology for the human sciences: Systems of inquiry.* Albany, NY: SUNY Press.
Smith, J. (2017, July). Are we there yet? Theoretical convergence, part I. *Integrative Therapist, 3* (3), 16–19. Retrieved from www.sepiweb.org/?page=news_about.

Preface

This book aims to show how psychotherapists can draw upon multiple, perhaps all, domains of knowledge—from neuroscientific, behavioral, cognitive, biophysical, developmental, and systemic to psychodynamic, existential-humanistic, cultural, and spiritual—in order to more comprehensively understand and more effectively counsel the patients[1] who seek our help. As a psychotherapist, educator, supervisor, researcher, and theorist, I have strived to understand how to integrate research findings and other forms of knowledge from different disciplines and different therapy approaches that are not only apparently contradictory, but often hostile to one another. As Prochaska and Norcross wrote, "a healthy diversity has deteriorated

---

1 As I have written elsewhere:

> Even though many nonmedical mental health professionals (counselors, counseling psychologists, social workers, etc.) have been taught not to use the term "patient" because it is associated with the medical model, the word *patient* is etymologically derived from the Latin *patiens*, which means *one who suffers*; in contrast, the etymology of the word *client* refers to *one who is dependent on another*, as with a peer-contractor or consumer of expert services (Partridge, 1958). I think it is worthwhile for mental health professionals to consider using the word *patient*, rather than *client*, while also being clear that this does not imply that patients are necessarily "sick" or "disordered." Paraphrasing Sadler, being a patient implies a certain woundedness, and words such as *client* or *consumer* are poor fits for this: "*client* and *consumer* aren't simply inappropriate terms; they are dehumanizing; they make a human existential need more closely akin to a desire for a business transaction, placing health care in the ethos of conspicuous consumption" (2005, p. 144). This is the spirit in which I use the word "patient." For more on the patient–client distinction, see Sadler (2005, pp. 142–144). (Ingersoll & Marquis, 2014, p. 535)

into an unhealthy chaos. Students, practitioners, and patients are confronted with confusion, fragmentation, and discontent" (2003, p. 2).

I hope this book demonstrates not only the relevance of a vast array of theoretical, empirical, and practical/clinical perspectives, but also how they interrelate and complement one another, forming something of a unified whole. Such a unified perspective is important because, without it, therapists and researchers view humans in fragmented ways that fail to honor their complexity and multidimensionality. If therapists systematically devalue, deny, or ignore some aspects of human experience—whether cultural, experiential, environmental, cognitive, biological, or spiritual—there is no way they can be maximally helpful to the full diversity of patients who seek their services. Thus, I will provide the reader with an elegant framework that fosters holistic, comprehensive, and effective conceptualizing and therapeutic intervening.

Psychotherapy scholars are increasingly emphasizing unifying, metatheoretical models as the future of psychotherapy (Henriques, 2011; Magnavita & Anchin, 2014; Wolfe, 2008; Millon & Grossman, 2008; Marquis & Wilber, 2008). With an excess of 1000 "named" psychotherapies, therapists need a conceptual framework capable of organizing and providing a systematic way to understand the plethora of extant psychotherapeutic approaches. A mature unifying model must be capable of addressing—with coherently interrelated constructs—issues that span from dynamics of healthy human development, the assessment process, and the development of psychopathology to pertinent methodological research issues and the processes and techniques of psychotherapeutic change (Magnavita, 2006; Henriques, 2011; Marquis, 2013). The integral model (Wilber, 2000a) is capable of addressing all of the above with only a handful of constructs, and that is what this book does. As such, it will integrate theory, research, and practice and is written for practitioners, scholars, students, and researchers in the fields of mental health (clinical and counseling psychology, counseling, psychiatry, marriage and family therapists, and clinical social workers). Although a few other books have addressed such unifying, comprehensive models of psychotherapy (i.e., Magnavita & Anchin, 2014; Henriques, 2011), the integral approach does so in a different way. With its exquisitely parsimonious model, integral psychotherapy (iPT)[2] is capable of both assimilating and accommodating the entirety of psychology and psychotherapy while also allowing each practitioner or researcher to retain her own style, preferences, and previous training and expertise; simultaneously, the integral framework organizes all of the aforementioned within a coherent framework for understanding human beings and the psychotherapeutic process. I want to emphasize that this book is more of a skeletal framework than a fully fleshed out, complete unifying model (I am not sure if the latter is even possible). Thus, this book is a working *toward* unification; *in no way am I proposing the final word on what integral or unified psychotherapy is*. This book will also overview the

---

2 The "i" is lowercase in iPT to distinguish it from interpersonal psychotherapy (IPT).

most recent research on iPT, which has necessitated the revision of some iPT principles.

As an approach that attempts to embrace, bridge, and balance the major systems of psychotherapy as well as important insights from biological science, neuroscience, sociology, philosophy, and various (often contemplative) spiritual traditions, iPT offers a powerful way of conceptualizing human nature that simultaneously appreciates the formidable constraints of one's genetic makeup and early formative experiences while refusing to foreclose on the possibilities of transcending one's struggles and limitations. In short, iPT honors body, mind, and spirit (our highest capacities and virtues, not necessarily religious) as expressed in self, culture, and nature; what this means will be discussed throughout the book.

My research, teaching, and professional practice have all been informed by the agenda of developing and *applying* a metatheoretical framework capable of integrating and lending coherence to the vast numbers of theoretical schools, research methodologies, and practical interventions that pertain to counseling and psychotherapy. I have tried to strike a balance so that this book will be useful to both beginning therapists and graduate students, as well as seasoned professionals and psychotherapy scholars.

So that I do not have to continually make qualifications throughout this book, I want to emphasize that the integral psychotherapy that I am describing here is my personal and ever-evolving perspective; although it has been deeply influenced by Ken Wilber and others, some of my views are not necessarily shared by Wilber or all who identify as integral psychotherapists.

To be precise, what I practice is "integrally informed psychotherapy" but I will primarily use the term "integral psychotherapy"—because of how it "reads" and "comes off the tongue"—throughout this book. Please remember that iPT is not actually a discrete, prescriptive approach, but rather one *informed* by integral metatheory; this point will also be discussed in more detail throughout the book. Also, it may be relevant for the reader to know that I have practiced only in outpatient settings (various clinics and private practice), *mostly* with patients suffering from depressive disorders, anxiety disorders, personality disorders, and substance-related disorders as well as those struggling with everyday—but not insignificant—relationship distress and other "problems of living." In other words, I have not worked extensively with people with psychoses, antisocial personality disorder, or organically impaired or brain-injured individuals.

This book includes both new, original chapters along with adaptations of previously published works of mine, some of which appeared in professional journals that are not linked to psycINFO, ERIC, and other databases (and thus are not easily accessible to those who may be interested in this topic). In order to contextualize the emergence of iPT, chapter 1 provides a primer on the evolution of psychotherapy—from the many decades of single-system ("pure-form") approaches, to the emergence of eclecticism and integration, and finally to unified approaches to psychotherapy.

Chapter 2 introduces readers to the integral framework and its principle constructs: the four quadrants (which represent the intersection of two sets of contrasts: interior/exterior and individual/system), developmental dynamics (stages, states, and lines), personality types, and the self-system. In particular, the relevance of quadratic and developmental considerations to both clinical practice and psychotherapy research will be highlighted. For example, the quadratic model of integral theory posits that disparate aspects of people and their circumstances—from one's neurobiology and felt-sense of selfhood to cultural worldviews and social systems—are all critically influential to one's well-being or suffering, and therefore should be given thoughtful, considered attention in psychotherapy. Similarly, the "spectrum model" of integral theory spans from the earliest stages of human development to "the farther reaches of human nature" and informs the clinical decisions required to effectively treat people with conditions as distinct as psychosis, borderline personality disorder, and mild depression or adjustment disorder. An understanding of this chapter is essential to a deeper appreciation of all the subsequent chapters, which presume a working knowledge of integral metatheory.

Chapter 3 departs significantly from much of the previous iPT literature. A (if not *the*) central construct in Wilber's writings (i.e., 1999) and other iPT literature has been the importance of how a patient's developmental stage status should inform the specific therapeutic approach for that given patient. Consistent with the extant iPT literature, this chapter discusses the constructs of levels and lines of development, and how they are critically important to understanding human psychological development. However, based upon recent research of iPT (Marquis & Elliot, 2015), patients' developmental "center of gravity" (the developmental stage around which a person hovers, and which is best captured by their level of ego development; Loevinger, 1976) appears less *clinically* relevant than patients' moment-to-moment states of consciousness (i.e., affective, self-, or defensive states). Thus, this chapter overviews pertinent developmental dynamics (i.e., levels and lines) but emphasizes the critical importance of prioritizing the matching of therapeutic interventions to where a patient is in the moment, rather than what a standardized developmental assessment of their ego development suggests. I am aware that, being fundamentally theoretical, chapters 1–3 are fairly abstract. Please bear with them; the remaining chapters are much more concrete and applied. For those readers who are most interested in treatment applications, chapters 6, 7, and 8 could be read after chapter 2.

Given the significance of understanding the etiology and development of psychopathology for any model of psychotherapy—whether single-system, integrative, or unified—chapter 4 addresses the affordances offered by an integral perspective on this topic. Because I recently co-authored a book on this topic that exceeded 600 pages (Ingersoll & Marquis, 2014), I here focus only on anxiety disorders. I chose to focus on anxiety disorders not only because they are among the most prevalent of mental disorders, but also because many psychotherapy scholars (i.e., Barlow, 2004; Fosha, 2000; May, 1977; Wolfe, 2005; Yalom, 1980) have posited that a deeper understanding of them would shed light upon most other mental disorders. Etiological risk factors are surveyed by quadrant. The Upper-Right quadrant includes evolutionary, genetic, physiological, neuroscientific, and behavioral perspectives. The Upper-Left and Lower-Left quadrants include cognitive, existential, spiritual, attachment theory, and contemporary psychodynamic perspectives. The Lower-Right quadrant includes the role of family (parenting styles, child abuse and other trauma, role inversions) and larger social/systemic structures that are etiologically implicated in anxiety disorders.

Chapter 5 begins with a brief overview of some general assessment foundations and then demonstrates how to comprehensively assess patients in an idiographic manner. The chapter overviews several research studies that have examined the clinical utility of the Integral Intake (Marquis, 2008) as well as how integral psychotherapists actually use it to assess their patients and how it impacts the therapy they provide (Marquis, 2010).

Chapter 6 addresses the role of techniques and interventions in iPT. Given that therapists are confronted with literally hundreds of interventions to potentially utilize in their clinical practice—and a growing chasm separating research and practice—how do therapists decide which interventions to use with a given patient? This question is both epistemological in nature and immediately tied to practice. This chapter includes a figure that classifies more than 200 therapeutic interventions according to the "All-Quadrants, All-Levels" model of iPT, followed by a critical discussion of the clinical utility of such a taxonomy. The chapter ends with suggestions regarding how to use the integral taxonomy of therapeutic interventions with psychotherapy patients, the role and meaning of interventions, an algorithm describing how the interventions were classified, and a caution against the "tyranny of technique."

Given that iPT is guided by principles rather than rules, chapter 7 provides a host of principles that inform my practice of iPT. A brief overview of Mahoney's (1991) views of human change processes is provided, followed by a discussion of how integral theory informs treatment decisions, including conceptualizing and intervening by quadrant, the role of explicit theory and implicit/procedural knowledge, and the clinical relevance of patients' states of consciousness. Attention then turns to Wilber's thesis that awareness is the basic principle of therapeutic change, and amendments to that view are offered, including the vitally important role of emotions in the therapeutic process, as well as how to work with patients' defenses and resistance. The chapter concludes with the distinction between "integral psychotherapy" and "integrally informed psychotherapy" and suggests a reprioritizing of core iPT constructs in clinical practice.

Chapter 8 picks up where chapter 4 left off, addressing the treatment of anxiety disorders from an integral perspective. It begins with a brief overview of assessment issues relevant to patients with anxiety disorders, followed by general treatment goals and principles for this population. The chapter then surveys treatment approaches by quadrant: from behavioral, pharmacological, family systems, and the need to address a host of inequitable social systems to cognitive, contemporary psychodynamic, existential, spiritual, and integrative approaches such as Barry Wolfe's.

Chapter 9 begins with a brief overview of the long-standing controversies regarding the methods and processes used to study psychotherapy; it then considers various methodological issues pertinent to how psychotherapy—including a unified psychotherapeutic approach that is guided by a metatheory—can be systematically studied. The currently fragmented state of psychotherapy is reviewed, and attempts at unification are suggested as a solution to this problem. The epistemological disparities of different research paradigms are examined, including the role that one's methodology plays in constraining the types of questions asked and thus the types of answers one is likely to find (Cronbach, cited in Anchin, 2008). Alternatives to empiricist-quantitative methodologies are considered, highlighting the need for methodological pluralism, and one specific form of this—integral methodological pluralism—is outlined. For those who are particularly interested in epistemology and research issues, you may want to read chapter 9 immediately after chapter 2. Chapter 9 addresses not only research issues; it also adds a few layers of complexity to integral metatheory that were not addressed in chapter 2 (i.e., the eight "zones" that represent the inside and outside of each of the four quadrants).

Chapter 10 concludes the book by reflecting upon some of the most salient current perspectives on iPT as a metatheory for guiding counseling and psychotherapy, as well as the implications and challenges for practice that this approach presents. It reminds readers that this is an evolving approach that will continue to be developed and refined toward its ultimate goal of enhancing the effectiveness of psychotherapy for as many patients as possible. It also emphasizes a core tenet of this book: that people are complex and multidimensional; they inhabit different developmental worlds and their suffering derives from a multitude of causes, ranging from their neurobiology, lack of positive reinforcement for adaptive behaviors, maladaptive cognitions, being emotionally under- or over-regulated, to the choices they make and a host of unhealthy familial and sociocultural dynamics and inequitable social arrangements. If this is true, then therapists need to conceptualize and practice in a manner that brings together such multidimensionality; iPT facilitates this. The integral framework offers a parsimonious set of conceptual tools that facilitates an enhanced capacity to perceive and attend to phenomena spanning multiple dimensions and domains, and such attention to a wider range of data engenders more holistic, comprehensive, integrated, and unified treatment to better serve the needs of each unique person.

What I am here attempting is a daunting challenge, and you, the reader, will decide how successfully I have accomplished my aims. In writing a book that covers so many domains, I am unlikely to do complete justice to all of the detailed specifics of some of the approaches I attempt to unify. Like other books on unified psychotherapy (i.e., Henriques, 2011; Magnavita & Anchin, 2014), this book is about the forest more than the individual trees. I hope the reader will forgive me when I fail to do justice to the many important trees in the forest of psychotherapy. I am also aware of the multitude of professional books that you could choose to read and sincerely appreciate that you have chosen to read this one; I hope that you find it worth your time and attention.

Acknowledgments

I could not have written such an ambitious book without the help of many people and organizations. I would like to thank the Society for the Exploration of Psychotherapy Integration (SEPI), as well as their *Journal of Psychotherapy Integration* (*JPI*), for providing a forum for a rich cross-fertilization of ideas from many different perspectives—and for welcoming presentations and articles on the topic of unification in psychotherapy. SEPI and *JPI* were where I first met Jack Anchin and Jeffrey Magnavita, the co-founders of the *Journal of Unified Psychotherapy and Clinical Science*, a wonderful journal that I am proud to have published in; they have both been encouraging supporters of my work and I am very grateful to both of them. I want to thank Jeffrey for spearheading the Unified Psychotherapy Movement, and for introducing me to Gregg Henriques—a kindred spirit both professionally and personally. Gregg, Jack, and Jeffrey are among the most intelligent, "big thinkers" I have ever known, and they are also tremendously enjoyable to "hang out" with. I want to extend my thanks to the three psychotherapists who participated in my multi-year Integral Psychotherapy in Practice study: Sarah Hubbard, Janet Lewis, and Baron Short; my views of iPT have been significantly influenced by the years we regularly met to discuss their cases, their filmed sessions, and what it means to practice iPT. I also am grateful to Ari Elliot for his systematic qualitative and quantitative analyses for the Integral Psychotherapy in Practice study and his co-authorship of one of its manuscripts, from which I drew for several chapters of this book.

As the reader will encounter throughout this book, my views of psychotherapy have been more deeply influenced by Michael Mahoney than any single person; I continue to be grateful for his wisdom, love, and friendship. This book would not be possible without the original thinking of Ken Wilber, the founder of integral theory. Although I do not agree with a few aspects of Wilber's work, I am deeply indebted to him for his powerful and parsimonious AQAL model, which serves as the metatheoretical framework for all of this book and most of my professional work; thank you, Ken. I extend a warm-hearted thank you to Jack Anchin, Jeffrey Magnavita, Barry Wolfe, and Scott Warren for taking the time to review an earlier manuscript of this book; their feedback was invaluable and improved the product you are holding in your hands. Of course, I take full responsibility for any errors found within these pages. I would also like to express my appreciation for my colleagues at the Warner Graduate School of the University of Rochester, especially Kathryn Douthit and Raffaella Borasi. I am deeply appreciative of my editor, Anna Moore and her assistant Nina Guttapalle, for their openness to this book, their flexibility as I reorganized chapters from my original proposal, their competent professionalism, and their prompt responses to my many questions; they are a true pleasure to work with! Last but not least, I am grateful for my parents, my brother Ro, my "dog-son" Nelson, and my wife Erica Crane for their continued love, support, patience, friendship, and love of life.

PART I

Unifying Psychotherapy

Context and Theory

CHAPTER 1

Setting the Context
From Single Schools, Eclecticism, and Integration to Unification[1]

Introduction

In order to contextualize the emergence of integral psychotherapy (iPT),[2] I will provide a brief primer on the evolution of psychotherapy—from the many decades of single-system ("pure-form") approaches, to the emergence of eclecticism and integration, and, finally, unified approaches to psychotherapy. Until the latter part of the twentieth century, most psychotherapists were "purists" who practiced a single-therapy system, such as psychoanalysis, behaviorism, or person-centered therapy. In fact, rivalry and sectarianism characterized the different single-school psychotherapies for most of their history (Norcross, 2005a).[3] Given that differing schools of psychotherapy commonly incorporated knowledge and methods from diverse disciplines such as medicine, the natural and social sciences, and even philosophy and literature, it is particularly ironic that most therapists were ignorant of, or even hostile to, alternative psychotherapeutic systems. Gradually, a growing dissatisfaction with single-school approaches led many to begin seeing how they could enhance their effectiveness and efficiency by learning from other approaches (Norcross, 2005a), and indeed there are many different approaches to learn from.

Jumping to the present, there are now more than 1000 differently named psychotherapies (Garfield, 2006), but the majority of these are more variations on a handful of themes than genuinely novel approaches (Magnavita & Anchin, 2014). Of significance, very little research demonstrates the consistent superiority of one single-school approach or intervention over the others; examples to the contrary—such as the superiority of exposure approaches for specific phobias—are far more

---

1 Parts of this chapter are adapted from Marquis, A. (2015). Integrative therapies: Overview. In E. S. Neukrug (Ed.), *The encyclopedia of theory in counseling and psychotherapy* (pp. 546–552). Thousand Oaks, CA: Sage Publications.
2 The "i" is lowercase in iPT to distinguish it from interpersonal psychotherapy (IPT).
3 Even more concerning is that "To no small extent, a tribal mentality continues to exist among adherents to different theoretical orientations, whose different esoteric language systems contribute significantly to fractionation continuing to plague the field" (Magnavita & Anchin, 2014, p. 6).

the exception than the norm.[4] Given this situation, and because they perceive the limits and drawbacks of practicing solely within the parochial confines of any of those single school approaches to outweigh the benefits that such "pure form" therapies have to offer, the majority of English-speaking therapists have reported practicing eclectically or integratively for the last three decades. A review of a dozen recent studies in the United States revealed that eclecticism/integration is the most common therapeutic orientation (Norcross, 2005b), with some studies reporting 90% of therapists espousing an eclectic or integrative position (Norcross, Karpiak, & Sanotoro, 2005; Marquis, Tursi, & Hudson, 2010). Many current students of counseling and psychotherapy find it hard to believe how intolerant the preceding generations of therapists were of theories and interventions of approaches other than their own.

Context: From Single Schools, Eclecticism, and Integration to Unification

In 1950, John Dollard and Neal Miller significantly moved psychotherapy beyond single-system thinking by recasting psychoanalytic therapies in the concepts and language of behaviorism, which resulted in modifying traditional psychoanalytic technique. Frederick Thorne's work in the late 1950s is often considered the inauguration of eclecticism in counseling and psychotherapy, and a decade later Arnold Lazarus articulated a comparatively comprehensive technical eclecticism. In the early 1970s, Jerome Frank initiated what would become the common factors approach with his classic *Persuasion and Healing*; in it, he argued that change in psychotherapy involves *a healing setting* in which a special form of a *trusting, safe, emotionally charged relationship* is cultivated in which *therapeutic rituals*, which are based upon a sound *theoretical rationale*, occur. A few years later, Paul Wachtel authored the classic theoretical integration of psychoanalysis and behaviorism. In 1980, Sol Garfield and Marvin Goldfried published key integrative works (Norcross & Beutler, 2007). A thorough account of the developmental history of eclectic and integrative thinking can be found in Goldfried (2005).

Since the founding of the Society for the Exploration of Psychotherapy Integration in 1983, five different integrative approaches—each with numerous different subtypes—have been developed and are now well-established: eclecticism, common factors, theoretical integration, assimilative integration, and metatheoretical integration (the latter is involved with unified psychotherapies); these will be described in more detail subsequently. Integrative therapies consist of a broad range of approaches that are not confined by single-therapy systems. Although the variety of integrative psychotherapies is quite diverse, all of them share a similar goal—that of transcending a "one size fits all" mentality and incorporating manifold

---

4 And even in these relatively rare cases, the empirical literature is lacking with regard to how to help the approximately 50% of phobic patients who are not effectively treated with exposure-based interventions (Wolfe, 2005; Barlow & Wolfe, 1981).

ways of conceptualizing and intervening so that the applicability, effectiveness, and efficiency of psychotherapy is enhanced (Norcross, 2005a). Reflecting the steady growth of scholarly conceptual, clinical, and empirical work on integrative treatment approaches, the *International Journal of Eclectic Psychotherapy* was published from 1982 to 1986 and then changed its name to the *Journal of Integrative and Eclectic Psychotherapy* (published from 1987 to the present); the *Journal of Psychotherapy Integration* has been published from 1991 to the present; and the *Journal of Unified Psychotherapy and Clinical Science* has been published from 2012 to the present.

Eclecticism

Eclecticism, a common form of integration, includes technical eclecticism and systematic eclecticism. The eclectic practitioner attempts to provide a specifically tailored treatment for each individual and her specific issues. The determination of the treatment approach is guided not by theory, but by research and/or what has been beneficial in previous work with similar patients with similar problems; for this reason, its foundation has been described as "actuarial," rather than theoretical (Norcross, 2005a). Technical and systematic eclecticism evolved as a response to concerns pertaining to the haphazard nature of *un*systematic eclecticism (or syncretism); the former involves utilizing techniques derived from a theory other than one's own guiding theory, which affords the therapist an expanded and flexible technical repertoire that is drawn from the empirical literature. A limitation of eclectic approaches is their failure to provide a coherent (theoretical) rationale for *why* one uses specific treatments in one case but not in another, which is why they are considered more "actuarial" than "theoretical." Exemplars of eclecticism include the respective psychotherapeutic systems developed by Lazarus (2003), Norcross (1986), and Beutler and Clarkin (1990).

Common Factors

Followers of the common factors approach, the "commonians," argue that a significant percentage of the effectiveness of the different counseling approaches is due to what those diverse approaches have *in common* with one another, in contrast to their unique, specific differences. This position is corroborated by numerous meta-analyses of psychotherapy outcome studies that demonstrate that as little as 10–15% of patients' improvement is due to the specific interventions or single-school approaches to which many therapists hold allegiance (Asay & Lambert, 2003; Norcross, 2011). Some of the common factors that appear to be therapeutic to patients are: empathy; warmth; congruence; receiving feedback from the therapist; being helped to understand their problems; being encouraged to practice facing those things that disturb them; having the opportunity to speak to an understanding person; being helped to understand themselves; the personhood of the therapist; and the Hawthorne effect (people often improve due to having special attention devoted to them). Overall, the commonians believe that the most helpful forms of therapy will emphasize those elements that are common to all, or most, forms of psychotherapy—while also acknowledging and implementing theory-specific, unique interventions as needed. Limitations of the common factors approach include its failure to adequately answer the following questions: How does one systematically organize patients' reports and conceptualize patients' dynamics? How does one identify the specific goals of therapy? And what aspects of patients (thinking, feeling, behaving, relationships, culture, systems, etc.) should therapists emphasize? Moreover, like eclectic approaches, common factorists lack a systematic rationale for their counseling different individuals differently. Exemplars of common factors approaches to psychotherapy integration include the various therapeutic systems developed by Frank (1982), Garfield (2003), Beitman (2003), Wampold (2001), and Hubble et al. (1999).

Theoretical Integration

Theoretical integration has been characterized as both the most important and sophisticated integrative approach as well as overly ambitious; the latter is asserted because most theoretical approaches contain philosophical assumptions that are incompatible with other approaches. The theoretical integrationist attempts to *synergistically integrate the theories* of two or more single-system psychotherapeutic approaches, along with their associated interventions. Although it is usually impossible to integrate the totality of different systems, essential components of different theories can be *synthesized* into a new, internally consistent, coherent structure that differs from either of its constituent parts. The primary limitation of theoretical integration is that it tends to integrate only two or three of the multitude of approaches, many of which appear impossible to theoretically integrate due to incompatible philosophical assumptions. Exemplars of theoretical integration include the respective therapeutic approaches of Wachtel (1977) and Ryle (1990).

Assimilative Integration

Assimilative integration involves therapists who—while being firmly grounded in a single, preferred psychotherapy approach—include and incorporate (assimilate) interventions or perspectives from other approaches (provided that they do not contradict the premises and intentions of one's "home theory") into their preferred mode of theory and practice. If you recall Piaget's descriptions of assimilation and accommodation, you will recognize that this approach does not require therapists to fundamentally alter the theoretical conceptualizations of their "home theory"; this represents the primary limitation to this approach: "few have discussed the modifications in one's home theory that are made necessary by the successful application of techniques generated by another therapy orientation ... The examples of assimilative integration thus far published have tended to reinforce one's commitment to one's flawed home theory" (Wolfe, 2001, pp. 126–127). Exemplars of assimilative integration include the respective psychotherapeutic systems developed by Messer (2003), Safran (1998), and Stricker and Gold (1996).

Metatheoretical Integration

Metatheoretical integration is the most appropriate category for approaches such as transtheoretical therapy, integral psychotherapy, developmental constructivism, and the approaches of Henriques (2011) and Magnavita and Anchin (2014); although integral psychotherapy and developmental constructivism were once categorized as integrative, they are more properly conceived of as unified approaches (it is worth noting that metatheoretical integration and unification are not completely synonymous; technically, the former is a method for achieving unification). In simplest terms, a metatheory is a theory about theory (Magnavita & Anchin, 2014). "Meta" refers to that which is beyond, transcending, or more comprehensive. Thus, metatheories are theoretical frameworks of a more comprehensive order—at a higher level of abstraction—than traditional single theories. A key advantage of this higher level of abstraction is that, unlike single-system theories that necessarily disagree with or contradict other single-system theories on key points, metatheories operate from a conceptual space beyond the single-system theories such that relativism is transcended by conceptual frameworks that can unify the spectrum of psychotherapies. These approaches also allow utilizing, and capitalizing on, the strengths of both single-school approaches and integrative approaches. Unified psychotherapies—of which there are many—have in common the utilization of a metatheoretical framework that takes into account all (or as many as possible) levels of the human and its various ecological systems, as well as their complex interactions. A primary limitation of metatheoretical unification is that—precisely because it operates from a higher level of abstraction and attempts to be comprehensive—it is sometimes perceived as overwhelming, and thus those new to it are often unclear regarding its immediate clinical application; striving to be comprehensively unified also exerts quite a burden on the therapist to be knowledgeable and competent in domains as varied as neuroscience and cultural meaning-making systems. Exemplars of unified psychotherapies include the respective psychotherapeutic systems developed by Magnavita and Anchin (2014), Henriques (2011), Mahoney (2003), Brooks-Harris (2007), and Marquis (2008).

Is Unification the "Next Wave"?

Many psychotherapy scholars view unifying psychotherapies as the leading edge of the field of psychotherapy, and—after the evolution from single-system approaches and the rapprochement that characterized early eclecticism to the maturation of psychotherapy integration—as the fourth developmental wave in the history of psychotherapy (Magnavita & Anchin, 2014; Henriques, 2011; Wolfe, 2008; Millon & Grossman, 2008). This emerging trend is also apparent in the increasing number of books that demonstrate unified conceptions of personality, assessment, research, psychopathology, and psychotherapy; these books provide a metaframework with which to assess and organize the multidimensional and interconnected domains of humans and their systems and from which to provide psychotherapy (Allen, 2006; Mahoney, 2003; Magnavita & Anchin, 2014; Henriques, 2011; Marquis, 2008;

Ingersoll & Marquis, 2014; Brooks-Harris, 2007; Singer, 2005). Two of these books in particular—Henriques' *A New Unified Theory of Psychology* (2011) and Magnavita and Anchin's *Unifying Psychotherapy: Principles, Methods, and Evidence from Clinical Science* (2014)—clearly reveal how unifying approaches represent the leading edge of psychology and psychotherapy. Many of the extant unified approaches have been highlighted in special issues of journals published by the American Psychological Association focusing on issues of unification in psychotherapy: *Journal of Psychotherapy Integration* (2008) volume 18 (no. 3) and *Review of General Psychology* (2013) volume 7 (no. 2). In addition, the *Journal of Unified Psychotherapy and Clinical Science* (JUPCS) was recently inaugurated, and its goals include, but are not limited to:

a) organizing and systematically interrelating—that is, integrating and unifying— diverse bodies of evolving knowledge regarding different domain levels of the biopsychosocial matrix in both healthy and unhealthy states;

b) encouraging multidisciplinary, interdisciplinary, and transdisciplinary (Rosenfield, 1992) clinical theory and/or research which explores, illuminates, and explicates the complex webs of interconnectedness between structures and processes within and across different levels of the biopsychosocial system;

c) identifying and developing solutions to methodological issues associated with studying human personality, adaptive and maladaptive functioning, and being-in-the-world from a unifying perspective;

d) clarifying philosophical issues (e.g., associated with ontology, epistemology, and/or axiology) associated with unified psychotherapy and clinical science; and

e) developing principles of unified psychotherapy and associated methods of assessment, clinical strategies, therapeutic relationship processes, and interventions based on the growing body of unified knowledge about the biopsychosocial matrix along the continuum of adaptive to maladaptive states, and about multilevel processes that interactively influence movement and change in one direction or the other.

The Journal welcomes original manuscripts targeting these and other theoretical, empirical, methodological, philosophical, and/or clinical dimensions of a unified paradigm for psychotherapy and the clinical sciences. (Anchin, Magnavita, & Sobleman, 2012, pp. iii–iv)

As the goals of JUPCS demonstrate, unified psychotherapies represent a paradigmatic shift in the field's understanding of all domains of human functioning, their interrelationships, how they impact health and psychopathology, and how to most effectively intervene (Magnavita, 2008). Finally, even prominent figures in the psychotherapy integration movement who have not themselves developed unifying approaches, such as Stricker and Gold (2011), have suggested that unification "may in fact mark the end of psychotherapy integration as we know it" (p. 478).

Two more signals of the emergence of unification as the next wave of psychotherapy are the Unified Psychotherapy Project and the Unified Psychotherapy Movement, both founded and established by Jeffrey Magnavita:

> The Unified Psychotherapy Project (UPP) Task Force is an invited group of leading researchers, scholars, theorists, and clinicians who are devoted to advancing the field of clinical science and psychotherapeutics. The mission of the task force is to catalogue the methods and techniques of contemporary psychotherapy and organize them at four domain levels. The UPP is similar, although on a smaller scale, to the human genome project in that there currently is no comprehensive database which can be used by clinical scientists and clinicians. (www.unifiedpsychotherapyproject.org/)

In September of 2015, Magnavita convened the first Summit on Unified Psychotherapy in Cape Cod. The members of that meeting, including myself, created the following consensus definition: "The unified psychotherapy movement seeks to enhance practitioners' capacity to draw from the diversity of approaches, processes, techniques, and research findings by providing an evolving, comprehensive, and holistic framework." As you can see, momentum is gaining in the unified psychotherapy movement; those who are interested in joining us in this exciting new work are encouraged to contact us at http://unifiedpsychotherapy.net/.

How Are Integration and Unification Different?

The unified psychotherapy movement has emerged from the psychotherapy integration movement, but the former bears a number of characteristics that differentiate it from integration. In addition to striving to be as comprehensive as possible (including, but not limited to, domains from neuroscience and psychology to sociology and systems theory), a key difference is that psychotherapy integration typically begins by blending theory and/or therapeutic techniques. In contrast, unifying psychotherapies begin by viewing integration/unification as inhering in human nature rather than in our preferred theories and interventions; this leads to unification's emphasis on *organic holism* and its *dialectically* viewing phenomena from *multiple perspectives and paradigms* (Anchin & Magnavita, 2006). Thus, how a unified psychotherapist intervenes derives from their more comprehensive and metatheoretical understanding of the multidimensional nature of people and their ecologies. As Prochaska and Norcross—prominent figures in psychotherapy integration—write, "Lacking in most integrative endeavors is an adequate, comprehensive model that provides an intellectual framework for thinking and working across systems" (2003, p. 3). Mahoney (1993) wrote that most forms of integration can be contrasted with unification's emphasis on *wholeness*. Anchin and Magnavita similarly emphasize that, for unifying psychotherapies, "part–whole relationships are central, standing in dialectical contradistinction to reductionistic levels of analysis" (2006, p. 28).

People are unified; so too should be our therapies. Our patients inhabit different developmental terrains and their disorders and suffering derive from a vast spectrum of insults—from neurobiological and psychological to cultural and systemic. Given that most approaches emphasize and specialize in treating certain dimensions of patient problems (while neglecting others), only unifying approaches remind us to "keep all" perspectives in mind so that we can select an approach that is more likely to be optimal for this specific person, at this time. Anchin and Magnavita

> define unified psychotherapy as a metatheoretical framework—a metaframe— on human adaptation, disorder, and psychotherapy that encompasses all the major, presently identifiable component domain systems of human personality and functioning and their complex interactions...Unified therapy is by definition applicable to the entire spectrum of psychopathological adaptations seen in human systems, from microsystemic to macrosystemic forms of dysfunction. This unifying framework is also capable of organizing the vast assortment of empirically supported and clinically useful strategies and methods. (2006, pp. 27–28)

In addition, because unified psychotherapies view human nature as a complex, dynamic system, they appreciate the role of general systems theory, nonlinearity, and the novel phenomena that emerge with increasing levels of developmental complexity (Thelen & Smith, 1994; Mahoney, 1991; Henriques, 2011), as well as the interconnectedness and reciprocal influence of the different domain systems. A key tenet of integral metatheory is that dynamics from every quadrant (the four quadrants are one of the core constructs of integral theory; they will be explained in chapter 2) impact dynamics in every other quadrant. For example, maltreatment, abuse, and trauma in early childhood (an environmental, Lower-Right quadrant dynamic) clearly change brain structure (a neurobiological, Upper-Right quadrant issue), which then leads to changes in both the person's internal experience (a phenomenological, Upper-Left dynamic) as well as how they relate to others (a relational, Lower-Left dynamic). Thus, rather than focus on just cognition, behavior, affect, culture, brain, or systems; unified approaches seek to understand the whole by dialectically holding together diverse perspectives (Anchin, 2008).

Advantages of Unifying Psychotherapies

The primary advantage of unification is the manner in which a metatheoretical framework can enlarge our perspective (actually, it facilitates our dialectically holding many different perspectives together); this pertains to both how we assess and how we treat our patients. As Knoblauch wrote, "Unification, it seems to me, values keeping it all" (2008, p. 304), and to "keep it all" requires a "both/and"—rather than an "either/or"—mindset that "makes room" for all approaches. Working toward unification is fundamentally an attempt to comprehensively understand how our patients are affected by the many different domains and processes they are subject to (from various psychological dynamics that are the most frequently discussed by psychotherapists to biophysical aspects such as diet, sleep, and exercise, to sociocultural variables that span from exposure to toxins and other environmental traumas to the person's cultural meaning-making systems and choices).

Whereas integrative models inevitably leave out various domains that may be essential to a given patient's case, unified approaches remind us to keep the "big picture" view in mind. This more comprehensive view may conclude that, at times, what is most appropriate is a conventional, domain-specific intervention (i.e., exposure or cognitive restructuring); but even when domain-specific interventions are performed, they are used with the larger picture in mind. The dialectical thinking that is required by unifying approaches may also mean that, having conceptualized in a manner that takes everything from "neurons to neighborhoods" into consideration, under certain circumstances we ultimately deem it best to refer a given patient to a therapist who is less unified than us, but who specializes in the specific domains that that given patient needs the most.

As Mahoney emphasized, "the quest to unify is itself a search for meaningful order" (2008, pp. 367–368). As such, unifying metatheories not only urge us to take as many perspectives into consideration as we can,[5] they also *organize* the data that emerge from those different perspectives; whether this is done with a biopsychosocial systems model (Magnavita & Anchin, 2014), the unified component systems model (Henriques, 2011), or the "All-Quadrants, All-Levels" model of integral theory (Wilber, 1995; Marquis, 2008), unifying approaches facilitate organizing disparate bodies of data into coherent, unified wholes.

The multiple paradigms that unifying approaches incorporate are relevant not only to patient assessment and treatment, but also to research, as they encourage interdisciplinary research and the valuing of a pluralism of research methods. Far too often, researchers start with a method, rather than utilize a method that is most suited to a significant research question. Integral methodological pluralism (which will be discussed in detail in chapter 9) offers a parsimonious theoretical justification for why and how to apply dialectics as a method, recognizing that because different methodologies are capable of illuminating different, essential parts of the whole, each contains uniquely important elements of knowledge concerning the process or phenomena under consideration (Marquis, 2013; Anchin, 2008). In other words, because each methodological family (from empiricism and systems analyses to hermeneutics and phenomenology) is particularly attuned to different types of knowledge, the comprehensiveness of our understanding of any given phenomenon will be enhanced when we integrate multiple methodologies to investigate our specific research questions.

---

5 Janet Lewis described this as "listening on many different channels" (Marquis & Elliot, 2015, p. 21); it can also be thought of as "viewing the patient through multiple lenses," with each channel or lens bringing different phenomena and/or aspects of the same phenomenon into sharper focus.

Concerns Regarding, and the Difficulty of, Unification

In his commentary on unification in psychotherapy, Messer wrote that:

> The unification of psychotherapy entails the melting away of distinctions among current theoretical paradigms such as psychoanalytic, cognitive-behavioral, experiential/humanistic, and couples/family systems. Replacing them, presumably, would be the one true psychotherapeutic approach agreed on and practiced by all... I regard such a total unification as neither feasible nor fully desirable for reasons expressed below. At the same time, however, I believe that there should continue to be efforts made in this direction... even if they will inevitably fall short of full and universally accepted unification. (2008, p. 363)

At the aforementioned Summit on Unified Psychotherapy, none of the unified psychotherapy scholars were proponents of dissolving or minimizing the distinctions among different theoretical approaches to psychotherapy.[6] Rather, it is precisely because we see value in each major approach that we seek metatheoretical frameworks capable of coherently incorporating them all. Unification—to those in the Unified Psychotherapy Movement (UPM)—is not about denying important philosophical differences or creating a conceptual hegemony; it is about being on the lookout for, making room for, taking into account, and bringing together all of the perspectives that may be relevant to the patient sitting before you: "in other words at any given clinical moment, with any given patient how might bringing in versus keeping out disparate clinical approaches help the work?" (Knoblauch, 2008, p. 306). Although unificationists do not want to minimize distinctions between different approaches, we do see each single-system approach as being incomplete on its own (which is why we seek metaframeworks that remind us to view phenomena from as many perspectives as possible). Later in his commentary, Messer asked: "Can one strive for unification even while acknowledging differences? Yes, but not without difficulty" (2008, p. 364); I concur—it is both possible and difficult (more on this in a moment).

There are clearly many therapists who fear that a unified psychotherapy will become a hegemonic force (the "one true psychotherapeutic approach") that dictates "you must do therapy this way"; however, none of the unified scholars I know is of such a mindset (i.e., Henriques et al., 2015). To be a bit more specific, I think that what is most feared is what Mahoney (2008) referred to as unification by "forcing particulars":

> the potential risks and benefits of unification in psychotherapy depend critically on the kind of unification that is sought and how it is achieved. One form of unification operates at the level of particulars and the other at the level

---

6 I believe that Messer is misrepresenting—even if unintentionally—those of us in the Unified Psychotherapy Movement with this statement (from p. 363).

> of general principles; there are also 2 means of achieving unity: 1 by force and 1 by flow ... flowing unifying principles can embrace the essential tensions of diverse theories' and different paradigms' partial truths without resorting to forcing specifics or foreclosing on alternative possibilities. (p. 367)[7]

All of us in the UPM are advocates of flowing, general principles; we are not interested in forcing prescribed, manualized, highly specific procedures.[8] What we are interested in are metatheoretical models that recognize and honor *the unity within the diversity*. In fact, and as will be emphasized throughout this book, the integral approach is actually "content free"—it provides a framework that urges practitioners, theorists, and researchers to view any phenomenon from multiple perspectives, but how one does that is not prescribed; this will become clearer in chapter 2.

Another concern—expressed by Fisch (2001) and Carere-Comes (2001)—is that a unified theory will fetter our clinical openness to the unique complexity of each individual patient; in other words, these scholars think that working from a metatheory will interfere with open listening. Being less open would clearly be detrimental. However, I believe that metatheories are keys to remaining clinically open, open-minded to how any number of the vast array of theoretical perspectives—from biological psychiatry, behaviorism, family systems, and social justice perspectives to relational psychodynamics, diversity approaches, existential-humanism, and cognitive therapy, to name a few—may be most pertinent to the unique complexities of the patient with whom one is working.

"What I regard as most important," Messer writes, "is maintaining a continuing dialogue among many therapy perspectives ... One theory inevitably will emphasize some aspects of a concept or technique at the expense of others. Therefore, multiple, contradictory theories are necessary to capture them more fully" (2008, p. 365). I agree completely, and metatheoretical unification not only requires continuing dialogue among the multitude of *apparently* contradictory perspectives, it also brings meaningful order to what would otherwise be a dizzying, "buzzing confusion."

Life is difficult; so is unifying psychotherapy. After years of teaching psychotherapy unification, I think that its major obstacle is its inherent difficulty: "The challenge of a unified model of clinical science and psychotherapy puts a great deal of pressure on clinicians and clinical researchers to be conversant in the domains of systems from neurons to neighborhoods" (Magnavita, 2008, p. 287). Similarly:

> The challenge to the practitioner of unified psychotherapy is to be adequately familiar with it all (i.e., these theoretical, epistemological bases) so that when

---

[7] Mahoney (2008) offered the APA *Publication Manual*, the DSMs, and APA accreditation as three examples of forced unities that emphasize particulars.
[8] For that matter, we in the UPM are also advocates of each other's unifying work, as is evidenced by my strong endorsement of Henriques (2011) and Magnavita and Anchin (2014); they have likewise expressed appreciation of my work. Thus, I see no reason to believe that the forms of unification I am advocating will become hegemonic.

> he or she turns to clinical practice, methods can be adaptively matched to system levels of domains to supply as carpenters say "the right tool for the right job." (Knoblauch, 2008, p. 302)

Becoming "expert" in all of the domains that a comprehensively unifying approach entails is a virtual impossibility. As you will likely discover as you read this book, although I certainly use behavioral interventions (especially exposure with various phobias and anxieties) and systemic interventions (couples, families, and, to a lesser extent, macrosystemic interventions), I often do not spend equal amounts of time addressing all the different dimensions of patients; I tend, for example, to spend more time with patients' defenses and their emotional, meaning-making, and interpersonal lives. This could be appropriate in most cases, or it could be a reflection of my currently not fully manifesting the ideal of unification in practice. I continue to feel, at times, overwhelmed by the challenge of being as comprehensive and balanced as possible, and I certainly am not equally well-versed in all of the different domain systems. However, working from, and continually reflecting upon, a metatheoretical framework that can incorporate the diversity of extant and future theories, techniques, and research methodologies keeps me motivated to continue learning about approaches that I am currently unfamiliar with or less competent in performing. In other words, even though one may not be equally versed in *all* of the major approaches to psychotherapy, a metatheoretical framework underscores the relevance of all of them and hence can serve as a useful guide for directions that a given therapist's continued learning especially needs to take.

It also seems that some are put off or perhaps intimidated by the potential hubris of attempting such an ambitious project as unification. On this point, I think we should bear in mind what many have written on this topic: "This is not work for an individual but for a multitude—theoreticians, philosophers, methodologists, experimentalists, and practitioners" (Staats, cited in Anchin 2008, p. 312.)

Why the UPM and the Integral Approach Do Not Fall Prey to the Above Concerns

Key reasons that the UPM and iPT will not lead to the feared concerns just mentioned include their encouraging openness to multiple, traditionally competing perspectives as well as urging us to remain in dialogue with others from differing viewpoints. Perhaps even more important is that unifying approaches are inherently ever-evolving. Advocating for increasingly unified psychotherapies does not mean that we are at an endpoint of knowledge from which we want to exert dominance: "any system guided by principles of unification is necessarily an evolving one, and by its very metatheoretical nature is equipped with both the scope and continuing capacity to incorporate new findings" (Anchin & Magnavita, 2006, p. 28).

Because of its relative "youth," and because of the inherent impossibility of specifying or delineating exactly how to practice from any metatheoretical unifying approach,[9] it is in many regards more appropriate to refer to "integrally informed psychotherapy" or an "integral sensibility" than "integral psychotherapy" per se (more on this in chapter 7). I have recently referred to iPT as an approach "in the making" and as at an "embryonic" state of development (Marquis & Elliot, 2015); thus it is not anything like a precisely defined or highly operationalized approach. Rather, iPT provides a comprehensive metaframework that is largely "content-free" (see chapter 2). As such, I have emphasized the importance of not subjecting the iPT model to a premature definition or an excessive sense of certainty that could lead to reification; in other words,

> "it's being true to the integral endeavor to never absolutely put some period on it and say this is what it is" (Lewis [an integral therapist in the study]), but rather, "to have a model where there's room for continual growth" (Lewis) ... as iPT continues to be developed and refined, even claims that withstand theoretical challenge and empirical testing in showing themselves to be accurate and useful should still be considered "true but partial" discoveries. This is viewed as necessary due to the strong likelihood, if not inevitability, of future concepts and findings that expand upon, qualify, supersede, or even contradict earlier premises, including the Wilberian insights and theoretical frameworks that have provided the foundation upon which the iPT movement has continued to build. The integral perspective recognizes that there is always more to the picture, and thus in articulating the integral theory of today, no attempt is made at certitude regarding "what it's going to be tomorrow" (Short [an integral therapist in the study]). The aim is to continue adding clarity and specificity to a working model that remains flexible and open to ongoing expansion and revision in response to new theoretical perspectives and empirical findings. In this sense, iPT seeks to remain true to the spirit of science. (Marquis & Elliot, 2015, p. 19)

An integral approach does not aim to eliminate differences or to establish some sort of uniform, closed, or final system. Rather, a primary thrust of this book is to foster dialogue and to promote further exploration of the intricate dimensions involved in the attempt to bring unifying order and more coherent comprehensiveness to psychotherapy. As such, my work as an integral psychotherapist will always be an open-ended work-in-progress, and whatever "unifying" I am proposing is not meant to deny, eliminate, or minimize the critical importance of the very real differences between various approaches.

One of the strengths of the integral model is its ability to incorporate specific interventions that have demonstrable effectiveness. At the same time, perhaps

---

9 For example, different therapists can subscribe to the biopsychosocial model and yet the *specific* ways they assess and intervene at the biological, psychological, and social dimensions of their patients may vary considerably (i.e., some may address the psychological dimension more psychodynamically and others in a more CBT manner).

increased effectiveness is not the sole criterion by which the value of unifying efforts should be evaluated.

> If the goal of integration is not to produce a singularly "better" therapy, however, so much as to create a context of constructive dialogue and collaboration among scientists and practitioners of diverse viewpoints, then the process will necessarily remain open to future developments that cannot be either foreseen or strategically engineered. (Mahoney, 1993, pp. 7–8)

The same could be said of unification. As usual, I think a "both/and" perspective is useful here: the ideal for me would be to improve the effectiveness of the psychotherapy we provide by being more comprehensive and holistic while also engaging in constructive dialogue and collaboration with a diverse array of scholar-practitioners.

Under a heading titled "Addressing the basic fear that people have of unified theories" Wolfe wrote that:

> Unification is merely the next step in the evolution of psychotherapy. I do not expect that the evolution will end there ... psychotherapy theory will oscillate between states of unification and differentiation ... It is the oscillation between pluralism and unity, between assimilation and accommodation, and between analysis and synthesis that will fuel the continuing and continuous evolution of psychotherapy integration. (2008, p. 299)

Toward an Integral Unifying Psychotherapy: Theory, Practice, and Research

In addition to operating from a metatheory, emphasizing holism, and conceptualizing dialectically, a unifying psychotherapy must take those lenses and address issues of human development, clinical assessment, the development of psychopathology, therapeutic treatment interventions and change processes, and psychotherapy research; this book will do all this. However, because this book covers so much territory, I cannot delve into as much depth on every topic as one might hope; as it is, this book is longer than my editor/publisher requested. Consequently, some details or aspects of the above to which I have previously applied the integral approach could not be included here.[10]

---

10 For more details on many of these issues, the interested reader can consult Marquis (2008), Ingersoll & Marquis (2014), and the chapter on integral counseling in Fall, Holden, and Marquis (2004/2017); the latter is where I provided the first exposition of integral psychotherapy as a "fully-fledged" theory of psychotherapy, including a theory and model of both personality development and the process of therapeutic change. In that chapter I filled in many gaps left by Wilber's work, drawing upon other psychotherapy approaches and my own clinical experience as well as extrapolating theoretically to establish an integral approach that addresses all of the aspects of traditional psychotherapy theories: structural and functional/motivational aspects of the psyche; dynamics of personality and identity development; genetic and environmental influences on those processes;

I also want to emphasize that this is a work in progress: this book is my working "toward" unification; there are too many domains that I need to more deeply understand and be able to competently implement to declare this as a "fully mature" unifying psychotherapy. Nonetheless, I think there is more than enough value in what I am offering to make it worthwhile to "go to press" now. Even though it will surely be critiqued, "To fail to [attempt to] build such a unifying paradigm will keep us on the same unprogressive course that has plagued the field since time immemorial" (Millon & Grossman, 2008, p. 362; brackets added).

Fundamentally, because patients live and suffer within a complex, multidimensional world, it behooves therapists to conceptualize and practice from a model that accounts for, and can render comprehensible, such multidimensional complexity. A core thrust of iPT is to provide a parsimonious route to such comprehensive conceptualization and practice. Another strength of iPT is that it readily lends itself to drawing upon, and integrating knowledge from, not only the field of psychotherapy but also biomedical science, social psychology, sociology, general systems theory, critical theory, philosophy, contemplative spirituality, and so forth. I am of the position that each major single-system and each major integrative psychotherapy approach has its strengths and weaknesses; that the value of a theory resides in both its heuristic and practical consequences; and that integral theory provides a comprehensive metatheory with which to address issues pertinent to psychotherapy unification.

I confess that I am a "big picture" type, and more rational than empirical by temperament. I am more adept at thinking abstractly, holistically, and metatheoretically than I am at carrying out a reductionistic program of micro-level research. This in no way suggests that I devalue the latter; on the contrary, such detailed, focused research forms most of the knowledge that people like me attempt to unify in their "big picture" work. Important to the unifying work you will find in this book, what appears competing or contradictory from one angle (whether debates between quantitative and qualitative researchers or person-centered therapists and applied behavioral analysts) can often be recognized as complementary from a metatheoretical perspective. In this manner, sundry important-but-incomplete approaches can be holistically integrated into a coherent whole; such a unifying process demonstrates that the component parts are vital, essential elements even if they are partial in-and-of-themselves. To me, this honors the unity and the diversity, reminiscent of William James' pointing out the need to balance "the one and the many."

Like Mahoney, "I have long been a seeker of unifying principles that can embrace the partial truths of diverse theories and different paradigms" (2008, p. 373). To

---

definitions of what constitutes health and well-being in contrast to dysfunction and pathology; what motivates patients to seek therapy; what their capacity is to change; what their role is in the change process; what the therapist's role is in the change process; assessment and intervention strategies; how to address patient's resistance to change; and how integral theory interfaces with recent developments in the mental health field such as pharmacotherapy, managed care and brief therapy, diversity and multicultural issues, the relationship of therapy and spirituality, etc.

repeat, what I am offering in this book is *an* integral approach to unification in psychotherapy; I am not suggesting it is the only way to be unified or even the only way to be integral. And although it is an approach without much empirical corroboration (although the same can be said not only about other unifying approaches but also about most integrative psychotherapies; Glass, Arnkoff, & Rodriquez, 1998; Castonguay et al., 2015), it does appear to have face validity. At this point, let us delve into integral metatheory.

CHAPTER 2

Integral Metatheory and Integral Psychotherapy
A Model of Interrelationships[1]

People are complex, multidimensional, and unified; thus should be our theory.

Integral metatheory (Wilber, 2000a, 2000b; Marquis, 2007, 2008, 2013) is a conceptual framework that promotes and facilitates a more comprehensive, coherent understanding of any phenomenon; in my work, this has involved applying the integral framework to issues of human development and personality (Fall, Holden, & Marquis, 2004/2017), methodological and epistemological issues in psychotherapy research (Marquis & Douthit, 2006; Marquis, Douthit, & Elliot, 2011; Marquis, 2013), the development of psychopathology (Ingersoll & Marquis, 2014), the psychotherapy intake process (Marquis, 2008), and psychotherapeutic interventions (Marquis, 2009). Following Rychlak (1973), Magnavita (2006) emphasized that "a substantive theory of psychotherapy must include interrelated and consistent constructs about personality, psychopathology, and the process and techniques of psychotherapeutic change" (p. 885). Magnavita (2008) also stressed that such a unified theory is dependent on a *holistic framework* capable of revealing the interconnectedness of all of those constructs. A primary purpose of integral psychotherapy (iPT; Marquis, 2008; Wilber, 2000b; Ingersoll & Zeitler, 2010; Forman, 2010) is to do just that and, in the process, to foster the recognition that disparate aspects of people and their circumstances—from one's neurobiology and felt-sense of selfhood to cultural worldviews and social systems—are all critically influential to one's well-being or suffering and, therefore, should be given thoughtful, considered attention in psychotherapy.

In my view, the integral model meets the criteria outlined above by Magnavita (2006, 2008a) regarding a unified theory of psychotherapy. The integral model integrates fragmented, compartmentalized data from not only a plethora of divergent psychotherapy systems but also other related disciplines (such as biomedicine, sociology, public health, philosophy, and spirituality) into higher-order, unified

---

[1] This chapter is adapted from Marquis, A. (2013). Methodological considerations of studying a unified approach to psychotherapy: Integral methodological pluralism. *Journal of Unified Psychotherapy and Clinical Science*, 2 (1), 45–73, as well as from chapter 2 of Marquis, A. (2008). *The Integral Intake: A guide to comprehensive idiographic assessment in integral psychotherapy.* New York: Routledge.

wholes by providing a parsimonious conceptual scaffold within which to order the myriad psychotherapeutic approaches—from psychodynamic, behavioral, and cognitive to existential-humanistic, family systems, and constructivist—as well as the other disciplines mentioned above. A unifying metaframework such as the integral model is *not* intended to minimize the authentic significant differences we often find across cultures, systems, or between individuals from the same culture or family; this would clearly be a detriment to this approach. However, in addition to acknowledging that differences are salient, vital, and add spice to life; integral theorists also search for the deep pattern similarities that pervade striking surface variations between individuals and cultures (Wilber, 2000b). Thus, a primary goal of the integral approach is to understand and genuinely honor *unity within diversity*. As Staats (1991) put it, "It should be emphasized that the ability to see commonality, in principle, through thickets of superficial difference is at the heart of creating unified science" (p. 905). A primary advantage of discovering and/or constructing unifying patterns is to reconcile *apparent* contradictions between the various psychotherapies and related disciplines; to do so not only reduces redundancy, it may also result in more comprehensive, coherent, and effective theory and practice.

Although often referred to as integral "theory," the perspective presented in this volume is actually a *meta*theoretical framework. As such, integral metatheory simultaneously honors the important contributions of a broad spectrum of epistemological outlooks and practical procedures while also acknowledging the parochial limits and misconceptions of those perspectives. In other words, the integral model provides a metaperspective that allows us to situate diverse knowledge-approaches (from pre-modern to modern to post-modern) in such a way that they synergistically complement, rather than contradict, one another. What is this metatheoretical framework that we characterize as integral? Simply put: AQAL (pronounced *ah-kwahl*).

AQAL: All-Quadrants, All-Levels

AQAL refers to "All-Quadrants, All-Levels" but it also signifies attention to four additional components: *lines, types, states,* and the *self-system,* the meaning of which will be subsequently explained. *These six components reflect fundamental patterns and principles that appear to recur in multiple domains of knowledge.* Thus, "All-Quadrants, All-Levels" or "AQAL" is integral metatheory's shorthand signature phrase for the multiplicity of dimensions that any phenomenon discloses if investigated from the appropriate perspectives. I begin this discussion of integral metatheory with a description of the four quadrants.

All-Quadrants: The Four Quadrants

The four quadrants are a central component of the unifying model that Wilber (2000a) developed in response to the plethora of apparently contradictory assertions found among diverse disciplines and competing theoretical approaches within those disciplines. This metatheoretical model allows one to situate diverse perspectives such that they augment and complement, rather than compete with and contradict, one another. The four quadrants are formed by the intersection of two axes: interior–exterior and individual–collective (see Figure 2.1).

In other words, the four quadrants are aspects of, and perspectives on, our world that yield four interrelated yet irreducible domains/perspectives.[2] Integral metatheory posits that comprehensive description of any phenomenon requires that one account for these four irreducible perspectives:

- Upper-Left (UL) *experiential* (micro-subjective): the individual viewed from the interior
- Upper-Right (UR) *behavioral* (micro-objective[3]): the individual viewed from the exterior
- Lower-Left (LL) *cultural* (macro-intersubjective): the collective viewed from the interior
- Lower-Right (LR) *social* (macro-interobjective): the collective viewed from the exterior.

In a bit more detail, the four quadrants manifest as follows:

Upper-Left/Experiential: Interior-individual. This quadrant includes the subjective, phenomenal dimension of individual consciousness—any and all experiences, sensations, perceptions, feelings, and thoughts that can be phenomenologically described in "I" language. It also includes the spectrum of those impulses, emotions, and motivations of which the person is unconscious.

---

2 Although psychotherapists do not need to understand the following technical point to assess and practice effectively, integral theorists differentiate the "view from" and the "view through." Wilber (2006) stated that all sentient holons (a holon is a "whole/part"—that which is simultaneously a whole entity and also a component part of a larger whole entity; i.e., an atom is a whole that is also a part of a molecule, and a molecule is a whole that is part of a cell, etc.) possess four perspectives *through* which they touch or view the world; these are the four *quadrants* (the *view through*). At the same time, anything—whether a sentient holon such as a dog or a nonsentient artifact such as a guitar—can be *viewed from* those four perspectives, and technically, integral theorists term those views *quadrivia* (plural of quadrivium) (Wilber, 2006). In my attempt to balance theoretical precision with practical utility, and for the sake of simplicity and clarity, I will simply refer to the four dimension-perspectives as "quadrants."

3 I would agree with a critic that points out that there are few, if any, psychological constructs that are properly understood as being completely objective (Anchin & Magnavita, 2008). I recognize that even neurological measures such as PET scans and fMRI are not *completely* objective; that those methods are social practices that have emerged within socially constructed traditions that are subject to the dynamics of power and privilege (Gergen, 1985). Nonetheless, in comparison to the quality of lived, felt experience (UL), the amount of blood in a specific region of the brain or the number of times someone washes his hands (UR) is *relatively* objective—*by which I really mean "externally observable."* Thus, "*relatively* objective" is a phrase that I have used numerous times in other writings (Marquis, 2007, 2008), as well as in this chapter; I also stress in this chapter that "*the four quadrants represent the interiors and exteriors of both individuals and systems,*" which is more accurate than saying the "subjective and objective views of both individuals and systems." Importantly, this same "relatively" applies to all four quadrants.

Upper-Left (UL): Interior-Individual 1st person/Self/Consciousness/Subjectivity Freud, Rogers, Hegel, Piaget Validity Claim: Truthfulness, sincerity *Experience*—as felt "from the inside"	Upper-Right (UR): Exterior-Individual 3rd person/Organism/Brain/Objectivity Skinner, Beck, Hume, Locke Validity Claim: Truth (by correspondence or proposition) *Behavior*—as seen "from the outside"
• Any noteworthy patterns in the patient's self-experience • Self-image, self-concept • Self-esteem, self-efficacy • Instability–stability • Joy, zest, purpose, motivation • Depression, sadness, emptiness • Anxiety, "jitters", feeling "revved up" • Cognitions (e.g., thoughts, beliefs, attitudes, interpretations) • Imagery • Political, religious, and/or spiritual beliefs and/or experiences • Consciousness as experienced as *mind* • The *experience of*, for example, depression: sadness, loss of interest in pleasurable activities, fatigue, feelings of worthlessness, difficulty concentrating, frequent thoughts of death, suicidal ideation, etc. Also *how one interprets* events such as the death of a loved one, divorce, profound loss, or childbirth	• Any noteworthy patterns of behavior: what specific behaviors bring the patient to therapy and what specific behaviors will indicate successful outcome? • Medical disorders • Medication • Diet • Alcohol and/or drug use • Aerobic and/or strength training • Patterns of sleep and rest • Consciousness as described by neurotransmission and the functioning of *brain* structures • *Observable changes* in, for example, depression: appears tearful, no longer engages in pleasurable activities, significant weight loss or gain, psychomotor agitation or retardation, lower levels of available serotonin, social withdrawal
Lower-Left (LL): Interior-Collective 2nd person/Culture/Worldview/Intersubjectivity Stolorow et al., Wachtel, Habermas, Gadamer Validity Claims: Justness, mutual understanding *Cultural Worldview*—the group's experience "from the inside"	Lower-Right (LR): Exterior-Collective 3rd person/Social Systems/Environment/Interobjectivity Minuchin, Gottman, Marx, Parsons Validity Claim: Functional fit, systems theory web *Social Systems*—the group's behavior "from the outside"
• Patient's meaning-making system(s) • Patient's relationships with significant others, especially spouse/partner, boss, friends, and family • Patient's experience of ethnicity • Patient's experience of family dynamics • The medium of the therapeutic relationship and how both the patient and therapist experience their intersubjectivity • *Cultural meanings* assigned to, for example, depression: sick, lazy, irresponsible, heartbroken, hexed, bewitched, etc.	• Patient's socioeconomic status • Condition of one's neighborhood • Environmental stressors and/or comforts; layout of household • Analyses of interpersonal dynamics, including family history • Treatment contexts (setting—inpatient/outpatient and physical nature of therapy setting; frequency and length of sessions; modality—individual/group/family therapy) • *Social systems* that contribute to, for example, depression: economic, educational, and medical systems: poverty-, drug-, and gang-ridden neighborhoods; poor/dangerous schools; minimal access to medical care (brief therapy or none at all); racism, sexism, classism, ageism, etc.

Figure 2.1 Selected Aspects of the Four Quadrants Pertinent to Psychotherapy

Upper-Right/Behavioral: Exterior-individual. This quadrant includes the relatively objective perspective of individual structures, behaviors, events, and processes that are externally observable (whether observed with the five senses, measured with medical or scientific equipment, or captured by a video camera) and described in "it" language.

Lower-Left/Cultural: Interior-collective. This quadrant includes the intersubjective dimension of the collective. This perspective requires a sympathetic resonance common only to members of a given community—shared worldviews, customs, linguistic semantics, ethics, communal values, and other meaning-making activities that are mutually understood by members of a given culture (whether that culture is a dyad or consists of millions of people) and are subjectively described in "you/we" language. It also includes relationships with significant others, most notably one's spouse/partner, boss(es), friends, family, and therapist.

Lower-Right/Social: Exterior-collective. This quadrant includes the interobjective perspective of systems, addressing aspects of societies such as economic structures, civic resources (education systems, employment opportunities, available transportation), governmental systems, and city planning (architectural style, spacious vs. congested, available parks and other areas of natural beauty). Social phenomena are described in objective, third person, plural ("its") language. This quadrant also includes any observable or measurable interactions between the parts of a system or between systems.

For example, when seeking to understand a person in psychotherapy, each of these four perspectives yields different meanings and information necessary for a more complete understanding. This understanding, in turn, reveals that none of the four perspectives can be reduced to another perspective without violating the essential value of the former's point of view.

Hopefully it is clear that integral metatheory is a deeply contextual model (numerous and diverse contexts are inherent to the lower quadrants); it is equally important to emphasize that integral metatheory is an organismic model, and essential to such models is reciprocal interaction "between various parts or subsystems of the organism or between the organism, its subsystems, and the environment" (Schwartz, 1988, cited in Anchin, 2008, p. 337). Thus, dynamic processes from any of the quadrants influence processes and structures within that quadrant, as well as those in the other quadrants, in interdependent, nonlinear ways. In other words, as in all nonlinear dynamic systems, not only do different processes reciprocally influence one another via various feedback and feedforward processes, the system itself is autopoetic: "Complex systems are self-organizing and tend to replicate themselves at different domain levels" (Magnavita, 2006, p. 889). Thus, no single quadrant is considered more significant than the others; they are equi-primordial and dynamics within the system "tetra-arise"[4] (Wilber, 2006, p. 34). The

---

4 "Tetra-arise" refers to dynamics from all four quadrants arising or emerging as a function of each other. Because dynamics from the four quadrants reciprocally influence each other in this way, the distinction between them can become so blurred as to seemingly break down (Wachtel, 1987); this does not diminish the utility of these contrasts.

quadrants provide a model that reminds us of a basic assumption of all unified models: of holism in contrast to reductionism[5] (Magnavita, 2008).

In response to some of my publications, presentations, and informal discussions involving the quadratic model, a number of people have told me something along the lines of "that's just like the biopsychosocial model—what is there that's new about that?" First, the quadrants are not simply revealing the importance of biological (UR), psychological (UL), and sociocultural (LR, LL) influences on health and disorder; each of the four quadrants entails those dynamics but also much more. Part of the reason that the quadratic model discloses more than the biopsychosocial model is that it is not merely an "adding together" of different dimensions. Rather, the four quadrants are a function of interrelating two fundamental, contrasting perspectives that have been pervasive in human thought and experience: that of looking from within (interiors),[6] in contrast to observing from outside (exteriors), as well as a focus on the individual (in relative isolation), in contrast to a focus on contexts (group dynamics, systems, cultures, ecologies, etc.). Precisely because the quadratic model is capable of disclosing and dialectically unifying such a tremendous amount of knowledge from what have traditionally been competing and apparently contradictory perspectives, it is a remarkably parsimonious conceptual tool.

Each quadrant provides an alternative and legitimate perspective for a given phenomenon. The significance of these four perspectives may become clearer with an example. According to the *Diagnostic and Statistical Manual of Mental Disorders* (DSM-5; APA, 2013), a patient suffering from depression *experiences* (UL) sadness, loss of interest in pleasurable activities, fatigue, feelings of worthlessness, difficulty concentrating, frequent thoughts of death, suicidal ideation, and so forth. Also important from this experiential perspective is *how one interprets* events such as the death of a loved one, divorce, profound loss, or childbirth. At the same time, we can *behaviorally observe* (UR) that this patient may often be tearful, engages in fewer pleasurable activities, and displays psychomotor agitation or retardation. Additional data from this behavioral perspective often include significant weight loss or gain as well as lower levels of available serotonin. Another important dimension impacting patients who are depressed comprises the *cultural meanings* (LL)

---

[5] Although it might appear that holism not only competes with but ultimately is preferable to reductionism, these two approaches can also be seen as anchoring two ends of a dialectic, such that reductionism has its place, too, in scientific and clinical investigation. At the same time, holism *balances* reductionism's dissectiveness by underscoring that how the parts fit together and interact to create an integral whole is of equal importance to understanding a phenomenon. This distinction pertains to two *kinds* of understanding: analytic understanding (which is reductionistic) and synthetic understanding (which is holistic); see Anchin (2008).

[6] The issue of psychological phenomena having important interior dimensions is not a minor issue. As Staats wrote, "let us ask why psychology has made so little progress in unification ... Centrally, psychology studies phenomena that, in their number, range, and complexity are unique ... and many of them are *inside the organism*, where they are difficult or impossible to observe" (1999, p. 7, italics added).

assigned to depression, which vary from sick, lazy, and irresponsible to heartbroken, hexed, bewitched, and so forth. To underscore the interiority of these cultural meanings, many of the phenomena and processes in the LL quadrant are individual internalizations of cultural and relational meanings and values that do not emerge independently of one's culture, family, or relationships. Finally, *social systems* (LR) are clearly implicated as contributing to many patients' depression, and these vary from economic (poverty, drug- and gang-ridden neighborhoods), educational (poor, overcrowded, and dangerous schools; or a lack of education), familial (abuse, neglect, and unclear rules, roles, and/or boundaries), and medical systems (minimal access to medical care—brief therapy or none at all) to racism, sexism, classism, ageism, and so on. The experience of depression is thus inextricably constituted by UL factors including self-appraisals of worthlessness; UR factors such as sleep EEG abnormalities, dysregulated neurotransmitter systems, alterations of neuropeptides, and behavioral "shutdown"; LL factors that influence both the likelihood of developing a depressive episode (from an insecure attachment history and a lack of intimate relationships to a consumer culture in which energies are directed toward acquiring material goods rather than cultivating interior development and capacities for tolerance, acceptance, and compassion) as well as how the depression is interpreted (medical disease vs. inauthenticity vs. hexed); and LR factors such as living in poverty and being denied appropriate mental health care because HMOs and other managed care systems dictate such. Every event or experience irreducibly has a subjective, an objective, an intersubjective, and an interobjective dimension, and to dismiss or ignore one or more of these dimensions is to be reductionistic or incomplete. Accordingly, integral therapists understand an individual's psychological development—which many therapists view as a fundamentally individual, internal phenomenon (UL)—*not* as a merely isolated, internal process of increasing complexity, but as a phenomenon with at least four distinct dimensions (quadrants) that are mutually constitutive of one another.

Although I introduced the quadrants first, they are but one of the organizing constructs of an integral framework. The AQAL model stresses that dynamics from not only the quadrants, but all of the following components, reciprocally interact with each other.

All-Levels: The Spectrum Approach

According to integral psychotherapy (Marquis, 2008; Marquis & Wilber, 2008; Ingersoll & Zeitler, 2010; Forman, 2010; Wilber, 2000b), attending carefully to patients' developmental dynamics is a key factor in treatment planning—influencing which categories of interventions are likely to be optimal, neutral, or contraindicated. This is a relatively common notion in psychotherapy (McWilliams, 1994; Ivey, 1986; Kegan, 1982; Mahoney, 1991, 2003). The term "*all*-levels," however, refers to integral metatheory's integratively constructing what is arguably the most complete spectrum of human development, from the earliest stages of human development to "the farther reaches of human nature" (Maslow, 1971). As such, Wilber's spectrum model of human development spans three broad realms, each of which includes three to four distinct stages.[7]

According to Wilber (2000a), children typically spend approximately their first seven years of life developing through three stages of development that, together, constitute the *prepersonal realm*. The term "prepersonal" refers to those stages of development during which a coherent, relatively stable, individuated self-sense is, as yet, only in the process of emerging; hence Mahler's distinction between the *psychological birth* and physical birth of the human infant (Mahler, Pine, & Bergman, 1975). Newborn children enter the *sensoriphysical* stage in a state of psychological undifferentiation from their environment. During their first year and a half, they take their first tentative steps toward individuation by developing an identity as a *physical self*, separate from the environment. Then, in the *phantasmic/emotional* stage, toddlers develop a sense of their *emotional self* that perceives emotions differing from those of others and, thus, feel emotionally differentiated from others. At approximately 3 years of age, in the *representational mind* stage, the child's *mental self* emerges: what children had known only through their senses they are now able to represent mentally. Piaget (1977) classified this structure as preoperational, in which the capacity for symbols and language provides the child access to an entirely new world of objects and ideas in both the past and the future.

Because stages four through six involve the elaboration and stabilization of a more autonomous, coherent self, they constitute the *personal realm*. When children are approximately 7 years of age, they typically enter the *rule/role mind* stage, corresponding to Piaget's (1977) concrete operations. Here, the child develops the capacity to take the perspective (role) of others and thus assumes an identity as a *role self*, learning the rules associated with various social roles. Adolescence commences with the emergence of the *formal-reflexive* stage, corresponding to Piaget's formal operations. The young teenager is now able to think about thinking, which allows the person to introspect, marking the emergence of a *conscientious self*. Many people live their lives centered in this stage of development (some, in fact, never fully acquire formal operational thinking). However, young adults have the potential to develop into the *vision-logic* stage. Whereas the formal-reflexive stage involves dichotomized, either/or thinking, vision-logic is characterized by the capacity for dialectical thinking, allowing one to simultaneously embrace multiple, seemingly contradictory perspectives in one's attention and, through synthesis and integration, conceptualize networks of interactions among the various perspectives. At this point, cognitive development has greatly expanded, yet existential concerns often plague the individual.

---

7 As will be discussed in more detail in chapter 3, Wilber originally included four stages of trans- or supra-personal development, but his current model now includes four suprapersonal *states* of consciousness, each of which can potentially manifest at different stages of development. Chapter 3 will also discuss Loevinger's nine levels of ego development, which are incorporated within Wilber's developmental model.

Wilber (2000a) posited that if one continues to develop and/or cultivate various suprapersonal states of consciousness (usually through various meditative practices), one may enter the *suprapersonal realm*, which is *potentially* more *self-actualizing* or *spiritual*. In this realm, one may recognize that one's deepest self is not merely the separate, isolated-mind, individual self, but something including yet transcending the personal self, something more akin to a spiritual, though not necessarily religious, Self (Maslow, 1971); hence the term "*suprapersonal*."[8] Wilber has consistently emphasized that our deepest nature and ultimate identity is Spirit—the source, ground, and cause of all existence. In fact, one of the conceptual foundations of Wilber's integral theory (2000a, 2000b) is the *perennial philosophy*, which is often referred to as the essential core of the world's great spiritual, or wisdom, traditions. It is important to note that many integral scholars are, unlike Wilber, not committed to the particular suprapersonal model he has put forth. For more detail regarding developmental stages, see chapter 3 of this book; for even more detail, consult Wilber (2000b, 2000a), Mahoney (1991), Kegan (1982), and Loevinger (1976).

Wilber (2000b) used several different words to describe the basic "stages" of consciousness development. He uses the word "levels" to connote the qualitatively distinct nature of each stage of development; "structures" to underscore the integrated, holistic nature of each stage; and "waves" to emphasize the fluid, in contrast to rigid, nature of the stages. Importantly, these stages are not viewed as reified structures, but as *probability waves*, suggesting *not* a concrete structure residing within the individual; rather, an individual's developmental level is fundamentally a function of that person's residing in a *psychological space* from which the probability is quite high that the specific patterns of thinking, feeling, and acting that characterize a given level of development are present and observable, whether from within or without (Marquis & Wilber, 2008). Importantly, that psychological space is profoundly impacted by a variety of contexts (especially relational ones) and one's neurobiology, so again "psychology"—as used integrally—is not simply an Upper-Left issue, but an All-Quadrant affair.

When it comes to issues of stage-, structure-, or level-related conceptions of human development, it is important to differentiate a "theory of the person" (more akin to a personality theory or a theory of human nature) from a "theory of psychotherapy" (more akin to a theory of how to intervene to facilitate constructive change). Although I firmly believe in the utility and veracity of some stage theories

---

8 This is Wilber's (2000a) view; I and other integral scholars are agnostic with regard to the ontological structure of reality and our ultimate nature. Our position is that it is not necessary to believe these specific spiritual claims to identify as an integral therapist (Marquis, in press; Ingersoll & Marquis, 2014; Forman, personal communication, August 6, 2015). Nonetheless, spirituality—whether religious or of an atheistic/agnostic form—does occupy an important place in an integral conceptualization of human nature and optimal functioning; please see the Appendix: Integral Culture, Spirituality, and a Category Error, which addresses this issue in greater detail.

of human development (i.e., Piaget's (1977) stages of cognitive development, Loevinger's (1976) stages of ego development, Gilligan's (1982) and Kohlberg's (1969) stages of moral development; see also Mahoney (1991)), when it comes to understanding people and human nature, I have come to believe—in part due to research I have conducted (Marquis & Elliot, 2015; Marquis et al., 2015)—that stages or levels of development are less relevant to the moment-to-moment practice of psychotherapy than are the more rapidly changing *states* of a person (from affective and dissociative states to meditative or mystical states; these states and their relevance to psychotherapy will be discussed subsequently, and in more detail in chapters 3 and 7).

Although integral theory posits other important constructs to consider (i.e., developmental lines, states of consciousness, personality types, and the self-system), quadratic and developmental level components have traditionally been considered the essential foci in most of the integral literature; it is for this reason that Wilber's integral theory is also often referred to as "All-Quadrants, All-Levels" or AQAL (Wilber, 2000a, 2000b).

Lines, Types, States, and the Self-System

Integral theorists recognize that people have many different aspects—or lines—of experience and functioning that often are not equally developed. For instance, it is common to encounter people who are cognitively quite developed, but emotionally or interpersonally are much less so. Wilber (2000b) posited approximately two dozen different lines that develop, such as cognition, self-identity, object relations, morality, role taking, emotion, values, needs, worldview, creativity, psychosexuality, aesthetics, and spirituality. Attending to patients' developmental lines helps us narrow clinical attention to those aspects of our patients that are most implicated in their current struggles.

Different lines can, and often do, develop at different rates. Thus, although specific developmental lines and levels unfold sequentially, "*overall development* ... is far from a sequential, ladder-like, clunk-and-grind series of steps, but rather involves a fluid flowing of many waves and streams in the great River of Life" (Wilber, 2000a, p. xvii, original italics). Generally, Wilber (2006) notes that the cognitive line of development leads all other lines because cognition, broadly defined, determines what one can be aware of. The line of self or ego development follows cognition (of the things I can be aware of, what do I identify with?). Finally, there are self-related lines that hover around the self-sense or ego (e.g., values, ethics, needs, etc.); in other words, one's needs, values, and ethical development will have much in common with one's sense of self or identity (i.e., as one's sense of self develops and expands, so do one's values and ethics).

Although different lines of development disclose important aspects of a person's way of being-in-the-world, Wilber (2000a) and other integral theorists (Marquis, 2008; Cook-Greuter & Soulen, 2007; Ingersoll & Zeitler, 2010) consider the line of ego development to be the most illuminating single developmental dimension of a person—especially with regard to one's sense of self, worldview, cognitive and interpersonal style, and how one constructs meaning. Hundreds of studies have supported the soundness of the ego development construct (Loevinger, 1976; Cohn, 1991; Manners & Durkin, 2001).

The activity of being a person is the activity of taking an experience and organizing and constructing its meaning (Kegan, 1982). As one's sense of self evolves over time, one's "self-narratives" evolve as well. There are commonalities in the stories or meanings a person creates out of experience and the way these stories evolve. One's developmental "center of gravity" is the level of ego development that one tends to inhabit most of the time (Cook-Greuter & Soulen, 2007). It is important to note, however, that humans are dynamic—rather than static—and thus a given individual sometimes inhabits levels of development that are above or below her center of gravity. Additionally, ego development is hardly a straightforward affair. As one moves through levels of ego development, parts of one's self may become dissociated or split off and essentially remain stuck at lower levels of development (Wilber, 2000b; Rowan, 1993). These dissociated parts may involve different self-states with intense affective experience along with internalized representations/schemas; moreover, they can be activated by various circumstances. For example, a current interpersonal dynamic may trigger a dysfunctional schema from childhood and an individual may start to feel, think, and act in ways that are characteristic of early stages of development. More will be said about ego development in chapter 3.

Personality *type* refers to a given person's way, or style, of being-in-the-world. Tailoring a therapeutic approach to a given patient's personality type may be important in some instances because, by definition, different types of people emphasize different ways of being-in-the-world. Personality "types" are radically different from developmental stages or levels, in part because any type can manifest at any level (Wilber, 2000b; McWilliams, 1994). Although some personality typologies have demonstrated more reliability and validity (i.e., the five-factor model, attachment style, temperament) than others (i.e., the Myers-Briggs Type Indicator, the Enneagram), even the latter appear to be clinically useful at times, especially if recognized and used more as metaphors than as constructs with solid psychometrics (Ingersoll & Zeitler, 2010).[9] An integral approach posits that therapists will tend to better serve their patients if they assess their patients' types and attentively *work with, rather than against*, their patients' preferred styles of being-in-the-world.

On a less healthy note, people who meet diagnostic criteria for DSM-5 personality disorders can also be conceptualized as different types. In her classic *Psychoanalytic Diagnosis*, Nancy McWilliams (1994) somewhat jokingly boiled down understanding a patient from a psychoanalytic perspective as 1) How sick are they? (levels) and 2) In what way? (type or defensive style). Those who meet diagnostic criteria for borderline personality disorder display a relatively consistent (even if what

---

9 Another way of accounting for types is that of personality systematics (see Magnavita, 2009).

is consistent is their instability) way of being-in-the-world, just as those who meet diagnostic criteria for avoidant, narcissistic, or any of the personality disorders also exhibit relatively discernible, inflexible ways of being. However, with the exception of DSM-5 personality disorders, it is important to remember that no type is, in general, better or worse than any other.[10] However, different circumstances may be more easily handled or adjusted to by a certain type of person than another.

Whereas levels/stages of consciousness, as well as personality types, can be thought of as enduring structures or *traits*, by which I mean *relatively* stable patterns of events in consciousness, *states* of consciousness are more temporary and fleeting.[11] States of consciousness are another important component in integral psychotherapy. In fact, recent research (Marquis & Elliot, 2015) suggests that at least some integral psychotherapists attend more to patients' states (i.e., affective, self, regressive, dissociative states, etc.) than any other iPT construct. From any affective state to those states induced by drugs or contemplative practice; to an aspect of a patient's presenting problem (most episodes of depression, mania, psychoses, etc. are just that—episodic states—not permanent, enduring traits of patients); or to the states of consciousness of the therapist, if therapists do not pay attention to the shifting, varying states of consciousness of both patient and therapist, they will not recognize the actual experience of what it is like to be that person—how that person's "rubber actually meets the road." Depending on their state of consciousness, patients may be more or less open to certain counseling interventions (Fosha, 2000; Greenberg, 2011; Yalom, 2002). If they are too "revved up," they are unlikely to be able to "sit with" what is present and deeply process what they are experiencing. Conversely, "when we exist in the ontological mode—the realm beyond everyday concerns—we are in a state of particular readiness for personal change" (Yalom, 2002, p. 127). Obvious examples of the value of inducing altered states of consciousness can be seen in the work of Ericksonian Hypnosis (Erickson & Rossi, 1981), Eye Movement Desensitization Reprocessing (Shapiro, 2001), or dream work (Hill, 1996). Carl Rogers (1986) eloquently addressed how the therapist's own state of consciousness may have tremendous impact on the therapeutic process:

> When I am at my best . . . when I am closest to my inner, intuitive self . . . when perhaps I am in a slightly altered state of consciousness in the relationship, then whatever I do seems to be full of healing. Then simply my *presence* is releasing and helpful. (p. 198)

---

10 When a person's type meets criteria for a personality disorder, this is considered less healthy or "worse" because, by definition, it involves significant impairments of self-functioning and interpersonal relating that are pervasive in the person's life (APA, 2013).
11 This is not to deny the existence or significance of "steady states" (Anchin, 2008, p. 333), but rather to attempt to distinguish between phenomena that can appear very similar, but may arise from different processes.

Last but not least, integral therapists also attend closely to each patient's *self*: "The *self-system* or *self-sense* (or just the *self*)," in contrast to the quadrants, levels, lines, types, or states, "is where the action is" (Wilber, 2000c, p. 548, original italics). The self is the seat of a host of significant operations and capacities, such as *identification* (self-identity), *organization* (providing a sense of cohesion to one's experience), *will* (choosing and initiating action), *defense* (the employment of defense mechanisms), *metabolism* (psychological digestion of one's experiences), and *navigation* (one's journey through the developmental labyrinth). Not only is it the self that balances, integrates, and navigates the assorted levels, lines, states, and so forth, it is also the experiential center of each individual's psychological universe; but it is important *not* to reify the self into a "thing." In other words, although at any given moment in time, the objects of one's attention (what is currently occupying a person's mind) are composed of particular contents (i.e., nouns), the self is the *process or activity* of constructing one's sense of identity. Much more will be said about the self-system in chapter 3.

Some Additional Aspects of My Integral Psychotherapeutic Approach

Because iPT is by nature a metatheoretical approach to psychotherapy, the specific emphases in approaches of different practitioners of iPT will vary. For example, I draw heavily from psychodynamic (from McWilliams, 1994, 2004, Wachtel, 2008, and Fosha, 2000 to Davanloo, 2000, Frederickson, 2013, and Abbass, 2015) and existential (Yalom, 1980, May, 1977, Bugental, 1981) approaches; Janice Holden is informed more by cognitive therapy, schema-focused therapy, and Assagioli's psychosynthesis; Elliott Ingersoll is heavily existential and analytical (Jungian); Sarah Hubbard draws most heavily from psychodynamic and mindfulness-based approaches; Baron Short draws heavily from cognitive-behavioral and mindfulness-based therapies; and Janet Lewis draws heavily from humanistic and psychodynamic therapies.[12] The following are some other crucial aspects of my integral approach to psychotherapy; more principles that guide my work will be discussed in chapter 7.

---

12 I emailed all of the above integral psychotherapists and asked them: "Please let me know the one or two approaches you draw from most heavily." Mark Forman replied that he draws heavily from all the major approaches: behavioral, cognitive, trauma-focused, psychodynamic, interpersonal, Jungian, humanistic/existential, feminist, multicultural, and transpersonal. I asked the question the way I did (emphasizing the one or two approaches that most inform their work) to highlight the theoretical diversity within the iPT community. At the same time, the question I asked limited most of the responses I received. Although my "response"—psychodynamic and existential—is true of me, it leaves out other extremely important approaches I draw upon, such as behavioral exposure for anxiety-related problems (see chapter 8 of this book).

Process Even in the Context of Structure

As previously mentioned, although integral theorists frequently discuss various psychological "structures," it is critical to bear in mind that "structure" ultimately refers to a relatively stable *pattern* of events. Thus, even in the context of discussing structures, I stress *process* thinking—conceptualizing with verbs more than nouns and resisting temptations to reify psychological processes into static structures. "Structures" are not ultimately static or unchanging; the difference between structure and process is really a matter of the *rate* at which they change: "Steady states ... are not static. At any given moment in time, a steady state is also characterized by variation and flux" (Anchin, 2008, pp. 331–332; see also Mahoney, 1991).

A Few Constructive-Psychodynamic Points

Although many integral therapists work primarily from a cognitive-behavioral perspective, I have been deeply influenced by Mahoney's developmental constructivism (1991, 2003), as well as the relational psychodynamic tradition (Wachtel, 2008; Stolorow, Brandchaft, & Atwood, 1987; Fosha, 2000) and Intensive Short-Term Dynamic Psychotherapy (ISTDP; Davanloo, 2005, 2000; Frederickson, 2013; Abbass, 2015). Thus, any consideration of psychological life would be, from my point of view, incomplete without attention to unconscious processes. Consistent with Mahoney (2003) and relational psychodynamics, I view relationships as "the central process of human adaptation, function and dysfunction" (Magnavita, 2006, p. 887), as well as the attachment system being the foundation of our psychological lives (Fosha, 2000). I also view affect and emotion as central to human development and motivation, and consider various forms of emotional dysregulation to be central to most forms of psychopathology (Fosha, 2000; Greenberg, 2002; Magnavita, 2006; Mahoney, 1991; Mahoney & Marquis, 2002; Davanloo, 2000; Frederickson, 2013; Abbass, 2015; Smith, Lane, & Goldman, 2017).

Given that integral metatheory aligns so well with Mahoney's (metatheoretical) developmental constructivism (1991, 2003), I want to address the five basic themes and four "core ordering processes" of Mahoney's unifying system (the interested reader can also consult "Integral Constructivism and Dynamic Systems in Psychotherapy Processes"; Mahoney & Marquis, 2002). The five basic themes are: 1) active agency, 2) order/organization, 3) self/identity, 4) social-symbolic processes, and 5) dynamic dialectical life span development; before addressing these, I want to summarize some of the insights that Mahoney (1991, 2003) distilled and for which he is perhaps best known: "human change processes."

Human Change Processes

Human change processes are nonlinear—neither cumulative nor continuous, they usually involve gradual "baby steps" that are punctuated by sporadic regressions or larger leaps forward. Oscillations—between expanding–contracting, opening–closing, or engaging–disengaging—are also pervasive in human development.

Because novelty and disorder are essential for development, developmental processes involve periods of perturbation and disruption in functioning and experience; this disorder may or may not become problematic. Under conditions of novelty or developmental challenge that produce disorder and disorganization, a person may become maladaptively rigid or adaptively flexible. If the novelty is insufficient, the person may stagnate; if the challenge exceeds a person's capacities, the individual may "breakdown" into excessive disorder. Ideally, novel disruptions are optimally challenging to one's developmental capacities, resulting in a "breakthrough" transformation. Resistance to change is the norm—particularly if too much is changing too quickly; such resistance is a form of self-protection and, in general, should be empathically worked with, not against. Thus, the pacing and magnitude of such developmental challenges are critically important. Attentional skills are paramount, and new insights must be actively practiced. As such, techniques, homework assignments, and other structured experiments in living can function to promote and elaborate valued experiences. Relationships characterized by strong affective bonds, safety, and intimacy are especially potent crucibles for personal change. Likewise, a host of spiritual—not necessarily religious— practices appear to be significant in their potentials for personal transformation. Because compassion and care are among central spiritual practices essential to life, they are also essential to counseling and psychotherapy (Mahoney, 2003).

Active Agency

Human experience is a function of continuous and fundamentally anticipatory *activity*. In other words, we are active participants and creators of our lives, not mere passive pawns. Importantly, simply "paying attention" is a profoundly important act of agency (activity does not need to be externally observable). The practice of various attentional skills is often helpful to patients, ideally when engaged in regularly and paired with behavioral action.

Order/Organization

Human agency is fundamentally devoted to *ordering processes* (the organizing and patterning of experience) that are largely emotional in nature; they are primarily nonconscious, and they constitute the essence of meaning-making. Emotions function as ordering processes by directing our attention, shaping our perceptions, organizing our memory, and motivating adaptive action. Developmental constructivism views emotions not as unhealthy, bad, or dangerous; rather, the pervasive denial or avoidance of them is usually detrimental to health. Although challenges to our ordering systems are phenomenologically disruptive and disorganizing, they are essential to learning and development. For example, although the experience of losing one's faith in the orthodox doctrines of one's religion may be psychologically and socially painful and disruptive, coming to view one's self, others, and the world in a less confined manner may ultimately result in a greater sense of possibility, compassion, and engagement.

Self/Identity

The organization of experience is essentially recursive or self-referential, which results in a phenomenological sense of personal identity or *selfhood* as the center of our psychological universe. One's sense of self is usually linked with one's sense of reality, and one's relationship to one's self is indicative of, and plays a determinative role in, one's life quality. Importantly, this self is a process, or verb—not a noun; moreover, it is not isolated or separate. In other words, the self is a coherent yet fluid perspective from which we experience life, and it emerges from and changes predominantly within emotional relationships with others.

Social-Symbolic Processes

Social-symbolic processes are pervasive influences on how we obtain and maintain order and meaning. We are embedded within webs of relationships and other social discourse practices that are mediated by language and other symbol systems. Although the Western notion of self usually implies individuality, selfhood (as well as meaning) emerges only within (intersubjective) relationships; as such, we are as much "embedduals" as we are individuals (Kegan, 1982).

Dynamic Dialectical Life Span Development

Humans can potentially develop throughout the entire course of their lives. Development always involves the *tensions of contrasts* (good–bad; possible–impossible; approach–avoid; me–not me; us–them; able–unable) and oscillations between opening (expanding) and closing (contracting) are common. Extreme contraction is a natural response to overwhelming challenges to our current organizational processes, and periods of disorganization are usually required in the reorganization and integration that is involved in healthy human development.

Core Ordering Processes

Core ordering processes (COPs) are deeply abstract and nonconscious processes that are central to our psychological experiencing and meaning-making. When a person changes in important, long-lasting ways, what changes most are her COPs. However, being so central to our experience, COPs tend to be rather stable and difficult to change. The four COPs, which are not completely separate from each other, are: 1) reality, 2) value, 3) self, and 4) power. *Reality* refers to a person's worldview—the individual's perceptions and constructions along dimensions such as real–unreal, meaningful–meaningless, and possible–impossible. *Value* refers to valuing processes—constructing emotional judgments (which require assigning a *val*ence—positive or negative) along dimensions such as good–bad, approach–avoid, and right–wrong. *Self* refers to that with which one identifies, constructed along dimensions such as me–not me, body–world, and us–them. *Power* refers to a sense of control and agency, constructed along dimensions such as engaged–disengaged, hopeful–hopeless, and in–out of control.

Theory and Practice

A new theory without new practices is akin to a map without a territory (Wilber, 2006). Thus, integral metatheory urges one not only to conceptualize differently, but also to practice and/or research differently; subsequent chapters will demonstrate this. I want to emphasize that an integral approach consists of a network of practices that allows us to honor the value of a vast array of approaches (from epistemological issues in research to practical interventions in psychotherapy), while also recognizing that each approach is optimal in specific situations, and less so in others. Thinking integrally also provides a potentially self-correcting reminder to conceptualize from, and work with, all four dimensions (all-quadrants) of our patients' being-in-the-world, at the most appropriate developmental level of consciousness (all-levels); it will also continually prompt us when we are not honoring an important mode of our own or others' being-in-the-world: all-quadrants, all-levels, all-lines, all-types, and all-states.

Integral metatheory affords an unusually comprehensive way of conceptualizing, researching, and practicing psychotherapy because it honors the validity of each major psychotherapy theory and its associated set of methodologies and techniques while simultaneously recognizing the incompleteness and blind spots of each. Thus far, I have in several places mentioned the value of "keeping all" perspectives, "making room" for all approaches, or honoring the validity of each psychotherapy theory. However, this must be understood with the caveat that I am referring to the *major* approaches to psychotherapy and that there are other, less widely accepted approaches that may be simply wrong, ineffective, or harmful (i.e., aromatherapy, holding therapy, past-life regression, rebirthing; Neukrug, 2015), and this may be illustrated by way of historical examples. In the not-too-distant past, bloodletting and humoral balancing,[13] phrenology, mesmerism/animal magnetism, and lobotomies were all considered sound scientific and medical practices. In fact, Antonio Egas Moniz shared the 1949 Nobel Prize for Physiology or Medicine for discovering the use of the lobotomy. However, these practices have all been discredited as scientifically unsound or more harmful than helpful. It was only with sustained scientific scrutiny and continued research that they were recognized as faulty or unsafe. It is likely that some of today's psychotherapeutic approaches will likewise eventually be recognized as essentially faulty, as less effective than other therapies, or as appropriate for only a small subset of patients. Unfortunately, it is currently difficult to ascertain which aspects of which therapeutic approaches are not helpful or at least less helpful for specific conditions. One thing is clear: Simple lists of

---

13 The four humors—black bile, yellow bile, blood, and phlegm—supposedly represented different temperaments—melancholic, choleric, sanguine, and phlegmatic, respectively.

"Empirically Supported Treatments" are far from infallible guides in such matters (see chapter 9 and Marquis & Douthit, 2006). It seems that the best we can do is to continually and critically evaluate not only the empirical literature but also the assumptions and rationales underlying therapeutic approaches that have not been subjected to well-designed research.

As one example of a major psychotherapy approach either having "blind spots" or being "true but partial," most of the cognitive therapy I have observed—whether watching "expert" videos, conference presentations, or reading clinical examples from highly regarded cognitive therapists such as Aaron Beck (in Wedding and Corsini, 2010)—focuses more on patients' self-talk, their automatic thoughts and assumptions, and examining the evidence for and against various thoughts than it focuses on working to change patients' maladaptive schemas; Wachtel and Greenberg (2010) made a similar point, and see also Henriques (2017, p. 18). Obviously, this is not true of all cognitive therapy, but Gregg Henriques (who worked with Aaron Beck for four years and published 15 articles with him) agrees that cognitive therapists far more often work to help patients with coping skills than with the deeper schema work that is required to remedy more chronic depression, anxiety, or personality disorders (personal communication, April 7, 2017).[14] This is not to suggest that helping patients cope is unimportant, but equally important is acknowledging what type of interventions are best suited to what types of patient problems (coping or deeper characterological change). In the case of patients with chronic problems, more deeply experiential work—whether experiential psychodynamic approaches, emotion-focused therapy, or cognitive-based yet experiential approaches such as Jeffrey Young's schema therapy—appears to be needed (Fosha, 2000; Greenberg, 2002; Young, Klosko, & Weishaar, 2006; Osborn et al., 2014).

Integral metatheory takes a step beyond most pluralistic stances by revealing *how* the diversity can be unified in a more encompassing and compassionate framework (AQAL) that salvages the validity of each stance by relieving each of its absolutisms. When the various theories, methodologies, and interventions are unified, we have a transformation *from a partial pluralism to an integral holism* (Wilber, 2006). The remaining chapters in this book will reveal how this is done— with regard to issues of research, assessment, human development, and the etiology and treatment of psychopathology.

Whereas the translation of theory to practice for single-system/pure-form therapies is somewhat straightforward, for a *metatheoretical* approach such as integral psychotherapy that *attempts* to be *comprehensively unifying* (integrating not only intrapsychic, interpersonal, and behavioral approaches, but also neurobiological, cultural, and systems perspectives as well as other metatheories such as

---

14 This is also a primary reason that Michael Mahoney—who was one of the pioneers of the "cognitive revolution"—ceased calling himself a cognitive therapist and adopted "developmental constructivism" as the term to describe his more experiential approach to psychotherapy (Mahoney, 2000, 2003).

developmental constructivism), it is difficult, if not impossible, to *do in practice* everything that the theory suggests; as a consequence, the translation of integral metatheory into psychotherapy practice thus far has been somewhat general. As I have stated in previously published works (Marquis, 2008, 2009) and have recently demonstrated empirically (Marquis & Elliot 2015; Marquis et al., 2015), most courses of integral psychotherapy with a given patient do not attend to every construct previously discussed (quadrants, levels, lines, states, types, self); however, any one of those constructs may be central to a specific patient's struggles and positive change.

Integral metatheory can help us heal the wounds and mend the fractures of an increasingly fragmented and suffering world by providing a systematic, coherent, and consistent framework that not only allows one to draw upon the entire gamut of psychotherapeutic theories and practices but also urges therapists to heal more than just psyches. In other words, quadratic thinking reveals the dire need to transform not just the thoughts and self-experience of individuals (UL), but also the social systems (LR) that contribute to human suffering. This means that, as professional helpers, we may need to begin to work toward transforming the unjust systemic structures that promote human suffering. As someone who was trained as a psychotherapist, I admit that I am not well-versed in how to effect large-scale transformations in social structures such as poverty, racism, and classism, but I suspect that at least some, if not most, readers agree that truly comprehensive therapy must address all of the sources of our patients' distress and, clearly, such systemic forces generate tremendous suffering (Wachtel, 2017).[15]

Conclusion

This has been a brief overview of integral metatheory, a unifying conceptual framework that Walsh and Vaughan (1994) referred to as "systematic, broad-ranging, multidisciplinary, integrative, visionary yet scholarly ... perhaps unparalleled" (p. 18). Perhaps you have disagreed with some of the details, or perhaps you are concerned that developmental models can be used to marginalize certain people (a concern that I refer to as "developmental abuse," 2008, p. 97). If you think that Wilber or I have overgeneralized, that is possible. The attempt to unify such divergent approaches necessarily involves a level of abstraction that requires

---

15 One example of such social inequities is the fact that although

> people from all strata of society *use* drugs, enforcement of drug laws and incarceration fall more heavily on African Americans, Latinos, and those living in poor neighborhoods and/or inner cities (Beatty, 2010; Moyers, 1998) ... An all-too-common and unfortunate reality is that, for poor people who are caught using illicit substances, what they get is a stay in prison waiting for a placement in a rehabilitation center that almost never materializes. In essence, our public policy allows the wealthy person with a drug problem to go to Betty Ford whereas the poor person will likely go to jail (Moyers, 1998). (Ingersoll & Marquis, 2014, p. 290)

orienting generalizations that may not always do justice to the detailed specifics that are central to those therapists who specialize in single-system approaches or who treat patients with only one or a few disorders, or to scholars with more narrow research agendas. The voicing of disconfirming details will hasten our accommodating the integral model to "fit with the facts." That is, after all, a primary manner through which scientific knowledge develops.

CHAPTER 3

Developmental Dynamics and States of Consciousness[1]

> The complexity of human change processes merits appreciation. Human development rarely follows a simple, linear path. It is more often a zigzag course, with frequent sticking points, repetitive circles, occasional regressions, and a few startling leaps and falls. The particulars may seem dizzying in their diversity, yet *there are patterns. Patterns suggest principles. Understanding the principles of human development is essential to the task of psychotherapy.* (Mahoney, 2003, pp. 9–10, italics added)

Introduction

As the quote above suggests, issues of human development are central to psychotherapy. Moreover, human development—even though it is complex, manifests tremendously diverse particulars, and is influenced by myriad sociocultural contexts—does follow patterns and principles. Those principles and patterns (structures) are essential to better understand the nature of what it means to develop, influences on human change processes, milestones in those processes, and problems that can arise within the course of development.

Why are developmental theories—and particularly developmental psychology— important to psychotherapy? First and foremost,

> Psychotherapy *is* applied developmental psychology. The therapist uses his or her knowledge of normal development to reach some conclusions about the reason for a patient's malfunctioning and how one may enter the developmental spiral either to foster or to reinstitute a more productive, or at least less destructive, developmental process ... the model of the developmental spiral provides such a framework for gauging therapeutic interventions. (Basch, 1988, p. 29)

---

[1] Parts of this chapter are adapted from chapters 4 and 5 of Marquis, A. (2008). *The integral intake: A guide to comprehensive idiographic assessment in integral psychotherapy.* New York: Routledge.

Many of the troubles and challenges with which patients present are intimately related to issues in their development. Furthermore, meaning-making is a process that is central to human experience and successful counseling (Mahoney, 2003; Cook-Greuter & Soulen, 2007), and understanding how a given patient makes meaning is greatly aided by an understanding of various developmental processes, from cognitive and moral development (Piaget, 1977; Kohlberg, 1990; Gilligan, 1982) to ego and worldview development (Loevinger, 1976; Cook-Greuter, 2003; Wilber, 2000b). Essentially, people vary not only along dimensions such as personality *types*; they also differ significantly as a function of their developmental *levels* of meaning-making (Kegan, 1982; Cook-Greuter & Soulen, 2007). Whereas different types (such as the personality styles posited and assessed by the Myers-Briggs Type Indicator) are often emphasized as being equally valid styles, there are clear advantages, greater capacities, and more complexity associated with later stages of human development. To take an example, think of the activity of being a psychotherapist. Now compare how effective two differentially developed therapists would be: one who has little capacity for abstract thought (characteristic of Piaget's concrete-operational stage of development) and who has very little awareness of emotional dynamics (Goleman, 1995; Salovey, Brackett, & Mayer, 2004); and another who not only can think abstractly and dialectically—seeing patterns and principles that structure various patients' problems, even when they are apparently contradictory—but also has an exquisitely developed sense of intrapersonal and interpersonal dynamics that results in a highly integrated sense of emotional intelligence. Given equal training, which of the two therapists would be more effective? The answer is clear.

In several previous publications (Marquis, 2008; Fall, Holden & Marquis 2004/2017), I have expounded upon many of the developmental principles that Wilber (2000b) posited; those are often related to *stages* of development. For years, I have grappled with the issue of the value of stage models of development and how they pertain to psychotherapy. As an example, it seems incontrovertible that humans do, in fact, develop through stages of development (think of Piaget's stages of cognitive development or Loevinger's stages of ego development). On the other hand, Mahoney's (1991) magnum opus—*Human Change Processes*—discusses dynamics of human development for 455 pages and stages of development are seldom mentioned. My current view is that stage models of human development are essential to a "theory of the person" but that they are less relevant (though far from irrelevant) to the moment-to-moment practice of psychotherapy (which involves both a "theory of the person" and a "theory of change processes" within the person); my reasons for this position will be explained in the second half of this chapter. In short, any unified psychotherapy needs to have a unified theory of human nature, and the developmental model of integral theory is essential to that. This chapter will address how developmental dynamics and states of consciousness are involved in both human nature and the process of psychotherapy; these issues will be intertwined throughout the chapter.

A thesis of Wilber's that has been central to the extant iPT literature is the "spectrum of development, pathology, and treatment" (addressed in detail in

Marquis, 2008). Briefly stated, this thesis maintains that "at each stage of self development, an arrest, fixation, or dissociation from that stage results in a specific psychogenic pathology" (Marquis & Wilber, 2008, p. 355). Similar notions have been proposed by various researchers and therapists within psychoanalytic, psychodynamic, and other developmental circles (McWilliams, 1994; Kernberg, 1980; Kohut, 1984; Masterson, 1981; Fosha, 2000; Ivey, 1986; Mahoney, 1991). What distinguishes Wilber's thesis is the more comprehensive developmental spectrum that he addresses, which spans from the earliest developmental stages (Mahler, Pine, & Bergman, 1975) up through what he, for many years, referred to as transpersonal or suprapersonal stages (Wilber, 2000a, 2000b).[2] Perhaps even more significantly, Wilber suggests that different psychotherapeutic approaches are optimally suited for patients suffering from the psychogenic pathologies that derive from the developmental derailments associated with specific stages of development.[3] Although this notion has been posited by a variety of psychotherapy scholars—from McWilliams (1994) to Ivey (1986)—I will discuss why I think it is not of paramount clinical utility (again, in the second half of the chapter).

At the same time, applying a developmental perspective certainly *does* allow therapists to better understand, and empathize with, their patients. For example, one's ego development is central to how one makes meaning, and meaning-making is crucial to the experience of well-being and the "good life." Thus, failing to take a patient's level of ego development into consideration will likely result in a therapist projecting her own manner of meaning-making upon the patient, thus failing to accurately understand the patient and his problem(s). At times, a single

---

2   In the "Wilber–Combs Lattice" (W–C Lattice; Wilber, 2006, pp. 88–93; you can Google it to see the figure), this spectrum model of development was significantly revised. In the W–C Lattice, there are no transpersonal stages; rather, there are four distinct transpersonal *states* of consciousness (psychic, subtle, causal, and nondual), each of which can arise at any of the stages of development: "Thus, gross/psychic, subtle, causal, and nondual were no longer stages *stacked on top* of the Western conventional stages, but were states (including altered states and peak experiences) that can and did occur *alongside* any of those stages" (Wilber, 2006, p. 91). The W–C Lattice is a significant conceptual improvement over Wilber's preceding developmental model, but it seems that Wilber and some integral psychotherapists (i.e., Forman, 2010) still refer to transpersonal *stages* of development.

3   Here is what I wrote with Wilber in 2008, which I no longer find to be of very much specific help with regard to moment-to-moment clinical work:

> Corresponding to stages of development from birth to potential enlightenment, the psychogenic psychopathologies and their proposed corresponding treatment modalities are: sensoriphysical/psychoses/psychopharmaceutical and behavioral; emotional-phantasmic/borderline- and narcissistic personality disorders/structure-building approaches; representational mind/neuroses/uncovering approaches; rule-role mind/script pathologies/cognitive approaches; formal-reflexive/identity neuroses/Socratic dialogue; vision-logic/existential pathologies/experiential and existential approaches; psychic/psychic disorders/nature mysticism, subtle/subtle disorders/deity mysticism, and causal/causal disorders/formless mysticism. For an in-depth exploration of this issue, see Wilber (1999, vol. 4, pp. 80–160). (Marquis & Wilber, 2008, p. 355)

More on this issue will be discussed subsequently in this chapter.

developmental principle underlies a multitude of patient concerns; failing to take a developmental view renders one blind to such critical phenomena. For example, a patient of mine who was a freshman college student came to counseling because she no longer felt she fit in at home or church. Not only was Jennifer[4] experiencing more conflict at home and church, she also frequently argued with her boyfriend. In addition to the conflict and not feeling that she "belonged" in her home, church, or romantic relationship, Jennifer felt increasingly lonely and misunderstood in the same contexts that previously had so well met her needs. Some therapists might have implemented a "problem-solving" approach, perhaps teaching conflict resolution skills and so forth. Any number of her apparently discrete problems could have been the focus of her sessions with such a therapist. From a developmental perspective, however, I saw that Jennifer was transitioning from a previously conformist (rule/role) level of development into a more conscientious (formal reflexive) level of development. Her father was highly authoritarian and her Baptist church was likewise; her southern boyfriend upheld traditional gender roles.

It was no coincidence that she was finishing her second semester of liberal arts courses—which she reported were incredibly stimulating and were "opening up" her mind—when she began to question the rigidity and universality of the moral codes with which she had been raised. Encountering not only a diversity of students, she was now also engaged with new ideas and worldviews, which suddenly and rather drastically altered her perception of herself and the world around her. I conceived of her fundamental "problem"—and all of its associated challenges and pain—as a developmental one and communicated the following ideas to her (not exactly as in this monologue, but the same basic ideas):

> It seems to me that in some ways you are *outgrowing* your family, church, and boyfriend; which doesn't mean you don't still love, need, and want them—but that you are orienting or positioning yourself differently with them. Correct me if this doesn't fit, but it struck me that the very rules and structures in your family and church that you once felt most comforting and inspiring are now the very things you find the most constraining and irritating. Your previously adopting the codes of various groups—such as your family and church—without evaluating those codes for yourself was developmentally appropriate. It's also developmentally appropriate that you are now concerned with thinking for yourself, coming to your own conscientious decisions about how to lead your life, and expressing yourself even when your views differ from others. The difficulty rests in how to do that and maintain your ties to your family, church, and boyfriend; or you may choose to find a different faith community or boyfriend.

---

4 All names and other identifying information have been changed to protect the identities of patients who are discussed in examples throughout this book.

This patient felt liberated by my framing her "problem" as a normal developmental experience: "Developmental theory has been too long separated from clinical practice" (Ivey, 1986, p. 2). If she had seen a therapist that had construed her problems as merely relationship or family troubles and worked on communication skills, assertiveness training, or conflict resolution, a significant developmental opportunity would have been lost. Jennifer and I worked together for about 30 sessions and I had the pleasure of witnessing her blossom into a young woman who thought for herself, became more relativistic in her moral stances, and was excited to be alive. Her boyfriend could not tolerate her changes and they broke up. Likewise, she left her authoritarian church and began attending a Unitarian church. Though both of the losses were painful, she found enjoyment and meaning amidst her grieving. She continued to have "heated discussions" with her family and she was often simultaneously distressed and excited by the dissolution of rigid rules structuring how she related to her family. She felt "more alive" than she ever had when she terminated therapy. Much of my counseling with her was simply contextualizing her experience within a developmental framework, helping her process her experience via Socratic-type dialogue, and offering feedback and empathy along the way.

According to Ivey, "providing an appropriate therapeutic environment that is matched to the current developmental level of the client may be useful in facilitating growth and change" (1986, p. 141). Thus, with Jennifer's emerging formal-reflexive capacities, much of our work was introspective and philosophical in nature. She valued that our relationship was a place where she could "sort things out for herself"—that we discussed ideas and "examined the evidence" for various viewpoints. Though she did feel more anxiety than she used to (probably because she no longer benefited from the comforts of being associated with the "one true way" to follow), she was invigorated by her new quest to develop into the person she was becoming, and she experienced her newfound freedom as intoxicating.

Given that Jennifer was quite clearly transitioning out of a conformist/sociocentric worldview into a more conscientious/worldcentric worldview, what I offered her was very different from what I would provide a patient who was highly egocentric. In the latter case, encouraging the patient to take, and conform to, the perspective of his family and church members (provided that those perspectives were not harmful, pathological, etc.), and helping him see the downside of his acting only out of his own self-interests, would constitute more of the work of therapy. For him, developing an appreciation of the value of a structure beyond himself to which he could conform would be a major transformation; and that is also the very structure/stage that was confining Jennifer, and out of which she emerged as a more mature young woman. Thus, different interventions and approaches are needed both to support patients at their current level and also to "challenge" them at their current level, thus facilitating their developing into subsequent stages, wider worldviews, and further integration (Cook-Greuter & Soulen, 2007).

General Principles of Developmental Dynamics and Therapeutic Processes

Mahoney (1991) wrote that because life and human change processes are complex, so too must therapy be complex. Some of the developmental principles that are common to most stage theories—which may make the complexities a bit more manageable—include:[5]

- Development follows a repeated pattern of *differentiation* (separation, agency) and *integration* (connection, communion) (Wilber, 2000a; Mahoney, 1991; Kegan, 1982).
- Development can occur throughout one's entire life (Mahoney, 1991; Ivey, 1986).
- Development takes place in various sociocultural contexts, many of which we are not consciously aware of (Ivey, 1986; Mahoney, 2003; Wachtel, 2008).
- People at a given stage rarely (perhaps never) prefer the solutions (or ways of being) characterizing the previous stage(s) (Kegan, 1982, p. 56; Piaget, 1977).
- Each new stage or balance brings with it the capacity to see others more fully as they are in their distinct integrity (Kegan, 1982; Cook-Greuter & Soulen, 2007).
- Development involves a process of an unfolding of potentials that leads to greater understanding of dynamic phenomena and effective action, with worldviews evolving from simpler to more complex (Cook-Greuter & Soulen, 2007; Wilber, 1995).
- *Overall*, human development is teleonomic (having directionality without a specific endpoint or final goal), but there is also spiraling (plenty of regressions and nonlinearity; Mahoney, 1991).
- Each later stage is increasingly complex, holistic, enveloping, and holarchical (a holarchy is a hierarchy composed of holons; a holon is that which is simultaneously a whole entity and also a component part of a larger whole entity; for more detail on holons, see footnote 2 in chapter 2 on p. 21; Wilber, 2000a).
- "People's stage of development influences what they identify with, notice, or can become aware of, and therefore, what they can describe, articulate, influence, and change" (Cook-Greuter & Soulen, 2007, p. 184).
- Subsequent stages reveal an increase of: tolerance for ambiguity and diversity; reflection, flexibility, and skillful interaction in the world (Kegan, 1982; Cook-Greuter & Soulen, 2007).
- Development is a never-ending process: regardless of how developed we may become, our understanding and knowledge always remain partial and incomplete (Cook-Greuter & Soulen, 2007; Forman, 2010; Mahoney, 2003).

In a nutshell, later stages of development demonstrate more behavioral flexibility, increased cognitive capacities, and a greater sensitivity to others' experiences,

---

5 These bulleted, general principles will be elaborated upon throughout this chapter.

especially when those experiences are different from one's own; all of which tends to facilitate more intimate, satisfying, and therapeutic relationships, whether professional or not (Cook-Greuter & Soulen, 2007; Ingersoll & Zeitler, 2010). Although the following is a very general statement (and all generalization is, to some extent, overgeneralization), people functioning from later developmental levels can potentially understand people at earlier levels of development, whereas the reverse is not the case (for example, consider how someone with only concrete operational capacities will not be able to understand the abstract thoughts of someone with formal operational capacities; the same holds true for affective and other forms of development). Each subsequent developmental stage is also more differentiated, more comprehensive, and more effective in resolving dilemmas, problems, and other complexities than is its predecessors.

Many stage theories of human development have incorporated key Piagetian notions. For example, each stage of development includes a period of *preparation*, followed by a period of *relatively* stable achievement. According to Piaget, "development is spotty, local, and uneven. A concept may appear in one form, but take a year or more to extend itself over its possible range" (1977, p. xxv). This unevenness, or *decalage*, was thought by Piaget to be an explanatory principle for development: that the more highly developed structures *coexist* with the lower ones and this coexistence generates the conflict, disequilibrium, and dissonance that spur further growth. The concept of *equilibration* was central to Piaget's theory. Briefly, it refers to the individual's effort to keep his or her cognitive structures in balance. States of disequilibrium are inherently dissatisfying, and the organism will do what it can to re-equilibrate.

Humans clearly have needs both for relationships, connectedness, and belonging, on the one hand, as well as for autonomy, individuation, and agency on the other. Each stage of development thus constitutes something of a "balancing act," "dynamic stability," or "evolutionary truce" (Kegan, 1982, p. 44) between those mutually defining needs, with each stage representing a shift in the balance: one stage emphasizes connectedness, the next emphasizes separation, and so on (Kegan, 1982; Cook-Greuter & Soulen, 2007). Neither pole is better than the other. Both are needed; the tension between the two is part and parcel of evolutionary motion. In fact, according to Kegan (1982) the two greatest strivings in human experience are for 1) inclusion, connection, belonging, and *communion* and 2) independence, autonomy, separateness, and *agency*. These two yearnings may appear to be in conflict but it is actually their dialectical relation and generative tension that is most important. Thus, even if masculine types (whether male or female) tend to emphasize agency and feminine types (whether male or female) tend to emphasize communion, "both men and women exist as agency-in-communion (as do all holons)" (Wilber, 2000c, p. 588, parentheses in original); this duality of fundamental human motives, characterized in precisely these two terms—i.e., agency and communion—is also central to contemporary Sullivanian-based interpersonal approaches (e.g., Anchin & Pincus, 2010).

Development and Therapy

As therapists, we must be able to apprehend what it is like to be our patient (Rogers, 1961). Because others' (perceived) worlds and worldviews are in large part a function of their development (although their perception is also critically influenced by numerous contexts; Wachtel, 2008), one can far more readily and accurately apprehend their worlds and worldviews if one understands their developmental capacities: "If one is to understand others, one must understand their epistemology, or way of knowing the world ... It does little good to offer a formal operational therapy to a client who is unable to operate concretely upon the world" (Ivey, 1986, pp. 138–139).

If you recall the quote by Basch in the introduction of this chapter, he referred to his model of a developmental "spiral." Numerous developmentalists use the metaphor or model of a spiral (Kegan, 1982; Cook-Greuter, 2000; Mahoney, 2003; Wilber, 1999). Even though the specific contents of Basch's developmental spiral (decision-making, behaviors, self-esteem) differ from those of other developmentalists, the *principles* with which developmental therapists assess patients and then tailor approaches suited to where in a developmental model patients are stuck are the same: assess what normal developmental processes or tasks were not successfully accomplished/navigated and then facilitate the patient's successfully ameliorating that previous deficit (whether that deficit has more to do with the person's internal world or external holding environment, culture, or social system). Furthermore, such therapists use their developmental knowledge to more fully empathize with patients' self-experience. For example, people at different developmental waves are aware of vastly different *cognitive* possibilities (Piaget, Wilber), *value* different things (Graves), and *make meaning* via different processes (Kegan; Cook-Greuter). Thus, a therapist's ability to provide different forms of environments—different "cultures of embeddedness" (Kegan, 1982, p. 118)—based upon the developmental needs of each individual is essential to effectively helping a spectrum of people: "It is the environment the therapist provides that determines the future growth and development of the client" (Ivey, 1986, p. 131). For example, some patients need a therapeutic environment (relationship) that is primarily comforting and stabilizing, whereas other patients benefit more from a therapeutic relationship that is more challenging and de-stabilizing; more on these dynamics will be addressed in chapter 7.

Integral Principles of Developmental Dynamics and Therapeutic Processes

The Self-System

The self—or, more properly, the self-system—is central to any attempt to understand human nature (a "theory of the person"), and it is likewise fundamental to psychotherapy. As previously mentioned, the *self* is not so much a thing or noun as it is an action or verb—the dynamic and usually tacit *process* that holds together the developmental lines, constructing something of a cohesive whole that recursively serves as each person's psychological universe. Integral theory distinguishes between the self-sense (the self as experienced by a person from inside; phenomenologically experienced with a zone 1 methodology) and the self or self-system (the self as viewed and conceptualized from outside; structurally analyzed with a zone 2 methodology); see p. 222 for the eight zones and their respective methodologies.

Proximate and Distal Selves

Although constituting the same self-system, the distal and proximate selves are distinct constructs that have practical consequences for psychotherapy. If you consider your "self" you will notice two qualitatively distinct aspects: all of the things about yourself that you are capable of observing and describing (*distal self*; experienced as *me*; the *objects* of your awareness, such as being a husband, teacher, friend; enjoys outdoor activities, etc.) and also some observing self that is aware of those descriptive components of yourself (*proximate self*; experienced as *I*; the inner *subject* or witness of experience). With this in mind, Wilber summarized the fundamental developmental dynamic (which is also relevant to therapeutic dynamics) as:

> *The "I" of one stage becomes a "me" at the next.* That is, what you are identified with (or embedded in) at one stage of development (and what you therefore experience very intimately as an "I") tends to become transcended, or disidentified with, or de-embedded at the next, so you can see it more objectively, with some distance and detachment. In other words, the *subject* of one stage becomes an *object* [of the subject] of the next stage (2000b, p. 34, italics in original, brackets added).

For example, sensorimotor infants identify almost exclusively with their bodies and thus their bodies constitute who they are as subjects, or "I"s. As such, they are not capable of reflecting upon and observing their bodies as *aspects* of who they are; rather, they *are* body-selves. Once they develop the pre- and concrete-operational capacities of symbols and concepts, they begin to identify with mental concepts (mind becomes their subject or "I") and can then observe and reflect upon their bodies as objects of awareness. Their bodies are now the object of their new subject, mind. Thus (and to repeat): "*the 'I' of one stage becomes a 'me'* [or 'it' or 'mine'] *at the next*" stage (Wilber, 2000b, p. 34, italics in original, brackets added).

A technique that many integral psychotherapists use that involves the aforementioned principle is the process of making what one is currently embedded in (and thus *subject* to) an *object* of one's awareness. Rather than view and react to the world *from* various unacknowledged assumptions, schemas, or emotions, such assumptions, schemas, or emotions are made objects of one's awareness; in this manner, one can gain clarity and understanding about them such that one then has the freedom to potentially perceive and act differently with regard to, or change, such assumptions, schemas, or emotions. For example, I counseled a patient years ago who was court-ordered to attend therapy because of his history of violence. When I initially asked him to tell me about himself, the first words he spoke were "I'm a violent man"—as if that was the *whole* of who he was. Although it took a few months, he would later respond to that same query with "*part* of who I am is aggressive or violent, but those are really adjectives that do not describe the real me, which is more difficult to explain." In this case, what he was previously subject to, identified with, and embedded in—violence—became an object of his awareness with which he no longer exclusively identified. Wilber described this relationship between what is subject and what is object to oneself as a process in which "a *mode* of self becomes merely a *component* of a higher-order self" (1980, p. 81, italics in original).

Wilber has described the above process in a number of different ways. In addition to the notions that *what was subject becomes object* and *what was the whole becomes a part*, he has also said that "what is *identification* becomes *detachment* ... what is *context* becomes *content*" (1980, p. 81, italics in original). These dynamics were echoed by Kegan (1982) as the balancing act between subject and object. According to Kegan, development always involves a process of differentiating objects from the subject we are in the process of being and becoming, a process of emerging from prior embeddedness:

> The notion of development as a sequence of internalizations, a favorite conception of psychodynamic thinking, is quite consistent with the Piagetian concept of growth ... In fact, something cannot be internalized until we emerge from our embeddedness in it, for it is our embeddedness, our subjectivity, that leads us to project it onto the world in our constitution of reality. (Kegan, 1982, p. 31)

Kegan further described development as "the evolutionary motion of differentiation (or emergence from embeddedness) and reintegration (relation to, rather than embeddedness in, the world)" (Kegan, 1982, p. 39, parentheses in original). Kegan also made it clear that although developmental lines such as cognition and affect clearly develop or evolve, the context in which this evolutionary motion occurs is that of the self. That which has emerged from embeddedness (what we are in relation to) is the distal self. Whatever is currently identified with (that in which one is embedded) is the proximate self. Such an evolutionary or developmental conception of the self is pertinent to psychotherapy because how a person settles the matter of what is "self" and what is "other" actually construes the *psychologic* (the underlying psychological reasons) of that person's meaning-making (Kegan, 1982). To again underscore that human development cannot be understood apart from its many contexts and that stages are anything but rigid stabilities, Kegan writes:

> what is the subject–object relationship the person has become in the world? ... subject–object relations *become*; they are not static ... subject–object relations live *in the world*; they are not simply abstractions, but take form

in actual human relations and social contexts ... these self–other distinctions are in fact tenuous, fragile, precarious states. They are balances, I have said ... They are truces, I have said; chaos and a state of siege hang around the corner ... The "stages" in their seductive clarity ... [are] markers in an ongoing process. They mark those periods of relative balance in the lifelong process of evolution ... As important as it is to understand the way the person creates the world, we must also understand the way the world creates the person ... Each balance suggests how the person is composed, but each suggests, too, a new way for the person to lose her composure. (1982, p. 114)

Self-System Pathology: When the Subject/Object Balance Becomes the Subject/Other Dynamic

At this point, it may be helpful to point out that the statement about the subject becoming an object is a 3rd-person conceptualization of something that occurs within a 1st person (a zone 2 description). Phenomenologically (a zone 1 description), a person experiences "what was 'I' has become 'me' (or 'mine')." This is important in order to distinguish healthy from unhealthy development.

In healthy self-development, 1st-person "I" becomes 1st-person "me" or "mine" (Wilber, 2006). What is most significant about this process is that even though the me/mine (object) is no longer exclusively identified with (it is, in fact, *dis*-identified with), the *me/mine/objects are owned*. What was subject has become object, but not just any object, *my* 1st-person object, an object of *my* new subject.

In unhealthy self-development—by way of contrast—1st-person "I" becomes 2nd-person "you" or 3rd-person "it" (Wilber, 2006). Rather than assuming responsibility and ownership for aspects of oneself, the person dissociates from and projects those aspects onto others or the world at large. Although differentiation and dis-identification are essential to healthy development, that is the case only when what has been dis-identified with is still owned as an object of oneself. A great deal of psychological pathologies involve projecting, dis-identifying, or dissociating from parts of oneself without "owning" and integrating those parts.

To demonstrate how people project their disowned feelings, thoughts, etc. onto others or dissociate from them so that they are perceived as 3rd-person "its," recall the patient with violent tendencies mentioned above. During one of our sessions, he was in the process of becoming angry, as evidenced by a tense face, gritting his teeth, and clenching the arms of his chair so tightly that his knuckles were literally white. When I commented that he appeared angry, he burst out, "Me! I'm not angry, but *you* seem infuriated with me" (to the best of my self-monitoring/self-awareness capacities, I don't think I was angry; that session was videotaped and none of my supervision group that watched it thought I was angry either). Moreover, that same patient, especially in the beginning of our work together, often spoke not of "I became angry" but of "being overcome with anger [it] or violent thoughts [its]"—as if they were not part of him (3rd-person "its").

As can be seen from this discussion and the example, having a 1st-person dynamic (such as "I am angry") converted into 2nd-person ("I'm not angry, *you* are!") or 3rd-person ("the anger, *it* just took control of me") dynamics is usually unhealthy. Make note of the "**1–2–3**" process in the preceding sentence. Because disowning 1st-person qualities (projecting or dissociating them to 2nd persons or 3rd persons) is usually unhealthy, what is therapeutic is the reversal of that dynamic, what Wilber refers to as "the 3–2–1 process of (re)owning the self before transcending it" or more simply as the "3–2–1 process" (2006, p. 136). In its most skeletal form, the 3–2–1 process involves the patient's converting those 3rd-person "its" into 2nd-person "others" or "yous" with which they can then have a dialogue. In the case of the angry patient, he takes the 3rd-person anger that "overcomes" him, converts that into another (2nd) person who is angry (whether that is the therapist or anyone else) and then—à la empty chair work—has a dialogue with the 2nd-person "other" who is angry. After some insights into a given patient's issues and that which was disowned, projected, etc., the goal is for the patient to re-identify with the other voice (the 2nd person) as part of one's own 1st person, thus moving from a 2nd-person dialogue to a 1st-person monologue. The 3–2–1 process works with the repression barrier and the mechanisms of projection and dissociation (1–2–3), resulting in therapeutic ownership (3–2–1) of different aspects of one's being. For more details on the 3–2–1 process, consult Wilber (2006). To repeat and summarize: healthy self-development transforms I into *me* or *mine*; pathological self-development transforms I into *you* (an *other*) or *it*.

As was mentioned in chapter 2, psychological development is not simply an Upper-Left quadrant issue: genetics, developmental histories, and the cultures and systems into which one is born may severely constrain one's choices and freedom. Nonetheless, people, like other biological systems, do self-organize (Maturana & Varela, 1987; Guidano, 1987; Mahoney, 1991). As such, people can be viewed as self-organizing systems whose development throughout the lifecourse is substantially regulated by processes of differentiation and integration through structural organizations of increasing complexity (Guidano, 1987), and self-awareness and self-reflection play an essential role in this differentiation and integration process.

> Each time the self (the proximate self) encounters a new level in the Great Nest [one of Wilber's metaphors for the developmental spectrum], it first *identifies* with it and consolidates it; then disidentifies with it (*transcends* [*differentiates* from] it, de-embeds from it); and then includes and *integrates* it from the higher level. In other words, the self goes through a *fulcrum (or a milestone) of its own development.* (Wilber, 2000b, p. 35, italics and parentheses in original, brackets added)

The line of the proximate self is a particularly important line for integral therapists because "proximate self development is at the very heart of the evolution of consciousness. *For it is the proximate self that is the navigator through the basic waves in the Great Nest of Being*" (Wilber, 2000b, p. 35, italics in original). Wilber defined a "fulcrum" of development as a type of developmental milestone, and thus each new stage is a fulcrum. Analogous to the traditional definition of "fulcrum" (the point of support upon which a lever pivots), a developmental fulcrum involves the basic structures that support the generation of a new sense of self. Thus, one's fulcrum is the current probability wave around which one's functioning and way of being "teeters," sometimes reaching slightly forward, sometimes dipping slightly backward. However, "fulcrum" and level/stage/wave/structure are synonymous only with regard to the line of proximate–self development (Wilber, 2000b), which is most closely assessed in a formal manner with measures of ego development (Hy & Loevinger, 1996).

The Line of Ego Development

Ego development is inextricably involved with meaning-making, and, as Kegan notes, nothing we do as humans is more fundamental than make meaning from our experience:

> The activity of being a person is the activity of meaning-making. There is thus no feeling, no experience, no thought, no perception, independent of a meaning-making context in which it *becomes* a feeling, an experience, a thought, a perception, because we *are* the meaning-making context ... "Experience is not what happens to you," Aldous Huxley said, "it's what you *do* with what happens to you" (1972). And the most fundamental thing we do with what happens to us is organize it. We literally make sense. (Kegan, 1982, p. 11)

Loevinger's (1976; Hy & Loevinger, 1996) concept of *ego development* is a broad, holistic stage model addressing the development of a unitary personality construct throughout the life span. According to Loevinger (1976), ego is a holistic construct representing the fundamental structural unity of personality organization. Ego involves both the person's integrative processes in dealing with diverse intrapersonal and interpersonal experiences, as well as the consequent frame of reference that is used to create self-consistency and meaning. Ego (self-sense or identity) structurally develops through nine distinct stages in a hierarchical, invariantly sequential manner with an inner logic pervading their progression. The stages represent a reorganizing of the self-system at each level, resulting in greater: awareness of self and others, flexibility, personal autonomy, and responsibility (Loevinger, 1976; Hy & Loevinger, 1996).

The nine stages of psychological maturity through which ego develops include characteristics ranging from an external approach to oneself and the world (i.e., external sources of reinforcement, lack of insight into oneself, projection of blame) to an increasing internalization of one's experience, interests, and control (i.e., awareness of thoughts, desires, motives; emphasis on self-reliance and competence; and autonomy). Ego operates as an overarching master trait, broadly subsuming a number of other developmental sequences, including: 1) *character development*, which incorporates impulse control and moral development as the basis for moral preoccupations and concerns; 2) *cognitive style*, which incorporates levels of both cognitive complexity and cognitive development; 3) *interpersonal style*, which addresses the attitude toward interpersonal relationships and other people, understanding of relationships, and the preferred type of relationship; and 4) *conscious preoccupations*, which involve the dominant themes of the person's thoughts and behavior. Antecedent constructs from the psychological literature include Adler's "style of life" (Ansbacher & Ansbacher, 1956), Sullivan's (1953) "self-system," and Erikson's (1963, 1980) "psychosocial development."

Ego development represents a developmental characterology of psychological maturation beginning in childhood and extending throughout adult life (Loevinger, 1976). It is similar in structure to other significant developmental processes, such as cognitive development, in that it consists of a series of stages of maturation defined independently of chronological age. However, ego development does tend to increase with age fairly uniformly throughout childhood and then manifest differentially as a function of age sometime during adolescence and adulthood (Loevinger & Wessler, 1970). The age beyond which differential stages occur appears to be approximately 14, after which a wide spread of ego development levels may be found in any given cohort (Hauser, Powers, & Noam, 1991).

As an *organismic* approach, ego development theory is modeled on living systems, in contrast to machines; considers inherent properties and goals; and emphasizes the whole rather than the parts, the relations among the parts, and how the whole gives meaning to the parts (Miller, 2002). Organismic theories presume an active exchange between the self-system and the environment in which the self-system both selects particular environments and also acts from a repertoire of responses to accommodate itself to those environments (Blasi, 1976).

The self-system's *structure* provides the framework and horizon of both selectivity and possible forms of response. This concept emphasizes the underlying organizational processes that operate upon the diversity of specific content. Fundamentally, development consists of a change in the basic rules governing the various elements (Blasi, 1976).

According to structural developmental theory, the selectivity and flexibility—similar to Piaget's (1977) assimilation and accommodation—provided by each structure allow for the system's overall stability (Blasi, 1976). The foremost tendency of the system at each stage is to endure and remain the same, preserving the current structural characteristics. However, the system's stability may have limits. Structural tensions may arise as the result of internal processes or environmental pressures, wherein the flexibility of responses becomes inadequate to deal with the stressors of the environment. The result is a disequilibration, in which case the structure must shift (i.e., self-organize) in order to accommodate the tension, or the system will disintegrate. In psychological development, the impulse toward structure change is typically influenced by the desire to become more competent, satisfy one's needs more adequately, or grasp the world more fully (Blasi, 1976).

Currently, Loevinger's model consists of nine stages, although, for reasons explained below, one is not addressed by the Washington University Sentence-Completion Test (WUSCT). The following are brief descriptions of each stage—adapted from Loevinger (1976, 1998), Hy and Loevinger (1996), and Manners and Durkin (2001).

Pre-social/symbiotic (E1). Exclusive focus on gratification of immediate needs; strong attachment to caregiver(s); engaged in differentiating self and objects; because it is preverbal, it is not capable of being assessed via the sentence completion method; thus, this stage is postulated for theoretical completeness.

Impulsive (E2). Emphasis on physical needs and impulses; no sense of psychological causation; demanding; conceptually confused; self and others understood in simple dichotomies (good/bad, nice/mean, etc.); unable to distinguish emotional and physical malaise.

Self-Protective (E3). Wary; complaining; opportunistic; beginning to be capable of delay for immediate advantage; blame assigned to others, circumstances, or a part of themselves for which they are not responsible; preoccupied with staying out of trouble and not getting caught.

Conformist (E4). Conventional; moralistic; sentimental; identified with group or authority; rules accepted because they are the rules; friendliness and social niceness highly valued; behavior of self and others seen in terms of externals; conceptually simple; cooperative; loyal.

Self-Aware (E5). Increased, although limited, self-awareness and appreciation of multiple perspectives; exceptions for rules allowable, but only in broad demographic terms; slightly more focused on feelings, problems, and adjustment; banal reflections on life issues such as God, death, and relationships.

Conscientious (E6). Self-evaluated standards; "ought" differentiated from "is"; motives and consequences more important than rules; intense; responsible; empathic; long-term goals and ideals; rich and differentiated inner life; values achievement; striving for goals; attempts to improve self; thinking beyond personal concerns.

Individualistic (E7). Sense of personality as a whole or style of life; tolerant of self and others; inner self and outer self are differentiated; values relationships over achievement; awareness of inner conflicts without resolution; particular concern with emotional dependence; awareness of psychological causation and development; role differentiation.

Autonomous (E8). Recognition of others' need for autonomy; moral dichotomies no longer typical; free from excessive striving and sense of responsibility; high tolerance for ambiguity and recognition of paradox; relationships seen as interdependent rather than dependent/independent; values uniqueness; vivid expression of feelings; self-fulfillment; clear sense of psychological causation; existential rather than hostile humor.

Integrated (E9). Wise; broadly empathic; full sense of identity; broad differences in descriptions of qualified raters but probably best illustrated by Maslow's concept of the self-actualizing person who is growth motivated, seeking to understand his/her intrinsic nature and achieve integration; very rare (research suggests that less than 1% of adult populations in urban areas develop into this stage; Hy and Loevinger, 1996).

Since its initial development, Loevinger's model has been refined, extended, and validated through an extensive body of research (Loevinger, 1979, 1985, 1998; Manners & Durkin, 2001). Researchers have completed more than 280 studies to explore various aspects of ego development (Cohn, 1991). A comprehensive review of the literature continued to support the conceptual soundness of the theory (Manners & Durkin, 2001).

Ego Development and Psychotherapy

Given the nature of the domains (character development, cognitive style, interpersonal style, conscious preoccupations) that are theorized to be interwoven in the fabric of ego development in Loevinger's model, it would intuitively seem that considerations regarding the construct and its role in the practice of psychotherapy would be appropriate. For example, character development addresses the development of moral concerns and ethical decision-making, which are often foci in the practice of, and content addressed in, counseling and psychotherapy (Miller, 2004; Ingersoll & Marquis, 2014; Herlihy & Corey, 1996). Cognitive style encompasses cognitive complexity, tolerance for ambiguity, and understanding of psychological causation, all of which potentially have a bearing on a patient's manner of relating to distress and meaning-making activities. Finally, interpersonal style captures the nature of relationships, including the understanding of others and the types of relationships that are sought.

Holding Environments and Cultures of Embeddedness

All development occurs within a variety of social and cultural contexts (LR and LL), from caregiver–child bonds, family relations, peer groups, schools, religious institutions, work, and other community affiliations, all the way to national and global economic and political systems (Mahoney, 1991; Wachtel, 2008; Wilber, 2000b). Kegan (1982) describes in great detail the different "cultures of embeddedness"—including mothering, role-recognizing, mutuality, self-authorship, intimacy, etc.—that optimally provide the qualitatively distinct "holding environments" that individuals need at each stage of development. Kegan emphasizes the significance of our embeddedness to such an extent that he wrote that:

> In Winnicott's view the "holding environment" is an idea intrinsic to infancy. In my view it is an idea intrinsic to *evolution* ... They are the psychosocial environments which hold us (with which we are fused) and which let us go (from which we differentiate) ... There is never "just an individual"; the very word refers only to that side of the person that is individuated, the side of differentiation. There is always, as well, the side that is embedded; the *person* is

more than an individual. "Individual" names a current state of evolution; "person" refers to the fundamental motion of evolution itself, and is as much about that side of the self embedded in the life-surround as that which is individuated from it. The person is an "individual" *and* an "embeddual." (Kegan, 1982, p. 116)

Many of the most fascinating aspects of development entail the occurrences and experiences *between* two stages of development, when people are teetering or transitioning between different ways of identifying with and understanding themselves and the world. To actually emerge into a new evolutionary balance, one must both differentiate and integrate (not just differentiate):

the tolerance won out of the differentiation from the societal is not a balanced position from which to construct the moral world (how can you be tolerant of the intolerant?) precisely because it does not represent a new evolutionary truce. It is differentiation without integration. (Kegan, 1982, p. 66, parentheses in original)

Many developmental models refer to subsequent stages of development as "higher," a term against which many others react negatively. However, such terms are developmental judgments, not judgments about the value of people themselves. Thus, a teenager is not more valuable or worthy as a person than a toddler, but most teenagers are less egocentric and more capable of resolving more complex problems than toddlers are. Relative to this notion of height and altitude, integral theorists often describe development using the metaphor of climbing a mountain. First, most mountains do not have only one path to their peak. Thus, different types of people, or cultures, may develop with different emphases, just as one person may prefer a steeper, shorter path or hike up a mountain, whereas another prefers the longer, more gradual path. Second, some people's goal may not be the peak, but rather a beautiful meadow two-thirds of the way up the mountain. Third, some paths may afford views that other paths may not, just as both counseling, meditation, serving others, and conscious relationships can all foster development through very different experiences.

Despite those differences, the different paths that actually arrive at the summit must have passed through all of the same altitudes, and although the specifics (surface features) of the views from different paths may have varied, higher altitudes will disclose greater, not lesser, views. That is to say, as one's altitude/vantage point increases, more of the territory below is available to one's perspective: not only the beautiful valleys and streams below, but also the darker, shadow spots that were formerly hidden by trees and other life-scenery. As one nears the peak, and especially at the summit of one of the higher mountains in a mountain range, one can see beyond one's own mountain to other mountains and distant possibilities on the increasingly revealing horizon. "The more the hikers can see, the wiser, more timely, more systematic and informed their actions and decisions are likely to be. This is so because more of the relevant information, connections and dynamic relationships become visible" (Cook-Greuter & Soulen, 2007, p. 183).

However, higher altitudes are not increasingly free from problems and distress. Wilber termed this notion the "dialectic of progress," meaning that, in addition to resolving prior problems, further development confronts one with new, potentially more horrifying ones. For example, developing into an autonomous, formal reflexive thinker may free one from falling prey to a herd mentality, but it also opens one up to existential anxieties that do not exist (at least not nearly as intensely) at conformist levels. On this issue, Mahoney emphasized that "none of us can realistically hope to arrive at a level of development that is free of problems ... Development creates new levels of difficulties, to be sure, but development also begets enlarged capacities for embracing the overall process" (2003, p. 88).

Reality therapists (Glasser, 1990) have made the analogy that if humans are front-wheel-drive automobiles, then the front wheels (which we directly influence with our steering) are our thoughts and behaviors, whereas our feelings and physiology (which are more difficult to directly influence) are the rear wheels. I would add that larger systems, from economic and political to educational and religious systems, are the roads and highway systems that structure where and how we drive. Of course, there always seem to be a few, rare developmental leading edge "trail blazers" who drive off-road. Most of us, however, are largely constrained by these larger social and cultural systems, many of which operate outside of our conscious awareness.

A Few Distinctions

A key issue is that integral theory strongly maintains that stages of development are not rigid essences or molds; rather, they are like "evolutionary grooves or habits"—*relatively stable patterns* of events or ways of being.

Stages, Levels, Structures, and Waves

Recall from chapter 2 that Wilber uses the term "levels" to refer to the qualitatively distinct degrees of complexity or organization that characterize the different stages of development; "structures" to emphasize the holistic, integrated nature of each stage; and "waves" to underscore the fluid confluences with which the stages meet and join with one another. Does integral theory posit basic structures? Yes. Rigid, reified structures? No. Waves? Yes. Fluid? Certainly. Wilber definitely views humans as developing through stages. But what exactly is a stage model of human development? According to McCarthy (1978), stage models specify:

> An invariant sequence of discrete and increasingly complex developmental stages, whereby no stage can be passed over and each higher stage implies or presupposes the previous stages. This does not exclude regressions, overlaps, arrested developments, and the like. Stages are constructed wholes that differ qualitatively from one another ... ordered in an invariant and hierarchically structured sequence; no later phase can be [stably] attained

before earlier ones have been passed through, and elements of earlier phases are preserved, transformed, and reintegrated in the later. In short, the developmental-logical approach requires the specification of a hierarchy of structural wholes in which the later, more complex, and more encompassing developmental stages presuppose and build upon the earlier. (cited in Wilber, 1999, p. 50)

Although Wilber posits that each developmental line develops in an invariant sequence and that subsequent stages cannot be stably "attained before earlier ones have been passed through," people do not need to perfectly master all of the tasks associated with a stage of development in order to proceed to the next stage. Also, even when conceived of as integrated structures, those structures (patterns) are not reified. Rather, they are viewed as probability waves, full of complex dynamics such as lines, states, types, and subpersonalities. As Wilber has emphasized:

Please remember one thing: these stages (and stage models) are just conceptual snapshots of the great and ever-flowing River of Life. There is simply nothing anywhere in the Kosmos called the [place the name of any stage of development here] (except in the conceptual space of theoreticians who believe it). This is *not* to say that stages are *mere* constructions or are socially constructed, which is the oppositely lopsided view. Stages are real in the sense that there is something actually existing that occurs in the real world and that we call development or growth. It's just that "stages" of that growth are indeed simply snapshots that we take at particular points in time and from a particular perspective (*which itself grows and develops*). (2006, pp. 58–69; italics and parentheses in original; brackets added)

Stages of Development (Levels and Lines) and States of Consciousness

People are tremendously diverse; not all differences, however, are of the same nature. For example, Justin and Babatunde may differ because they were raised in very different cultures; or they may differ because one of them is much more developed with regard to logico-mathematical operations and the linguistic line and the other is more developed in moral and emotional lines; or they may appear different at this moment because they are experiencing highly different states of consciousness (i.e., one is intoxicated, panicked, or having a deeply emotional experience, whereas the other is in a rational, calm state of mind).

"*Development is the aim of counseling and psychotherapy* . . . Staying put, refusing or being unable to change are what development is not" (Ivey, 1986, p. 28, italics in original). I agree, and it is also important to recognize that not all change is developmental or transformative; hence Wilber's distinction between *transformation* and *translation*. Translation is *horizontal growth*—change or expansion *within* one's stage of development that modifies *surface structures* without fundamentally altering the *deep structures*.[6] Translation can entail learning new information, developing new skills, or transferring knowledge from one domain to another, none of which necessarily involves a fundamental shift in how a person interprets life and makes meaning (Cook-Greuter & Soulen, 2007). In contrast, transformation is *vertical development*—a transition to a new stage of development that fundamentally alters and shifts the deep structures of a person's being and functioning. Transformation involves the emergence of a new, more integrated perspective; it is much rarer in adults than is translation because it requires a literal transformation of one's view of reality, self, and others: "In general, transformations in awareness or changes in our mental modes are more powerful than any amount of horizontal growth and learning" (Cook-Greuter & Soulen, 2007, p. 182.).

In my experience, most patients seek translative, not transformative, change. Thus, integral therapists often work toward what Wilber (1999) called the *prime directive:* helping patients stabilize at their current level of development. That is to say, even if what a patient desires the most is transformation, he must first become fully grounded at his current level. Doing intensive transformative work (which may take the form of prolonged meditative and other potentially self-transcending types of spiritual practice) when one is not fully stabilized and grounded is like building a mansion without first laying a solid foundation.

The Spectrum of Development, Pathology, and Treatment

Whereas Wilber's spectrum of development, pathology, and treatment (which was mentioned on pp. 25–27) formed the center of the chapter devoted to developmental issues in my *Integral Intake* book (Marquis, 2008), research has tentatively suggested that it should not occupy such a central role in iPT (Marquis & Elliot, 2015).[7] First, the exact relationship between developmental stages and psychogenic pathology remains speculative and conjectural. Second, Wilber's treatment matching hypothesis—the thesis that particular theoretical approaches are differentially useful with various forms of psychopathology, the latter of which he posits correspond to specific levels of overall self-development (a person's developmental "center of gravity," the level of ego development that a person inhabits most of the time)—is likely more conceptually elegant than it is useful in informing moment-to-moment clinical decisions (i.e., it describes the "logic" of development more than the actual lived experience and "messy" dynamics of development; this

---

6 The *deep structures* represent the defining underlying, patterned organization of each stage and appear to be cross-cultural, largely invariant, and quasi-universal (Wilber, 1999). *Surface structures*, in contrast, are highly culturally influenced and thus are unique to specific types of people, locales, and so forth; more on this later in the chapter.

7 Recall, and perhaps revisit, the distinction made on pp. 27–28 of chapter 2 between a "theory of the person" and a "theory of psychotherapy." Although many of the preceding developmental considerations may not occupy a central role in the moment-to-moment practice of psychotherapy, they are, nonetheless, essential to fully understanding human nature ("theory of the person"), which cannot be neatly separated from the practice of psychotherapy.

distinction will be discussed subsequently in this chapter). Third, applying Wilber's spectrum of development, pathology, and treatment to clinical practice relies heavily on the notion of the patient's developmental "center of gravity," and the results of Marquis and Elliot (2015)—although perhaps not reflecting the view of all integral psychotherapists—suggest that the clinical utility of the "center of gravity" construct is not as significant as much of the extant iPT literature suggests. Before I offer critiques of Wilber's treatment matching thesis and the center of gravity construct, I will explain the former a bit further, though only in broad contours; I went into far more detail in Marquis (2008, especially chapters 4 and 7). Bear in mind that the following principles (in the next two paragraphs) that Wilber (2000b) posited are very general and suggestive rather than known with certainty; he further stated explicitly that they are not meant to be applied in a rigid manner.

Because *psychotic*, *borderline*, and *narcissistic* patients (disorders that ostensibly derive from the first two *prepersonal* levels of development in Wilber's model) lack the psychological structure (i.e., "ego" or "self") required to make their experiences cohere in a relatively stable manner—which promotes the sense of being an individuated self that is separate-yet-related to others—some form of "structure-building" approach is most helpful to these people. Common examples of structure-building approaches include those of Kernberg (1980), Kohut (1977, 1984), Masterson (1981), and Linehan (1993a, 1993b). For individuals struggling primarily with *neuroses*—in which disturbing symptoms arise that are symbolic of repressed, projected, or otherwise-defended-against emotions and impulses—"uncovering approaches" are more useful. A neurotic patient has developed enough psychological structure to repress, rationalize, etc.; that is, after all, why his or her issues are seeking expression in symbolic symptoms such as disturbing dreams, somatisized bodily pains, depression, anxiety, phobias, and so forth. Thus, these patients do not need to build structure (as do those patients with psychotic, borderline, and narcissistic *levels* of organization). Rather, neurotic patients will benefit more from *uncovering* what they have pushed out of their awareness; hence, the general category of uncovering approaches (which spans the entire spectrum of psychoanalytic, psychodynamic, and other "depth" approaches).

The next general category of treatments involves those patients who have developmentally acquired a relatively coherent and individuated sense of self, but are challenged with struggles revolving around the process of further elaborating and defining their autonomy and/or interdependence in terms of the rules and roles they abide by and by deeper answers to questions such as "who am I?" and "how can I live as fully and authentically as possible?" (disorders that ostensibly derive from *personal* levels of development). For patients with *script pathologies* and/or systematic biases in reasoning and thinking, cognitive approaches appear most effective (Wilber, 2000b). For patients with *identity neuroses*—in which the individual struggles with establishing autonomy and self-directedness rather than merely conforming to societal, cultural, and other collective standards—an introspective, philosophical approach will likely be most helpful (Wilber, 2000b). For patients whose primary concerns are *existential* in nature—such as deeply assuming responsibility for one's life, acknowledging one's mortality, isolation, freedom, and striving to live an authentic, self-actualizing life—existential-humanistic approaches (i.e., Yalom, Bugental, Perls, Rogers) are likely most effective.

In previous publications, I have stated that paying attention to the following will help one assess a patient's developmental center of gravity:

- their use of language, which reflects thought processes: Is the patient able to think abstractly? Is the patient open to examining the evidence for his thoughts and opinions? Is he willing and capable of changing those thoughts, opinions, etc.?
- the degree of differentiation and complexity in his meaning-making activities;
- how the patient relates to you (i.e., reciprocally or merely as an extension of himself; countertransferential reactions you observe in yourself that you think the patient is eliciting in you);
- the patient's most commonly used defenses;
- signs of developmental arrests or fixations, such as intense needs that appear regressive or age-inappropriate.

Critique of the Spectrum of Development, Pathology, and Treatment[8]

Although this thesis of Wilber's is potentially an important contribution, it also bears significant limitations. In short, it is overgeneralized when it comes to clinical practice. Importantly, Wilber (2000b) did not presume a precise one-to-one correspondence, noting that "it is not that a given therapy applies only to one level of development, but that, in focusing on one or two levels, most forms of therapy increasingly lose their effectiveness when applied to more distant realms" (p. 97). Nevertheless, the complexity of interactions between psychopathology, development, and psychotherapy is such that, even with the preceding caveat, the "on the ground" clinical reality is far messier than Wilber's thesis implies. Thus, while Wilber's thesis may be reasonable and reflect considerable truth value in a general sense, it is not at all neatly applicable within the "actual territory" of therapy.

Although I, like many psychotherapy scholars (i.e., Mahoney, 1991; McWilliams, 1994), agree with general principles such as not using uncovering approaches with borderline or psychotic patients (they would need some form of structure-building; a general form of treatment matching consistent with Wilber's thesis), McWilliams (1994) stated that

---

[8] The following critiques of Wilber's treatment matching thesis and the center of gravity construct derive largely from Marquis and Elliot (2015). I want to thank Sarah Hubbard, Janet Lewis, and Baron Short for all of the time, effort, and thoughtful reflections they contributed to the Integral Psychotherapy in Practice (IPP) study, some of which are reported here.

this way of conceptualizing degree of pathology is not without usefulness ... But it falls short of a comprehensive and clinically nuanced ideal ... The model is too gross to permit a sensitive practitioner to derive from it any *specific* ideas about what kinds of human relatedness will be therapeutic to what kinds of human beings. (p. 44; italics added)

McWilliams' quotation captures the views of the Integral Psychotherapy in Practice (IPP) study therapists perfectly: in a very general sense, Wilber's thesis has utility, but it is far too overgeneralized to be very helpful with the complexities and "messiness" of clinical realities. The notion of matching theoretically based treatments to a type of pathology and developmental level is an oversimplification precisely because it overstates the influence of stages and structure and understates the *variability* associated with patients' *states* and thus the fluidity and ambiguity inherent in the therapeutic process:

Describing people as characterized by a particular developmental level ... fails to ask *when* they manifest whatever is being attributed to them ... attention to these other (and often healthier and more adaptive) ways of being—and examination of when they do and do not appear (that is, of their contextual nature)—can greatly enhance our clinical work. (Wachtel, 2008, p. 73)

Wachtel's (2008) concept of *variability*—consonant with the integral construct of *states*—highlights that a given person's experience and behavior vary from context to context; it also informs the clinical imperative to attend to (and bring to the patient's awareness) the reality that he or she is *not always* x, y, or z, as if the person's qualities and capacities derived from only one developmental level.[9] For example, rather than speaking as if a patient is (developmentally) *unable* to relate authentically to significant others, the therapist can refer to the patient's *difficulty* of relating authentically, identify the dynamics that make it so difficult, and highlight those instances when he or she *is* able to actually do so.[10] This represents a dynamic—rather than static—formulation of the patient, and allows the patient

---

9 Some integral theorists might reply that neither Wilber nor they have written that a person's behavior and experience derive solely from a single developmental level. In fact, the "25-50-25" rule, which is frequently referred to among integral theorists (Marquis, 2008, p. 93), suggests that approximately 50% of a person's behavior and experience derive from their developmental center of gravity, and 25% derives from the level beneath and above that level. Despite such understandings in the integral literature, it was the opinion of all of the therapists in the IPP study that integral theorists and therapists frequently lapse into a tendency to describe people as "at" a given stage of development, thus failing to appreciate the complexity and *variability* characteristic of all of us.
10 "Psychological functioning is radically different in different relational environments: conditions of optimal safety and conditions experienced as threatening tend to evoke different ways of being ... We have all felt at ease and confident with one person one minute, only to feel shy and uncomfortable with someone else the next" (Fosha, 2000, pp. 106, 125).

to simultaneously acknowledge the less functional ways he can be, while not conceiving of those "self-at-worst" qualities as who or how he *always* is (Wachtel, 2008; Fosha, 2000). The tendency of some therapists to say things such as "This patient *is not capable* of intimacy" reflects a static, essentialist way of thinking. Similarly, when therapists describe a patient as, for example, borderline, they often implicitly assume or imply that all of his actions and experiences are borderline. Such static formulations are tied to the notion of patients being "at" a certain developmental level, and thus unable to transcend its structural limits. Wachtel emphasizes that thinking contextually, in terms of variability—in contrast to thinking structurally in terms of a given developmental level—does not and should not downplay or ignore patients' limitations and struggles:

> the tragedy in the lives of people with diagnoses such as borderline or narcissistic personality disorder does not lie in a complete absence of "higher level" functioning (see Westen, 1989), but in their terrible *vulnerability* to more problematic modes of functioning. Attending to the variations in their behavior and experience, finding the upward reaches, so to speak, of their personal capacities and modes of relating is not to engage in denial but to find the rungs in the ladder they need to climb. (Wachtel, 2008, pp. 289–290)

Contrary to the idea of a homogeneity of experience and behavior (as from a single developmental level), Wachtel's notion of variability highlights that although referring to someone as "at a given developmental level" may, in some ways, communicate an accurate description of certain key aspects of the person, it is a description without a therapeutic trajectory or narrative of possibility. Thus, it is more therapeutic to help a patient identify those contexts (LL, LR) in which he is less able to relate authentically, as well as the exceptions (i.e., when he *is* able to relate authentically); this facilitates his not feeling as chained to his "inability." Fortunately, the "contextual" quadrants (LL and LR) are already a part of the integral model; the task for integral psychotherapists is to give more attention to them and deeply appreciate that one's experiences (which most integral theorists place squarely in the UL quadrant) are equally a function of relational and systemic contexts (LL and LR) as they are the internal worlds of individuals (UL). In fact, an intersubjective field (LL) is neither a sharing of two or more individuals' experience (UL) nor a mode of experiencing; rather "it is the contextual precondition for having any experience at all" (Stolorow, Atwood, & Orange, 2002, p. 85). Although, on the one hand, it may be helpful to think of contrasts such as interiors and exteriors (the Left- and Right-hand quadrants) and individuals and collectives (the Upper and Lower quadrants), there is another way in which such boundaries are artificial and illusory (Wachtel, 1987; Mahoney, 1991); and even though integral theory posits that the four quadrants "tetra-arise" and mutually influence each other, there is nonetheless a tendency to reify the boundaries between the quadrants that renders some prone to failing to see how contexts influence psychological experience, and thus how variable a person's behavior actually is.

Developmental Dynamics 63

An intimately related issue in some of the iPT literature (as well as much of the psychotherapy literature in general) involves a tendency to view psychological structures as residing in a person's interiors (his "inner world"; UL) *in a manner that is largely sealed off from the many relational (LL) contexts in which he interacts*.[11] In contrast, a deeply contextual, or intersubjective, perspective is sensitively attuned to how a patient's experience does not simply unfold or emerge from "within"; rather, an individual's psychological structures and experience continuously and reciprocally interact with the relational world (Orange et al., 1997). Now, on the one hand, the four quadrants, and the Lower-Left quadrant in particular, point to an understanding of the significance of intersubjective contexts; however, all of the therapists in the IPP study agreed that the iPT literature has thus far failed to adequately address the relational, intersubjective dimensions of psychotherapy. It is important to emphasize that relational thinkers do not exclude or minimize the significance of what is generally conceived of as "intrapsychic"; however, what they do is contextualize such experiences, personality styles, and other characteristics (Wachtel, 2008; Stolorow, Atwood, & Orange, 2002). In contrast, "concepts such as internalization, developmental level, and developmental arrest direct attention inward, to tendencies that are implicitly treated as more or less context-free properties of the single individual" (Wachtel, 2008, p. 57). Developmental levels, like other psychological structures, are not static and do not operate independently from current contexts. "Who" or "what" emerges from "inside" is not determined merely from within; what emerges is also a function of various contexts, even if one is alone. Significantly, aloneness itself is a context; even when alone, we orient ourselves in relation to others (Wachtel, 2008).

There are many clinical implications for such an intersubjective re-contextualization of psychotherapy (which involves underscoring the LL quadrant), one of the more significant involving a recognition of the centrality of *affect* as experienced (by both patient and therapist), in contrast to the primacy of *drive*—as (objectively) observed and theorized by the therapist alone (in isolation):

> Unlike drives, which originate deep within the interior of a Cartesian isolated mind, affect is something that from birth onward is regulated, or misregulated, within ongoing relational systems. Therefore, locating affect at its center automatically entails a radical contextualization of virtually all aspects of human psychological life. (Stolorow, Atwood, & Orange, 2002, pp. 10–11)[12]

---

11 Wachtel and I *do* believe there are structures within individuals. The point is that those structures cannot be known in an objective manner; whatever resides "within" the person will be influenced by the relational context in which the therapist gains access to it: "We can never discover what was lying buried before we entered the scene because our entering the scene inevitably changes the person's experience of the world ... There is no 'immaculate perception' (Nietzsche, 1885) whereby we may simply see the person as he or she 'is,' divorced from our own role in the investigative process and our own point of view" (Wachtel, 2008, pp. 25–26, 36).

12 The central role of affect as a pervasive motivational and organizational process within the child–caregiver system has been corroborated by many developmental psychologists, neuroscientists, and

Before addressing the paramount importance of patients' affective states, some limitations of the center of gravity construct should be addressed. Briefly, the concept of "center of gravity" implies a considerably greater level of functional stability and consistency than actually exists; this is due in large measure to fluctuations in various affective (and other) states. Thus, despite the psychometric soundness of Loevinger's stages of ego development (Manners & Durkin, 2001), the clinical reality—moment-to-moment—is that many patients do not perceive and act from a single stage of development. Thus, it is more therapeutic to tailor our interventions based upon their current *state* (in a given moment), rather than their center of gravity. Wilber has acknowledged that states fluctuate, but also contends that individuals tend to hover around a particular center of gravity. The consensus from the IPP study was that patients' dynamics are much more fluid and messy than the center of gravity construct suggests. If indeed everyone has some lines that are less developed than their center of gravity, then treatment may be more aptly focused upon underdeveloped aspects of the person than upon their level of overall development.

In short, Marquis and Elliot (2015) suggest that actual moment-to-moment treatment is—and should be—driven first and foremost by patients' affective (and other) states. In other words, iPT might be better characterized less as treatment matched to a patient's center of gravity, and more as a relatively fluid process involving shifts in the therapeutic approach and the use of different interventions that correspond to changes in a patient's states in a given session and over the course of therapy.

States and State Work

The Prominence of States

One of the most consistent and pronounced themes to emerge from Marquis and Elliot (2015) was the prominent role of patients' states and "state work" within psychotherapy. This finding is intriguing in part because it stands at odds with the original theoretical assertions of the iPT model, in which states of consciousness have been ascribed less significance than developmental stages/levels, quadrants, and even developmental lines. The IPP study session coders indicated that, at least explicitly, the therapists attended to states more frequently than to quadrants or levels, and this observation was corroborated by the therapists' own perceptions of their work. A clear consensus emerged that states were more salient than other integral constructs in the moment-to-moment therapy process and that attending to and working with patients' states occupied the "lion's share" of therapists' actual intervention.[13]

---

interpersonal neurobiologists (Stern, 1985; Beebe and Lachman, 1994; LeDoux, 1996; Siegel, 2010; Schore, 2003); more on this in chapter 7.
13 It is important to bear in mind that the revisions I am making to Wilber's theory regarding states and their greater prominence than developmental stages in influencing actual moment-to-moment

The Nature of States

"State work" includes clinical attention to patients' affective states (Fosha, 2000; Greenberg, 2002; Davanloo, 2005; Frederickson, 2013; Abbass, 2015; Osborn et al., 2014), "self states" (Wachtel, 2008), dissociative states (van der Kolk, McFarlane, & Weisaeth, 1996; Lanius, Paulsen, & Corrigan, 2014; McWilliams, 1994), and so forth. States may be viewed through several different lenses within integral theory. They correspond to different psychological and physical dimensions, such as motivational, cognitive, affective/emotional, and physiological states. States may also be conceptualized within a quadratic framework; for example, phenomenological (UL) states (e.g., feeling overwhelmed or terrified), neural and behavioral (UR) states, and intersubjective/relational (LL) states.[14] Regardless of how one conceives of or labels states, they are clearly of paramount importance to psychological functioning and iPT; they will be discussed in further detail in chapter 7.

State "Fluidity" and a "Witnessing Capacity" as Markers of Healthy Psychological Functioning

It appears that healthy functioning is characterized by a capacity for fluid movement between states depending on the context, a capacity to be consciously aware of one's state in a given moment, and a capacity to juxtapose different states.[15] Similar to Greenberg's (2002) definition of an adaptive emotion, such context-dependent state fluidity promotes adaptive responding to the environment, in contrast to a relative rigidity and inflexibility of states across situations and events.

---

in-session clinical work are based on consistent findings in several systematic, intensive single-case studies; further research is essential regarding the generalizability of these findings.

14 As has been emphasized throughout this book, changes in the structure or processes of one quadrant impact phenomena in the other quadrants. An excellent example of this is Porges' (2011) polyvagal theory, which has identified and demonstrated how the autonomic nervous system (UR) regulates affective states (UL) and consequent social behavior (LL/LR) (see also Lanius, Paulsen, & Corrigan, 2014).

15 According to Fosha (2000):

By discovering the link between particular self states and others who tend to evoke them ....:

- The patient learns that any bad state is just that, a bad state, and that other states of mind are available. A given state does not have to carry the weight of completely representing the individual's identity. *"I am no good"* changes into *"For now, I'm in a state where I feel I am no good."* The heightened awareness of multiple states often reduces the shame and self-contempt that accompany pathological, self-at-worst configurations.
- With experience, the patient comes to know the features of environments in which positive self states are more likely to be evoked, and those in which negative self states are more likely to come to the fore ...
- Over time, the patient becomes able to give up negative self labels; he comes to understand his more compromised functioning in the context of particular emotional situations and habits of mind resulting from best efforts in difficult earlier situations. (pp. 262–263)

Other aspects to consider in evaluating the relative health of a given state include: the degree of control the patient has over the state; the degree to which the patient remains aware of the environment while in the state; the degree to which the patient is able to communicate while in the state; the patient's sense of identity during the state; and the degree of organization of the patient's inner experience of the state (Walsh, 2007, as cited in Ingersoll & Zeitler, 2010).

State Work: Facilitating Integration

Part of iPT involves facilitating a process in which patients increasingly learn to recognize and observe their multiple states and to move between them more consciously and effectively, a process that may require the integration of previously fragmented and isolated states.

> Being able to rapidly identify such states in himself allows him the greatest leeway to shift states, and if that proves too difficult, at least be clearly aware that this is a state and not a permanent way of being. Optimally, he will acquire a facility and fluency regarding his own patterns, as well as those of others. (Fosha, 2000, p. 269)

It must be emphasized that state work is inherently relational as well as intrapsychic, given that the subjective experience of a state is influenced by different contexts (Stolorow, Atwood, & Orange, 2002).

In spite of the foregoing reservations and potential limitations, and while overgeneralized as a whole, certain aspects of Wilber's treatment matching thesis do have practical traction. For example, with diagnoses reflecting different levels or degrees of severity (e.g., borderline personality organization, neuroses, and self-actualization concerns), differences in the nature of optimal treatment do appear to exist, and those differences tend to follow the structure proposed in Wilber's thesis. Thus, I still advocate that developmental considerations are important to the practice of iPT. A key premise conveying the significance of developmental concerns is that psychological disturbances such as depression, as with life events in general, are experienced and interpreted differently as a function of both one's many contexts and one's developmental center of gravity.

Clarifications and Cautions

Many, if not most, psychotherapy approaches are easily caricatured and distorted. Understanding developmental principles and dynamics provides powerful sources of insight into our patients and the source(s) of their suffering, not to mention the insights we gain into ourselves. However, simply reading about developmental theories will not foster improved clinical skills, and implementing the principles suggested in this chapter requires far more than merely inserting "stage-relevant interventions" into the therapeutic process. Integrating an intellectual understanding of developmental theories with your clinical practice will improve your effectiveness as a therapist; mere reading will not. Ideally, after a period of focused study of developmental literature (i.e., Mahoney, 1991, 2003; Kegan, 1982, 1994; Ivey, 1986; Loevinger, 1976; Cook-Greuter, 2003; Cook-Greuter & Soulen, 2007; McWilliams, 1994; Wilber 1999), one *practices* these principles, then *reflects* upon one's practical experience, continues practicing developmentally while continuing to reflect, and so on. I consider a skilled developmental clinical supervisor indispensable in this learning process, and the supervisor does not need to identify with integral theory in order to be of immense help; most psychodynamic clinicians conceptualize and practice developmentally and individuals like Ivey and Mahoney represent developmentalists from the cognitive therapy tradition. In the same way that mental health practitioners-in-training optimally hone their clinical skills in practica and internships under skilled clinical supervisors (rather than in theoretical courses or without the benefit of seasoned supervisors), learning to practice developmentally is optimally accomplished by counseling many developmentally diverse people under the supervision of a seasoned developmental supervisor.

Many of the cautions and clarifications regarding misuses of iPT involve common misconceptions of stage theories in general. The next sections will explore five common critiques of—or concerns about—stage theories of development: the universality of stages; the irreversibility of stages; the idea of progression itself; linear/ladder models as oversimplifying; and the dangers of hierarchical stage theories. Although the following sections are more pertinent to a theory of human nature than they are to a theory of psychotherapy, they do have implications for the practice of psychotherapy.

Stages: Universal or Context-Bound?

Yes and yes. Although the idea of universal stages of development is currently about as out of vogue in academic social sciences as phrenology is in personality research, integral theory posits that the *basic structures* of consciousness are cross-cultural and universal, or at least quasi-universal. *The basic structures/stages/waves of consciousness represent the degree of consciousness that characterizes any given phenomena*; in our case, these phenomena are people and their development. The basic structures are to consciousness what altitude is to a mountain; both are content free, yet both also set parameters on what is possible:

> The altitude markers themselves (3000 feet, 8000 feet, etc.) are *without content*—they are "empty," just like consciousness per se—but each of the paths can be measured in terms of its altitude up the mountain. The "feet" or "altitude" means degree of development, which means degree of consciousness ... using "altitude" as a general marker of development allows us to refer to general similarities across the various lines, yet altitude as "meters" or "inches" or "yards" **itself has no content**; it is empty. "Inches" is a measure of wood, but nothing in itself. You do not go around saying, "I had to stop building my house today because I ran out of inches." ...

68 Unifying Psychotherapy

> Likewise with "consciousness" when used in this fashion. It is not a thing or a content or a phenomenon ... In particular, consciousness is not itself a line among other lines, but the space in which lines arise. Consciousness is the emptiness, the openness, the clearing in which phenomena arise, and if those phenomena develop in stages, they constitute a developmental line (cognitive, moral, self, values, needs, memes, etc.). The more phenomena that *can* arise in consciousness, the higher the level in that line. Again, consciousness itself is not a phenomenon, but the space in which phenomena arise. (Wilber, 2006; pp. 65–68; bold and italics in original)

As such, Wilber's basic structures are simply markers referring to some of the *relatively stable patterns* that developmental psychologists have observed as they assessed people across their life spans. According to integral theory, the basic structures are not permanently fixed or unchanging essences; they are more akin to evolutionary patterns than pre-given molds (Wilber, 2000b).

> To return to the question of the universality of the stages/structures, the basic structures have deep (universal) structures and surface (local) structures ... (although I usually call these "deep features" and "surface features" to avoid confusion with Chomsky's formulations; also, deep and surface are a sliding scale: deep features can be those features shared by a group, a family, a tribe, a clan, a community, a nation, all humans, all species, all beings. Thus, "deep" doesn't necessarily mean "universal"; it means "shared by others," and research then determines how wide that group is—from a few people to genuine universals. The preponderance of research supports the claim that all of the basic structures, and most of the developmental lines, that I have presented in the charts [of the book *Integral Psychology*], have some universal deep features. (Wilber, 1999, pp. 651–652, parentheses in original, brackets added)

Thus, the deep features of the basic structures represent the defining underlying organization of each level (as in the case of Piaget's sensorimotor, preoperational, concrete-operational, and formal-operational stages, all of which are themselves content free) and appear to be "largely invariant, cross-cultural, and 'quasi-universal'" (Wilber, 1999, p. 50). In contrast are surface features, which are highly culturally influenced and unique to specific locales, types of people, and so forth. For example, whereas Piaget's stages of cognitive development (*deep features*) are universal, the *surface features* of the basic structures—how individuals *use* their cognitive development, the specific *contents* of their thinking, and the *value* assigned to different ways of thinking and knowing—will vary tremendously; they are anything but universal. Thus, two people may share the deep feature of formal-operational thinking, yet express it completely differently: one does calculus; the other writes a novel—two apparently different activities, neither of which could manifest without the capacity for formal-reflexivity.

Although research has revealed cultures in which most adults do not exhibit formal-operational thinking, I am aware of no research that has found Piaget's stages to emerge in an order other than the one he proposed. Regardless of how a culture expresses symbols, concepts, and rules, symbols emerge before concepts, and concepts emerge before the rules that apply to those concepts.[16] Likewise with moral development: conventional stages emerge after preconventional stages, and post-conventional stages emerge after them, whether assessed with Kohlberg's or Gilligan's protocols. Most definitely, the details of various stage models can—and *should*—be critiqued and continually revised to accord with the data. Because they are constructions, there will always be a modicum of arbitrariness regarding where the demarcations are drawn between stages. However, even if future research finds a qualitatively distinct structure of cognition between two of Piaget's stages, or that two of the stages that we previously conceived of as distinct can be understood to operate on a similar principle (and thus represent only one stage of cognitive development), that would not alter Piaget's more central point that children think in symbols before they think in concepts, and that if they are now thinking conceptually, they previously thought symbolically. One of the defining criteria for asserting that a given phenomenon has, fundamentally, a universal, quasi-universal, or cross-cultural deep structure is that the specific sequence of stages emerges in a particular (invariant) order.

To summarize, surface structures will exhibit tremendously diverse variations in the expression of a universal, cross-cultural, or "quasi-universal" deep structure. The basic structures are like a skeletal system, upon and around which tremendously different human bodies express themselves. According to integral theory, the emergence of the basic structures is sequential, but it is also less like a fixed mechanical process than it is like an organic, living habit.

Stages: Irreversible?

Yes and no. The directionality and irreversibility of stage emergence is central to stage theories. Referring, for example, to the transition from Kohlberg's preconventional morality to conventional morality, Kegan captures this notion: "If children develop and change their notion of what is fair, it is *always* in the direction from this instrumentality (stage 2) to interpersonal concordance (stage 3), *never the reverse*" (Kegan, 1982, p. 56, italics added). On the other hand, we would do well to remember Piaget's admonition regarding preparation and *decalage*: "development is spotty, local, and uneven. A concept may appear in one form, but take a year or more to extend itself over its possible range" (1977, p. xxv). Because aspects of different levels of structural organization coexist, of course people's behavior and experience will not all stem from a homogeneous stage of structuralization. In fact, when developmentalists such as Kegan (1982) claim that an individual is, for example, "at stage 4," what they mean is that her center of gravity is at stage 4 and thus approximately 50% of her behaviors, thoughts, feelings, etc. reflect the

---

16 This is consistent with Werner's (1940) orthogenetic principle.

70 *Unifying Psychotherapy*

characteristics of stage 4, whereas about 25% of them will reflect stage 3 and about 25% will reflect stage 5:

> To say that the self has identified with a particular wave in the Great Rainbow [rainbow emphasizes how the colors/basic structures blend into one another rather than being rigidly discrete stages as in a "staircase" or "ladder"] does not, however, mean that the self is rigidly stuck at that level. On the contrary, the self can be "all over the place" on occasion. Within limits, the self can temporarily roam all over the spectrum of consciousness—it can regress, or move down the holarchy of being and knowing; it can spiral, reconsolidate, and return. (Wilber, 1999, p. 467, brackets added)

Perhaps even more relevant to the notion of the irreversibility of waves than the above points is the crucial distinction between the logic and dynamics of stage models (Habermas, cited in Visser, 2003). Whereas the *logic* of a stage model explicates a linear, sequential unfolding of stages, the *dynamics* of those same stage models reflect how development actually emerges with people in their lived worlds. Of course no one actually develops as smoothly and simply as a stage model is depicted on a page; the "messiness" of human change processes (all of the various complications, regressions, fixations, etc. that arise in the course of one's life) is what the *dynamic* aspect of developmental theories addresses, and what any therapist or parent can attest to; more will be said about this subsequently. Most critiques of the linear aspect of stage models are focusing exclusively on the logic of the model, rather than the dynamics of how that logic unfolds in a given person.

A Progression of Stages: Are Later Stages Better or More Valuable?

Yes and no. The fundamental idea in this critique is the notion that later, "higher" stages of development are uniformly more valuable or better than earlier, "lower" stages. On the one hand, many of the developmental theories that are integrated into integral theory (from Piaget to Loevinger to Kegan) do in fact posit that subsequent stages are not merely different but more effective (along various dimensions) than previous stages (Cook-Greuter & Soulen, 2007), and that those at a given stage "never" prefer solutions to problems based upon the logic of previous stages (Piaget, 1948; Kegan, 1982, p. 56). From this perspective, subsequent stages include, yet transcend, the prior stages (this is why I prefer conceiving of developmental stages not as a linear ladder but as a series of nested, concentric spheres or circles—with each larger circle or sphere including and transcending the smaller, previous ones); because of this, people at subsequent stages are capable of understanding people at earlier stages, while the reverse is not true. Thus, subsequent stages tend to be more inclusive; more dynamic and flexible; more differentiated; more comprehensive; more complexly organized; more tolerant of diversity and ambiguity; less preprogrammed and automatic; and more capable of effective action in a rapidly changing and increasingly complex world. Consider that if a preoperational child's perception of a stable object changes because the child's perspective has changed, that child will declare that the object itself has changed. In contrast, a child who has developed an understanding of how one's own perspective influences one's perception of an object will recognize that the object itself has not changed; only one's perception of the object has changed, which is closer to the truth than the preoperational child's assertion. As Cook-Greuter has argued, higher is believed to be better because the more differentiated and autonomous persons become, the more they can claim they have a relatively nondistorted (true) and realistic view of themselves and the world. Equally important, "Yet no matter how evolved we become, our knowledge and understanding is partial and incomplete" (Cook-Greuter & Soulen, 2007, p. 184). In Wilber's words:

> I have rarely, if ever, used the term "progress"; I have used the terms "development" and "evolution." There is a big difference: "progress" tends to imply that development is necessarily and in all ways a positive or beneficial affair, an idea I absolutely reject. "Evolution" or "development," on the other hand, implies that, in the course of the emergence or growth of various phenomena, there is indeed a discernible differentiation and increase in certain structures and functions, but these increases *can* be used malevolently as well as benevolently... In short, there is a price to be paid for every increase in consciousness, and only that perspective, I believe, can place humankind's evolutionary history in the proper context. (1999, pp. 283–284)

Thus, Wilber and other integral theorists do not deny that along with the evolution of our species came the downside of "progress," including increases in the magnitude of exploitation, war, and oppression; these represent evolutionary advances (such as technological development) used for malevolent purposes.[17] Unfortunately, humankind's internal—particularly moral—development has not progressed as rapidly as our external technologies have. Moreover, any developmental sequence may include "good" and "bad" aspects. For example, as one develops the capacity for formal-operational thought, one may use one's emergent reasoning powers to deny, repress, or dissociate from one's bodily sensations and emotions, whereas young children are often very attuned and sensitive to these experiences. In summary, an integral view of development acknowledges the *dialectic of progress*: at the same time that development affords constructive and beneficial potentials and capacities, those potentials and capacities may be utilized to achieve a host of destructive, harmful ends.

---

17 At the same time, Pinker (2011) provides much data that violence has declined over millennia and that our current age is likely the most peaceful our species has ever experienced; moreover, the decline in violence is enormous in magnitude. Pinker argues that this is contrary to what most people perceive because of the increased coverage of violence in the media that has resulted in the vanishing communication gap.

Are We as Simple as Stage Models Suggest?

Of course not. In fact, the opening quote of this chapter emphasizes that not only is human development exceedingly complex, it more often than not is characterized by regressions and spirals than a simple linear path. Nonetheless, there are patterns, and Wilber's (2000b) basic structures represent some of the more salient contours of the great River of Life, through which all humans appear to flow.

Essentially, whereas individual lines of development do unfold or emerge, in general, in a sequential manner, an individual's *overall development is more characterized by nonlinear, fluid, flowing streams and waves; it is not rigidly linear.* This is due, in large part, to the fact that people can ride different waves (levels) in different circumstances; have various streams (lines) that flow through different waves (not all of their *lines* are equally developed); have different personality *types* that journey through the same basic waves with different emphases; and have different *subpersonalities* that may surf different waves.

Recall that the fields of counseling and counseling psychology founded the practice of their professions upon developmental bases; and *the phenomena of human development are exceedingly more dynamic and complex than most traditional theories have suggested* (Mahoney 1991; Thelen & Smith, 1994; Wilber, 2000b). Not only will clinical cases rarely unfold in as conceptually clear a manner as the logic of stage theories often suggests, *developmental theories are themselves in the process of developing*, and integral theory and iPT are attempting to stay abreast of these complex dynamics.

Dangers of Hierarchical Systems

Many social scientists and educators today have strong negative reactions to the notion of hierarchy, primarily because they equate normal, "actualization" hierarchies—which are found everywhere in nature and complex systems (i.e., atoms are wholes that are parts of molecules, which are wholes that are parts of cells, which are wholes that are parts of organs, and so forth)—with what Wilber has called "pathological" or "domination" hierarchies, in which "one holon assumes agentic dominance to the detriment of all. This holon doesn't assume it is *both* a whole and a part, it assumes it is the whole, period" (2000b, p. 31). Given that the basic structures, waves, or stages are holons, their organization actually comprises a holarchy, a hierarchy composed of holons.

As I mentioned in chapter 2, using hierarchical stage models to suggest that others are inferior, or to oppress or marginalize them, is not integral or developmental practice; it is *developmental abuse*, a form of pathological hierarchy (Marquis, 2008). Moreover, from an integral perspective, a person is not conceived of as being "at" a particular stage of development, although for ease of communication such discourse is sometimes used; rather, the entire spectrum of development is a potential, awaiting emergence and unfolding, with every human being.[18]

---

18 The use of "emergence" and "unfolding," as used here, in no way implies that various contexts are not critically important to a given person's developmental course. Unlike Wachtel's (2008) insightful

It is also inappropriate to use stage descriptions in a concrete, reifying, reductionistic way. It is a rare patient who perfectly matches the description of a single stage. On the other hand, the stage component of integral theory serves valuable heuristic functions, and the other components (quadrants, lines, states, types) remind us that how people think, feel, and act varies tremendously not only as a function of their psychological development, but also as a function of relational, cultural, social-systemic, biological, and other circumstances.

Tailoring an individualized therapeutic approach to a specific patient is a complex process. The potential danger in models, figures, and tables is that their *logic* oversimplifies what are, in fact, highly complex issues. Integral psychotherapy involves far more than merely implementing a stage conceptualization of human development.

Conclusion

By assessing patients' developmental dynamics, therapists can more fully attune themselves to patients' experiences and how they make meaning, more fully comprehend the nature of the sources of their distress, communicate in such a way that fosters mutual understanding, and perhaps more skillfully tailor *developmentally sensitive treatment plans* that are more likely to meet each patient's unique needs. At the same time, it is critically important to not let one's conception of a patient's developmental status impede one's attention to their shifting states of consciousness, the latter of which should usually determine the type of intervention one uses moment-to-moment.

---

critiques on this matter, the use of these terms does not suggest that development is purely an internal, individual process; rather, it is an all-quadrant process, and LL and LR contexts may be as influential as are UR and UL processes.

CHAPTER 4

The Development of Psychopathology
An Integral Perspective on the Etiology of Anxiety Disorders[1]

Introduction

Given the significance of understanding the development of psychopathology for any model of psychotherapy—whether single-system, integrative, or unified—this chapter will address the affordances offered by an integral perspective on this topic. However, given that I recently co-authored a book on this topic that exceeded 600 pages (Ingersoll & Marquis, 2014), I will focus only on anxiety disorders. I chose to focus on anxiety disorders not only because they are among the most prevalent mental disorders, but also because many psychotherapy scholars have posited that a deeper understanding of them would shed light on most other mental disorders (Barlow, 2004; Fosha, 2000; May, 1977; Wolfe, 2005; Yalom, 1980). Etiological risk factors will be surveyed by quadrant, and pertinent developmental dynamics are also addressed.

> There is no question that the problem of anxiety is a nodal point at which the most various and important questions converge, a riddle whose solution would be bound to throw a flood of light on our whole mental existence. (Freud, *Introductory Lectures on Psychoanalysis*)[2]
>
> I would say that learning to know anxiety is an adventure which every man [*sic*] has to affront if he would not go to perdition either by not having known anxiety or by sinking under it. He therefore who has learned rightly to be anxious has learned the most important thing. (Kierkegaard, *The Concept of Dread*)[3]

---

[1] This chapter is adapted/reprinted from Ingersoll, R. Elliot & Marquis, Andre, *Understanding Psychopathology: An Integral Exploration*, 1st Ed., © 2014, pp. 266–313. Reprinted by permission of Pearson Education, Inc., New York.
[2] Cited in May, R. (1977). *The meaning of anxiety*. New York: W. W. Norton & Company, p. xxi.
[3] Cited in May, R. (1977). *The meaning of anxiety*. New York: W. W. Norton & Company, p. xxi.

Etiology of Anxiety Disorders

It is almost universally accepted that the capacity to experience fear and anxiety is adaptive, enabling, as it does, rapid and energetic response to imminent danger or preparation for more distal challenges. However, *the nature of maladaptive fear and anxiety remains controversial, and despite many hopeful leads, there is still no consensus about the etiology of any of the anxiety disorders* ... Indeed, the current anxiety disorders ... are characterized by enormous etiological heterogeneity. (Poulton, Pine, & Harrington, 2009, pp. 111–112, italics added)

Anxiety disorders are among the most overdetermined symptom-sets with which patients present (Whiteside & Ollendick, 2009). As is the case with many, if not most, mental disorders, different professional fields—from counseling, social work, and psychology to psychiatry and neuroscience—debate what the exact source and cause of anxiety disorders is. I recognize true but partial claims in all of these positions and posit that anxiety stems from complex interactions of genetic, affective, cognitive, and existential factors as well as interpersonal, cultural, and systemic factors. Thus, based on the evidence currently available, I do not believe there is adequate warrant to speak of a simple, unilateral *cause* of anxiety disorders. As you will soon see, there appear to be a plethora of contributing factors that influence the likelihood of a person developing the symptoms that would lead to being diagnosed with an anxiety disorder. Moreover, whereas the DSM-III and the DSM-IV were strictly descriptive and purportedly atheoretical, many researchers and clinicians suggested that the DSM-5 attempted to develop and communicate etiological knowledge (Andrews et al., 2009). Unfortunately, it does not appear that the DSM-5 has provided insight into the etiological complexities involved in most mental disorders.

David Barlow has put forth a well-supported "triple vulnerability model" positing that the development of anxiety disorders usually requires the interaction of *generalized psychological vulnerabilities* (i.e., external locus of control; highly reactive temperament; behavioral inhibition; Kagan, 1997; Muris, 2006; Rotter, 1975) and *generalized biological vulnerabilities* (genetic traits such as being nervous, highly biologically reactive to environmental changes, and "high-strung") with *specific psychological vulnerabilities* (i.e., people with Panic Disorder tend to be hypervigilant to suffocation cues or other somatic sensations that make them intensely afraid, perhaps that they are dying; Barlow, 2004). Once again, the integral model provides an excellent framework within which to organize these manifold etiological factors. An example of how the integral model is helpful, especially in reminding us not to be reductionistic, is offered with regard to the following quote of cognitive therapists Freeman and Simon: "We *experience* the emotion of anxiety because of the physiological correlates" (1989, p. 347, italics in original) such as those occurring within respiratory, circulatory, gastrointestinal, dermal, or muscular systems. Integral theory posits that the dimensions of the four quadrants emerge together; in other words, no single quadrant consistently has more ontological significance or etiological influence than the others—they all influence one another. If you look back at the Freeman and Simon quote, you can see that they are privileging the Upper-Right quadrant—which is the domain of physiology, as well as genes, neuroscience, and other more objective perspectives—by writing that the *reason* we experience anxiety is "*because*" of physiology. However, there are many individuals whose physiologies include tachycardia, increased sweating, and gastrointestinal problems, yet these individuals do not experience anxiety problems. Thus, physiology is not a unilateral cause of anxiety so much as it is one of many influential factors. Let's go through the four quadrants and explore the numerous theories of etiology from each of those perspectives.[4]

Individual-Exterior (Upper-Right) Perspectives: From Genes to Behaviorism

Evolutionary and Genetic Views

Anxiety and fear are intimately involved in various forms of escape from, or avoidance of, potential danger. From an evolutionary perspective, possessing "anxious genes" that lead to more "false positives" or false alerts to danger—rather than "false negatives" in which actual danger is not noticed—is a biologically adaptive trait (Beck & Emery, 1985; LeDoux, 1996). Many fears/anxieties (i.e., of heights, animals, the dark) actually decrease the likelihood of suffering harm. For example, an animal that is more vigilant and responds to the slightest danger cue is more likely to escape from a dangerous situation than a less vigilant, less danger-sensitive animal.[5] We can observe similar "avoidance-of-potentially-dangerous-situations" processes occurring in many of the anxiety disorders. For example, a heightened concern of being humiliated and negatively evaluated by others (as in Social Anxiety Disorder) could function to deter behaviors that could lead to social alienation. Likewise, an individual with an anxious attachment history may exhibit agoraphobic responses in an attempt to maintain a bond with her "secure base," a notion with clear adaptive value. In addition to helping a person or animal escape from a dangerous situation, there is also evidence that those who are more vigilant also seem to learn more quickly and easily (Barlow, 2004):

---

4 Although dozens of etiological factors are involved in the development of anxiety disorders, it will become clear throughout this chapter that researchers and scholars from highly divergent perspectives—from physiology and neuroscience (LeDoux, 1996; Porges, 2011; Lanius, Paulsen, & Corrigan, 2014) to a host of psychological and psychodynamic views (Barlow, 2004; Wolfe, 2005; Fosha, 2000; Davanloo, 2005) to those who study social systems (Whiteside & Ollendick, 2009)—converge on the idea that *trauma* is of central importance to the etiology of anxiety disorders.

5 At the same time, evolutionary biology posits some balance to this. If an animal were to flee every time there was a rustle in the grass, it would be undernourished at the end of each day. If an animal were to completely disregard such potential danger, it would sooner or later end up in a predator's stomach. Thus, the natural selection of genes "settles on a judicious balance between the risk-averse Scylla and the laid-back Charybdis" (Dawkins, 2015, p. 339).

The vigilant animal, occupied as it is with future threat, is concerned with what is going to happen in the immediate future. In a very fundamental sense, the animal is planning for that future by taking an orientation to the future best characterized by the question "What happens next?" The planning function is apparent. In humans, this is extremely adaptive. (Barlow, 2004, p. 9)

It is now widely accepted that our genes contribute between 30% and 50% of the variance in the expression of generalized anxiety traits (Barlow, 2004). However, genes do not operate in a vacuum; gene expression is largely a function of environmental factors. In fact, the virtually universal, even if not highly specific, consensus is that gene–environment interaction is involved in the development of anxiety disorders. In addition, research by Fanous and Kendler (2005) suggests that some genes operate as "modifier genes" that affect the course and clinical features of an anxiety disorder, in contrast to "susceptibility genes" that influence the likelihood of developing an anxiety disorder. Again, Poulton and colleagues conclude that:

Despite promising developments in the field of psychiatric genetics, we still know little about how genes and their products (RNA, polypeptides, proteins) interact with one another, let alone how they interact with a host of environmental factors impacting people at different points across the life course. (Poulton, Pine, & Harrington, 2009, p. 117)

Of critical importance:

the strong consensus is that anxiety and related emotional disorders (such as depression) have a *common* genetic basis, and that specific differences in these disorders are best accounted for by environmental factors ... there is no reasonable evidence to date confirming the existence of a specific "anxious gene." Instead, weak contributions from many genes in several different areas on chromosomes (i.e., a polygenic model) seem to contribute to a generalized biological vulnerability to become anxious. (Barlow, 2004, p. 253, italics added)[6]

Despite the strong consensus just mentioned, research by Hettema and colleagues suggests that genes may be implicated in individuals' tendencies to develop one of two broad categories of anxiety disorders, the specific phobias or the panic-generalized-agoraphobic disorders (Hettema et al., 2003). However, for every study that seems to suggest specificity, there are others suggesting a more common genetic vulnerability. For example, one study reviewed 23 twin studies as well as 12 family studies involving the comorbidity of anxiety and depression; their results showed that a *shared/common genetic vulnerability* for both anxiety and depression

---

[6] Research exploring the underlying genetic and environmental risk factors in anxiety disorder comorbidity among men and women suggests that both men and women share a similar underlying structure with regard to environmental and genetic risk factors (Hettema et al., 2005).

explained the comorbidity found in the twin studies. Whereas some of the family studies support that conclusion, other family studies highlight that one of the two disorders is an epiphenomenon of the other—in other words, that anxiety symptoms are often secondary and derivative of the depression, or vice versa (Middledorp et al., 2005). In either case—whether anxiety and depression share a common genetic basis or are epiphenomenal of each other—from a genetic perspective, they do not appear to be as distinct as the DSMs suggest.

In short, there are evolutionary and genetic reasons for us to be anxious. At the same time, excessive anxiety not only diminishes life satisfaction; the *cumulative* consequences of pathological anxiety can actually result in death. This is one of the paradoxes of anxiety and it poses the question: How could the accumulation of adaptive genes result in such a negative state of affairs? One response to this question is offered by the notion of *preparedness*. Martin Seligman (1971) demonstrated that laboratory-conditioned fear in rats bore some striking differences from human fear. For one thing, animals in labs will quickly extinguish prior avoidance conditioning if their avoidance response is prevented and they don't experience punishment. In stark contrast, most phobias in humans are far more resistant to extinction. Seligman proposed that the key difference involved the *arbitrary* stimuli used in lab experiments (buzzers, flashing lights), in contrast to the very meaningful (nonarbitrary) situations or objects that humans fear (heights, snakes, spiders, bears, etc.). Summarizing Seligman's view, LeDoux stated that "perhaps we are prepared by evolution to learn about certain things more easily than others, and that these biologically driven instances of learning are especially potent and long lasting. Phobias, in this light, reflect our evolutionary preparation to learn about danger and to retain the learned information especially strongly" (1996, p. 236).

The work of Susan Mineka and colleagues (1984) strongly supports preparedness theory. Mineka demonstrated that what was believed to be monkeys' genetically inherited fear of snakes was actually *learned* by observing other monkeys' fear reaction to snakes (if presented for the first time with a snake in the absence of other monkeys, monkeys do not display a fear reaction). However, consistent with preparedness theory, monkeys learn this (prepared) fear reaction extremely quickly, yet they do not learn about nondangerous stimuli in such an efficient manner, "suggesting that there is something special about biologically relevant stimuli that makes them susceptible to rapid and potent observational learning" (LeDoux, 1996, p. 237). Albert Bandura has likewise demonstrated that observational learning—similar to that in Mineka's study with rhesus monkeys and notions of preparedness—is often involved in the development of pathological anxiety (as cited in LeDoux, 1996). Numerous researchers have stressed that this evolutionarily endowed tendency to learn avoidance of certain stimuli more rapidly and potently than others must be genetic in nature (Mineka et al., 1984; Ohman, 1986). Ohman demonstrated that humans' conditioned fear responses to dangerous stimuli that have existed for millennia (e.g., snakes) are far more resistant to extinction than responses to modern fear-relevant stimuli (e.g., guns), evidence that insufficient time has passed since guns were invented for evolution to have "prepared" us to fear them. In addition, Ohman was able to use conditioned stimuli that were not consciously perceived by participants to demonstrate prepared conditioning without participants' awareness of the conditioned stimuli (as cited in LeDoux, 1996). Thus, even from a behavioral perspective, phobias can be learned without conscious awareness of their origins; consistent with integral theory's positing five different forms of unconscious processes (Wilber, 1983; Marquis, 2008, pp. 160–164), not everything we are unconscious of is due to repression.

Physiology

The behavioral component of fear and anxiety has been described as "fight or flight" or more recently as "freeze, flight, fight." Autonomic and endocrine processes that increase blood flow to the leg and arm muscles and the brain and decrease blood flow to other organs and tissues support such "fight-or-flight" behaviors (Debiec & Ledoux, 2009).

Various physical symptoms are associated with a significantly increased likelihood that someone will meet the criteria for an anxiety disorder: chest pain (even without significant cardiovascular disease), unexplained faintness, palpitations, dizziness, and irritable bowel syndrome correlate with Panic Disorder; and chronic respiratory illness, vestibular abnormalities, and gastrointestinal symptoms correlate with other anxiety disorders (Barlow, 2004). However, Mahoney stressed how important it is to note that, despite there being various physiological *correlates* to what individuals with anxiety disorders experience, those experiences "cannot be reduced to mere physiological 'arousal'" (Mahoney, 1991, p. 180).[7] This caution not to reduce etiology to physiology involves notions of appraisal and choice, which will be addressed in the Upper-Left perspectives. Nonetheless, there are important statistics involving various physiological dimensions (e.g., panic is more likely to occur in those who are supersensitive to carbon dioxide; LeDoux, 1996). According to Barlow (2004), although the process of assessing and measuring the psychophysiological aspects of anxiety is complex and methodologically difficult, two findings have garnered consensus. First, chronically anxious individuals tend to have persistently elevated sympathetic functioning, which fosters the likelihood of interpreting potentially threatening situations as, in fact, threatening; these individuals also demonstrate a relative lack of autonomic flexibility. It also appears that individuals experiencing anxiety and panic have more asymmetrical patterns of brain activity compared to nonanxious people.

Neuroscience

Anxiety disorders—according to neuroscientist Joseph LeDoux—involve a loss of cortical control of our evolutionarily adaptive fear system. However, that is a very

---

7 For more details on this point, see Dienstbier (1989) and Neiss (1988).

general and simple description of what is a set of highly complex neurobiological processes. The past decades have witnessed an explosion of research investigating the role of various brain systems and neurocircuitry in the development of anxiety and panic (Barlow, 2004; LeDoux, 1996). Whereas neurobiological research in the 1970s through the early 1990s tended to focus on single, relatively isolated segments of brain functioning, usually on a single neurotransmitter system, current trends involve studying the *interaction* of specific neurotransmitters and neuromodulator systems with emotions such as anxiety, particularly the neurobiological processes of the HPA axis as a neuromodulator of anxiety.[8]

There is little doubt that exposure to severe and/or prolonged stress results in long-term changes in the neuroendocrine and neurotransmitter functioning implicated in many anxiety disorders (Barlow, 2004; Moreno, Lopez-Crespo, & Flores, 2007). Based upon research by Lang (1994), Gray and McNaughton (1996), and LeDoux (1996), Barlow stated that, even after the new emphases of current research paradigms, "fine-grained neuroanatomical exploration will never offer a full explanation, even at a basic neurobiological level, of the workings of emotions" (2004, p. 43). What Barlow means by such a statement is that because neurobiology (i.e., biological stress response systems, neurotransmitters, etc.) is particularly susceptible to the effects of stressful environments during earlier developmental periods—when brain circuits are more highly plastic and synaptic connections are more rapidly being elaborated and refined—a comprehensive description of the etiology of anxiety must include not only neuroscience but also an understanding of how environmental experiences, psychology, and other such variables interact with neurobiological processes in the development of anxiety disorders. Nonetheless, an integral perspective views neuroscience as an important, although partial, component of understanding the etiology of anxiety disorders, so I will briefly discuss some of the prevailing views.

Very briefly, when a person perceives danger, the amygdala sends a message to the hypothalamus, which signals the pituitary gland to release the stress hormone ACTH (adrenocorticotropic hormone). With its connections to the hypothalamus, the amygdala can activate the HPA axis and the sympathetic nervous system (SNS). Whereas the amygdala is signaling danger, the hippocampus is part of a control system regulating the amounts of pituitary and adrenal stress hormones that are released; more on control systems and neurotransmitters in a moment. Information involving potential threat can be relayed to the amygdala via two different pathways. In the first, which LeDoux (1996) terms the "low road," signals proceed quickly from the thalamus to the amygdala; by bypassing cortical processing, this brain circuitry allows for immediate action. In contrast, in what LeDoux (1996) terms the "high road," information travels from the thalamus to the cortex and then to the amygdala; although this pathway does not allow for as

---

[8] HPA axis stands for hypothalamic-pituitary-adrenal axis, which is constituted by the interactions of the hypothalamus, the pituitary gland, and the adrenal glands. As part of the neuroendocrine system, it is responsible for regulating reactions to stress, emotions, and moods, among other things.

immediate action, it does result in more considered action, probably by recalling memories of similar potentially threatening situations.

Experimental studies with rats demonstrate that, under too persistent or intense stress, the hippocampus fails to control the release of stress hormones. The effects of such excessive stress on the hippocampus are also likely responsible for different sorts of memory failures that are associated with traumatic experiences. Bruce McEwen has demonstrated that severe but transitory stress causes the dendrites in the hippocampus to shrivel. However, this shriveling is reversible—provided that the severe stress is not prolonged; if it is prolonged, hippocampal cells irreversibly degenerate and memory loss—according to McEwen—appears to be permanent (McEwen, 1992).

Severe stress can also alter the prefrontal cortex, which, like the hippocampus, is involved in controlling the amount of stress hormones released by the adrenal and pituitary glands. Morgan and LeDoux (1995) demonstrated that damage to the medial prefrontal region resulted in what they termed "emotional perseveration"— the failure to extinguish conditioned fear responses. As LeDoux (1996) points out, different individuals' brains are differentially predisposed to develop an anxiety disorder. Those who are more likely to develop a phobia appear to have an amygdala that is hypersensitive to certain prepared stimuli or have frontal lobes that lead them to develop anxiety reactions that resist extinction, even in the absence of prepared stimuli.

Another important brain circuit involved in fear and anxiety is the behavioral inhibition system (BIS; McNaughton & Gray, 2000). Triggered from the brainstem by any potentially threatening cue—from external audiovisual cues to internally felt visceral changes—this circuit connects the limbic system with the frontal cortex. When activated, the BIS prompts behavioral freezing, cognitive vigilance regarding danger, and the experience of fear and/or anxiety (Barlow & Durand, 2002).

Various neurotransmitters are involved in the control and regulation of fear and anxiety responses. Although selective serotonin reuptake inhibitors (SSRIs) are sometimes helpful in treating the symptoms of anxiety disorders (i.e., several serotonin agonists appear to reduce anxiety), research into serotonergic activity as a basis for anxiety and panic has been inconclusive (Barlow, 2004); it seems most likely that SSRIs are not targeting anxiety per se, but rather are merely temporarily inhibiting emotional arousal in general (Breggin, 1997).

Norepinephrine is also involved in anxiety. Both norepinephrine (synonymous with noradrenaline) and epinephrine (synonymous with adrenaline) are central to the flight-or-fight response that is regulated by the locus coeruleus, a small brain structure consisting of neurons that project to most other norepinephrine neurons in the brain. The locus coeruleus appears to be one of the players involved in directing attention to threat-relevant stimuli. By triggering the release of norepinephrine, the locus coeruleus can stimulate the SNS, resulting in increased heart rate, sweating, tremors, and the experience of anxiety.

In the late 1970s, researchers began exploring the role of benzodiazepine receptors in anxiety. Much of the supporting evidence for the benzodiazepine system derives from the effects of that class of anxiolytics as demonstrated in research involving the provoking of fear and anxiety in animal studies. One hypothesis is that there is an endogenous benzodiazepine molecule that binds with receptor molecules to reduce anxiety, and that a deficiency of this causes anxiety disorders. Even if this is the case (which has yet to be conclusively demonstrated), it will be an important but only partial explanation for the development of anxiety disorders.

GABA, perhaps the predominant inhibitory neurotransmitter in the brain, seems quite certainly involved in anxiety disorders.[9] One example of research supporting the notion that GABA binding decreases anxiety is the laboratory finding that GABA antagonists increase anxiety in animals (Gray, 1985). However, similar to what we have encountered before, other researchers point out that the diversity of functions that the GABA system plays make it more likely to be a general inhibitory transmitter, rather than specifically anxiolytic (Zillman & Spiers, 2001). Likewise, benzodiazepines may be less specifically anxiolytic and more reducing of emotion or arousal in general (Lader, 1988). It now appears that not only is the benzodiazepine–GABA system more complex than had been previously supposed, it is also more intricately involved with other systems than had been appreciated a few decades ago (Barlow, 2004). Adrenocortical functioning is not completely understood either; a series of well-designed studies found normal or even decreased adrenocortical functioning among people with anxiety disorders. As a result of these inconsistent findings, research into neuroendocrine function lost vitality during the late 1980s and early 1990s (Barlow, 2004). It has become increasingly clear that many if not all of these systems—from serotonergic and noradrenergic systems to the benzodiazepine–GABA system—function more globally, rather than specifically, in alerting to potential threat. Thus, neuroscientists are now studying not isolated systems but networks and interactions of systems. Finally, it is important to remember the logical error of "reasoning backward from what helps"; this logical fallacy may become clear from the following example: "When I take aspirin, my headache goes away. Thus, the reason I get headaches is because my aspirin level is too low" (Abramowitz et al., 2009). In other words, the finding that increasing the level of a neurotransmitter decreases anxiety does not necessarily mean that the fundamental cause of the anxiety was a deficiency of that neurotransmitter.

Interestingly, in the past decade, several neuroscientists have made statements along the lines of "Psychotherapy: Just another way to rewire the brain" (LeDoux, 1996, p. 263) or "Therapy is just another way of creating synaptic potentiation in brain pathways that control the amygdala" (LeDoux, 1996, p. 265).[10] These statements involve the concept of neuroplasticity, or the brain's capacity to form new neuronal connections in response to various changes in the environment, whether that environment is physical or social, or even in response to "mental force"

---

9 GABA stands for gamma-aminobutryic acid, which is the primary inhibitory neurotransmitter in human and other mammalian nervous systems.
10 See also Damasio (1999) and Siegel (2007).

Development of Psychopathology   83

(Schwartz & Begley, 2002). Thus, and consistent with an integral perspective, it is not that either neuroscience is correct or psychological theories are correct, but rather they are more complementary than adversarial, both offering important but incomplete explanations; more on psychological perspectives subsequently.

Behaviorism

From a behavioral perspective:

> Anxiety is the primary learning problem in psychopathology. Once anxiety is established as a habitual response to specific stimuli, however, it can undermine or impair other aspects of behavior and lead to secondary symptoms... These secondary symptoms [from sleep disturbances and sexual dysfunction to tension headaches and stomach upsets] themselves may elicit anxiety because of their painfulness, their association with learned fears of physical or mental disorder, or simply their embarrassing social consequences. If these secondary problems produce additional anxiety, then new learning may occur, and a "vicious circle" is created that leads to more complicated symptoms... Over time, the primary complaint is no longer anxiety but the phobias and drug abuse patients have developed in order to avoid anxiety. Of course, a drug habit itself can produce anxiety and can lead to further drug abuse in order to reduce the new anxiety, and the vicious circle goes on. (Prochaska & Norcross, 2003, pp. 285–286)

In the simplest of behavioral terms, *anything that reduces a person's anxiety is highly reinforcing*. It is important to remember that what is being avoided can include both *external events* (i.e., avoiding going to a social event and thus the anxiety of possibly acting foolishly and being rejected) and *internal events* (i.e., defense mechanisms, mental maneuvers, or any other intrapsychic actions that distract one from anxiogenic thoughts, as well as unconscious memories that signal real or imagined danger). The (negatively) reinforcing avoidance of anxiogenic situations simultaneously diminishes felt anxiety in the moment, while perpetuating and entrenching the anxiety disorder because such patterns of negative reinforcement lead to a reduction of seeking novel experiences. Unfortunately, this diminishes the likelihood of new learning that could potentially disconfirm the anxiogenic representations and expectations that the person so vigilantly anticipates or "feeds forward."

High anxiety levels also interfere with accurate information processing and tend to cloud the clarity of thought an individual may be capable of when experiencing low to moderate anxiety, all of which tend to confirm the person's previously established anxiogenic expectations (Gold, 1993a). Barlow (2004) summarized large bodies of research and concluded that the vicarious (social) learning of anxiety, and how that anxious apprehension is focused on specific objects (from somatic experiences in those with panic, to specific feared objects in those with specific phobias, to the potentially threatening aspects of social situations in those with Social Anxiety Disorder), are clearly implicated in the development of specific psychological vulnerabilities, which interact with generalized biological and psychological vulnerabilities to produce anxiety disorders.

Despite the formidable constraints that genetics, physiology, brain chemistry, and learning histories exert upon people with anxiety disorders, not all of the etiological influences are externally observable. For example, referring to the behavioral approach he had used in his earlier work with phobic patients, Wolfe was "increasingly struck by the irony that unconscious conflicts were being elicited by a therapeutic approach that denied their existence" (2003, p. 374). Moreover, neurobiological researchers, having provoked and studied panic in laboratories for decades, have more recently confirmed that it is mediated primarily by psychological factors, of which lacking a sense of control—which derives from early developmental experiences—appears central (Barlow, 2004).

Interior Perspectives (Upper-Left and Lower-Left Quadrants): From Cognitive and Psychodynamic to Existential and Spiritual

Cognitive Perspectives

Aaron Beck has argued that the core of anxiety disorders is a sense (not always accurate or grounded in good evidence) of vulnerability, "defined as a person's perception of himself as subject to internal or external dangers over which his control is lacking or is insufficient to afford him a sense of safety" (Beck & Emery, 1985, p. 67). Beck views acute anxiety as particularly paradoxical in that it increases the likelihood that the feared situation will come to pass. Consistent with his approach, Beck emphasized a component of anxiety that had traditionally been neglected: the cognitive dimension. Beck has also posited a specific cognitive profile for many mental disorders. For many of the anxiety disorders, Beck notes that core beliefs involve themes of excessively persistent and exaggerated concerns about impending threat/danger (whether the perceived threats 1) are internal or external; 2) involve one's sense of individuality, identity, and freedom; or 3) involve social acceptance, bonding, and belonging) as well as an excessive devaluing of one's actual coping skills. Moreover, the distorted cognitions not only reflect but also perpetuate systematic biases in information processing (Beck & Weishaar, 2008). "This bias takes several characteristic forms, called cognitive distortions, that can be detected beneath the voluntary thought level of the client's cognitive system—in his automatic thoughts, intermediate thoughts, and core beliefs" (Fall, Holden, & Marquis, 2010, p. 274). Some of the cognitive distortions that are implicated in anxiety disorders include:

- Arbitrary inference: jumping to conclusions despite a lack of adequate supporting evidence or in the face of contradictory evidence. For example, an "A" student makes one bad grade on an exam and persistently worries that he is not cut out for college.
- Selective abstraction: thinking about a situation by focusing on one aspect of the situation and ignoring other important aspects. For example, at a social

gathering, most people smile at and laugh with John; however, one person grimaces at him and John believes that no one at the party liked him because all he can think of is that one unpleasant interaction.
- Overgeneralization: taking a general rule from an isolated incident and applying it to unrelated situations. For example, one of Erin's professors gives what she thinks is an unfair exam and Erin concludes that professors can't be trusted to be fair.
- Dichotomous thinking: black-or-white thinking in which any shade of gray is labeled either white or black. For example, Bill struggles with Social Anxiety Disorder and considers any social situation either completely safe or completely dangerous, with no middle area that would be uncomfortable but unlikely to cause serious danger to him.

Another cognitive variable that appears to be implicated in the etiology of anxiety disorders is *anxiety sensitivity*: believing that sensations associated with anxiety (such as autonomic arousal) will result in negative physical, social, and/or psychological consequences (Schmidt, Zvolensky, & Maner, 2006; Taylor et al., 2008). Whereas many researchers have pointed to the role that anxiety sensitivity plays in the development of anxiety and depression, one study demonstrated that several parental behaviors that have been viewed as pathogenic (hostile, threatening, and rejecting behaviors) appear to predict children's overall level of anxiety sensitivity (Scher & Stein, 2003). Thus, while acknowledging that those parental behaviors are implicated in the development of anxiety, those behaviors are also implicated in the development of anxiety sensitivity, the latter of which may function as a mediating variable between childhood experience and anxiety.

Other cognitive factors relevant to anxiety disorders include false beliefs about worry, intolerance of ambiguity, cognitive avoidance, negative problem orientation, selective attention, judgmental bias, and lacking a sense of control (Kindt & Van Den Hout, 2001; Rheingold, Herbert, & Franklin, 2003). Whereas it is widely acknowledged that anxiety amplifies selective attention, Kindt and Van Den Hout reported research pointing to the role that selective attention plays in increasing anxiety levels as well as the fact that those with anxiety disorders struggle to inhibit selective attention. Thus, selective attention appears to play a maintenance—even if not an etiological—role in anxiety disorders. Judgmental biases regarding threat-relevant stimuli have been shown to be implicated in Social Anxiety Disorder: one study found that adults with Social Anxiety Disorder exaggerated the likelihood that a negative social event would occur, as well as rating it as more distressing, than did a nonanxious control group (Rheingold, Herbert, & Franklin, 2003).

Numerous researchers have demonstrated the significant role that one's sense of control plays in the development of anxiety disorders. In short, the more internal one's locus of control, the more one is able to mitigate the intensity of anxious apprehension. Conversely, higher levels of external locus of control correlate with higher levels of experienced anxiety. This is readily understandable in that one's perception that one is incapable of controlling or impacting one's environment naturally leads one to feel less secure and more anxious. As will soon be suggested, although anxiety is *experienced within* a person (subjectively), it often *originates between people* (intersubjectively or interpersonally), as in the case of abuse, neglect, unresponsiveness, abandonment, and so forth—all of which are interpersonal in nature. Consistent with the multidimensional nature of the etiology of anxiety, one's sense of control (upper-left [UL] quadrant) is powerfully influenced by one's caregivers' parenting styles (lower-right [LR] quadrant) and the perceptions children have of their relationships with caregivers (lower-left [LL] quadrant), which leads us to attachment theory.

Attachment Theory

According to attachment theory (Bowlby, 1987, 1988; Fosha, 2000; Gold, 1993a; Guidano, 1987), anxiety is the felt experience of a threatened attachment bond. From this perspective, optimal psychological development requires that children have a predictable and secure relationship—a "secure base"—with their caregivers. According to Sroufe (1990), when caregivers fail to change their behavior in response to an infant's cues of need and/or distress (i.e., if the caregivers' behavior is not *contingent*), the developing child is likely to internalize a lack of control over the environment, which is a component of a generalized psychological vulnerability. Thus, it is the caregivers' contingent responsiveness to the infant's cues—and the sense of safety and security that such responsiveness endows—that affects the "attachment representations" that children develop. Fosha stated that: "If there is no feeling of safety, anxiety, the mother of all psychopathology, takes hold. Anxiety is a reaction to the nonavailability or nonresponsiveness of the caregiver and is rooted in the feeling of being alone in the face of psychic danger" (2000, p. 47).

According to attachment theory, insecure attachment histories are major etiological factors in subsequent anxiety disorders. Infants and children who lack a "secure base"—an available, sensitive, empathically attuned and responsive caregiver—are more likely to suffer from anxiety and less likely to explore their external environments (physical or social) or capacities (external or internal; Bowlby, 1987, 1988; Fosha, 2000). Of significance, psychological aloneness amplifies any anxiety that one may experience. Thus, feeling alone (UL)—whether with others or not—and the poor attachment histories that often accompany feelings of pervasive aloneness are viewed as causally implicated in anxiety disorders.

Although not completely comprehensive from an integral perspective, the theories of attachment theorists from Bowlby and Guidano to Gold and Fosha posit that one can usually trace a patient's anxiety disorder to problematic attachment histories with early caregivers (Guidano, 1987). The idea here is not that attachment dynamics are the sole cause of anxiety disorders, but rather they are central to the psychological vulnerabilities (stress) that must interact with a genetic vulnerability (diathesis) to produce an anxiety disorder:

> Once attachments or exploration are structuralized in negative and dangerous terms, a considerable portion of the person's activity is organized around identifying threats to the tenuous ties to safety which exist in his or her own

experiences, thoughts, wishes, and behavior, and in the actions of others. As even the possibility of such a threat can be the stimulus for tremendous anxiety, a hypervigilant and protective perceptual set is established, along with an overemphasized need for control or protection in those areas of life which represent, actually or symbolically, the person's subjective point of vulnerability to loss, abandonment, irrevocable separation, or to the surrender of autonomy and independence. (Gold, 1993a, p. 295)

Support for attachment theory perspectives is not just theoretical. In a study examining the reciprocal influence of attachment status, child-rearing styles, and temperament on anxiety, van Brakel and colleagues found that higher levels of insecure attachment and parental control correlated with higher levels of both anxiety symptoms and disorders (Van Brakel et al., 2006). Bosquet (2001)—in a longitudinal dissertation using a developmental psychopathology perspective to examine the course of anxiety symptoms among a high-risk community sample from infancy through adolescence—found that those children who lacked confidence in their secure base and who had struggled with stage-salient developmental tasks were the most likely to develop anxiety symptoms (the risk factor of lacking a secure base was greater for females than males). Moreover, those who initially had anxiety symptoms but also perceived a secure base were more likely to have their anxiety symptoms remit. Another long-term study reported that anxious/resistant attachment at 1 year of age correlated with anxiety disorders at age 17, even after controlling for each mother's anxiety and each child's temperament (Warren et al., 1997).

"Exploration" is among the most important constructs in attachment theory. Those with insecure attachments, like those with anxiety disorders, tend to explore less, whether that exploration is external (trying new behaviors in the world, such as initiating conversations, public speaking, or confronting any feared situation) or internal (allowing a more fully felt visceral experience of emotion rather than defensively excluding emotions because one is afraid of being overwhelmed or being out of control). The unfortunate irony is that people with phobias or other anxiety disorders need to explore and confront what they fear in order to overcome their problem, but their lack of security makes it more difficult for them to do this.

Other Psychodynamic Views

In general, psychodynamic approaches view phobias and other anxiety disorders as primarily rooted in unconscious conflicts stemming from early childhood trauma that—although sometimes is sexual or aggressive in nature—is more often a function of caregivers' unreliability, unavailability, unresponsiveness, lack of empathic attunement, neglect, or abandonment. To varying degrees, these approaches also posit that the phobogenic or anxiogenic situation is symbolically related to repressed traumas and/or other intrapsychic conflict, and that transferring one's fears or anxieties to a more concrete, often external, situation renders the fear or anxiety more manageable (Wolfe, 2005).

In reference to childhood trauma, I concur with Kohut, Bowlby, and Wolfe that the occurrence of "real traumas" is far more common than most psychotherapists acknowledge; however, what constitutes "trauma" is far less often the dramatic episodes of sexual or physical abuse than repeated experiences of having self needs left unmet, whether due to caregivers' own psychological deficits, the child's temperament, or other cultural, social, and family structures—as well as the interactions of some or all of those (Kohut, 1984). Such childhood trauma, whether more overt abuse or sustained neglect, reaps a heavy toll on one's sense of self and contributes to the ensuing sense of tenuous, if any, connection to safety, security, and reliable and attuned responsiveness from others. Although all of this may sound rather different from behavioral views of anxiety disorders, both perspectives share the notion (even if they use different terminology) that anxiety disorders derive from various traumatic or otherwise aversive learning experience(s).

Essential to attachment theory and psychodynamic theories of psychopathology is the fundamental role that anxiety plays in influencing behavior, thinking, and feeling. "Central to both is the tenet that contact with the attachment figure counteracts anxiety, whereas the experience of aloneness exacerbates it. The experience of aloneness in the face of what is experienced as psychically dangerous is at the core of AEDP's understanding of psychopathogenesis" (Fosha, 2000, p. 37).[11] Moreover, dynamic theorists from Sullivan and Horney to Fosha and Wachtel posit that personality is fundamentally a function of the person's experience of anxiety and the defensive maneuvers enlisted to quell it (Fosha, 2000; Horney, 1945; Sullivan, 1953; Wachtel, 2008). The internal working models—or internalized representations of self and others—that become structuralized in childhood as a result of child–caregiver interactions not only influence the person's regulation of affective experience and subsequent relating/attaching to others, they profoundly impact all exploratory behavior. Children will defensively exclude not only thoughts and behaviors that lead them to feel anxious, *they will also*—in order to decrease the likelihood of their caregivers' turning away in unavailability—*exclude those aspects of their experience that their caregivers cannot tolerate*. I agree with Fosha's conceptualization regarding how dependent a child's self development is on caregivers' capacity to establish secure attachment with the child and the concomitant feelings of safety that ensue. "In secure attachment, fear and anxiety are kept at bay as a result of reliable, responsive caregiving; in insecure attachment styles, fear and anxiety are kept at bay through reliance on defense mechanisms" (Fosha, 2000, p. 41). Similarly, Greenberg (2002) views childhood and other relational experiences that were unpredictable or characterized by a sense of lacking interpersonal control as causal in many maladaptive anxieties, particularly those involving issues of intimacy, fears of abandonment, and other relational anxieties. Whereas Greenberg (2002) views fear as "a compelling

---

11 AEDP stands for Accelerated Experiential Dynamic Psychotherapy, which was created by Diana Fosha.

survival-oriented signal to escape from danger or seek protection ... Anxiety, on the other hand, is a response to 'threats' sensed in the mind—symbolic, psychological, or social situations rather than an immediately present, physical danger.... Fear and anxiety operate tacitly and automatically" (p. 143).

I already mentioned that any behavior a person engages in to avoid the anxiogenic situation will simply sustain the underlying pathology—for the simple reason that the reduction of anxiety is inherently highly (negatively) reinforcing. Thus, anxiety disorders are rarely a function of only intrapsychic (UL) dynamics. Although not the norm, I have counseled patients with Social Anxiety Disorder (previously referred to as Social Phobia) whose anxieties significantly diminished after only a few weeks of social skills training (LR), lots of role plays, and lots of behavioral (interpersonal) homework outside of the sessions. More commonly, people with Social Anxiety Disorder simply avoid the feared situation and this avoidance is then reinforced by diminished anxiety.

Wachtel (1982) has demonstrated how internalized representations of self and others (UL) interact with real-world experiences (LR) in "vicious circles" (p. 259). For example, if Bob attempts to face his feared situation and actually asks a woman for a date, a "vicious circle" might manifest as Bob's anticipatory anxiety—experienced viscerally as shortness of breath, trembling, sweating, and tachycardia (UR) and cognitively as expectations of rejection and appraisals of oneself as unattractive, incompetent, and undesirable (UL)—influencing Bob to actually behave in an odd, uncomfortable manner that makes the woman more likely to avoid or reject him (LR). Thus, Bob's real-world behaviors and his interactions with others—both of which can be observed "from the outside" (UR, LR)—seem to confirm his intrapsychic representations of himself as an unappealing, unattractive, undesirable failure that no one will love (UL), as well as negatively influence the meanings he assigns to his inability to establish a romantic relationship (LL). In short, it's not all intrapsychic (UL) or neurochemical (UR). Whatever occurs culturally, socially, and interpersonally, including the person's actual social skills, profoundly influences many of the anxiety disorders. Bob also demonstrated secondary anxiety (also called meta-anxiety): the tendency to suffer anxiety or other painful emotions in response to the primary anxiety:

> First, they become anxious either for some unknown reason or because of the situation in which they currently find themselves; second, they become anxious about being anxious ... the fear of fear rapidly escalates the intensity of the original fear and may well be a specific catalytic process by which anxiety spikes into panic. (Wolfe, 2003, pp. 376–377)[12]

Interestingly, the *Psychodynamic Diagnostic Manual* conceptualizes Generalized Anxiety Disorder not as one of the other anxiety disorders but as a personality

---

12 Barry Wolfe (2003) prefers to call this "metappraising."

disorder, primarily because, in addition to it being chronic and pervasive, it can be the primary psychological organizing experience of the individual suffering from it (PDM Task Force, 2006, pp. 56–57, 96–97).

Existential Views

From the perspective of existential philosophers and existential psychotherapists, anxiety is an absolutely unavoidable aspect of human existence that stems from our awareness of, and confrontation with, the "ultimate concerns of existence" (also referred to as the "givens of existence"): death, freedom, meaninglessness, and isolation.[13] From this perspective, *existential anxiety is necessary for mental health* because such anxiety is often a sign that one is not realizing one's potentials as a free and responsible human being (Yalom, 1980). Therefore, avoiding one's existential anxiety results in living a life that is relatively vapid, hollow, and inauthentic.

In general, existential therapists agree with Freud's dynamic structure of anxiety (drives → anxiety → defense mechanisms), but believe that the ultimate sources of anxiety are less the threat of acting out our sexual and aggressive impulses and more a function of our confrontation with the "ultimate concerns" (awareness of ultimate concerns → anxiety → defense mechanisms). Other points of agreement with psychodynamic conceptualization are that people resort to a host of defense mechanisms in order to ward off or lessen anxiety and that each individual's configuration of defenses constitutes his or her psychopathology; even though the defenses provide a sense of protection and safety, they ultimately restrict the person's experience and development (Yalom, 1998). Importantly, existential anxiety itself is not considered pathological; rather, its absence or avoidance is (Frankl, 1985).

Critical to the existentialists is distinguishing existential anxiety from neurotic anxiety.[14] One thing that both forms of anxiety share in common is conflict. However, whereas neurotic anxiety involves conflict between what the id impulsively would like to do and the retribution that would result from society or one's superego, existential anxiety involves the conflict generated by the givens of existence: conflict between being and nonbeing; conflict between wanting to live with the comfort and security afforded by the conventions of society versus living as an authentic, self-transcending individual; and so forth. In order to become aware of existential anxiety, it is often necessary to first confront and clarify one's neurotic anxieties, or to realize that one is concerned with them as a defense against the

---

13 Kierkegaard (1954) and Tillich (1952) pointed out that although existential anxiety is inevitable, it is tempered by the activity of self-reflection and courageously assuming authorship of one's life. They further emphasized that to not even recognize one's existential anxiety is a far greater form of dread and despair.

14 Existentialists such as Rollo May often use the word "normal anxiety" synonymously with "existential anxiety," which I consider somewhat unfortunate because anxiety regarding one's outcome on a final exam, a social performance, etc. (what most would refer to as "normal" anxiety) is a far cry from the depths of existential anxiety.

more terrifying existential anxieties from which they stem (more on this in chapter 8).

Importantly, existential anxiety is not one emotion among others, such as anger, happiness, or sadness. Rather, *existential anxiety is an ontological characteristic of being human*. In other words, *we don't merely have existential anxiety*—it is not merely a part of the human condition—rather, *existential anxiety is an essential aspect of who we are as human beings* (May, 1958, 1977). Unlike neurotic anxieties, existential anxiety is never peripheral: "[existential] anxiety is *the experience of the threat of imminent non-being* ... this threat of dissolution of the self is not merely something confined to psychotics but describes the neurotic and normal nature of anxiety as well" (May, 1958, p. 50, italics in original; brackets added). Whereas *fears* can be objectified (made an object of one's awareness) and thus made to not subsume a person, *existential anxiety*—as ontological—assaults the core of one's being:

> Anxiety is ontological, fear is not. Fear can be studied as an affect among other affects, a reaction among other reactions. But anxiety can be understood only as a threat to *Dasein* ... It is an experience of threat which carries both anguish and dread, indeed the most painful and basic threat which any being can suffer, for it is the threat of loss of existence itself. (May, 1958, pp. 51–52)[15]

This notion is captured by Binswanger's claim—which Heidegger previously posited—that "the source of anxiety is existence itself" (Binswanger, 1958, p. 206).

As previously mentioned, a fundamental source of anxiety stems from our awareness and fear of our mortality and other ultimate concerns such as our freedom and the need to create meaning from our experience. Although the bulk of North American culture, as well as most Western psychology, operates from a denial of *death*, deep down we know that our existence (as well as that of those we love) will end and this death anxiety pervades much of our lives, even if at largely unconscious levels (Becker, 1973).[16] Although many laypeople do not attribute negative connotations to the concept of freedom, it is because of *freedom* that we are responsible for ourselves, and because we often do not assume such responsibility, we live in "bad faith," Sartre's (1943) term for the condition in which a person denies his freedom and deceives himself of the fact that he is always responsible for his choices. This condition of *inauthenticity*, in which one passively and uncritically thinks and acts like the majority (under the "tyranny" of the masses, crowd, or "herd"), rather than with authenticity—responsibly, creatively,

---

15 *Dasein* is a term used most famously by the existential phenomenologist Martin Heidegger. Although it is in many regards "untranslatable" into English, it denotes the quality of human beings' mode of existence (Ellenberger, 1958).
16 For more on this issue, consult Yalom's (2009) book: *Staring at the Sun: Overcoming the Terror of Death*. As you can glean from the title, the entire work is devoted to the issue of death anxiety and how it often masquerades under many other guises.

and courageously choosing to live in accord with one's individually chosen values and commitments—is *a primary source of anxiety*. Inauthenticity is a signal that one is not living as a fully free human being. "In order to pass from inauthentic to authentic existence, a man [sic] has to suffer the ordeal of despair and 'existential anxiety,' i.e., the anxiety of a man [sic] facing the limits of his existence with its fullest implications: death, nothingness. This is what Kierkegaard calls the 'sickness unto death'" (Ellenberger, 1958). When existentialists refer to the ultimate concern of *meaninglessness*, they do not mean that there is no meaning to human life. Rather, they assert that we must imbue our lives with meaning; in other words, meaning is not inherent—as most traditional religious views maintain—in existence. Another primary source of our anxiety is *isolation*: "The experience of separateness arouses anxiety; it is indeed the source of all anxiety" (Fromm, 1956, p. 7). From a spiritual perspective, and echoing one of the Upanishads of Hinduism, "where there is an other, there is fear." In other words, if we are exclusively identifying with a sense of self that is separate from existence, it is perfectly reasonable to be afraid; after all, something out there can hurt and kill you!

Rather than directly facing and dealing with such ultimate concerns, which we can never completely solve or resolve, people often displace the anxieties stemming from them onto more concrete and surmountable things, which is what Kierkegaard meant when he wrote "the nothing which is the object of dread becomes, as it were, more and more a something," and Rollo May meant when he wrote "anxiety seeks to become fear" (as cited in Yalom, 1998, pp. 193–194). Paraphrasing Rollo May (1958), it is not so difficult to see that neurotic forms of anxiety develop (at least in part) because one has been unable or unwilling to accept and deal with the existential dimensions of anxiety.

Sartre (1943) posited that, even in the most extreme circumstances, people have the freedom to choose, even if those choices are limited to how they will view their circumstances. Although a whole host of circumstances—from the genes we inherit to the political and socioeconomic conditions into which we are born—may place severe constraints upon us, they cannot force a free being to choose one option over another. The fact that we know that our choices have consequences for which we are responsible leads to anguish and dread—in other words, anxiety. Related to existential anxiety, when an individual denies or fails to fulfill her potentials, she may experience existential guilt—feeling guilty against herself for failing to realize what she has been given as a human being. To illustrate that such claims involving freedom are not mere abstractions, let us briefly consider the life and work of another existential therapist, Victor Frankl.

Frankl was a psychiatrist and a prisoner of Nazi concentration camps during World War II, in which his mother, father, brother, and wife were killed. During his time in the concentration camps, Frankl (1985) came to believe that humans' most fundamental need is for the "will-to-meaning." Consequently, Frankl's *logotherapy* is primarily concerned with the individual's creation of, and engagement with, meaning—a position highly consonant with Nietzsche's (1954) dictum that "He who has a why to live can bear almost any how." Under such terrible conditions, Frankl could have easily fallen into despair and resolved that his life was meaningless, but he didn't. Despite his body being imprisoned, he nonetheless exercised his freedom to choose how to relate to his circumstances and created meaning in his life by helping (loving) his fellow prisoners.

Although some integral theorists have differentiated existential and transpersonal stages of development, existential concerns are present throughout the life span. For the purposes of this chapter, I do not believe the spiritual dimensions of anxiety need to be treated completely discretely from the preceding discussion of existential anxiety, although certainly there are some unique features of spiritual anxieties depending on the specific spiritual culture, beliefs, and practices a person is from and/or engaged in. Before delving into some of the spiritual dimensions of anxiety, it is important to know that, from an integral perspective, all spiritual traditions have both legitimate and authentic dimensions.

According to Wilber (1997), *legitimate spirituality* (also referred to as translative spirituality) is the more common form and function of religion, which involves fortifying one's sense of self. Through a system of beliefs and rituals, people are helped to understand and minimize the inherent suffering of the separate self; thus, legitimate spirituality fosters feelings of security, comfort, consolation, protection, and fortification (Wilber, 1997). Legitimate spirituality is so called because it provides a certain sense of legitimacy to one's beliefs about the world and one's place therein. In contrast, *authentic spirituality* (also referred to as transformative spirituality) constitutes a less common function of religion: to transcend (include and develop beyond) one's sense of self:

> Rather than consoling, fortifying, or legitimizing the self, it dismantles, transmutes, transforms, and liberates the self—ultimately from its illusion of separateness—through a series of deaths and rebirths of the self into ever more inclusive developmental waves [stages]. Authentic spirituality inquires into legitimate spirituality and concludes that the latter tends to entrench a person in one's current wave of development and, thus, prolong—even if more comfortably—the illusion of separateness that is, ironically, the actual source of suffering. (Marquis, Holden, & Warren, 2001, p. 227, brackets added)

From an integral perspective, both legitimate and authentic spirituality are important. Equally important, however, is distinguishing the two because of their different goals and processes. It is worth emphasizing that a key feature of authentic spirituality is that it facilitates developmental transformation via self-transcending practices. Thus, given the heavy emphasis on self-transcendence by many existentialists, you can probably recognize the spirituality inherent in existentialism: "*Self-transcendence*, I would say, is the essence of existence; and existence, in turn, means the specifically human mode of being" (Frankl, 1967, p. 74). As Albert Einstein put it: "What is the meaning of human life, or for that matter of the life of any creature? To find a satisfying answer to this question means to be religious" (as cited in Frankl, 1967, p. 93). And finally:

> If we are to understand a given person … we cannot avoid the dimension of transcendence … *transcendere*—literally "to climb over and

beyond"—describes what every human being is engaged in doing every moment when not seriously ill or temporarily blocked by despair or anxiety. (May & Yalom, 1995, p. 267)

What does all of this have to do with spirituality and anxiety? At the heart of most, if not all, authentic spirituality is the activity of transcending one's self (that with which one identifies), which confronts one directly with the dread of nonbeing. Whether through Zen meditation, Christian centering prayer, or selfless service, one is encouraged to let go of oneself. In fact, the dynamic involved in the transformation from any developmental stage to the next involves dis-identifying with one's current self-sense (read: dying to one's current sense of self), identifying with the subsequent developmental sense of self, and then integrating the two (Wilber, 2000a). What makes this process more terrifying at transpersonal or post-post-conventional stages of development is the lack of solidity of the potential future selves, not to mention that many spiritual teachings emphasize that one should let go of *all* forms of self-identification. In other words, authentic spiritual practice is often about meeting the death of one's self-sense head-on! Is it any wonder that intense, sustained, self-transcending spiritual practice can produce its own class of anxiety?[17]

With regard to legitimate spirituality, anxiety of a different nature is often involved, some of which is relatively neurotic and some of which is more existential in nature. Consider, for example, a person who is questioning her faith. This produces a whole host of anxieties, many of which share similarities to the DSM-5 *Religious or Spiritual Problem*, involving the anxiety-provoking nature of doubting spiritual values relating to one's religious upbringing or institution, questioning or losing one's faith, or converting to a new faith.

Wolfe's Integrative Perspective: Experience and Meaning-Making as Central

In previous sections, I reviewed research suggesting that not only the different anxiety disorders but even other categories of mental disorders (i.e., depression) share a common genetic basis. Barry Wolfe's (2005) integrative approach suggests that an important differentiating variable with regard to which of the different anxiety disorders manifest in a given individual is that of the cognitive, somatic, or affective strategies people develop in an effort to protect themselves in the face of potential threats and dangers. Although these strategies offer short-term buffering of the anxiety, they also entrench it, at the same time that the strategies themselves come to constitute part of the disorder itself (Wolfe, 2005). While not denying the contribution of genetics and other biomedical factors, Wolfe's integrative approach

---

17 For in-depth discussions of the issue of spiritual anxieties, consult Wilber (2000a), Walsh and Vaughan (1993), Walsh (1999), Steindl-Rast (1984), and Keating (1986).

posits that troubled self-perceptions and experiences (UL)—what he calls "self-wounds"—are the foundational source of anxiety disorders. Moreover, both the explicit as well as implicit meanings that the anxiety has for each patient need to be addressed. Commonly, patients are aware of only the explicit meanings, which often derive from secondary reactions stemming from some perception of anxiety. Underlying such secondary reactions are the implicit meanings, which usually involve fears of catastrophic danger to the self that themselves derive from the patient's "self-wounds"—perceptions of one's self as defective, worthless, unlovable, incompetent, and so forth. Because such subjectively perceived (UL) self-wounds are as equally involved in the etiology of anxiety disorders as the more genetic, physiological, and behavioral (UR) aspects, they deserve to be understood and addressed in each patient.

Thus, even though genes and stressful childhood experiences predispose one to anxiety disorders, the actual development of an anxiety disorder requires a perception of one's self as somehow "wounded"—inadequate, vulnerable, defective, incompetent, unlovable, inferior, unable to control, and so forth—suggesting a self-concept that is unable to cope with the demands of everyday life. With such a self-perception, the person enlists various coping strategies—from behavioral avoidance and emotional constriction to cognitive rituals—in an effort to defend against anxiety and other intolerable affective states, which simultaneously preclude the person's directly facing those demands as well as usually producing interpersonal consequences that reinforce the person's negatively skewed self-perceptions (Wolfe, 2005). According to Wolfe, if our activity of meaning-making is given a central focus,[18] then *anxiety disorders are fundamentally disorders of (usually unconscious) anticipated dangerous, if not catastrophic, meanings.* However, many approaches fail to see this because they focus solely on the explicit, secondary aspects of the anxiety symptoms. As you probably surmise, Wolfe's treatment approach pays very close attention to patients' subjective experiences and how they make meaning of them; more on this in chapter 8.

Collective-Exterior (Lower-Right) Perspectives: The Role of Family and Other Social Systems in Anxiety

> Anxiety disorders ... result from various factors only some of which are internal to the child. Considerable evidence suggests that bioecological and ecobehavioral influences are evident ... Children are highly dependent on their families, schools, and communities, and, not infrequently, these contextual influences occasion and maintain anxiety in them. (Whiteside & Ollendick, 2009, p. 318)

---

18 Wolfe is far from alone on this point; Mahoney (2003) and Kegan (1982), among others, emphasize that the essence of who we are as human beings is the activity of meaning-making.

96 Unifying Psychotherapy

The effects of stressful environments on brain function have been demonstrated in numerous studies. This body of research reveals the profound effects that early stressful experiences (traumatic events or environments) have upon neuroendocrine functioning, especially with regard to basal cortisol levels and hypothalamic-pituitary-adrenal (HPA) axis and corticotrophin-releasing factor (CRF) activity (Barlow, 2004). As one example, correlations between childhood sexual abuse and subsequent anxiety disorders have been reported in several studies (McCauley et al., 1997).[19]

Recall that earlier in this chapter I mentioned that genes contribute between 30% and 50% of the variance in the expression of generalized anxiety traits. While this is true, it is equally important to bear in mind that

> the neurobiological processes underlying anxious apprehension that may emerge from this biological (genetic) diathesis seem to be influenced substantially by early psychological processes, contributing to a generalized psychological vulnerability. In this sense, *early experiences* with controllability and predictability, *based in large part* (but not exclusively) *on interactions with caregivers,*" . . . contributes to something of a psychological template, which at some point becomes relatively fixed and diathetic. Stated another way, this psychological dimension of a sense of control is possibly a mediator between stressful experience and anxiety, and over time this sense becomes a somewhat stable moderator of the expression of anxiety." (Barlow, 2004, pp. 277–278, parentheses in original; italics added)[20]

Jang and Shikishima (2009) posed the following question: "As previous research has shown, if the same genes ostensibly influence unique disorders such as GAD [generalized anxiety disorder] and major depression, what causes them to express and manifest as GAD, depression, or both?" (p. 139). They proceeded to answer that the action and interaction of the environment is responsible for such differential pathologies. For example, whereas depression seems to be largely associated with "loss events" (such as the death of a loved one or job loss), GAD appears to be predominantly associated with "danger events" (such as those that could potentially harm the person).

It appears that studies of gene–environment interactions are yielding impressive results. For example, Stein and colleagues

> found a statistically significant interaction between levels of childhood emotional (or physical) maltreatment and 5-HTTLPR genotype. Specifically,

---

19 It is important to note, however, that this relationship does not appear to be specific to anxiety; rather, a wide range of psychopathology correlates with childhood sexual abuse.
20 "Diathetic" is the adjective form of diathesis, which refers to a genetic or constitutional tendency or predisposition to manifest a given pathological condition. The stress-diathesis model states that, in order for many pathologies to manifest, this diathetic predisposition must combine or interact with stressful experiences (Kendler, Myers, & Prescott, 2002).

people who carried two short forms of the serotonin transporter polymorphism (5-HTTLPR) allele and experienced higher levels of maltreatment had significantly higher levels of anxiety sensitivity than subjects in other groups. These results provide evidence of a specific genetic influence on anxiety sensitivity—an intermediate phenotype for anxiety (and depressive) disorders. This effect is modified by severity of childhood maltreatment, and is consistent with the notion that 5-HTTLPR operates broadly to moderate emotional responsibility to stress. (as cited in Jang & Shikishima, 2009, pp. 140–141)

Although I have already highlighted the role of the family and caregivers in the development of anxiety disorders in the discussion of attachment and psychodynamic theories, those perspectives are far from the only ones highlighting the profound role that caregivers play in children's psychological vulnerabilities that predispose them to later develop anxiety disorders, and many of these studies of family systems have been performed by observing those interactions externally, hence a Lower-Right quadrant view. According to Rapee and Bryant (2009), "A tremendous amount of retrospective research has pointed to an association between specific parenting styles and adult anxiety disorders" (p. 204). Moreover, Rapee and Bryant concluded that behavioral genetics research supports this view. Chorpita and Barlow (1998) reviewed much of this research and stated that parenting styles that are helpful in buffering pathological anxiety include encouraging the child's autonomy, consistently being supportive and expressing warmth and sensitivity, and responding to children contingently (based upon the child's present experience, needs, and abilities) rather than in a rigid or fixed manner. Conversely, intruding on the child's sense of autonomy, being overcontrolling and/or overprotective, having negative or critical attitudes, and being more intrusive or enmeshed and less socially engaged are associated with a lower sense of control and hence an increased psychological vulnerability for developing anxiety and other related disorders. Other implicated systemic/environmental factors include a lack of social interactions, role inversion during childhood, and vicarious learning from a relative with an anxiety disorder (Rapee & Bryant, 2009).

Parental control as a factor influencing the development of anxiety disorders appears to have almost universal consensus (Ballash et al., 2006). Much of this should seem similar to, and consistent with, attachment perspectives. However, a child's external locus of control does not necessarily result solely from separation and/or loss experiences, or even from excessively stressful experiences; a child's cognitive vulnerability for anxiety may also derive from an overly involved, overprotective, controlling parenting style (Barlow, 2004).

Another observable family variable is that first-born children tend to have higher internal loci of control than their later-born siblings (Hoffman & Teyber, 1979). Despite the large bodies of research supporting the notion that a variety of specific family system factors contribute to the development of anxiety disorders, one review of this literature concluded that although there are clearly associations between anxiety disorders and family factors such as attachment styles, parental control and other child-rearing strategies, and family functioning dynamics (i.e., marital conflict, sibling relationships, etc.), relatively little of that research clearly indicates that those family factors are implicated specifically in anxiety disorders; rather, those family factors appear to be implicated in the development of psychopathology in general (Bogels & Brechman-Toussaint, 2006).

Another social/systemic factor involved in anxiety is social support. Experimental research on monkeys suggests that the presence of social support from one's peer group leads to significantly fewer anxiety reactions, compared to those monkeys reared in isolation (Mineka, 1985). As you can probably imagine, this finding is readily transferrable to humans, and perhaps most interesting here is that it is not only the receiving but also the giving of social support that appear to reduce anxiety. Along similar lines, and particularly interesting from a social (LR) perspective, are the studies that Rachman (1979) reviewed in which children in a variety of "high-risk" environments were enlisted to help others—individuals and families in their community—with substantial adversities. The children were called upon to help others cope as well as they could amidst difficult circumstances. This focus on others' well-being produced a measurable "steeling" or "toughening" effect in the children who were providing the help and support (as cited in Barlow, 2004).

Although most of the details remain to be discovered, virtually all researchers in the arena of anxiety disorders acknowledge a complex interaction of biological predispositions with various psychological and environmental dynamics in the etiology of anxiety disorders; this notion is well captured by Barlow's triple vulnerability model (described on p. 75).

A topic with much less consensus involves the relative influence of shared, in contrast to nonshared, aspects of the environment: some studies suggest that the largest influence derives from *nonshared* aspects of the environment (i.e., one of four kids in the family had a life-threatening illness or received a nationwide award), whereas other studies highlight the profound influence of *shared* aspects of the environment (i.e., all four of the kids in the family were severely disciplined, had high expectations placed upon them, and experienced intrusive control from their parents). For example, much of the research studying twins with anxiety disorders suggests that an individual's *nonshared* environment is far more influential than *shared* environmental factors (Asbury et al., 2003). In contrast, many other studies have highlighted the significant roles that *shared* environmental dynamics play in some anxiety disorders. As one example, children with similar generalized biological vulnerabilities are more likely to develop anxiety disorders if their parents encourage avoidant behaviors in the face of anxiety, compared to similarly genetically vulnerable children who are not exposed to such parental encouragement (Hudson & Rapee, 2008). Moreover, research by Boer and colleagues (2002) suggests that shared negative life events have a more significant impact than nonshared life events on anxious children, and that such negative life experiences are what most clearly differentiate clinically anxious from nonclinical populations.

A potentially significant etiological mechanism deserving further research is that of *epigenetic inheritance,* which involves the transmission of gene expression (phenotype) even after the genes themselves (genotype) have been passed on. It appears that parents can transmit their phenotypic responses to stress and other environmental challenges to children even in the absence of the children's exposure to those stressful situations (Harper, 2005).[21] However, we currently have an incomplete understanding of exactly how this occurs, specifically with regard to:

1. the effects of parents' psychopathology on children's development across a broad range of domains, including both positive and negative outcomes;
2. the mechanisms of risk transmission;
3. the reasons for discontinuities in the transmission of risk for psychopathology across generations;
4. the role of mothers' and fathers' mental health in children's development; and
5. the bidirectional nature of parents' and children's relationships—that is, children have effects on their parents just as parents have effects on their children. (Poulton, Pine, & Harrington, 2009, p. 117)

So far in this discussion, much of the environmental (LR) impact on anxiety has focused on the family system. However, large social systems, and the stressors associated with them, are also implicated in the development of anxiety disorders.[22] According to Ingersoll and Rak (2006), a few of the sociocultural forces in America that contribute to heightened anxiety include the terror of 9/11 and the potential for future terrorist attacks in our country; the continued lack of equal rights for all Americans; an increasing distrust of politicians; a declining economy; and the disintegration of traditional values. It should be emphasized that the environmental stressors and trauma that people experience in most of the world far exceed those that most Americans face.

Contemporary America is often referred to as a "consumer culture," one in which many, if not most, of us distract ourselves from various interpersonal, occupational, familial, political, existential, and spiritual concerns with material goods, hobbies, travel, and so forth. This culture of "having" (consuming) rather than "being" offers endless possibilities to "escape from freedom" and the painful consequences of being responsible for one's choices (Fromm, 1941, 1976). Thus,

---

21 I am not a biologist or geneticist; thus, I am simply conveying my relatively limited understanding of some of the pertinent epigenetic literature. I think it is important to mention Richard Dawkins' (2015) critique of cross-generational transmission. Whereas epigenetics most commonly refers to phenotypic changes (changes in gene expression) that result from environmental factors (rather than a change in the genome itself), "transgenerational effects may occasionally happen and it's a quite interesting, if rather rare, phenomenon. But it's a shame that, in the popular press, the word 'epigenetics' is becoming misused as though cross-generational transmission was a part of the very definition of epigenetics, rather than a rare and interesting anomaly" (Dawkins, 2015, p. 402).
22 Scholars have differing positions on this point. For example, Frances (2013) emphasized that humans evolved in environments that were always full of stress and danger; despite the stresses that many of us experience today, he argued that environmental stress is less severe now that it has been throughout most of our evolutionary history.

many trade their freedom and responsibility for comfort and (illusory) security. I have counseled many patients who have remained in unsatisfying corporate jobs because they felt comfortable, and their hefty salaries provided them the opportunity to travel and buy culinary, electronic, automotive, and other "toys" that kept them distracted, even if only temporarily. Compounding the matter, the United States is so wealthy that many can afford to distract themselves in endless ways until their anxiety builds to such a point that it finally bursts through acutely. One patient of mine, in particular, illustrates this point. Dan was a successful businessman with two large homes, several luxury and sports cars, a yacht, and endless other "toys." Dan was referred to me by one of his family members who, from prior conversations with me, thought that I might be a good "fit" for him; otherwise, he likely would not have sought psychotherapy. Despite the fact that he had achieved "success" in the business world and had all the luxuries a person could want, Dan was quite miserable. It turns out that he was wracked with existential guilt and anxiety. According to Sartre (1943), he was living in bad faith. In our work together, he realized that although he had previously thought that what was most important to him were the conventional definitions of success that he had achieved, he had become deeply unsatisfied with how he was living (i.e., inauthentically). He now saw himself as a relatively shallow fraud, not in touch with the ideals that he remembered once having in his later teens and early twenties. After he realized that his unhappiness was a function of his not leading a life he could be proud of—or that his children could truly admire—he began reorienting himself, his time and his energies, toward artistic and service activities and his existential anxiety and suffering diminished greatly.

Notions about the etiological impact of larger systems in anxiety disorders do not merely "make sense"—they also have empirical support. For example, one study examined the association between mood and anxiety disorders with participants' perceptions of work stress and the degree of imbalance between work and their personal and family lives. Multivariate analyses revealed that both imbalance between work and their personal/family lives and work stress were independently correlated with both anxiety and mood disorders. In fact, those in the most stressful work situations and most imbalanced work–personal/family circumstances were four to five times as likely to have had an anxiety disorder in the last month, compared to those in the least stressful, least imbalanced circumstances (Wang, 2006).

Also relevant from a social point of view is the powerful influence that managed care exerts regarding the most appropriate treatment (which usually means what is most cost-effective).[23] Thus, today's market forces and the influential corporations of the managed-care industry push for psychopharmacological interventions that rarely result in maintained benefits or a deeper understanding of oneself and what is most meaningful in one's life (anxiolytics are among the most frequently prescribed psychotropic medications in Western societies; Ingersoll & Rak, 2006).

---

23 Because of this, managed care is often referred to as "managed cost" or "mangled care."

Because people with anxiety disorders often appraise themselves as vulnerable and inadequate to the demands of a social system that is so competitive, fast-paced, and perpetually dissatisfied (always needing more progress, growth, and development), they often end up trading a life of passionate engagement with what they—in their deeper selves—deem important and meaningful for comfort and security. Thus, such people often lead restrictively avoidant lives that diminish their sense of vitality, authenticity, and self-efficacy while increasing shame, guilt, self-condemnation, and self-alienation; all of which is compounded by an increasing lack of felt-community and, with it, concomitant psychological isolation.

Developmental Dynamics in Anxiety Disorders

According to the authors of *Stress-Induced and Fear Circuitry Disorders: Advancing the Research Agenda for DSM-5,* although a developmental research framework was essential to the task of making the DSM-5 a substantial improvement over the DSM-IV, they doubted whether such a framework would be successfully advanced (it was not), largely because they argued that current etiological understandings of anxiety disorders are rudimentary at best (Poulton, Pine, & Harrington, 2009). Although children, adolescents, and adults do not always, or necessarily, comprise a sequence of development (because many teenagers are more developed than some adults, based upon tests of ego, cognitive, and moral development, and so forth), what the DSM-5 has to say on this point is not without value.

According to the DSM-5, children and adolescents with GAD often worry about their competence and how well they perform; this occurs not only with their grades, sports, and so forth, but also in the absence of any external evaluation. They also frequently worry excessively about things on a spectrum of importance—from issues as "small" as their punctuality; to their needs to conform, obtain approval, and be "perfect"; to catastrophes such as war, tornadoes, and hurricanes. In contrast, adults with GAD tend to be anxious about a host of things, from minor daily events to career, children, health, and the state of local and world affairs, as well as existential concerns of authenticity, purpose, meaning, responsibility, death, isolation, freedom, and all of the many choices that must be made on those fronts. Other research has corroborated, to some extent, the general notion that fears and anxieties are differentially expressed across the life course. For example, one study found that separation anxieties are most common from ages 6 to 9; death and bodily danger fears are most common from ages 10 to 13; and fears of failure, criticism, and other social anxieties predominate from ages 14 to 17 (Weems & Costa, 2005).

The *Psychodynamic Diagnostic Manual* (PDM) has a section devoted to classifying developmental disorders in infancy and early childhood; in it, Anxiety Disorders and Developmental Anxiety Disorders are both classified as Interactive Disorders: "challenges in which infant- or child–caregiver interaction patterns play the major role" (PDM Task Force, 2006, p. 320). Importantly with regard to these disorders, the PDM emphasizes the need to take into account how contributions from 1) functional, emotional, and developmental capacities; 2) regulatory-sensory processing capacities; 3) child–caregiver and family patterns;

and 4) medical and neurological diagnoses all interact to produce these disorders. The PDM emphasizes that, particularly in children, the primary source and meanings of anxiety may not be clear. In its discussion of the presenting pattern of *Anxiety Disorders* (code IEC101), the PDM states that, for very young children who cannot verbally communicate, the anxiety is often of a generalized nature: excessive fearfulness, agitation, tantrums, worries, panic reactions, and avoidance are persistently evidenced, even in the absence of possible separation from their caregivers. Infants only 3 to 4 months old may appear hypervigilant, overly reactive, and frequently frightened, even in the absence of danger. In contrast, older children who can verbalize their fears and anxieties may show fight-or-flight or freezing reactions and tend not to respond to reassurances (PDM, 2006).

When discussing *Developmental Anxiety Disorders* (code IEC102), the PDM begins by stating that developmental processes themselves may produce substantial anxiety, especially in children who have difficulty dealing with the changes inherent in developmental transitions. In more severe cases, the anxiety may be intensely disruptive, as in cases of children with insecure attachment styles, who may be terrified when their caregiver must separate, and consequently avoid exploring anything new, whether play activities or interacting with other children (PDM, 2006).

Consistent with the psychodynamic conceptualization that any personality or character type (i.e., dependent, histrionic, obsessive, or, in this case, anxious) can exist at any developmental level or degree of pathology (neurotic, borderline, or psychotic), the PDM discusses and gives examples of anxiety manifesting at different levels of personality organization (McWilliams, 1994). *Neurotic*: "My mind is deluged with all sorts of frightening thoughts and images. My body is all nerves. I can't sit down for any period of time ... At my job I can't do a thing; I just feel I can't go on." *Borderline*: "My sense of self was hollow, like I didn't have a self, like I was outside myself ... There are all these characters who feel separate, not part of me, and they start fighting. I can't stop them or integrate them." *Psychotic*: "They have been blowing poison gas through the keyhole. It's destroying me and obliterating my thoughts" (PDM Task Force, 2006, pp. 98–99). In the neurotic quote, the type of *neurotic anxiety* that has been much discussed thus far in this chapter is evident. In the borderline quote, *fragmentation anxiety* is present: a fear of self-disintegration that, in small amounts, can be normal and tolerable; when chronic and intense, it can be unbearable and a key feature of borderline personality organization. In the psychotic quote, *annihilation anxiety* is present: a fear of being catastrophically overwhelmed, invaded, or destroyed.

Working from a different developmental perspective—one that emerged from Jane Loevinger's work with *ego development*—Susanne Cook-Greuter described the characteristic anxieties most frequently observed in people who scored differently on her test of ego development, the Sentence Completion Test integral (SCTi). At conventional/conformist stages of development, the chief anxiety revolves around being "not-me"; "if they lose a sense of themselves as 'me-as-accepted-by-others' they lose their sense of self" (Cook-Greuter, n.d.). For those who have recently grown beyond a conformist self, anxieties often revolve around concerns that they will not be strong enough to maintain their own views and commitments—that they may be drawn back to conformity. These anxieties and vulnerabilities often manifest as having an extra-strong front. For a more postconventional ("conscientious") individual, anxieties tend to revolve around the challenges involved with integrating different aspects of oneself (i.e., rational and emotional); people at this stage often feel confused by their multiplicity of selves. As people become increasingly autonomous, anxieties revolve around not fulfilling one's potentials and/or not acting in accord with one's individually chosen commitments. As a person becomes increasingly more developmentally complex, there are necessarily fewer people who can understand their experience; thus, their anxieties often involve not feeling understood.

In contrast to other sources, such as the PDM, it is surprising how little attention is given to developmental data in the recent DSMs, especially when one considers that most adult mental disorders, including the variety of anxiety disorders, have their origins in early childhood (Kim-Cohen et al., 2003; Pine et al., 1998; Poulton Pine, & Harrington, 2009; Whiteside & Ollendick, 2009). Given the considerable consensus on this point, Widiger and Clark (2000) stressed that "the amount of life span information that is provided in DSM-IV is only the tip of the iceberg of what should in fact be known" (p. 956).[24] In all fairness, the DSM is not alone in its dearth of developmental data: Poulton and colleagues (2009) searched the developmental literature regarding the etiology of anxiety disorders and reported "no studies that explicitly tested for etiological stability across the juvenile and adult period" (p. 113).

Ideally, a developmental perspective on anxiety disorders would also examine *cumulative risk*, both in terms of total risk-factor burden as well as duration of time exposed to such risk factors. For example, a study by Koenen and colleagues found that, of those members in the "Dunedin" study who had at least three childhood risk factors, 58% developed Post-Traumatic Stress Disorder (PTSD; which was categorized as an anxiety disorder prior to the DSM-5) in the aftermath of experiencing a trauma, in contrast to only 25% of those members with no childhood risk factors who experienced a trauma (as cited in Poulton, Pine, & Harrington, 2009, p. 115). An optimal developmental framework would also be flexible enough to integrate new knowledge as it emerges.

> If diagnosis *is* prognosis, then it seems that too little attention has been paid to developmental aspects of anxiety disorders or to considering how the interplay of biology and environment influence course, both singularly and across disorders. The current DSM [DSM-IV] provides a multiaxial system that recognizes cross-sectional heterogeneity. DSM-5 requires a developmental equivalent. (Poulton, Pine, & Harrington, 2009, p. 118, brackets added)

Again, unfortunately, such a developmental equivalent is not to be found in DSM-5.

---

24 I contend that this applies to the DSM-5 as well.

It is important to recognize the large amount of heterogeneity *within* many DSM diagnostic categories, because this represents a significant problem for a categorical system. A developmental perspective, however, "explicitly posits the existence of heterogeneous subtypes *within* disorders that follow quite distinctive developmental trajectories, reflected in age of onset (early versus late) and subsequent course of symptoms over time (temporary versus persistent)" (Poulton, Pine, & Harrington, 2009, p. 116, italics and parentheses in original).

Summarizing the results of a study by Kim-Cohen and colleagues that examined the degree to which adult mental disorders are derivative of juvenile disorders, Poulton, Pine, and Harrington (2009) wrote that "adults with anxiety disorders had also had anxiety disorders in childhood or adolescence. However, adults with anxiety were also at elevated risk of having had juvenile externalizing-spectrum diagnoses of attention-deficit/hyperactivity disorder (ADHD) and conduct disorder (CD) or oppositional defiant disorder (ODD)" (p. 108). This is yet another example that highlights the *nonspecific* dimensions regarding the etiology and continuity of mental disorders.

A fundamental and misleading problem is that a great deal of research looks for various statistical correlations between variables (in this instance, the presence of a juvenile anxiety disorder and the likelihood of having an adult anxiety disorder) and because some researchers look at so many possible correlations, they frequently find some, often by chance alone, which is why 1) the results of those studies are often not replicable and 2) other studies often report highly contradictory findings. In this particular case (the study by Kim-Cohen et al.), if we are to accept the validity of the conclusion regarding the continuity of anxiety disorders in childhood, adolescence, and adulthood, we also must accept that anxiety disorders are not necessarily discrete entities—due to their high comorbidity rates with other disorders. At the same time, other research suggests that Panic Disorder, GAD, and the phobias do have distinct biological (e.g., neurochemical or neuroendocrine) signatures (Yehuda, 2009).

Summary and Conclusion

As we have seen, there are many different notions about the etiology of anxiety and anxiety disorders. An integral perspective acknowledges that each of these perspectives contains a vital component of the overall picture while also recognizing that each is also incomplete in its explanation of the origins and causes of these disorders. Thus, I concur with Poulton and colleagues (2009) that future research should no longer focus upon a traditional risk-factor approach that examines only a single or, at best, several risk factors but rather move toward approaches that aim to assess cumulative risk from as many quadratic and developmental perspectives as possible. (See Figure 4.1 for a summary of the etiology of anxiety disorders from a quadratic perspective.)

This chapter illustrates how applying the integral model to virtually anything—in this case, the etiology of anxiety disorders—produces a more comprehensive understanding of the multidimensional, interacting domains and processes

UPPER-LEFT (UL): INTERIOR-INDIVIDUAL	UPPER-RIGHT (UR): EXTERIOR-INDIVIDUAL
• View of self as vulnerable, weak, incompetent, unlovable, etc. • Views of the world and others as excessively dangerous, threatening, untrustworthy • Fear, apprehension, and other distressing concerns regarding one's capacities to meet future demands • High anxiety sensitivity • Uncertainties about the future and a sense of (even if markedly inaccurate) one's own vulnerability, inadequacy, and/or inferiority result in varying degrees of apprehension and vigilance • Many anxious people experience life as a relatively continuous struggle to avoid pain and other dangers • Not assuming responsibility for living up to one's potentials as an authentic human being • Confronting the "ultimate concerns" of existence	• Biological and genetic predispositions (Barlow's generalized biological vulnerabilities) • Physical tension and increased sympathetic nervous system activity • Avoidance of feared situations • Extensive efforts to meet life demands and develop self-control are common • Neurobiological processes of the hypothalamic-pituitary-adrenal (HPA) axis and corticotrophin-releasing factor (CRF) activity • Loss of cortical control of the brain's fear system • Direct and vicarious conditioning • Preparedness theory
LOWER-LEFT (LL): INTERIOR-COLLECTIVE	**LOWER-RIGHT (LR): EXTERIOR-COLLECTIVE**
• Insecure attachment histories • Psychological aloneness amplifies any anxiety that one may experience: "The experience of aloneness in the face of what is experienced as psychically dangerous is at the core of AEDP's understanding of psychopathogenesis" (Fosha, 2000, p. 37) • Lack of intimate relationships that function as secure bases to help one mitigate the inevitable anxieties in life • Internalized representations of others as unavailable, unreliable, and unattuned • Maladaptive meaning-making systems (e.g., you'll go to hell for masturbating; some forms of religious education or otherwise rigid, harsh, and intolerant codes of conduct at home or school, etc.)	• Parenting styles that are overly controlling, overly protective, intrusive, nonattuned, nonresponsive, and noncontingent • Childhood abuse and other traumas • Parents with insecure attachments styles and incoherent life narratives are much more likely to have children with insecure attachment styles • Lack of social interactions or role inversions during childhood • Vicarious learning from a relative with an anxiety disorder • Actual interpersonal interactions that confirm anxiogenic thoughts • Systemic structures such as both parents working, which leads them to be more stressed and tired so they have less time to foster secure attachments • Fast-paced, long work days/weeks; we work more than most countries; we relax less and have less vacation time • A society that is highly competitive; many are isolated/alienated and thus lack intimacy, belongingness, and social support

Figure 4.1 A Quadratic Summary of the Etiology of Anxiety Disorders

involved.[25] Even though it has not led to a definitive "THIS is what causes anxiety disorders," it has demonstrated the complexities involved, and once it is truly clear that such complexities are involved, it obliges us to do our best to understand them, and with that understanding to then attempt to treat those aspects that are at the root of a given patient's disorder and suffering. I will return to the treatment of anxiety disorders in chapter 8, after discussion of assessment, interventions, and principles of treatment in integral psychotherapy.

---

[25] This chapter, even together with chapter 8, still constitutes a truncated version of the anxiety chapter in *Understanding Psychopathology: An Integral Exploration* (Ingersoll & Marquis, 2014); for example, the etiology and treatment of the five most common anxiety, or anxiety-related, disorders (Panic Disorder, Specific Phobia, Social Anxiety Disorder, Generalized Anxiety Disorder, and Obsessive-Compulsive Disorder) are also addressed there (page constraints did not allow that material to be included here). If you would like to read analyses of the etiology and treatment of an array of mental disorders, I encourage you to consult that book. I am grateful to Pearson for allowing me to adapt the anxiety chapter from Ingersoll and Marquis (2014) into these two chapters here.

PART II

Treatment

CHAPTER 5

Assessment in Integral Psychotherapy
The Integral Intake[1]

Most therapists begin the process of psychotherapy with some sort of intake assessment, whether formal (structured interviews or paper-and-pencil instruments) or informal (semi-structured interviews; Persons, 1991; Shertzer & Linden, 1979). This chapter will describe the Integral Intake as a tool for assessing patients in an idiographic manner, and research has suggested that it is the most comprehensive, clinically helpful, and efficient of the extant theoretically based intake instruments (Marquis & Holden, 2008). Understanding patients in such a comprehensive manner facilitates tailoring individualized, culturally sensitive, balanced, and holistic treatment plans appropriate to each unique patient. Two research studies examining the Integral Intake will also be reviewed. The first study asked experienced psychotherapists to evaluate the clinical utility of the Integral Intake in comparison to that of the other two (at that time) published intake instruments that are grounded in a theory of psychotherapy. The second study inquired into how experienced integral psychotherapists actually use the Integral Intake to assess their patients and how it impacts the therapy they provide; the advantages and disadvantages of using it as well as what they deem its most and least helpful aspects; and what else is needed—that the Integral Intake does not provide—to understand patients and create treatment plans.

The Need for Holistic Assessment

According to Anchin and Magnavita (2006), "the provision of effective psychotherapy depends significantly on the vitality and capacity of clinical assessments and their implications for treatment" (p. 31). Most psychotherapy theorists and practitioners agree that comprehensive assessment, in which information encompassing as many aspects of the patient as is reasonable to obtain, is essential and

---

[1] Parts of this chapter are drawn and adapted from chapters 1 and 3 of Marquis, A. (2008). *The Integral Intake: A guide to comprehensive idiographic assessment in integral psychotherapy*. New York: Routledge.

crucial to successful psychotherapy (Hood & Johnson, 1991; Marquis, 2008; Magnavita & Anchin, 2014). Moreover, "the ability to assess an individual is a basic skill required of all psychotherapists regardless of the setting in which they practice" (Shertzer & Linden, 1979, p. 3). *Not assessing is an impossibility*; even humanists such as Carl Rogers assessed clients along dimensions, for example, such as congruence-incongruence, openness-closedness, inner vs. outer focus, and so forth. Thus, the issue at hand is a matter of *what constructs* and *how formally* one assesses those constructs.

Patient intake represents one crucial point for assessment in the psychotherapy process. Although integral psychotherapists will at times administer standardized (nomothetic) assessments, the Integral Intake is *idiographic*. Also called self-referent or ipsative, idiographic assessment uses each individual as his or her own reference point; thus, idiographic instruments are not standardized. As such, idiographic instruments are more concerned with individual differences and the uniqueness of each person and his or her culture and systems, thus being more consistent with diversity, multiple systemic contexts, and other issues that are increasingly recognized as essential to understand in order to be of maximal help to patients. As Hood and Johnson (1991) wrote, "nomothetic techniques can be more readily interpreted, but they may not be as relevant or as penetrating as idiographic methods" (p. 7). From an integral perspective, the predominance of standardized assessments in psychotherapeutic practice is a reflection of what Wilber (2000a) termed "flatland:" the dismissal, reduction, or devaluing of internal, phenomenological, interpretive practices in favor of external, quantifiable, and other "empirical" practices.

Improving the effectiveness of psychotherapy depends in part on research, and research related to initial patient assessment would be potentiated by the development of an intake form that can accommodate a diversity of patients as well as the many theoretical approaches that psychotherapists use. Because of pressure by managed care and other work setting factors to maximize the efficiency of patient contact time (Glosoff et al., 1999), an instrument that patients can complete on their own time and at their own pace appeals to many psychotherapists, as well as patients. In addition, because of psychotherapists' diversity in theoretical approaches, an instrument based on a metatheory that incorporates all the major psychotherapy approaches into an overarching system of thought would likely have the greatest universal appeal to practitioners. Moreover, an intake instrument that assesses patients' strengths and resources as much as their struggles and deficits in a culturally sensitive, nonpathologizing manner should appeal to many psychotherapists.

Key Aspects of the Integral Intake

Of particular significance, the Integral Intake pays explicit attention to patients' cultures, spirituality, social systems, development, and other aspects of diversity that other intake instruments fail to assess (Marquis & Holden, 2008). In fact, approximately half of the Integral Intake is devoted to cultural and social/systemic issues. Thus, explicit attention is focused on how issues of race, ethnicity, gender, socioeconomic class, disability, sexual orientation, spirituality, religion, and other dynamics of power or social injustice contribute to the struggles that many patients face, which, in turn, influences their suffering and seeking of counseling and psychotherapy. The Integral Intake complements these sociocultural dimensions with detailed inquiry into biomedical, behavioral, and other observable factors as well as the lived experience of each person. Perhaps even more important than "covering a lot of ground," the Integral Intake will help both therapists-in-training and experienced therapists *organize* a tremendous breadth and depth of clinically relevant information so that richer understandings of patients and their problems inform the planning of therapeutic courses of treatment. The Integral Intake consists primarily of open- and closed-ended questions, Likert-scale questions, and checklists; it is available on a CD that accompanies Marquis (2008) in English, Spanish, French, and Psychiatric versions. Before discussing the Integral Intake in more detail, I will address the issue of assessment as a process (not solely something that occurs at the beginning of therapy) and the importance of attunement.

Assessment as a Process

Although assessment begins with the initial contact between therapist and patient, it certainly does not end there. "Actually," writes Garfield (2003), "assessment and treatment are intertwined and continue throughout therapy" (p. 175). Moreover, in many ways, assessment *is* a form of intervention; it is the beginning of a process of evaluating what patients feel, how they experience themselves, what they think is disturbing them, and what their strengths, resources, and best options are (Persons, 1991; Mahoney, 2003). Based upon an *initial*—and hopefully comprehensive—assessment, the therapist constructs a *tentative* treatment plan. As the therapy progresses, patient and therapist periodically evaluate (an ongoing assessment process) how well the treatment is working and "revise the treatment plan as needed, using an empirical hypothesis-testing approach that involves a continual interplay between assessment and treatment" (Persons, 1991, p. 100).

My approach to assessment is highly resonant with Persons' (1991) "case formulation" approach in which the information gleaned from the initial assessment process is used to construct a working hypothesis regarding the nature of the potential factors, issues, and/or mechanisms underlying the patient's presenting symptoms and problems. The case formulation provides the basis from which the therapist chooses the particular approach and specific interventions that he or she deems optimal for a specific individual with his specific issues. Importantly, the case formulation is a working hypothesis that should be continually reassessed based upon information that is obtained from each subsequent session, and revised as needed. Importantly, just because two patients have the same DSM-5 diagnosis does not mean they have the same case formulation. Moreover, patients change over the course of treatment. Thus, therapists should respond not to a fixed diagnosis or conceptualization, but to an ever-evolving person, requiring a sensitive attunement to each individual's change process. I further agree with Mahoney (2003) that the primary goal of assessment is to understand patients in such a way that will ultimately serve their immediate concerns and lifelong development. Mahoney (2003) and Yalom (2002) also emphasized that knowing one's self (deep self-awareness; "therapist as instrument") is intimately related to deeply knowing others; this is another factor that impacts one's assessment process.

Attunement

The initial contact that is established in the first session is critical to successful patient outcomes. Whether described as building rapport, establishing a therapeutic relationship, creating an I–thou relationship, or forming a therapeutic "we," the early aspects of "coming together" are of paramount importance. As such, intake interviews (the first session) ideally constitute a form of mutual exploration of compatibility. Not only are therapists evaluating the nature of patients, their problems, and their contexts, patients are also assessing whether or not they feel a compatibility and confidence in the therapist's capacity to help them. Thus, patients should be given the opportunity to ask any questions they have—either about the process and nature of therapy in general or about how a specific therapist works (including theoretical assumptions and specific interventions used). If therapists do not feel confident that they can be of help to a given patient, they should refer that patient to others who are more competent with that patient's problems, unique circumstances, and so forth. The skill of referral deserves more attention and research, focused for example on not only recognizing when it is appropriate to refer a specific patient, but also how to optimally communicate that decision (Wachtel, 1993; see also Mahoney, 2003, pp. 52–54).

In the first session, many therapists opt not to work from a clipboard and a standardized intake form, and many will not take notes in-session (Fosha, 2000; Garfield, 2003; Frederickson, 2013). Although I inquire into and listen for any cues regarding concerns that could demand immediate attention, my overall intention for the initial session is to be as authentic and present as possible, hopefully providing patients with a form of human relating that is experientially distinguishable from those to which they are accustomed. Although I try to remember as many of the details of the patient's presentation as I can, I am not overly concerned with tracking all of the details; patients will return repeatedly to their central concerns throughout a session or the course of therapy (Fosha, 2000; Wachtel, 1987; Mahoney, 2003).

As the first session approaches its end, I ask patients how they feel about working together with me. If we have a sense of mutual optimism, I provide them with the Integral Intake and ask them to complete it before their next session. (Occasionally, I have mailed it to patients prior to their first session if, while speaking on the phone, they express a desire to do anything they can to "speed up" the process and consent to answering personally sensitive questions prior to establishing a sense of trust with me; other ways of using the Integral Intake will be discussed subsequently.) I tell patients that we will continually evaluate how our work together is progressing and I encourage them to engage in as much self-observation and self-monitoring (of thoughts, feelings, actions, interactions, etc.) as possible.

Clinical Interviews

Clinical interviews provide a unique condition for gathering certain types of information that would be difficult to obtain with a paper and pencil instrument, such as follow-up questions that search for more detailed descriptions of the patient, her circumstances, and her experiences. Interviews also afford the therapist's observation of interpersonal styles and any discrepancies between verbal content and nonverbal behavior. With these points in mind, Beutler (1995b) described the Integrative, Semistructured Interview, which

> occupies a central role in evaluation but does not carry the burden of being the only or even the primary tool ... This conception of the interview as part of a comprehensive clinical evaluation invites the clinician to incorporate the semistructured interview into an integrative battery of assessment procedures. (p. 97)

Such an interview is essentially what occurs between therapist and patient after the therapist has perused the patient's completed intake form. This will be addressed further later in this chapter.

Clinical Flexibility

The issue of whether, and, if so, when, to have patients complete intake forms is a complicated matter. Examples abound of patients who leave waiting rooms, never to return, because they "couldn't go through" the process of writing such personal information on an impersonal form. Thus, exactly *how* to use the Integral Intake is up to each clinician. If you tend to have most or all of your patients complete intake forms, you can have them do that with the Integral Intake, either before or after the initial interview. For those therapists who rarely or never have patients complete such forms, the theoretical framework of the Integral Intake can be used either to structure a comprehensive semi-structured clinical interview or to help remind you to eventually "touch all the bases" of those dynamics and factors that are relevant to each patient's challenges and strengths. Essentially, therapists have considerable freedom regarding exactly how to use the Integral Intake; therapists can tailor their use of it to fit their preferred style.

Beutler (1995a) pointed out that the preferences in human sciences for quantitative measurements and methodologies have come primarily from researchers in academia. Mahoney (1991, 2003) lamented that numbers and "quantophilia" often still hold more scientific capital and authority than idiographic, qualitative assessment. Although nomothetic measures often provide valuable means for conceptualizing patients' problems and patterns, they are far from infallible: "the limitations of numbers to capture important qualities is [sic] readily apparent when it comes to the measurement of meaning, particularly personal meaning. Quantifiable measures of persons are plentiful, but meaningful measures are elusive" (Mahoney, 2003, p. 39). Mahoney and I are not bashing numbers, mathematics, or nomothetic assessments. In any integral system, as many perspectives as possible are valued and included, yet their limitations and partiality are also recognized simultaneously; and a primary limitation of nomothetic assessment is the virtual impossibility of its adequately capturing and conveying patients' personal meanings and realities in simple summary numbers, statistics, and labels.

In contrast to the "quantophilia" of many academicians are clinicians who "have become disillusioned with quantitative methods and have criticized academic psychology and measurement theorists for the failure to attend to individual idiosyncrasies" (Beutler, 1995a, p. 81). Clinicians tend to believe that idiographic assessments, such as multidimensional biographical inventories, capture more accurately the complexity of what it is to be human, attempting to attend to the whole person and her environment.

It is important to emphasize that the Integral Intake was constructed in order to be pragmatically helpful—to increase clinical effectiveness; it was not designed for assessment purposes in standardized research. Nonetheless, although outcome assessment is not what the Integral Intake was designed for, a study by Farnsworth, Hess, and Lambert (2001) found that patient self-reports (the form of data obtained with the Integral Intake) are the most common source for outcome data in psychotherapy research. For more on general assessment issues (from idiographic and nomothetic assessments and the nature of multidimensional biographical inventories to diversity and multicultural issues) as well as detailed illustrations of how different patients' completed Integral Intakes lead to vastly different treatment approaches, see Marquis (2008).

The Need for Integral Assessment

Accurate assessment is critical not only in iPT but in all counseling and psychotherapy, for the simple reason that different people—with different quadratic issues and at different stages of development—face different struggles whose resolution demands different approaches and interventions. The research of Van Audenhove and Vertommen (2000) revealed that:

> In most cases the psychotherapist's theoretical framework determines the specific form of intake and this in turn strongly predetermines the kind of treatment selected for a client ... There is no *metatheoretical* framework in which problems and complaints are conceptualized so that the choice of the most appropriate method for a specific client can be made. (p. 288; italics added)

As discussed in chapter 2, integral theory is just the sort of *metatheoretical* framework that Van Audenhove and Vertommen (2000) stated is needed to assess patients with the least theoretical bias possible—so that the most appropriate treatment is delivered to each patient, rather than providing similar treatments to all patients.

Numerous scholars have noted that assessment inventories seldom address patients' *cultural* (ethnic-, racial-, gender-identification, sexual orientation, etc.), *environmental* (socioeconomic status, environmental stressors, experience of discrimination, treatment contexts, etc.), and *spiritual* (religious and other meaning-making systems as well as one's experience of the sacred and/or altered states of consciousness) factors that might influence patients' problems and difficulties (Karg & Wiens, 1998; Pressly & Heesacker, 2001; Shertzer & Linden, 1979), all three of which are explicitly addressed by the Integral Intake. It is imperative that therapists proactively seek a greater understanding of diverse patients' cultural backgrounds; their worldviews and meaning-making systems greatly impact how they understand and respond to both their struggles and their strengths/resources. Moreover: "A clinician who is unfamiliar with the nuances of an individual's cultural frame of reference may incorrectly judge as psychopathology those normal variations in behavior, belief, or experience that are particular to the individual's culture" (APA, 2000, p. xxxiv). Whether these errors involve misinterpreting specific religious beliefs or spiritual experiences as psychotic or assessing an African American, Latina, or Native American as unmotivated, inhibited, or repressed, insensitivity to patients' diversity and other ethnocentric biases profoundly interferes with our optimally serving diverse patients. Bear in mind that many of these diverse patients who are seeking help feel systemically oppressed and marginalized from power differentials in society at large. At a more iatrogenic end of the assessment spectrum, therapists who are not mindful of how their position of power as a professional—especially with regard to how one acquires sensitive information during the initial phases of therapy—can impact those who already may feel vulnerable, marginalized, or oppressed can reproduce in therapy the very things that are responsible for patients seeking professional help in the first place.

Most assessments "have concentrated on the individual and the individual's specific traits, states, aptitudes, and attitudes. Little attention has been paid to the environments in which individuals function" (Hood & Johnson, 1991, p. 168). The environment (including both interobjective/systemic and intersubjective/cultural dimensions) is, of course, the bottom half of integral theory's four quadrants. The Integral Intake will thus help provide an overview of not only the patient, but also her environment (both cultural and social).

Similarly, most assessment instruments fail to adequately inquire into religious and spiritual dimensions of patients (Marquis, 2002). Prochaska and Norcross stated that therapists are increasingly integrating religious and spiritual issues with their psychotherapeutic treatment, and they assert that "in the future religion and spirituality will be incorporated more specifically and overtly into therapy. Clinicians will include religion and spirituality as a standard dimension of clinical assessment, especially as a potential strength and social support" (2003, p. 556).

An Overview of Quadratic Assessment

Although developmental levels, lines, states, and types are by no means ignored,[2] the Integral Intake emphasizes *quadratic assessment*: assessing the experiential,

---

2 Although the Integral Intake does not assess the following (because few patients would be able to

bio-behavioral, cultural, and social-systemic dimensions of patients and their distress. A critical aspect of iPT is an accurate and comprehensive assessment of a patient's life, including the reasons they are seeking help, the resources they bring with them, and their varied contexts and meaning-making systems. Therapists then use this information to construct their case formulation, which helps to prioritize phenomena to be addressed when initiating collaborative goal setting and treatment planning with each patient.

Before inquiring into information specific to the four quadrants, the Integral Intake requests certain basic data that virtually all effective therapists inquire into in the initial session; issues such as whether or not the patient has had any previous experience in psychotherapy and what her expectations and goals of the present therapy experience are. Other questions that are commonly asked of patients during the initial session are: "What do you hope to accomplish during your work with me?", "What brings you here?", "Why does that issue bring you here *now*?", "What dimensions of your life are going well?", and "What would you most like to change?" Questions that therapists should ask themselves during and after the initial session(s) include: "Does this person need counseling and/or psychotherapeutic services?", "Am I the best therapist for this patient or should I refer him elsewhere?", "Does this patient need a medical consultation?", "What type of counseling focus (symptom remediation or deep characterological change) and modality (individual, family, or group) is optimal for this person?", "Is there a risk of suicide?", "How much time and what resources does this person have and are these sufficient given my initial assessment of him, his struggles, and his life circumstances?", "What hidden agendas may this patient have that I am not yet aware of?", and "How is this patient's problem related to other dynamics such as his thinking, feeling, and behavior patterns; biophysiology; family of origin and other cultural dynamics; and large-scale systems?"

Experiential Items: Individual-Interior (UL)

The experiential dimension involves those aspects of assessment pertaining to the patient's phenomenological experience. It assesses each patient's self-experience (including but not limited to body image; self-esteem; self-concept; capacities for

---

accurately report them on a pencil-and-paper form), I believe it is critical to also assess: First, is the patient's problem a symptom neurosis (a discrete neurosis that has not pervaded most of the patient's life) or a character neurosis (a character consistently permeated by neuroses as in a personality disorder)? Second, McWilliams (1994) emphasizes the imperative need to further assess two different dimensions of the patient: his developmental level of organization (psychotic, borderline, neurotic) and his type or style (paranoid, compulsive, phobic, etc.). The first dimension can be thought of as "how psychologically unhealthy is the patient?" and the second dimension can be thought of as "and in what way?" (McWilliams, 1994). In addition, and to the extent that the therapist is able to do so, it is also helpful to understand the patient's psychological defensive organization and the nature of his resistance; his capacity to feel and tolerate aversive emotion; and his discharge pattern of anxiety (Davanloo, 2005, 2000; for more details on this, see chapter 7).

self-comforting, self-compassion, and self-reflection; self-criticism; self-hate); cognition and imagery; religious/spiritual beliefs and experiences; as well as the spectrum of emotions, motivations, and impulses of which the patient is unaware (aspects of which the patient is unaware will need to be inferred by the therapist because the patient will not be able to provide them on a self-report instrument).

Behavioral Items: Individual-Exterior (UR)

The behavioral dimension involves those aspects of assessment pertaining to the patient's observable behavior and other relatively objective dimensions (anything that can be measured, quantified, or captured with a video camera) of patients that relate to their distress and potential resources for coping; for example, medical disorders, medications, diet, alcohol or drug use, exercise, hobbies and recreation, and patterns of sleep and rest. Often times, patients seek therapy because of specific behaviors such as substance abuse, depression-driven interpersonal withdrawal, or anxiety-fueled avoidant behaviors. Even more frequently, patients' goals and views of successful therapy often involve specific behaviors (whether a decrease in eating, smoking, drinking, or aggression; or an increase in exercise, social activity, kindness, or intimacy).

Cultural Items: Collective-Interior (LL)

The cultural dimension involves those aspects of assessment pertaining to each patient's cultural experience, which among other factors includes not only ethnicity, religion/spirituality, sexuality, gender, age, etc. but also interpersonal relationships (including with the therapist), systems of meaning-making, and all other *intersubjective* dimensions that are disclosed through some form of mutual understanding or sympathetic resonance that is common only to members of given cultures, communities, or groups. A unique feature of the Integral Intake is its assessment of each patient's culture; thus, diversity and multicultural considerations are given substantial, structured attention from the outset of integral psychotherapy.

Social/Systemic Items: Collective-Exterior (LR)

The social, also called systemic, dimension involves those aspects of assessment pertaining to patients' environments and systems (from familial and local to national and global) that influence the onset, course, and treatment of their problems and struggles. As mentioned in chapter 2, these systems include economic, medical, corporate, and governmental systems; civic resources (educational and employment opportunities; transportation systems); city planning (available parks and other recreational areas; aesthetics of architecture, etc.); as well as smaller systems such as those characterized by family dynamics or working conditions. Thus, the patient's socioeconomic status; environmental stressors; poverty, unemployment, or unsafe living conditions (i.e., raising infants and young children in an old home with peeling lead paint or in a violent neighborhood); as well as any noteworthy observable interactions between parts of any social systems are addressed in iPT along with Upper-Left (experiential) and Upper-Right (behavioral) concerns that constitute the dominant focus of traditional psychotherapy.

Research on the Integral Intake

In the first study examining the Integral Intake (Marquis, 2002; Marquis & Holden, 2008), 58 experienced psychotherapists comparatively evaluated the Integral Intake (II), the Multimodal Life History Inventory (MLHI), and the (Adlerian) Lifestyle Introductory Interview (LSII).[3] Details of the study are available in Marquis and Holden (2008). Participants evaluated the II highest on all three *instrument dimensions (overall helpfulness, comprehensiveness, and efficiency)* as well as four of the eight *patient dimensions (culture, spirituality, what is most meaningful to the patient,* and *physical aspects of the patient's environment)*; they evaluated the MLHI highest on four of the eight *patient dimensions (thoughts, emotions, behaviors,* and *physical aspects of the patient)*. Noteworthy is that participants' evaluations of the Integral Intake as their preferred assessment tool—in comparison with the other two instruments—regarding patients' culture, patients' spirituality, and what is most meaningful to patients were statistically significant (Marquis & Holden, 2008). Considering the burgeoning attention in counseling and other psychotherapy professions to multiculturalism (Sue, Arredondo & McDavis, 1992), spirituality (Miller, 1999), and meaning-making (Carlsen, 1988), these features particularly endorse the Integral Intake for use by psychotherapists with diverse patients.

The results of this study (Marquis & Holden, 2008) have several implications. Of primary interest is that experienced mental health professionals evaluated the Integral Intake, in its first draft, as the best overall instrument compared to the other two published, theoretically based, idiographic intake inventories, each of which had been through several revisions. These findings were particularly notable in light of the participants' theoretical orientations: "the overall endorsement of the Integral Intake was predominantly by mental health professionals 'abandoning' the inventory associated with their identified theories and favoring, instead, an inventory the content of which arose from another theory" (Marquis & Holden, 2008, p. 83); this is a function of only four of the 58 participants identifying as "integral," in contrast to 21 as Adlerian and 12 as Multimodal. This finding is in alignment with the *metatheoretical* quality of integral psychotherapy; it genuinely values and includes important aspects of all major psychotherapy approaches and

---

[3] A review of the professional psychotherapy literature revealed that only four idiographic intake instruments have been published that are grounded in a theory of psychotherapy: the MLHI (Lazarus & Lazarus, 1991), the LSII (Eckstein, Baruth, & Mahrer, 1992), the (Constructivist) Personal Experience Report (PER; Mahoney, 2003), and the Integral Intake (II; Marquis, 2008). This research was performed as my dissertation in 2002, before Mahoney's (2003) PER was published; coincidentally, Mahoney was a member of my dissertation committee.

thus can potentially appeal to psychotherapists of any theoretical orientation, from single-school and eclectic to integrative and unified. This perspective was supported by the study participant who commented that the Integral Intake appeared "more objective and less theoretically-biased" (Marquis & Holden, 2008, p. 83).

Along with the Integral Intake's overall favored status, results from Marquis and Holden (2008) also indicated directions for its improvement. Marquis (2008) attended to the feedback from Marquis and Holden (2008) as well as added items that assess not only the four quadrants but also, to some extent, all of the five primary components of integral theory: developmental dynamics (levels and lines), states of consciousness, and personality types, all of which are discussed at length in Marquis (2008).

Despite the encouraging results from this first study, no research had examined how practitioners actually use the Integral Intake. In other words, issues of preferred method of administration (from paper-and-pencil formats to be completed at home to using it as a guide to a structured or semi-structured interview), how interpretation of patients' responses is used to contribute to the formulation of case conceptualizations, and ways in which the Integral Intake is used in the creation of treatment plans had not been the subject of inquiry. To address these issues, a follow-up study was performed; published as Marquis (2010), it was the first phase of the Integral Psychotherapy in Practice (IPP) study. Five "expert" integral psychotherapists were interviewed with attention to how they use the Integral Intake to gather information about a patient at the beginning of treatment.

In general, results revealed that the Integral Intake facilitated therapists' becoming aware of clinically relevant aspects of patients (especially *quadratic factors* such as their standard of living, their relationships, their primary stressors, their use of drugs and medications, and how they deal with strong emotions; *states of consciousness,* from ordinary emotional states such as anxiety to more severe, dissociative states; and negative *experiences in previous therapy,* i.e., not feeling listened to) that allowed them to complement, rather than fundamentally change, the way they provided therapy, which facilitated their addressing the unique needs of each patient (Marquis, 2010). For more details on the methods, analyses, results, and limitations of this study, consult Marquis (2010). What follows are selected—not comprehensive—findings from the study, structured around three of the interview questions.

Results[4]

Question 1. The first interview question was "*How, specifically, did you use the Integral Intake to help you formulate your case conceptualizations and to create a treatment plan?*" The major codes that emerged from the responses included:

---

4 This section is adapted from Marquis, A. (2010). The Integral Intake: Results from phase one of the "Integral Psychotherapy in Practice" study. *Journal of Integral Theory and Practice, 5* (3), 1–20.

different methods of administering the Integral Intake; indexing or "formalizing" specific concerns, issues, or factors to address in therapy; periodically referring back to it; and using information obtained from the Integral Intake (that standard assessments and intakes did not yield) to inform their treatment approach. A more detailed description of each of these codes follows.

Different methods of administering the Integral Intake. Examples of responses for this code ranged from patients completing it at home prior to their first session to using it to guide a semi-structured interview. One of the therapists who normally gathers intake information via a semi-structured interview (that her clinic requires) commented that her patient responded in more detail to the Integral Intake that she completed in a pencil-and-paper format than to similar intake questions she was asked in-session,[5] and this was particularly salient with the question on the Integral Intake that asks "Have you ever been a victim of, or witnessed, verbal, emotional, physical, and/or sexual abuse? If yes, please describe." Another comment along the same lines was: "even though I have asked some of the same questions to clients, I think they tell you more on the Integral Intake form than they might tell you to your face." In contrast to this potential advantage of pencil-and-paper administration, another therapist commented that it seemed awkward to ask sensitive, complex questions on a form rather than in the context of a developing, humanistic relationship. This therapist (who was using the Integral Intake for the first time) commented that using the pencil-and-paper format "was a tough shift for me and I have some concern about it disrupting the process [of therapy] or sending a wrong message about what the process is, because the process is not just this information exchange."

Indexing or "formalizing" specific concerns or factors to address in therapy. Examples of responses for the major code "indexing or 'formalizing' specific concerns" included: "The Integral Intake formalized the quadratic 'content' to address. Specifically, I knew ... [the therapist goes into detail about quadratic content as well as developmental lines and subpersonality information]"; "The Integral Intake provided an indexing of the various dimensions of her being, which allowed me to stay more present with her, build the alliance and then move into other exploratory areas as they continued to arise in session"; and "When you read through a client's completed Integral Intake, certain responses just 'jump out at you' and you know that's an important dimension to focus on in therapy." This last comment alludes to the subcode of creating a "hotspots" sheet (Ingersoll, 2002) which, in essence, is a sheet of paper with the quadrants drawn in, upon which the therapist lists the primary problems, apparent causes, client strengths, and so forth that will need to be addressed in psychotherapy. In the words of one of the therapists who has used the Integral Intake for years, "In the first session, I go over these [hotspots] with the client and we highlight the ones the client wants to

---

[5] The hospitals and clinics in which the therapists in the IPP study provided treatment required the therapists to administer their standard intake instruments and procedures in addition to those used in the IPP study.

address first; that will make up the remainder of the first session. From then on, I'll use a 'hotspot' sheet for notes and we'll adjust session by session as needed."

Periodically referring back to the Integral Intake. Examples of responses for this code included: "I've gone back and referred to it a lot over the last few sessions, to inform what she tells me in-session . . . as well as the clinical impressions that I'm getting from her in-session" and "so far it's been most useful for me in periodically going back to it to check things out." This major code included the subcode: referring back to the Integral Intake to "confirm or re-affirm different aspects of their treatment choice;" an example of one therapist's responses for this subcode was:

> The Integral Intake reaffirmed her symptoms, the diagnoses, and the extent of her problems . . . it was nice to have that reaffirmed and getting that reaffirmed was particularly reassuring for me in justifying the intensive treatment she's getting . . . it's reassuring to me that any third party can look back on this and there shouldn't be much of a question about the justification for the treatment.

Information obtained from the Integral Intake to inform their treatment approach. In addition to the participant who generally noted that "when you read through a client's completed Integral Intake, certain responses just 'jump out at you' and you know that's an important dimension to focus on in therapy," examples of responses for this code included: medically related items (i.e., medications, head injuries, diseases, etc.); "I have never inquired into a client's salary, their standard of living, or how satisfied they are with those circumstances . . . getting that type of information is helpful" and "I really like the question about subpersonalities; none of the intakes I've used before addressed that." This major code included the subcode of "previous therapy" questions (the Integral Intake includes five questions about the patient's previous therapy and another question regarding what the patient expects from the current therapist and their work together). Examples of responses for this subcode included: "I've found particularly useful the part of the form that asks about previous experiences in therapy" and "although I've used other intakes that asked about previous therapy, none of them had several questions like the Integral Intake does and I often get really important information about what to do and not to do from those questions."

Question 2. The second interview question was "*Which items on the Integral Intake yielded the most clinically relevant/helpful data?*" The major codes that emerged from the responses included: previous therapy questions; Upper-Left questions; Upper-Right questions; Lower-Left questions; and *how* patients respond to the items. The majority of participants responded that the questions about patients' "previous therapy" experiences yield very important information.

Upper-Left questions. Examples of the most clinically helpful items for this code included: "How would you describe your general mood/feelings?"; "What emotions do you most often feel most strongly?"; "How do you deal with strong emotions in yourself?"; "What are your strengths?"; "What are your weaknesses?"; "What is your happiest memory?"; "What is your most painful memory?"; the abuse question previously mentioned and Likert-scaled questions that ask "In general, how satisfied are you with your life?"; "In general, how do you feel about yourself (self-esteem)?"; and "In general, how much control do you feel you have over your life and how you feel?" Examples of other items from the Upper-Left quadrant include:

- Are you aware of recurring images or thoughts (either while awake or in dreams)? Yes/No If yes, please describe.
- Where in your body do you feel stress (shoulders, back, jaw, etc.)?
- Are you *presently* experiencing suicidal thoughts? Yes/No If yes, please describe.
- What are the ways in which you care for and comfort yourself when you feel distressed?
- How do you respond to stressful situations and other problems?
- Do you have ways in which you express yourself creatively and/or artistically? Yes/No If yes, please describe.
- Describe your leisure time (hobbies/enjoyment).
- Have there been any serious illnesses, births, deaths, or other losses or changes in your family that have affected you? Yes/No If yes, please describe.
- Have you ever been a victim of, or witnessed, verbal, emotional, physical, and/or sexual abuse? If yes, please describe.[6]

Upper-Right questions. Examples of the most clinically helpful items for this code included: "Please list any medications you are presently taking (dosage/amount and what the medication is for)"; "When was your last physical? Were there any noteworthy results (diseases, blood pressure, cholesterol, etc.)?"; "Have you ever suffered a head injury or other serious injury? Yes/No If yes, please describe"; "What other significant medical problems have you experienced or are you experiencing now?"; "Describe your current sleeping patterns (When do you sleep? How many hours per 24 hrs? Do you sleep straight through or do you wake up during sleep time?)"; "Do you engage in some form of exercise (aerobic and/or strength building)? Yes/No If yes, please describe"; and a checklist of the following behaviors (followed by a checklist of bodily feelings) that are true of the patient: drink too much, use illegal drugs, eat too much, eat too little, neglect friends and family, neglect self and your own needs, difficulty being kind and loving to yourself, act in ways that end up hurting yourself or others, lose your temper, seem to not have control over some behaviors, think about suicide, have difficulty concentrating, spend more money than you can afford to, crying, any other behaviors you would like me to know about. Headaches, menstrual problems, dizziness, heart tremors, jitters, sexual preoccupations, tingling/numbness, excessive tiredness, hear or see things not actually there, blackouts, do you have any other bodily pains

---

6 The justification and rationale for why specific items are placed in a given quadrant are explained in detail in chapter 3 of Marquis (2008). I will subsequently give two examples of such justifications (the next two footnotes) with regard to the Upper-Right and Lower-Left quadrants.

or difficulties? Yes/No If yes, what are they? Examples of other items from the Upper-Right quadrant include:

- Describe your drug and alcohol use (both past and present).
- Describe your usual eating habits (types of food, and how much).[7]

Lower-Left questions. Examples of the most clinically helpful items for this code included: "Describe your relationships, including friends, family, and coworkers"; "Which emotions were encouraged or commonly expressed in your *family of origin* (family you grew up with)?"; "Which emotions were discouraged or not allowed in your *family of origin*?"; "What emotions are most comfortable for you now?"; "What emotions are most uncomfortable for you now?"; "How did your *family of origin* express love and care?"; "How does your *current family* express love and care?"; "How did your *family of origin* express disapproval?"; "How does your *current family* express disapproval?"; "Do you have a religious/spiritual affiliation and/or practice? Yes/No If yes, please describe." Examples of other items from the Lower-Left quadrant include:

- Have you ever been a victim of any form of prejudice or discrimination (racial, gender, etc.) or felt that you were disadvantaged in terms of power and privilege in society? Yes/No If yes, please describe.
- In general, how satisfied are you with your friendships and other relationships?

  Not at all   1   2   3   4   5   6   7   Very

- In general, how comfortable are you in social situations?

  Not at all   1   2   3   4   5   6   7   Very

- How do you identify yourself ethnically? How important is your ethnic culture to you?

---

[7] Although the relevance of the above items is probably evident and clear with regard to why they belong in the behavioral (individual-exterior) quadrant, I will add that many patients' presenting symptoms may be due *not* to a mental illness but to a medical disorder. For example, hypothyroidism, brain tumors, and cardiac conditions can produce many of the symptoms associated with, respectively, depression, manic episodes, and panic disorders. Thus, it is imperative that biomedical conditions be screened out so that therapists and patients do not waste time with psychotherapy when what is more contributive to patients' distress is biomedical in nature. On the other hand, most therapists, and especially integral therapists, acknowledge the importance of the biopsychosocial model (Engel, 1977, 1980; Anchin, 2008): that biological, psychological, and social dimensions all play important roles in illness and health and that each influences the others. The reader may recognize some similarities between an integrated biopsychosocial formulation (Campbell & Pohrbaugh, 2006; Magnavita & Anchin, 2014) and a quadratic formulation. Without considering levels and lines of development, different types of people, and various states of consciousness, a quadratic formulation could be termed a bio-behavioral (UR)-psycho-existential-spiritual (UL)-cultural (LL)-systemic (LR) formulation; it doesn't exactly roll off of the tongue. Hence, I term it a unified quadratic formulation.

- Describe your sex life. How satisfied are you with your sex life?
- Describe any political or civic involvement in which you participate.
- Describe any environmental activities in which you participate (recycling, conserving, carpooling, etc.).
- Describe your romantic/love relationships, if any.
- What beliefs do you have about sex? How important to you are those beliefs?
- What are some of your most important morals? How important to you are those morals?
- In general, how satisfied are you with your religion/spirituality?

    Not at all   1   2   3   4   5   6   7   Very

- What is important and meaningful to you (what matters the most to you)?[8]

Interestingly, none of the participants in this study (Marquis, 2010) listed any of the items from the *Lower-Right quadrant* as yielding the most clinically relevant/helpful data. Nonetheless, examples of items from this quadrant include:

- What sort of support system do you have (friends, family, or religious community who help you in times of need)?
- What aspects of your life are stressful to you? Please describe.
- Describe your current *physical* home environment. For example, describe the layout of your home, and other general conditions, such as privacy, is it well-lighted?, do you have A/C?, heating?, etc.
- Describe your neighborhood. (Is it safe/dangerous, nice/unpleasant, quiet/loud, etc.?)
- Describe your current *social* home environment (how would an outside observer describe how you get along with those who live with you?).
- Describe your work environment (include co-workers and supervisors who directly affect you).

---

8 Whereas most readers probably agree that meaning-making (religion and spirituality are primary, though far from the only, meaning-making systems) is not something disclosed to observation from the outside—and thus agree that it belongs to one of the left-hand quadrants—some of you may wonder why it wasn't placed in the Upper-Left (individual-interior) quadrant. Although religious beliefs, worldviews, and other life philosophies reside within the minds of individuals, meaning-making activities are so inseparable from the religious/spiritual, ethnic, political, moral, and other *cultural* traditions in which individuals are embedded that to conceptualize an individual's meaning-making as a merely individual (in contrast to embedded in multiple *cultural contexts*) activity denies the vast web of *intersubjective worldspaces* out of which mutual understanding, and even self-understanding, emerge. Even though what is meaningful to me discloses itself to my experience (UL), that meaning would not—and could not—emerge and be sustained without a vast network of contextual norms and practices as well as linguistic and semantic structures that form a shared culture. Thus, if a patient speaks to you in a language you don't understand, or about cultural practices with which you do not resonate, you will not understand the meanings about which the patient is speaking, even though all of the words are entering your ears and brain (Wilber, 2000a).

Assessment in Integral Psychotherapy 125

- Do you have a romantic partner? Yes/No Have you been married before? Yes/No If yes, please describe.

How patients respond to the items. Examples of responses encompassed by this code included:

> What I find helpful is not just the content the patient provides, but *how* they choose to answer some of the questions, such as how descriptive they are about their inner life ... those who respond to questions like "How do you deal with strong emotions in yourself?" with "I don't know" or "What do you mean by that?" tend to have a poorer prognosis in psychotherapy with me.

Along similar lines, another therapist commented that:

> For this client it's really interesting; you see the difficulty she has with affect—her language is quite simple—you know—"happy" emotions ... It's pretty black and white; there's not a lot of complexity or differentiation in her affective expression. On the question about which emotions are least comfortable for her, she wrote "all of them, but especially the happy ones." This nicely confirms what she's been telling me in-session.

Often times, what patients *don't* write is more clinically informing than what they do write. For example, one of the patients in this study, when asked to "Describe your romantic/love relationships, if any" wrote "Married to Eric" (with no description of the quality of that relationship, which was consistent with her never discussing him in her psychotherapy sessions). Similarly, another therapist commented that:

> I've found it helpful to keep going back to it ... what can be interesting is what's *not* said as much as what's said. It's almost like a projective test with regard to how they answer the questions ... I hadn't expected I would use it that way, but it is.

Question 3. The final interview question was "*Is there anything else you want me to know about the pros and cons of using the Integral Intake as an assessment tool and its role in helping you formulate your case conceptualizations and to create a treatment plan?*" The major codes that emerged from the responses included: its clinical helpfulness; complaints regarding its length; its face validity; it captures only what patients know about themselves; and the tensions between comprehensive information gathering and humanistic relating.

Clinical helpfulness. Examples of responses for this code included: "I find it incredibly helpful and complete"; "It's a nice way to collect a lot of information; it decreases the time spent getting that information while with them in the first sessions, so you can focus on the relationship"; and "it makes conceptualization and treatment planning really, really easy."

Complaints regarding its length. Examples of responses for this code included: "Some patients feel overwhelmed by the length, so I tell them to just fill out what they can or what they think is most important for me to know, but most patients fill out the entire thing" and "the only complaint I've heard is its length, but what I've found to be really effective to get people to complete it is to tell them it's saving them money. It's more efficient for them to fill this out on their own time than for us to have to cover all that information verbally in-session."

Face validity. Examples of responses for this code included: "I see it as a face valid instrument, so I read what they wrote down and take it as valid information to guide my initial impressions" and "the intake gets the information that it's supposed to get. I know some therapists these days want assessment instruments that yield scores and diagnoses but you can't measure meanings and other types of rich information that the Integral Intake gets."

It captures only what patients know about themselves. Examples of responses for this code included:

> One important thing that you can't obtain with any intake is the client's characterological style. I can get that only from how they interact with me. I guess you might be able to get that if you administered the intake as an oral interview, but I prefer to have my first impressions of a client come before I read their Integral Intake.

A more elaborate example of this same idea:

> Any kind of intake form is just going to gather information about things the patient can "see," as opposed to personality dynamics that you can learn only by how they actually relate to you. I mean, if I just looked at this client's Integral Intake, I could see a lot of depressive stuff, a lot of traumatic stuff, but I wouldn't know that this woman goes in and out of some very different states of consciousness, which I learned in-session with her. There's just no way I'm going to get that with any kind of intake form, and yet in my way of thinking about this case, it's one of the most important things. So a pitfall might be that some clinicians might not appreciate the distinction between what a client can answer about herself and what she doesn't know about herself. Thus, if someone tries to conceptualize the client and create a treatment plan *just* from the intake form, they aren't recognizing that such forms can get only the information the client sees about herself and it's often the case—especially with clients with personality disorders—that what's most important is what the client does *not* see about herself, what the client is not yet able to think about, and, you know, a therapist has an important role in helping somebody recognize and think about the things they don't know about themselves. As far as the information that a piece of paper can get, it's great, but nothing can get at these other things except what you observe in your interactions with the client. So a pitfall could be a clinician using the form to support partial ways of thinking about a case. For instance, in my clinic you have to have behavioral

goals for the treatment plan. So, by definition, these behaviors are things the client can see about herself. But if that's all the therapist considers, they're misusing the intake. So a concern is the "use and potential misuse" of an intake.

Discussion

What follows is a brief discussion of four themes: the variety of ways to use the Integral Intake; the "shadows" of paper-and-pencil assessment; assessing feelings, anxiety, and defenses moment-to-moment; and idiographic, interpretive assessment in an age of flatland (refer to page 110 for a description of "flatland"). For a complete discussion of the study's findings, consult Marquis (2010).

A variety of ways to use the Integral Intake. As evidenced by the results, there is considerable variation in how clinicians use the Integral Intake. It is worth noting that three of the five therapists in this study were using the Integral Intake for the first time. Thus, they were both inexperienced in its use and were also reporting how they used it with only one patient. In contrast, the other two therapists had used the Integral Intake extensively for many years. Whereas four of the therapists reported using the information gathered by the intake to assist them in conceptualizing their patients and to facilitate their treatment planning, one of the therapists (who works from an integrally informed humanistic, psychoanalytic perspective) reported using it primarily as a reference aid—to confirm what she was thinking about the patient and what she was actually doing with her.

Three of the five therapists mentioned advantages and potential disadvantages of relying exclusively on paper-and-pencil administrations of the Integral Intake, in contrast to having it guide a structured or semi-structured interview. Previous research (Marquis & Holden, 2008) highlighted the potential drawbacks of paper-and-pencil administrations (i.e., potentially adverse consequences as a result of asking for sensitive information on an impersonal, clinical instrument prior to establishing trust and rapport with the patient, and one therapist in this study reported similar concerns).[9] In contrast, two therapists commented that their perception was that their patients responded in *more* detail to the questions via a paper-and-pencil format than they would have in person.

Those therapists who are familiar with integral theory and the Integral Intake (or those who are comfortable having a copy of the Integral Intake with them as a guide) can assess patients in a structured or semi-structured interview, using the items on the Integral Intake as interview questions; this process is described in Marquis (2008). Briefly, the benefits of this approach include the opportunity to

---

9 On this subject, it is worth mentioning that Marquis (2008) includes an "Introductory Letter to New Clients" that not only describes the purpose of the intake, and informs patients that all of their responses will be kept strictly confidential, but also specifies that if they feel that some of their responses are too personal or complicated to put down in writing at that time, they are welcome to leave those lines blank.

128   Treatment

empathically respond not only to the content patients respond with, but also to how each patient experiences being asked for such information. Thus, rapport and trust can be built simultaneously with assessment procedures.

The "shadows" of paper-and-pencil assessment. Perhaps the most significant "shadow" of paper-and-pencil assessment is the fact that instruments that ask patients to respond to various questions can glean only information that patients know about themselves. Three therapists commented that no written intake form that patients complete outside of a psychotherapy session, regardless of how comprehensive it is in content, can provide insight into patients' characterological styles. In other words, when a patient provides responses to questions on a form, the responses are inherently a function of what the patient is aware of about herself (the objects of her awareness). In the case of personality disorders or other ego-syntonic dynamics, much that is important to understand about a patient will become known only by interacting with the person, in-session. This limitation may be overcome by using the Integral Intake as a guide to a structured or semi-structured interview. Provided that therapists remain mindful of this, they can complement what the Integral Intake provides with information obtained by how patients relate to them within the therapeutic relationship.

Assessing feelings, anxiety, and defenses moment-to-moment.[10] Given that my work is heavily influenced by the psychodynamic tradition, including many of the short-term dynamic therapies (STDPs), I also often assess patients moment-to-moment using the triangle of conflict and triangle of persons (see chapter 7, pp. 176–177). Introduced by Malan (1979), the triangle of conflict demonstrates how unconscious emotions trigger anxiety, and how anxiety triggers defenses, and how many patient symptoms are caused by their chronic reliance on defenses. Intensive Short-Term Dynamic Psychotherapy (ISTDP; Davanloo, 2000, 2005) excels in the moment-to-moment assessment of psychotherapy patients. Very briefly, if a patient is asked, for example, how she feels toward her husband for hitting her and she responds either with anxiety in the striated muscles[11] or with a defense, the ISTDP therapist will point out the anxiety and/or the defenses as detours from feeling and redirect the patient to her feeling. If the patient's anxiety is too high, it will manifest in her smooth muscles or in cognitive disruption or perceptual disturbance;[12] if this occurs, the ISTDP therapist regulates the patient's

---

10 This theme did not emerge from the IPP study; I include it here because it is an important dimension of assessment and it informs my practice of iPT.
11 Examples of anxiety manifesting in striated muscle include: fidgeting; tension headaches; tension in the intercostal muscles of chest (sighing or hyperventilating); tension in arms, shoulders, neck, legs, feet; jaw clenching, biting, etc. (Frederickson, 2013).
12 Examples of anxiety manifesting in smooth muscle include: bladder urgency; gastrointestinal spasm, stomach pain or nausea, bowel symptoms such as diarrhea or Irritable Bowel Syndrome; migraine headache, hypertension or other vascular symptoms; bronchial symptoms: asthma or difficulty breathing (because intercostal muscles are not operating automatically); feeling faint or dizzy: "jelly legs" (unsteady gate due to lack of tension in striated muscles) or slumping in chair and feeling weak. Examples of cognitive disruption or perceptual disturbance include: blurry vision,

anxiety until it returns to her striated muscles and then continues to explore the patient's feeling (specific ways to regulate patients' anxiety are discussed in chapter 7, especially footnote 23 on pp. 178–179). When the patient responds with a feeling, the therapist encourages her to feel that feeling more deeply so that they can understand the root of her difficulties. For more on how ISTDP therapists assess or "track" patients in the moment, consult Davanloo (2000, 2005), Frederickson (2013), and Abbass (2015).

Idiographic, interpretive assessment in an age of "flatland." It is important to re-emphasize that the Integral Intake is an idiographic—not a standardized or nomothetic—assessment tool. Part of what this means is that it does not yield a score, diagnosis, or statistical result; for this reason, reliability and validity (which are critical in the development of nomothetic instruments) are not capable of being established for idiographic instruments. Another practical implication with regard to using the Integral Intake—as is the case for any idiographic instrument—is that its use requires interpretation and clinical judgment. Today's marketplace—with increasing demands to deliver manual-based therapy matching a DSM diagnosis that often must be made after the first 50-minute session—reflects "flatland" trends that are, unfortunately, increasingly common. Likewise, most therapists working in clinics or needing third-party reimbursement must also demonstrate quantifiable, externally observable treatment goals in their treatment planning, while administering only "empirically validated treatments" or "best practices."

In contrast to objectivist approaches—which are concerned primarily with exteriors and other Right-Hand phenomena—are depth-oriented traditions that consider meanings, lived-experience, and other phenomenological and inter-subjective dynamics to be paramount. All such interior, Left-Hand approaches require interpretation (Wilber, 2000a). Unfortunately, the training that many mental health professionals receive today—whether psychiatrists, psychologists, counselors, social workers, or marriage and family therapists—emphasizes a narrow form of empiricism more than it does interpretation and the development of clinical judgment. Attempting to address this circumstance, Marquis (2008) includes five chapters discussing the theoretical rationale for why the various quadratic, developmental, states, and types items are included in the Integral Intake; it also includes a 70-page chapter devoted to two very different patients' actual completed intakes, the treatment plans that were created, and how the actual courses of psychotherapy proceeded. For those readers interested in more details regarding how to interpret patients' responses to the Integral Intake, how to formulate treatment plans from them, and the role of clinical judgment in that process, Marquis (2008) is a guide to effective use of the Integral Intake form itself.

---

tunnel vision, blindness; ringing in the ears; falling asleep, freeze response, fugue states, dizziness; thought blocking and/or a genuine inability to think; hallucinations; dissociation, confusion, losing track of thoughts, poor memory; anesthesia (sudden loss of feeling in areas of the body); and passing out (Frederickson, 2013).

Conclusion

Many courses of integral psychotherapy do not address all of the dimensions of patients that the Integral Intake discloses—primarily because of time restraints or other pragmatic constraints. Integral psychotherapists do, however, use the AQAL framework reflected in the Integral Intake to help them scan for as many potentially relevant factors as possible in each patient's struggles, as well as for specific interventions that may address those struggles (see chapter 6).

Integral treatment plans are designed in large measure as a function of each patient's most salient *quadratic* features. When scanning for quadratic variables or dynamics that are likely implicated in—or exacerbating—the patient's struggles, integral psychotherapists consider, for example, the patient's social support system as well as any environmental stressors, social oppression, or lack of access to economic, medical, or educational systems (LR); the quality of the patient's relationships as well as any ethnic/religious/political beliefs and other relevant cultural meaning-making systems (LL); any medical conditions, observable behaviors, or patterns of diet, exercise, or drug and alcohol use (UR); and the patient's strengths and weaknesses, as well as any noteworthy patterns in the patient's self-experience, from empty feelings of depression to chronic worrying or panic attacks (UL).

In phase one of the IPP study, the Integral Intake facilitated therapists' use of the AQAL framework to complement—rather than fundamentally change—how they assessed, planned treatment, and counseled. In essence, by using the Integral Intake to help you scan each patient's AQAL matrix (quadrants, levels, lines, states, types), you may observe relevant features of a patient's life that will add to and enhance the type of psychotherapy you already provide. Because iPT recognizes value in all of the major psychotherapy approaches, you can retain your theoretical and practical preferences. Honoring the multidimensional complexity of patients, the Integral Intake contextualizes patients' struggles and strengths within a comprehensive framework, facilitating psychotherapists' understanding of, and service to, patients in their processes of healing and flourishing in body, mind, and spirit, as each manifests in self, culture, and nature.

CHAPTER 6

An Integral Taxonomy of Therapeutic Interventions
The Role of Interventions in Integral Psychotherapy[1]

Introduction

The taxonomy presented in this chapter classifies more than 200 therapeutic interventions[2] according to the "All-Quadrants, All-Levels" model of integral psychotherapy, followed by a critical discussion of the clinical utility of such a taxonomy. I will discuss the value of such a classification system, including suggestions for how to use the Integral Taxonomy of Therapeutic Interventions (ITTI) with psychotherapy patients, the role and meaning of interventions, an algorithm describing how the interventions were classified, and a caution against the "tyranny of technique."

As discussed in chapter 1, the limits and drawbacks of practicing solely within the parochial confines of a single-system approach have gradually outweighed the benefits that such "pure form" therapies offer. Moreover, with only a few exceptions, we have very little definitive research that demonstrates consistent superiority of one single-school approach or intervention over the others (Asay & Lambert, 2003). Now that the majority of therapists report practicing eclectically or integratively (Jensen, Bergin, & Greaves, 1990), most of us have an overwhelming number of psychotherapy interventions, or techniques, to draw from. Confronted with this plethora of interventions—and a growing chasm separating research and practice (Miller, 2004)—how do therapists dispel the confusion that so many of us feel as we confront these fragmented heaps of technique? In short, how do we decide which interventions to use with a given patient? This question is both epistemological in nature and immediately tied to practice; after all, epistemologies have concrete clinical consequences (Stolorow, Atwood, & Orange, 2002).

---

1 This chapter is adapted/reprinted, with permission, from Marquis, A. (2009). An integral taxonomy of therapeutic interventions. *Journal of Integral Theory and Practice, 4* (2), 13–42.
2 There are 171 "bullets" in the taxonomy, but because many of those bullets contain more than one specific intervention, there are actually more than 200 interventions classified. For simplicity, I will refer to them as 200 interventions.

Although the five main categories of eclectic or integrative practice (eclecticism, common factors, assimilative integration, theoretical integration, and metatheoretical integration) each address the above questions and have contributed to the field's evolution, each of those approaches also has noteworthy limitations or drawbacks: incompleteness, restrictedness, leading to an excessive proliferation of integrative therapies, not including enough of the diversity of extant approaches and interventions, and operating from too-high of a level of abstraction, respectively (Norcross & Newman, 2003; Lampropoulos, 2001; Stricker, 1993; Marquis, Tursi, & Hudson, 2010). As I have been arguing throughout this book, integral metatheory provides a comprehensive yet parsimonious model and conceptual framework able to accommodate varying and highly divergent therapeutic systems, thus aiding therapists in their decisions regarding what interventions to use with which patients.

Given that the primary purpose of this chapter is to provide a classifying system with which to lend order and coherence to what has become a gargantuan heap of technique, I want to emphasize how imperative it is to retain a sense of humility when we assess and evaluate the therapeutic impact of our interventions; this is because our appraisals remain conjectural. A thorough critique of "empirically supported treatment" (EST) and "evidence-based practice" (EBP) research protocols would fill this entire book (see Marquis & Douthit, 2006; Marquis, Douthit, & Elliot, 2011; Messer, 2001; Miller, 1998; Persons, 1991; Polkinghorne, 1999; Slife, 2004; Slife, Wiggins, & Graham, 2005; Westen, Novotny, & Thompson-Brenner, 2004). This is not an expression of pessimism or nihilism, but rather an honest realism peering into the human condition, which is tremendously complex, multidimensional, and multiply-determined. In that mysterious region where facts and meanings mingle, our traditional scientific methods (especially the controlled clinical trials used in EST research) often seem to gaze in confusion at the shining surfaces, where they either remain mostly silent or hubristically pretend to know more about core, depth-level human change processes than they actually do (Foucault, 1973; Mahoney, 1991). It is almost certain that a frame of reference of a different order than that of the biomedical model alone (and its associated controlled clinical trial research) is required to understand the workings of the human heart and mind; what is needed is a more comprehensive, holistic, integral perspective.

The four quadrants are the primary construct organizing this ITTI, the guiding idea being that by including therapeutic interventions from each quadrant, we can identify those contexts in which each intervention is most effective. For example, when counseling an anxious, financially upper-class man whose family life and career are what he had always hoped they would be, we would likely begin with those interventions that facilitate our understanding of his inner world (primarily UL and LL interventions). After all, from an "exterior" perspective, he does not appear to be systemically disadvantaged. On the other hand, when a patient presents with anxiety and her systems are not meeting her basic needs (living in poverty and marginalized due to social class and race issues), we will often intervene with social liberation as more of an overall goal, working more as a systems consultant or resource advocate (primarily LR interventions) than as an intrapsychic excavator. This should become clearer as you peruse the ITTI and the discussion that follows it.

In chapter 3, I mentioned Wilber's thesis that different therapeutic approaches are optimally suited to patients as a function of their developmental center of gravity. As one example of how treatment modalities differ depending upon patients' developmental levels, "uncovering approaches/processes" (such as working through defenses and resistance) are ideal for a neurotic patient who has repressed certain aspects of herself, perhaps to accommodate an authoritarian, narcissistic father, and now a similar husband. However, those same uncovering processes may be iatrogenic to a person with a borderline or narcissistic level of personality organization. This example is corroborated by object-relations and self-psychological approaches that have demonstrated that patients with borderline or narcissistic personality organization need to develop their egos/selves such that they are capable of the relatively mature defense of repression, compared to less mature defenses such as splitting, projective identification, delusional projection, and so forth (Kernberg & Aronson, 1980; Kohut, 1977, 1984). Thus, it is commonly understood that patients struggling with "disorders of the self" need structure (ego/self) building approaches (supporting and reinforcing acts toward autonomy, encouraging differentiation), not uncovering approaches. For any therapist who works with patients who routinely split, express narcissistic rage, or enter the dissociated darkness of rigid, hostile perspectives and overwhelming sadistic impulses, knowledge of such differential courses of action in how to attune to and help patients is essential. At the same time, the "graded format" of Intensive Short-Term Dynamic Therapy (ISTDP)[3] is a modified version of Davanloo's (2000) "standard format," and he developed it to be able to work with highly fragile and resistant patients who often lack emotion regulations skills. When pressured to access their feelings, such patients' anxiety will often exceed what is tolerable; thus, continued pressure or challenge would be iatrogenic. Thus, "The graded format's goal is *building* capacity—also known as *restructuring* [what I called structure building above]—by shifting back and forth, based on the patient's *signaling* [i.e., is the patient's anxiety discharging in the striated muscles or in smooth muscle/cognitive-perceptual disturbance?], between phases of mobilization [mostly pressure] and phases of *anxiety regulation*" (Kuhn, 2014, p. 116; brackets added).

An Integral Taxonomy of Therapeutic Interventions

An ITTI is an ordered system for classifying the procedural methods and practical skills used by therapists to facilitate their patients' healing, growth, and well-being. I chose the word "therapeutic" instead of "counseling" or "*psycho*therapeutic" because a patient's healing and well-being may require changes that revolve more

---

[3] ISTDP will be discussed in greater detail in chapter 7.

Upper-Left (UL): Interior-Individual	Upper-Right (UR): Exterior-Individual
Body • Gendlin's focusing and attunement to immediate "felt-sense" • Self-comforting and basic centering exercises *Mind* • Awareness/consciousness raising • Dialogues with parts of self *Spirit*[4] • Meditation/contemplative prayer • Cultivating mindfulness, gratitude, love, compassion, forgiveness, etc.	*Body* • Self-management programs; self-monitoring and recording • Pharmacotherapy *Mind* • Cognitive restructuring • Reality therapy's WDEP system *Spirit* • EEG biofeedback and brain/mind machines that help induce theta and delta states of consciousness • Yoga
Lower-Left (LL): Interior-Collective	**Lower-Right (LR): Exterior-Collective**
Body • Attending to and mending ruptures in the therapeutic bond • Finding stability in relationships *Mind* • Establishing the therapeutic relationship • Role playing *Spirit* • Compassionate understanding as the heart of counseling • "Selfless service": compassion	*Body* • Basic session management skills and structure of sessions • Involving the patient's social support system in at least one session *Mind* • Social skills training • Genogram analysis *Spirit* • Serving others: advocacy of social justice; social liberation • Relating responsibly to the environment

Figure 6.1 A Mini Integral Taxonomy of Therapeutic Interventions

around diet, spirituality, or more societally systemic issues than the merely intra- and interpersonal changes that characterized counseling and psychotherapy for much of their histories.

Ideally, I would display the ITTI on a single, large sheet of paper. In my attempt to be thorough, the number of interventions is too great to fit on a single page of a book. Bear in mind that although Figure 6.2 spans four pages, it represents the four quadrants (refer to Fig. 6.1), with three levels/developmental realms within

---

4 As discussed in chapter 2, although the "spirit" I am referring to here can be conceived in religious terms (for religious patients), it can also be conceived of secularly (Solomon, 2002; Harris, 2014), which is my personal preference; as I use these three terms, I think of 1) body, 2) mind, and 3) our deepest or highest self; our highest values and capacities; or Maslow's "farther reaches of human nature."

Upper-Left (UL): Interior-Individual

Body
- Gendlin's focusing and attunement to immediate "felt-sense"
- Basic centering techniques: slow, deep breathing; breath counting; pause breathing; release breaths; alternate (control vs. surrender) breathing
- Body balance and other embodiment exercises: standing center, one-leg stand, range of movement/stretching
- Rhythm exercises: walking meditation; music listening, participation, tapping a beat; dance (both spontaneous and/or choreographed)
- Structure-building approaches (especially Kernberg, Linehan, and Kohut for borderline and narcissistic disorders)
- "Distress-tolerance skills" and other emotional/affect regulation skills
- Following flow (i.e., Tai Chi)
- Catharsis, abreaction, dramatic relief
- Self-comforting exercises
- Therapeutic touch: massage therapy; Rolfing; self-massage; handcrafts such as woodwork, needlework, etc.
- Voicework: laughing/crying meditations, singing, voice play, yelling/screaming exercises

Mind
- *Awareness* or consciousness raising: this general process is emphasized by more approaches than any other, the counseling relationship notwithstanding
- Mindfulness meditation; facilitating "de-hypnosis" and "de-automization"; "de-conditioning of old habits"; "thought stopping"; and controlling disturbing thoughts/panic management
- "Relaxing into center" and other relaxation exercises/scripts
- Facilitating the patient's assuming personal responsibility for one's self and experiences (owning and accepting one's feelings and reactions)
- Narrative reconstructions, "re-storying"
- "Turning points exercise" (Mahoney, 2003, p. 103)
- Assessing early recollections and personality priorities
- Guided imagery
- Adlerian lifestyle investigation
- Here-and-now immediacy: experiencing and processing present experience
- Dream interpretation and interpretation in general
- "Staying with the feeling" exercise; exaggeration exercise (Corey, 2001, p. 215)
- Confronting patients, especially with the idea that they are not merely victims; that they can *choose* how to respond to trauma and tragedy
- Confronting the patient with Yalom's four "givens of existence"—death, freedom, isolation, meaninglessness—and deeply pondering them
- Therapeutic double-binds
- Analyses and interruptions of patients' games; script analyses; script reversals
- Analyses of the strokes the patient is receiving from the games she plays
- Reframing

- Dialogues with parts of self/disowned subpersonalities or others: empty chair with underdog/topdog or unfinished business; two-chair dialogue (for conflict splits within a person that need integrating)
- Patient self-evaluation/reflection
- Free association/stream of consciousness
- Therapeutic writing: personal journaling, unsent letters, life review exercises, and narrative reconstructions
- Bibliotherapy: self-help; inspirational; wisdom/religious traditions; stories of others who have endured and emerged healthily from similar experiences
- Mirror time
- "Identity clarifications" (Mahoney, 1991)
- "Kindly self-control"
- Teaching self-relational skills
- Fantasy and dreamwork
- Brainstorming possible solutions/alternatives
- Personal experiments and considerations
- "Catching oneself"
- Push-button technique
- Art therapy: sand tray, clay, painting, music, etc.
- Giving up demandingness
- Changing one's languaging from needs, musts, and shoulds to preferences and conveniences
- Confronting irrational beliefs, expectations, and demands
- Visualizations; imagery; cognitive rehearsal
- "Deserted island fantasy technique" (Lazarus, 1995, p. 346)
- Desensitization - in fantasy with mental images
- Restructuring self-image
- Use of projective assessments such as Rorschach and Thematic Apperception Test

Spirit
- Meditation: concentrative/centering; awareness/insight/decentering
- Prayer/contemplation
- "Self-inquiry" and the intense pondering of profound questions such as "Who am I?", "How shall I live?", "Am I really living the values I claim to hold?"
- Tonglen, a meditation of compassion, and teaching patients about self-compassion
- Forgiveness
- Jungian dream interpretation
- "Coming home to process" (Mahoney, 2003, p. 104)
- "Spiritual skills and personal development" (Mahoney, 2003, pp. 161, 256)
- Practicing compassion for one's self
- Morita therapy's acceptance, reattribution, dereflection, and active engagement
- Cultivating mindfulness, concentration, calm, equanimity, love, compassion, forgiveness, gratefulness, etc.
- The person/being of the therapist and her ability "to enter a variety of distinct states of consciousness" (Sollod, 1993, p. 241)
- Having patients write their epitaph (Yalom, 2002)
- Identity clarifications and personal epilogues (Mahoney, 1991, p. 314)

Upper-Right (UR): Exterior-Individual

Body
- Behavioral techniques (in general); more specifically:
- Problem identification and assessment
- Behavioral analysis and assessment/self-monitoring: keeping detailed records of the specific situations in which the maladaptive behavior is more likely to occur; analysis of antecedents and consequences of the behavior; keeping detailed records of specific activities, events, and reactions; frequency counts
- Exposure therapy (exposure and response prevention; *in vivo* desensitization): graduated or flooding
- Operant conditioning
- Behavioral rehearsals
- Self-management programs: self-monitoring; self-reward/reinforcement
- Physiological recording: monitoring and recording heart rate, skin temperature, etc. (regarding anxiety, sexual dysfunction, etc.)
- Relaxation training (also UL): deep breathing; systematically tensing and releasing/relaxing all muscle groups; *systematic desensitization*
- Resistance exercises/strength training: weight training, isometric exercises
- Cardiovascular exercise
- Yoga
- Bioenergetics – breath and movement work
- Eating a healthy, balanced diet, possibly including vitamin/mineral supplements
- Pharmacotherapy
- Regular and sufficient sleep
- Self-control strategies such as restricting caloric intake, alcohol/drug use, etc.
- Sensory pleasuring
- Shaping: small steps/improvements (successive approximations)

Mind
- Cognitive restructuring (in general; see "A Few Clarifications" in the Discussion section); more specifically:
- Help patients learn to identify maladaptive automatic thoughts and record them, as well as accompanying feelings, events, etc.
- "Empirical disconfirmation": analyze the evidence supporting automatic thoughts and assumptions
- Modifying dysfunctional, maladaptive assumptions and schemas
- Decatastrophizing, reattribution, redefining, de-centering
- Diversion techniques, used to reduce strong emotions and decrease negative thinking: physical activity, social contact, work, play, visual imagery, etc.
- Scaling, cost/benefit analysis, "examining criteria," "defining terms," double standard technique, "downward arrow technique," 3-column technique (Fall et al., 2017, pp. 300–301)
- REBT's ABC analysis
- Disputing patient's irrational beliefs
- Various cognitive homework assignments
- Reality therapy's WDEP system
- Developing "positive addictions"
- BASIC ID analysis
- Modality assessments and modality profiles
- Bridging
- Tracking
- Adlerian "task setting"
- Eye Movement Desensitization and Reprocessing (EMDR)
- Standardized, nomothetic assessment instruments such as the Minnesota Multiphasic Personality Inventory (MMPI-2); California Personality Inventory (CPI); Sixteen Personality Factor Questionnaire (16PF)

Spirit
- EEG biofeedback and brain/mind machines that help induce theta and delta states of consciousness
- Yoga

Lower-Left (LL): Interior-Collective

Body
- Attending to and mending ruptures in the therapeutic bond
- Finding stability in relationships
- Petting and playing with pets
- ISTDP's pressure and challenge

Mind
- Establishing the therapeutic relationship
- Therapist's capacity to enact and *communicate* empathy, genuineness, positive regard (listening, understanding, accepting, prizing)
- Creating a climate of safety and trust
- Basic attending skills: eye contact, facial expressions, minimal encouragers, body posture, etc.
- Role playing (role reversal, role switching), role playing "as if"
- Dramatic enactments/psychodrama
- George Kelly's fixed role therapy
- Encouraging social interest
- Silence (see "A Few Clarifications" in the Discussion section)
- Experiments in directed awareness
- Metacommunicating; disengaging; and "unhooking" (Stricker, 1993, p. 536)
- Transference: emergence and analysis/interpretation
- Analysis/interpretation of resistance
- Confronting patients about incongruences, denying responsibility, etc.
- Socratic dialogue
- Guided discovery
- I-thou relating: authentically engaging patients
- Therapist's use of self-disclosure, especially regarding how she experiences the patient (countertransference)
- Therapist's *presence* and use of authentic self in the here-and-now encounter
- Gender-role analysis and interventions
- Family sculpting
- Circular questioning
- Encouraging social, political, and civic action

Spirit
- "Compassionate relationship as the heart of psychotherapy" (Mahoney, 2003, p. xv)
- Being "recruitable" (Kegan, 1982, pp. 16–17)
- Presence, "invoking the actual," "vivifying and confronting resistance," and "meaning-creation" (Schneider & May, 1995, pp. 174–175)
- Therapist's giving/instilling affirmation and hope "into" the patient
- The therapist's self-awareness and development: her capacity for empathy, presence, unconditional positive regard, genuineness
- Selfless service: compassion; social interest/generativity
- Encouraging patients to consciously create maximally empathic, compassionate, loving relationships with their friends, families, co-workers, etc.
- Helping those in need

Lower-Right (LR): Exterior-Collective

Body
- Basic session management skills: maintaining the therapeutic structure, framework, or "container"; opening and closing sessions
- How sessions are structured: number, frequency, and consistency of sessions
- Therapeutic stance: face-to-face vs. couch; "blank screen" neutrality, anonymity, "objectivity" vs. self-disclosing, transparent, authentic encounter, intersubjectivity
- Stimulus control and other environmental manipulation by therapist and patient
- Involving the patient's social support system (family, friends, significant others) in at least one counseling session (Beck, cited in Fall et al., 2017, pp. 292–293)
- Home visits (Yalom, 2002, p. 171)
- Encouraging patients to exercise responsibilities to the earth such as consuming fewer resources and recycling
- Social advocacy
- Providing patients with appropriate referrals (to other therapists; to city and/or state welfare agencies and/or other social services; to appropriate legal services so that they are not being taken advantage of in ways that violate their constitutional rights; etc.)

Mind
- Role induction (regarding the roles of patient and therapist)
- Therapist as model of appropriate, functional behavior
- Skills training: assertiveness training; social skills training; role training
- "Typical day" exercise (Corey, 2001, p. 397)
- Family therapy in general; more specifically:
- Genogram analysis
- De-triangulation
- Defining roles and boundaries within a family system
- Family sculpting
- Joining and accommodating
- Family mapping
- Family reconstruction
- "Disequilibriating" techniques: blocking, boundary marking, reframing, etc.
- Enactments
- Use of directives
- Paradoxical injunctions
- Satir's family life chronology

Spirit
- Serving others: friends and family; community agencies such as Hospice, Big Brothers, Big Sisters, etc.; visiting people in nursing homes; helping any person in need: "Inasmuch as you do this to the least of my brethren, you do this to me"
- Relating responsibly to nature/the environment, whether this involves recycling, advocating for more stringent standards for corporations' polluting the environment, etc.
- Social liberation: working as a systemic change agent to promote social justice, and encouraging patients to do the same: encouraging people to engage in social activism according to their own sense of justice, provided it is from a world-centric (in contrast to ethnocentric) perspective

Figure 6.2 A Preliminary Integral Taxonomy of Therapeutic Interventions

each quadrant; as will be discussed subsequently, four quadrants × three levels yields 12 dimensions of human beings. Furthermore, space constraints prohibit my describing most of the interventions. However, descriptions of more than 95% of these interventions can be found in three books: Corsini and Wedding (1995), Mahoney (2003), and Corey (2001). A few of the remaining interventions are taken from Yalom (2002), Fall, Holden, & Marquis (2017), and Lambert (2004). Bear in mind that, like Mahoney, "I cannot offer a simple rule for when to offer which of the following techniques" (2003, p. 131).

Discussion

I am well aware that the unifying order in this taxonomy reflects my inclination toward integral theory (see the "Taxonomies and Classification" section below). Nonetheless, I think that even those readers who do not subscribe to integral theory can still find the ITTI clinically helpful, both heuristically and by its organizing a large number of commonly used therapeutic interventions. A relatively quick scan through the ITTI suggests numerous general courses of action as well as specific methods and interventions to utilize with a given patient. Yes, some of the quadratic placements are contestable. As but one example, Stolorow, Atwood, & Orange (2002) compellingly contend—contrary to the continuing ascension of the biopsychiatric model (UR)—that the entire domain of counseling and psychotherapy is intersubjective (LL). In a very real sense, all psychotherapy interventions, because they occur *between* a therapist and one or more patients, are relational (LL) acts (Prochaska & Norcross, 2003). Thus, I expect some disagreement and dialogue regarding my assigning interventions to a particular quadrant, which may be perceived as "pigeonholing." Thus, it may be more accurate to think of which quadrant a given intervention *emphasizes* rather than which quadrant it resides in. Moreover, many of these interventions apply to more than one level; for example, practices such as yoga or meditation can be accurately described as spanning all three of the levels/realms. They are primarily bodily when used to relax and calm the body or reduce bodily tension; primarily mental when used to observe thoughts or images or to reduce anxiety; and primarily spiritual when used to cultivate virtues such as compassion, mindfulness, gratitude, forgiveness, and so forth. I further discuss the rationale behind my placement of interventions subsequently (see "An Integral Algorithm for Classifying Therapeutic Interventions" section below). Bear in mind that the primary goals of this ITTI are to incorporate the interventions of each major single-system approach into a more unified system of care and treatment and to prompt thoughtful dialogue that may heuristically serve the mending of our fragmented health professions. I will structure this discussion around eight themes: taxonomies and classification; the "gist" of the ITTI; the role and meaning of interventions in counseling and psychotherapy; suggestions regarding implementing some of the interventions; how to use the ITTI; attempts to clarify reactions that I anticipate among some readers; a preliminary algorithm; and a caution against the mechanical implementation of interventions.

Taxonomies and Classification

Classifying involves sorting things or processes into categories; the sorting is nonarbitrary because it affords the basis upon which communities dialogue about those things that are classified as the same. Classifying is also classified as natural or artificial,[5] with the former supposedly reflecting nature's internal order and assuming other naturalistic philosophical assumptions, whereas the latter is more often associated with specifically human intentions and thus reflects an external order that derives from humans' needs and purposes (Sadler, 2005). Traditionally, taxonomies have referred to specifically "scientific" classifying systems. In contrast, folk taxonomies are scientifically "agnostic" in that they are not necessarily scientific, although neither are they necessarily nonscientific (Sadler, 2005); Flanagan and Blashfield (2002) argue that the DSMs are folk taxonomies. Given that what I am classifying are artifacts—therapeutic interventions—rather than "givens" in the natural world, the ITTI is most accurately an artificial classification, or perhaps a folk taxonomy. Nonetheless, because psychological and psychiatric literatures often use *taxon* (the group of things constituting a category in a given classification scheme) and *category* interchangeably (Sadler, 2005), I chose to refer to my classification as a taxonomy.

The "Gist" of the ITTI

There are a lot of therapeutic interventions! As always, therapists should use only those interventions with which they have competence, based upon education, training, supervised experience, study, consultation, and/or professional experience (American Psychological Association, 2010; American Counseling Association, 2014). I am *not* suggesting that one needs to use most of these interventions in order to be an effective therapist; I certainly do not. There are some therapists and some approaches—Gestalt comes to mind—that use a great many interventions; when used judiciously, such an approach can work quite well. On the other hand—and as Perls and colleagues (1977) noted—merely using lots of techniques or exercises can be very gimmicky, ineffective, and even abusive. As Yalom (2002) has emphasized, many therapists make the mistake of developing a "grab bag of exercises" to reach into when they feel the need to "jazz up" the therapy. Part of developing as a therapist is learning and appreciating that often times "less is more": at times, sitting in silence with an unconditionally accepting presence is the best response; at other times, following a clinical hunch is best (Yalom, 2002; Mahoney, 2003; Welwood, 2000).

Again, a four-quadrant, three-level classifying scheme such as this ITTI does *not* imply that a therapist needs to use most of the 200 interventions indexed here; nor does it suggest that each therapist needs to regularly use interventions from each

---

5 As I wrote this sentence I was reminded of a humorous phrase attributed to Schopenhauer: "There are two kinds of people in the world: those who believe that there are two kinds of people in the world, and those who do not."

of the 12 dimensions (4 quadrants × 3 levels). What it does suggest, however, is that therapists *conceptualize their patients as having these 12 dimensions as part of their wholeness as human beings*. Thus, therapists will likely benefit their patients by asking themselves questions such as "Am I addressing these 12 dimensions in my patients? If not, why not?" and "Have I overlooked how one or more of these 12 dimensions may be significantly implicated in this person's struggles and healing?" In those cases in which a particular therapist is more of a specialist in three or four of those dimensions and doesn't feel competent to address the others, an indexing scheme such as this ITTI can also goad such a therapist to be humble and not to pretend to be comprehensively attending to the complete fullness of what it is to be human. A key point of this ITTI and this chapter is to encourage therapists to be aware of, and to attempt to "touch base" with, each of these 12 dimensions—as needed—in the people they serve.

You may be asking yourself "Exactly how many important dimensions of people are there?" Although I can't answer that question, there are probably at least several dozen, if not more. However, one simple conceptual framework I suggest using is AQAL; and even if we're using a "scaled down" version with only 12 dimensions (4 quadrants × 3 levels; in contrast to—for example—4 quadrants × 7 levels × 10 lines × 3 states × 3 types!), it will still urge us to consider and be aware of as many dimensions of human wholeness as we can, and thus not ignore or reduce important aspects of a person's being-in-the-world. This ITTI is intended to—first—help therapists approach each patient as a full, whole person (even if that person is experiencing problems in some of the dimensions of their wholeness) and each person has at least these 12 dimensions. Second, this ITTI will hopefully help therapists to open themselves to understanding and empathically resonating with all of the different aspects of human beings. Fundamentally, *the purpose of a classifying scheme such as this ITTI is to remind us of the whole human being*, and these 200 interventions are a reflection of that wholeness.

Importantly, theorists and practitioners have devised interventions in each of these 12 dimensions—I didn't create any of the 200 interventions indexed here—because 1) these 12 dimensions actually exist; they have a reality that the theorists or practitioners recognized; 2) each of these dimensions can be relatively functional or relatively dysfunctional in any given person; and 3) interventions in each of these dimensions are geared toward ameliorating the dysfunctions that arise within those specific dimensions within a given person. It is also important to recognize that these 12 dimensions are not a full expression of an AQAL approach. This ITTI incorporates the four quadrants and three levels within each of those quadrants. It does not address the eight zones (the inside and outside of each quadrant; see p. 222), or lines, states, and types. However, the utility of this ITTI and its 12 dimensions highlights an appealing and practical aspect of integral theory: its scaleability. Although the 12 dimensions of this ITTI will make most therapist's conceptualizations and practice more comprehensive, one could still be more comprehensive by including more of the other dimensions of human nature that are addressed by integral theory.

To be a bit more concrete, the ITTI can be clinically helpful to you if it assists your noticing that most or all of the interventions you use fall primarily within one or two quadrants, or primarily within one or two levels; in such cases you may increase your effectiveness merely by using interventions that address other dimensions—whether quadratic, developmental, or state-related—of your patients. This is one of the simple meanings of an AQAL approach—being aware of the multiple dimensions of ourselves and our patients and attempting to address all those elements implicated in a given person's struggles.

Although incorporating some of the spiritual interventions into your patients' treatment plans may serve their well-being, one contraindication involves the use of insight meditations (often called *vipassana*) with patients suffering from psychotic, borderline, or narcissistic levels of personality organization. Similar to the previous discussion of how such patients require structure-*building* approaches (whether more behaviorally or psychodynamically oriented) rather than uncovering approaches, insight meditations have as their aim the dissolution of psychic structure (ego, self), which is the worst possible "treatment" for such patients. Concentrative meditations, however, may be highly calming, soothing, and distress-ameliorating for such patients (see Boorstein, 1997; Epstein, 1995). Likewise, Mahoney's stream of consciousness, identity clarifications, and/or personal epilogue techniques are contraindicated or strongly cautioned against in the following situations: with patients who are struggling to maintain, recover, or develop an integrated, personal sense of self; with patients who are feeling highly unstable, emotionally vulnerable, or suicidal; with patients who have recently experienced a trauma; with patients who are reluctant to engage in experiential, process-level work; with patients who are not skilled in centering or regaining their sense of psychological balance; in early sessions prior to the establishment of a therapeutic alliance; or late in a given session or late in the course of therapy, when there may not be sufficient time afterward to adequately process the experience (Mahoney, 1991, pp. 296, 314–315; Mahoney, 2003, p. 143).

Another appealing aspect of an integral approach to therapy that the ITTI makes quite clear is that you do not have to abandon your preferred single-school or integrative approaches and their associated interventions to practice integrally. After all, an integral approach to therapy includes and values *all* of the interventions in the ITTI, while situating them within a more comprehensive conceptual framework. However, certain clinical situations will call for an emphasis or de-emphasis on different classes of interventions, as noted in the previous paragraph.

The Role and Meaning of Interventions

It has been argued that therapy, at its best, is spontaneous, dynamic, and creative. Yalom has gone so far as to say that we should "create a new therapy for each patient" (2002, p. 33). Additionally, he stated that therapy is

> grotesquely distorted by being packaged into a formula that enables inexperienced, inadequately trained therapists (or computers) to deliver a uniform course of therapy. One of the true abominations spawned by the

managed-care movement is the ever greater reliance on protocol therapy in which therapists are required to adhere to a prescribed sequence, a schedule of topics and exercises to be followed each week. (Yalom, 2002, p. 34)

What *is* paramount is empathic attunement to our patient's experience such that the therapeutic relationship—which is itself a primary component of the change process—is fostered (Hubble, Duncan, & Miller, 1999; Norcross, 2011), which is *not* to suggest that evidence-based approaches or the specific interventions in this ITTI are unimportant. Rather, the potency of any intervention greatly increases when used within a genuine, caring, attentive engagement with the *patient-as-person*, not as object of our "expert gaze" (Foucault, 1973) and technical mastery. Regarding this issue, Frankl wrote that:

> the two extremes, encounter and technique, seem to be a matter of theoretical importance only. Live practice hovers between the extreme poles. Neither should be looked upon contemptuously or disparagingly ... [However,] Technique, by its very nature, tends to reify whatever it touches ... Worshipping technique at the expense of encounter involves making man [sic] not only a mere thing but also a mere means to an end ... Seeing in man [sic] a mere means to an end is the same as manipulating him. (1967, p. 80, brackets added)

Like drives from contemporary psychoanalytic points of view (which primarily serve to maintain object relations, as every drive is always directed toward some object), interventions have been suggested as primarily functioning to establish, maintain, and deepen the therapeutic relationship (Gold, 1993a; Yalom, 2002). In addition to whatever power and effectiveness interventions may have in and of themselves, interventions serve other functions: from ideological functions (distinguishing therapists from the uninitiated and untrained) and ritualistic functions (providing a sense of control, competence, comfort, and hope through repetitive action) to justifying the ongoing interaction of the participants such that the relationship continues and develops (Gold, 1993a). In contrast, some behavior therapists have claimed that because their treatments and interventions derive from specific and powerful behavior change technologies, theirs is the only approach that transcends the common factor of "persuasion" that Frank (1961) maintained as the heart of psychotherapy. However, studies have revealed that when patients who undergo behavior therapy are asked what they think has been most helpful from their treatment, they do not appear to report very differently from those who undergo other (more relational) forms of therapy; they, too, most often emphasize relational and interactional factors (Sloan et al., 1975; Gold, 1980).

Given the apparently essential importance of the therapeutic relationship, integral therapists practice embodying Roger's "core conditions" of empathy, genuineness, and positive regard. According to Kegan, the best therapists are those who deeply resonate with a patient's phenomenological experience, "rather than to help solve the problem, or try to make the experience less painful" (1982, p. 274). Kegan emphasized that good therapy requires far more than merely implementing techniques: "Its delicacy lies in the fact that the therapist is actually trying to join another person in an extraordinarily intimate way; he or she is trying to become a helpful part of the person's very evolution" (1982, p. 278). Kegan also stresses that the therapist's "recruitability"—the ability to *care* for patients such that the therapist is vulnerable and moved by their "interbeing"—is as important in helping patients as is the therapist's professional, technical knowledge.

A related issue involves the different meanings that interventions, or "techniques," have for novices and experts. I remember my first clinical supervisor, John Garcia, saying "techniques are what you'll use until the therapist arrives"— meaning that until we became truly effective therapists (in part due to our abilities to form safe, trusting, empathic, intimate relationships; as well as developing a— relatively—unconditional healing presence that is augmented by our own consciousness development), we would have to rely solely upon techniques—a far cry from what optimal therapy is. Yalom (2002) used a musical analogy to explain this notion: a pianist needs technique to play, but to play beautifully one must transcend technique and trust one's intuition and creativity. Mahoney (2003) often likened techniques to languages. Obviously, one is more likely to successfully communicate with more of Earth's peoples if one knows more languages. At the same time, the language is not equivalent to a meaningful message; just because someone can speak many languages does not mean he is saying something important! Just as someone can graduate with a PhD and have received supervised training in numerous techniques and still not practice in a genuinely therapeutic manner.

Essential aspects of constructive integral practice involve experimenting, exploring, and constructing novel experiences in order to challenge patients' old patterns of activities. This technical "risking" often demands a spirit of adventure and creativity from the integral-constructive practitioner (Mahoney & Marquis, 2002). As Mahoney stressed, "that creativity and spirit cannot be formalized in a particular procedure ... [Likewise,] *constructive practice recognizes that the power to change lies in processes* rather than specific procedures" (2003, p. 58, italics in original, brackets added). For example, the *process* of learning to relax can be acquired from numerous different *techniques*, from meditation, yoga, and self-massage to progressive muscle relaxation, autogenic training, and guided imagery. The dynamic tensions between human change processes that unfold in the company of novel encounters in contrast to applying techniques as they are expounded in training manuals are essential tensions with which all therapists and educators of therapists must struggle. Although I will later caution against "technolatry," the "tyranny of technique," and what Rogers referred to as the "appalling consequences" of reducing helping to a mechanical use of technique (1980, p. 139), bear in mind that most therapeutic practice, as Frankl and Yalom suggested, involves integrating technique and genuine encounters with another human being.

A Few Suggestions

Most of the above interventions will be more effective if both the patient and the therapist are *prepared* for them and in an appropriate state of consciousness. Thus, it is helpful for therapists to prepare for powerful, experiential interventions (empty chair work, affect-focused work, etc.) with some form of centering method, which might involve a few deep breaths, a few moments of silent contemplation, and the setting of positive intentions (Mahoney, 2003). Also important is the patient's informed consent (rationale) about the intervention itself. Allowing plenty of time after the intervention in order to process the experience with the patient and reflect upon the meanings it disclosed is also essential.

Another caveat regarding powerful, experiential interventions: it is helpful if the therapist has experienced these as a patient. In other words, the maximally ethical therapist has not only studied and practiced such interventions under supervision, she also has first-hand knowledge of what these interventions stimulate within the person on the "receiving end," which helps the therapist appreciate the resistance that patients often display when asked to participate in such interventions. Regarding pharmacotherapy, it is best for therapists to work *collaboratively* with psychiatrists (see Ingersoll & Rak, 2006).

How to use the ITTI

Integral psychotherapy is an "All-Quadrants, All-Levels" activity. It is important to remember, however, that the acronym "AQAL" refers also to "all-states, all-lines, and all-types" of the patient's self-system. Due to space constraints, however, I will address only quadratic and developmental issues, beginning with the latter; attending to patients' lines, types, and states is discussed in Marquis (2008) and "state work" is also addressed in chapter 7 of this book.

As discussed in chapter 3, Wilber has posited that patients suffering from struggles associated with specific developmental stages will be optimally helped by interventions that are most appropriate to those particular developmental dynamics. As an example involving common clinical sense, consider that although philosophical introspection and Socratic dialogue may be very helpful for a patient capable of formal-operational thinking who is in the process of establishing a relatively autonomous identity (Wilber's formal-reflexive stage), using such methods, or speaking in complex metaphors, will be far less helpful to someone who has yet to grow into those developmental capacities. With a patient who thinks very concretely (Wilber's rule/role mind stage), one would likely use more concrete cognitive approaches (cognitive therapy, reality therapy, REBT, etc.). However, although such cognitive interventions are of some help to patients struggling with more profound disturbances, strictly cognitive approaches are not as helpful as uncovering approaches and structure-building approaches are for patients with neurotic and borderline/narcissistic personality organizations, respectively. Whereas many integral therapists suggest using those interventions that target each individual patient's "developmental center of gravity," I think it is most appropriate to match interventions to the patient's current, in-the-moment (self-, affective-, defensive- etc.) state (as discussed in chapters 3 and 7).

On the other hand, because mental health is not completely separate from physical or spiritual health, anyone's well-being may be enhanced by engaging practices from each of those three domains. With regard to exercising one's body, some people respond better to weight-lifting, others to swimming or hiking. Similarly, the same diet is not optimal for all people. The concept Integral Life Practices (ILPs; Wilber et al., 2008) emphasizes the cultivation of practices that celebrate and nurture the entire human being—from the body, emotions, and mind, all the way to the "farther reaches of human nature"—as *each* unfolds in self (UL), culture (LL), and nature (UR and LR). Thus, independent of how developed one's *lines* are (cognitive, affective, moral, interpersonal, etc.), one strives to be as "All-Quadrants, All-Levels" as one can be. The basic idea is that we are most likely to optimize our health and well-being if we exercise, nourish, and cultivate as many dimensions of our being as possible. Thus, we can assist our patient's choice of a practice or two from each domain of body (ideally one physical and one more emotion-oriented), mind, and "spirit" and encourage them to engage those practices as consistently as they can. Although we need additional research to more specifically ascertain which domains (such as body, mind, spirit, as well as ethics, interpersonal relationships, defense work, etc.) are most effective for which specific types of people to exercise, some research suggests that (analogous to athletic "cross training") when we engage practices addressing many dimensions of our being simultaneously, their positive influence increases synergistically (Murphy, 1995; Leonard & Murphy, 1995).

Analogous to exercising each dimension of body, mind, and spirit, paying attention to each patient's "quadratic balance" is also important. For example, someone who is excessively preoccupied with himself (UL) may be self-absorbed or what laypeople call narcissistic. Such an individual will often benefit by devoting time, energy, and attention to more collective endeavors, whether that is a systemic activity (LR) such as engaging in civic action or working to reduce their carbon footprint or a cultural activity (LL) such as empathically listening to others or helping someone in need of assistance. Conversely, someone who is inordinately concerned about her "we," or her place within various groups/collectives (LL), is likely to be excessively conformist. This person may benefit from spending more time alone, whether in nature, meditating, exercising, or engaging in some form of art, music, reading, or any other solitary activity that provides enjoyment and meaning to the individual. Finally, excessive focus on, or preoccupation with, solely the exterior, or the more objective, dimensions of life (UR and LR) can produce dissociation from oneself or from one's groups. Such a person could be served by interventions from the UL or LL quadrants: Gendlin's focusing; dialogues with parts of self or others; personal journaling; or developing better relationships by cultivating empathy and compassion for friends, family members, co-workers, and so forth. In short, as integrally informed therapists, we scan which quadratic dimensions each patient tends to ignore, avoid, or devalue, and then select specific interventions from the ignored, avoided, or devalued quadrant(s) that seem most likely to be a good fit for that individual.

A Few Clarifications

What many patients describe as their "problems" are situations or feelings that, in one way or another, "knock them off" their center of balance. Thus, it is helpful to teach and encourage the practice of centering skills throughout the duration of therapy. Life will always throw us curves, and rest assured, we *will,* even if only temporarily, lose our balance. If we have cultivated our capacities to regain our own balance and center, those moments of distress will be fewer, or at least briefer. This applies not only to our patients, but to ourselves as well. I am here reminded of Wilber's comment that we should not strive to rid the ocean of life of its waves; rather, we should learn to surf, which requires considerable balance indeed. Consistently practicing basic centering skills is as vital for therapists as it is for patients (Mahoney, 2003).

Although I personally react against the hegemony that cognitive-behavioral approaches are currently enjoying due to problematic and/or misguided conceptual, methodological, and political dimensions of EST research protocols (Marquis & Douthit, 2006; Shedler, 2010), I also recognize therapeutic value in both cognitive and behavioral methods. Regarding cognitive restructuring: the basic notion here is that much of what we experience is mental and much of our mental activity, especially in the form of thoughts and images, influences how we feel and act. Moreover, what we tell ourselves (self-talk) is critical to our processes of change and our awareness of what *is.* The success of cognitive-restructuring interventions depends in large measure upon creating and strengthening patterns of thinking that serve the individual's well-being. "Maladaptive" thought patterns are thus to be replaced with more adaptive ones. However, before individuals can replace dysfunctional thoughts with functional ones, they must be aware of those thought processes. Thus, training in introspection or other attentional processes is a helpful component to cognitive methods; after all, you cannot change negative self-talk and catastrophizing imagery if you are not first aware of them. This is corroborated by research by Segal, Williams, and Teasdale (2002), who demonstrated that integrating mindfulness meditation with cognitive therapy increases the latter's efficacy, particularly its long-term effectiveness and the prevention of depressive relapse.

The essence of cognitive restructuring involves the following four steps:

1. *Pay attention and observe your feelings,* particularly when your feelings change. This requires a certain degree of skill in moment-to-moment awareness, or mindfulness. The ability to notice that you are becoming anxious or angry *as that feeling is emerging* is a skill that most patients do not possess upon entering therapy. More often, they are likely to become pre-reflexively absorbed in, and by, the anxiety, depression, or anger and it may be minutes or hours before they are aware that they are upset. Thus, encourage patients to train their attention! (There is more on this in chapter 7.)
2. *As soon as you become aware of your feelings* (especially when they have just changed, either positively or negatively) *notice what was passing through your mind in the form of thoughts or images.*
3. *Evaluate those thoughts and images*: Do they make sense? What do they mean or imply? Would you want someone you love to hold onto such thoughts and images?

4. If your feelings are distressing or are headed in that direction, can you *imagine alternative ways of thinking about your situation/self?* Can you imagine and truly entertain *counterarguments* to your manner of thinking/imagining? Can you come up with more functional options that you will systematically attempt to replace the dysfunctional ones with? Until a patient can imagine constructive alternatives, change is unlikely. A useful way of determining if a patient can imagine her life without her problem(s) is Adler's "miracle question": "What would your life be like (what would you *specifically* observe and experience) if a miracle occurred during your sleep and you woke up without your problem?" Some patients organize their lives around problems and crises to such a degree that either they fail to conceive of such a possibility or they find the idea (of being without their problems) intensely distressing. (adapted from Mahoney, 2003)

Some key behavioral points to teach patients include: *be actively engaged*; *pay attention to the consequences of your actions/behaviors* and "control" your behavior with a much greater percentage of rewards than punishments; *small steps* are more likely to be maintained than dramatic changes; *practice* those small steps *as consistently as possible* (consistency and regularity is what creates habits). Homework assignments are a useful way to encourage patients' consistent practice of what they are learning in therapy. Moreover, we not only adapt ourselves to our environments, we also shape our environments to meet our needs and preferences. It is important to explore how aware patients are of how their environment influences them. Patients are more likely to succeed in a new behavioral regimen if they can anticipate environmental "hazards." For example, with a patient trying to eat healthier and lose weight, it is helpful to have healthy, low-calorie foods readily visible in his cupboards or refrigerator. The more salient and "within reach" the "junk" food is, the more likely he will consume it. Also, teach patients about how much of our behavior is a function of our associating two events, even if we are often unaware of those associative processes. For example, if a patient observes that he is usually watching TV when he binges on junk food, he may want to try minimizing TV viewing and find another activity that provides a similar function for him, or he may want to begin consciously eating only healthy, smaller portions of food while he is watching TV.

You may wonder what is therapeutic about writing one's epitaph/personal epilogue or "deeply pondering" existential givens such as death and isolation. Perhaps it seems morose to meditate on death. However, deeply understanding death can potentially free our hearts, illuminating the futility of our false projects that function to console, distract, and delude ourselves. Thus, deeply contemplating our mortality can be an ideal way to realize and *will* what is most important to us. These interventions, however, are contraindicated for patients who are depressed, psychotic, or struggling to maintain or develop an integrated self-sense.

An important caveat for the therapist who works with patients' suprapersonal issues is that she needs to know not only suprapersonal theories (which are fundamentally the same as transpersonal theories), interventions, and diagnostic issues and to practice these under supervision; she must also be engaged in her own inner work: "for transpersonal therapists, undergoing their own in-depth, transpersonally oriented psychotherapy and long-term practice of transpersonal disciplines such as yoga or meditation are invaluable . . . part of a lifetime practice" (Walsh and Vaughan, 1993, p. 154). In fact, the therapist's being, presence, empathy, compassion, and acceptance may be as helpful as any other therapeutic elements, and these are largely a matter of the therapist's own spiritual work (Epstein, 1995): "To whatever degree my personal [spiritual] practice keeps *me* loving, keeps *me* compassionate and empathic, to that degree therapy proceeds most effectively" (Boorstein, 1997, p. xvi; brackets added).

Although integral therapists will focus on the specific problems of patients and also work within the constraints of managed care, we are, in general, more *awareness-focused* and *development-focused* than problem-focused. With many patients, simply identifying and removing the obstructions to growth and development are sufficient to help them lead more healthy, fulfilling lives (Yalom, 2002). I am also highly cognizant of how the constraints of different patients bear on the services we provide. For example, I work in a much more direct, solution-focused manner with patients who have the resources for only a few sessions than those who have the time, money, and personal investment of many months or years of therapy.

An Integral Algorithm for Classifying Therapeutic Interventions

I anticipate that a reaction of some readers may involve disagreement, or perhaps even some confusion, regarding the placements of the various interventions in the ITTI. Thus, this section attempts to clarify how I classified the interventions. Regarding the quadratic placements, recall that *the four quadrants represent the interiors and exteriors of both individuals and systems.* Although many therapeutic interventions clearly involve more than one quadrant (such as empty chair work), most of them emphasize or focus on a dimension-perspective characterized by a single quadrant. Take, for example, the first intervention in the UL quadrant (interior-individual; see Figure 6.2). Gendlin's method of "focusing" involves a patient directing her attention internally to her inner "felt-sense." Hopefully, this is a good example of this "integral algorithm": the focus is on an *individual* (in contrast to a family system, relationship, culture, or society) and the therapeutic work of the individual is done *internally*, with her sensations and feelings (in contrast to her experimenting with a new behavior, which could be observed from the exterior, and thus would be one of the more objective, "right-hand" quadrants). To explicate the difficulty of placing empty chair work in a single quadrant (which I classified in the UL), consider that such an intervention *can* be observed from the exterior; the patient's actions could be captured with a video camera. The patient, after all, sits in one chair and speaks to an empty chair in which the patient is imagining a subpersonality of his or another person with whom he has unfinished business. However, I consider this more of an *internal* intervention because the power, meaning, and therapeutic value of empty chair work depend primarily on the patient's ability to enter certain psychological (internal) spaces in which his subpersonality or another person is vividly imagined to occupy that chair, as well as the emotional courage to dialogue about what is most important to the patient. Why, you might ask, if the person is "talking to another person" (such as an imagined parent) is this not a collective quadrant? Because the other with whom the patient is dialoguing is "there" only to the extent that the patient is holding the other within his own psyche; thus my placement in the UL.

Another counterintuitive placement involved my classifying cognitive interventions in the Upper-Right quadrant. Are not cognitions "inside" the individual and therefore belong in the Upper-Left quadrant? The reasoning behind my placing them in the UR involves a primary thrust that has characterized the cognitive therapy approach, which is striving to be as empirical and objective as possible, and a concomitant belief that information processing can be reduced to the associations of sensations, which is another quintessential characteristic of empirical/*externally observable*, as opposed to rational/internal, ways of acquiring data (Anchin, 2005). As Wilber has discussed, orthodox cognitive theorists have usually defined cognitions as internal (mental) acts upon external objects, thus essentially reducing cognition to sensorimotor objects (personal communication, February 3, 2007). Moreover, Beck modeled his approach after—and teaches his patients to practice on themselves—the scientific method: patients "are taught to treat their beliefs as hypotheses and to gather additional information and conduct behavioral experiments to test their accuracy" (Hollon & Beck, 2004, p. 448). All of the above characteristics signify "gaining distance from" one's thoughts—as *from the exterior* looking in—so that one is not so involved with the matter that they cannot see their thoughts as they "really are," which is what "objectivity" is all about. Gergen (1985) highlighted an irony that characterizes cognitive approaches to psychology and therapy: by privileging approaches that are objective—in an experimental manner that is valid independent of subjective appraisal—cognitive researchers devalue the very processes that they ultimately propose are most significant in our understanding of human nature.

Many of the interventions are difficult to classify solely in one quadrant because their placement is often a function of how the intervention is viewed or conceptualized. Take, for example, relaxation training. Literally hundreds of studies have documented the physiological changes and benefits of practicing various forms of meditation and/or relaxation. To the extent that those changes are measured externally (whether via blood pressure, galvanic skin response, EEG, or frequency of fidgeting), we can place such interventions in the UR/behavioral quadrant. However, if we endeavor to illuminate the phenomenological experience of relaxation and other altered states of consciousness, those same interventions are more accurately placed in the UL/experiential quadrant. Thus, some of the confusion and apparent contradictions stem from the goals with which a specific intervention is used and/or evaluated. Again noting that much of this is a matter of emphasis rather than strict placement, and also highlighting Wilber's notion of how the quadrants "tetramesh," a society (LR) that encourages meditation or other contemplative practices will increase the percentage of its members who engage in such practices (UR), which will likely lead them to have certain phenomenological experiences (UL) that will tend to play out in how they relate and understand one another (LL), which in turn can have an externally observable impact on that society's structures (LR) and on and on ... Thus, the quadrants not only co-arise with one another; they mutually constitute one another.

Another potentially controversial placement involves assigning structure-building approaches to the UL quadrant. Intersubjective field theorists such as Stolorow, Atwood, & Orange (2002) would argue that because psychic structures (ego, self) never develop independently of an intersubjective matrix of object relations, such approaches belong in the LL/cultural quadrant. Wilber and I agree that human psychology emerges within intersubjective contexts and thus all of our psychological dimensions are powerfully influenced by intersubjective and other contextual and cultural dynamics. Wilber's point—regarding why structure-building approaches are most appropriately placed in the UL quadrant—is that *a given psychic structure exists not within a collective, but rather within the interior of an individual*, hence the UL placement (personal communication, February 9, 2006).

A final quadratic issue involves placing behavioral methods in the UR. One could argue that the LR is a more appropriate placement because most behaviorists have stressed that behaviors are not initiated from within the organism, but rather are either elicited by environmental (systemic; LR quadrant) stimuli and/or reinforced or extinguished by their environmental consequences. Wilber, however, suggests the UR placement because behavioral methods have as their goal a change of (externally observable) behaviors *in the individual*; the goal of behaviorists is usually not simply to change the environment (personal communication, February 9, 2006) without regard to its effects on the individual.

My decisions regarding developmental placements were even more difficult and less than clear-cut, primarily because many interventions can influence or work upon different dimensions of our being. In general, I classified interventions according to which dimension of body, mind, or "spirit" they target or aim to impact the most. For example, it will hopefully be generally agreed that catharsis, pharmacotherapy, distress-tolerance skills, and behavioral methods primarily target the level of body (which includes emotions, because emotions are *actually felt* within one's body). Likewise, consciousness raising, cognitive restructuring, and narrative reconstructions primarily target dimensions of mind. Finally, contemplative prayer; cultivating love, compassion, and gratitude; serving others and working for their social liberation are dimensions that most therapists would categorize as spiritual (again, I use the term "spirit" and "spiritual" to refer to our highest virtues and capacities, without any necessarily religious connotations).

Prime examples of interventions that impact multiple dimensions of our being and development are meditation and yoga. Although these two practices are probably most strongly associated with spirit, in contrast to body or mind, they both positively influence all levels of our being. Some types of yoga[6] or meditation

---

6 For the sake of simplicity, I am subsuming many different types of yoga under the single category of "yoga" when, actually, there are distinct types of yoga that specifically address physical, mental, and spiritual dimensions. Interested readers can consult Feuerstein (1997).

may emphasize bodily postures and energies, others will emphasize mental processes, while others focus on spiritual dimensions. These interventions can be placed in more than one developmental category because, although they are not panaceas, they do often have significant positive outcomes for people who practice them appropriately (usually under a competent teacher's guidance) and ardently. Nonetheless, although meditation has been shown to affect the brain's physical structure (body; Schwartz & Begley, 2002; Austin, 1999), and although meditation also clearly influences our mental states (mind), I believe that the most powerful and unique contributions of meditation are directed toward states of consciousness and development dynamics that are best described as spiritual ("spirit").

Regarding my classification of silence as a therapeutic intervention, I can think of the use of therapeutic silence as also involving all three levels of body, mind, and spirit. During silence, awareness of felt-experience may be heightened (body); thoughts may be further processed (mind); or a mental quietude may open to a deeper realization of that which transcends the individual in some sort of universal manner ("spirit"). Frequently, powerful therapeutic moments include those of silence; not awkward, dead, or paralyzing silences but healing silences pregnant with meaning and possibilities. "This healing silence, which is an untouched natural resource for the practice of psychotherapy" (Epstein, 1995, p. 187), is possible only when the therapist can be with a patient without an agenda, simply being present to the intersubjective field arising between therapist and patient. This capacity is greatly augmented by the therapist's own meditative or contemplative practice. I chose to place silence at the level of mind in the LL because, in psychotherapy, silence is always occurring between two or more people, and in my experience as a therapist the most frequent dimension that patients discuss after silences are mental (insightfully making connections or realizing patterns in their lives), though often emotional as well. Aware that many readers may feel strongly that, for example, silence more frequently elicits bodily or emotional reactions, I titled Figure 6.2 a *preliminary* ITTI, rather than a *final* ITTI. I welcome reactions to, and feedback regarding, this taxonomy.

A Cautionary Appeal

In my experience as an educator and supervisor of therapists, it is all too common for mental health professionals to fall prey to the *tyranny of technique*, and too often what we think is a therapeutic "groove" is more a mechanically employed, technical rut: "the art of human helping will not be found in specific words or meticulously repeated rituals, unless those words and rituals reflect something deeper than their own surface structure" (Mahoney, 2003, p. 168). Similarly, Frankl wrote that: "What matters is not the technique applied but the doctor who applies it, or more specifically, the spirit in which he [sic] applies it" (1967, p. 81). Thus, integral psychotherapy is not defined by the specific interventions that are used, but, rather, by 1) the AQAL perspective from which, and within which, patients are viewed and therapy is practiced; 2) basing one's practice—as much as is feasibly possible—upon research grounded *not* in reductionistic "EST" research, but rather a pluralism of research designs and methods; and 3) the therapist's self, awareness, and *being* and her capacity to compassionately *"be-with"* those who are suffering. Regarding the significance of the therapist's self (UL, spirit), it is common to find this or similar ideas posited in many, if not most, books on psychotherapy practice, and it is well addressed by Yalom, who stated that the therapist's most valuable "instrument" is herself and that it follows, therefore, that:

> Personal psychotherapy is, by far, the most important part of psychotherapy training ... therapists must show the way to patients by personal modeling. We must demonstrate our willingness to enter into a deep intimacy with our patient, a process that requires us to be adept at mining the best source of reliable data about our patient—our own feelings ... I believe there is no better way to learn about a psychotherapy approach than to enter into it as a patient. (2002, pp. 40–41)

In a similar vein, Miller states boldly that the person of the therapist is "the primary therapeutic tool in any therapeutic encounter" (2004, p. 254). I further agree with Perls when he wrote that, in and of itself, "a technique is a gimmick ... We've got enough people running around collecting gimmicks, more gimmicks and abusing them" (1959, p. 1).[7] Kegan echoed this sentiment when he stated that, "like any technique, it can only stop being a technique when it is embodied by a person with a specific set of ideas and hopes which he is himself trying to bring to life through the medium of 'technique'" (1982, pp. 277–278).

Conclusion

I have argued that the "All-Quadrants, All-Levels" model of integral theory is a prime candidate for lending order to the multitude of extant therapeutic interventions and that the ITTI is merely one example of integral psychotherapy's clinical utility. Regardless of your theoretical orientation, the ITTI provides a fairly comprehensive classification of therapeutic treatment practices and hopefully a conceptual aid in your process of choosing among the many therapeutic interventions. You and your patients may be served by your consulting the ITTI and considering whether or not some of the interventions from different quadratic or developmental dimensions might be appropriate to your patients' specific struggles.

A primary point of this ITTI is that our patients are highly multidimensional and complex, that they have *at least* these 12 dimensions, and that suffering and/or dysfunction can arise within any of these 12 dimensions. An indexing system such as this ITTI is not meant to pigeonhole or marginalize any system of psychotherapy or any patient; it is meant to continually remind us of the richness, fullness, and

---

7 I will once again highlight a dialectical tension. On the one hand, I agree with what I have written in this section. At the same time, it also appears that some techniques and interventions (i.e., those of ISTDP) are unusually powerful and effective when performed with the requisite knowledge and skill.

wholeness of human beings everywhere. This ITTI also affirms that many therapists have created interventions to address problems in each of these 12 dimensions of people.

Integral theory and this ITTI are *both complexifying* (in that they integrate and unify more domain systems than most approaches) *and simplifying* (in that they bring parsimonious order to the cacophony of disparate dimensions of humans). This ITTI reminds us of—and hopefully helps us hold in both heart and mind—the rich fullness of what it is to be human. An AQAL approach and this ITTI are, thus, prompts to always look for all of the important dimensions of each patient and not to reduce anyone to just an id, ego, superego, information processor, passive product of reinforcements and punishments, merely the product of social systems, and so forth.

As most of us continue laboring to improve our ability to serve our patients, let us not forget the paramount priority of therapist self-care. What might an inability to be understanding, gentle, and compassionate with ourselves imply about our capacity to care for others? And how might that influence our work with patients? This is particularly critical in light of recent reports on "therapist impairment" (Rollins, 2005). Furthermore, to what degree are we, as therapists, willing to be vulnerable to the unforeseen consequences of practicing "the dangerous recruitability" that Kegan (1982) stresses is inherent in optimal psychotherapy? And to what extent are we practicing a *life-wisdom*, in contrast to merely accumulating information and mechanically repeating interventions? Deeply pondering such questions is a vital element of professional helping. As such, an integral approach to psychotherapy rests upon *phronesis*—the practical wisdom of the therapist's being—more than *techne*, the type of knowledge involved with machinery, crafts, and production. The notion of counseling practice based upon a "tyranny of technique" is misguided and potentially harmful (Mahoney & Marquis, 2002).

With its mission to embody a psychotherapy approach that integrates compassionate recruitability with the most current, sound, scientific psychotherapy outcome and process research, integral psychotherapy attempts to marry not only the heart and mind, but also the patient's experience and capacity to choose (UL); biomedical perspectives and the individual's behavior (UR); culture and meaning-making systems (LL); and the social systems in which we find ourselves (LR). I hope this ITTI helps therapists honor and nurture each patient's body, mind, and spirit (one's highest, most virtuous self), as each unfolds in self, culture, and nature.

CHAPTER 7

Principles of Treatment in Integral Psychotherapy

Give yourself and your client permission not to know and not to fully understand. Life is much more than figuring things out; effective therapy does not require complete understanding or definitive explanations ... Let your heart lead your helping. (Mahoney, 2003, p. 262)

The realities of our work do not fit that [fine-tuned empirical] model, and often we find ourselves improvising as we and our patients stumble together on the journey toward recovery. I used to be unnerved by that, but now, in my golden years, I whistle softly to myself as I marvel at the complexities and unpredictability of human thought and behavior. Now, rather than being rattled by uncertainty, I realize that it is pure hubris to posit specificity. (Yalom, 2015, p. 81)

Introduction

For many years, a goal of mine was to write a manual of iPT that would delineate exactly what iPT is and how to implement it, which would then afford the possibility that iPT could participate in outcome research studies. I no longer believe that such an iPT manual is possible; this is due in part—as I mentioned in chapter 2—to its metatheoretical nature and its attempt to unify all the major systems of psychotherapy. It is also due to what the two opening quotes of this chapter address: that human nature and change are too complex, multidimensional, and unpredictable to allow the delineation of specific interventions that apply to all individuals and circumstances. As will be further discussed in this chapter, there simply is not one way to implement iPT: one therapist may conceptualize and practice more psychodynamically, whereas another does so in a more CBT fashion; provided that they take into account the four quadrants, developmental dynamics, patients' moment-to-moment states, and so forth, they both may rightly claim to be integral therapists. In fact, research suggests that it may be more appropriate to say that one practices "integrally informed psychotherapy" or that one practices with an "integral sensibility" than to say one practices "integral psychotherapy" (Marquis & Elliot, 2015).[1] Thus, rather than attempt to explicate

---

1 Much more will be said about this toward the end of this chapter.

precisely how to implement iPT, this chapter will provide *orienting principles* that will facilitate your practicing psychotherapy in an integrally coherent and comprehensive manner.

As mentioned in chapter 6, because integral (or integrally informed) psychotherapy is not so much a distinct theoretical approach as it is a *meta*theoretical approach, integral therapists draw from the entire spectrum of psychotherapeutic techniques: from exposure (Richard & Lauterbach, 2006) and empty chair work (Greenberg, 2002) to analysis of transference (Clarkin, Yeomans, & Kernberg, 2006) and cognitive restructuring (Beck, 1976). Moreover, based upon any number of quadratic, developmental, or other dynamics that different patients manifest, the same integrally informed therapist may be quite person-centered with one patient and quite behavioral and directive with another.

As a sensibility (rather than a prescriptive, manualized approach), the form or process of integral psychotherapy can vary tremendously—from very brief and coping-focused to long-term, transformative depth work; from heavily influenced by one's prior CBT training to more psychodynamic or existential in nature. Integral psychotherapy also varies as a function of whether the focus of therapeutic work is geared more toward coping and/or *translation* (horizontal growth that involves changing surface structures within the patient's current developmental stage) or deep characterological work and/or *transformation* (vertical development that involves changing deep structures, which entails a shift to the next developmental stage). More often than not, what is most relevant and feasible is to help patients stabilize and optimize their functioning at their current level of development, which is translative work. In part because it is fairly new, but more because of its metatheoretical, unifying perspective, *integral theory provides principles* to guide one's conceptualization and practice *without exact prescriptions for how to practice.*

Integral Psychotherapy Is Guided by Principles Rather Than by Rules[2]

Integrally informed psychotherapists are far from a homogeneous group. Not only do they vary in terms of their prior training in psychodynamic, family systems, existential-humanistic, diversity, or cognitive-behavioral approaches; they also differ in relational style and degree of collaboration, which may vary as a function of patient variables or as a matter of the therapist's general style. This is consistent with the "content-free" nature of integral metatheory, in which a unifying framework provides the parameters within which to conceptualize and practice, without prescribing the specifics of how to do so (Marquis, 2013; Anchin, 2008). This is highly consonant with the argument of Levitt and colleagues (2005) that

---

[2] This section and some of what follows are adapted from Marquis et al. (2015). Integral psychotherapy in practice part 3: Three case studies illustrating the differential use of integral metatheory in informing unified treatment. *Journal of Unified Psychotherapy and Clinical Science, 3* (1), 41–79.

psychotherapy should be guided by principles rather than by rules. Although both rules and principles function to regulate conduct in a specific domain, rules offer specific prescriptions whereas principles offer more general, nonspecific instructional guides (Levitt, Neimeyer, & Williams, 2005). This does not mean that, at times, an integrally informed therapist cannot closely follow a manual, especially if no contextual or other data suggest otherwise. However, in general, the six primary constructs of iPT (quadrants, levels, lines, states, types, and self-system) orient integrally informed therapists in a relatively general and principled-yet-abstract manner that aligns with Mahoney's statement that "open, complex systems express endless, dynamic exchanges. They follow rules of order that can never be completely specified, predicted, or controlled" (2008, p. 370). For this reason, Mahoney (2008) wrote that quests toward unification should focus on general principles rather than "forced particulars." Levitt and colleagues highlighted that one of the detriments of rule-based systems is that they tend to disregard contextual dynamics within specific interactions. The quadrants, on the other hand, are fundamentally about contextualizing all phenomena within a larger metaframework—always considering multiple perspectives from the inside and outside of both the individual and her systems; thus, contextualizing is at the heart of iPT. One of the principles that emerged from the Integral Psychotherapy in Practice study (Marquis & Elliot, 2015) is that integral psychotherapists tended to be guided most prominently by their patients' in-the-moment states (affective, defensive, self, etc.), although quadratic and developmental variables also weighed heavily in their assessments and interventions (lines, types, and self-system constructs guided their work somewhat, but less pervasively). A fundamental reason why the cases of iPT reported in Marquis et al. (2015) were so different from one another is because, being principle-based, iPT is highly sensitive to the idiographic and contextual features of each patient, thus allowing for a nearly endless host of pragmatic differentiations of how to be guided by various iPT constructs; this inevitably leads to flexible and highly individualized clinical practice. For all of these reasons, this chapter will discuss *general principles* of treatment in iPT, rather than anything approximating a manual of highly specified procedures.

A Brief Overview of Human Change Processes[3]

No one has influenced my work as a therapist more than Michael Mahoney, who was my teacher, mentor, colleague, and friend, and arguably one of the world's experts on "human change processes" (1991). Thus, much of this section is heavily influenced by his work. First, "we are wise to appreciate the self-protective conservatism of change processes. We resist change even more passionately than we seek it" (Mahoney, 2003, p. 2). Kegan and Lahey (2009) emphasize the same point: if we

---

3 Parts of this section are adapted from Marquis, A. (2015). Developmental constructivism. In E. S. Neukrug (Ed.), *The encyclopedia of theory in counseling and psychotherapy* (pp. 278–283). Thousand Oaks, CA: Sage Publications.

want to be able to help people change, the most important things we must understand are all the reasons and ways people are committed (even, and maybe especially, if unconsciously) to not changing. Mahoney (2003) made the analogy that—similar to our brain, heart, and lungs being protected by our skull and ribcage—our psychological "core ordering processes" (one's sense of self/identity, one's perception of reality, one's values/emotions, and one's sense of having power/control) are similarly highly protected and are thus self-perpetuating and resistant to change. Also relevant to this point are all the ways that patients manifest defenses and resistance (more on this subsequently). People's change projects are difficult, in part, because so many of our ordering and organizational processes occur outside of our awareness, even when they are not being defended against (Mahoney, 1991). For all these reasons, iPT appreciates that many patients endure tragedies, struggle tremendously, and suffer great losses of meaning; thus, quick fixes and easy solutions are not promised. Rather, compassion and hope, along with psychological knowledge and therapeutic competence in interventions that have been intensively evaluated, are offered in the context of an I–thou encounter.[4]

I try to prepare for each session with some form of brief centering technique, setting an intention to be of maximal service to my patient. Following Mahoney, I caution against presuming to understand patients too quickly, rather than honoring each individual's uniqueness, including their capacities and pace of change.[5] In other words, I try to understand the uniqueness and complexity of each person I counsel. Although I certainly see value in psychoeducation and include it with many patients, my practice of iPT is largely an experiential approach; thus, patients are encouraged to *actually feel* their emotions rather than merely talk about them. It follows that Fosha's (2000) construct of "affective competence" is a prerequisite to this type of psychotherapy. Patients' safety is paramount, but their growing edges also need to be challenged with individually tailored explorations and experiments (discomfort is not the same thing as being unsafe). Finally, I teach self-care, encourage forgiveness (see Lewis, 2005), and emphasize patients being compassionate with themselves and others.

Integral psychotherapy involves an approach that is developmentally tailored to each patient; thus, there is no single therapeutic process that applies across all cases. That being said, there are some general principles. My overarching goal is to serve my patients' immediate and future developmental needs and well-being; this requires a deep understanding of the patient as a person—his or her experiences,

---

4 Regarding the importance of the therapeutic relationship, Yalom writes that: "The most important thing I, or any other therapist, can do is offer an authentic healing relationship from which patients can draw whatever they need" (2015, p. 209).

5 At the same time, it does appear that some therapists—Perls, Davanloo, Frederickson, and Fosha come to mind—are/were capable of homing in quite quickly on patients' core issues. This is one of the many dialectics I try to hold: the general notion of not presuming to know the patient too quickly and also trusting certain dynamics and processes (ISTDP comes to mind) and acting on them as quickly and efficiently as possible.

strengths, weaknesses, defenses, how the patient has been hurt and helped in the past, what the patient believes is possible, his or her worldview, sense of self, emotional life, and what provides meaning to his or her life.

In general, I begin sessions by being present and attuning to the patient. I then assess the patient's current situation while trying to maintain continuity between sessions. Sustained empathic attunement to patients' in-the-moment experiencing helps me balance the comfort and challenge I offer. I assist patients in practicing various techniques or exercises pertinent to their struggles and process their experience of those exercises. I offer affirmations, alternative perspectives, and usually homework (experiments in living), and try to end each session with good will. Comfort and challenge are among the important contrasts in iPT, a point to which I now turn.

Important Contrasts in iPT

Mahoney was fond of Schopenhauer's aphorism that there are "two kinds of people in the world (those who believe there *are* two kinds of people in the world and those who do not)" (2003, p. 13). He enjoyed it so much because humans *do* organize themselves and their experiences by means of contrasting categories. Thus, I will here discuss some of the important contrasts that Mahoney believed, and I believe, are important to help one tailor appropriate interventions to a given patient at a given time.

An integral-constructive approach (Mahoney & Marquis, 2002) suggests thinking in terms of two fundamental and interrelated dimensions: opening–closing and comforting–challenging. When a person is excessively closed, he or she is cut off from certain forms of exchanges with his or her world. When a person is excessively open, the person may exceed his or her capacity to metabolize what she is experiencing. Constructive change requires openness to novelty, but not too much too quickly; it is the therapist's responsibility to help the patient balance his or her cycles of opening and closing. Even when novelty is satisfying or rewarding, the self-system will commonly contract, close itself off, or pull back for at least a while; and if a new challenge is overwhelming, the person may become disorganized or completely shut down. Importantly, it is not that being open is good and being closed is bad; just as we need both activity and rest, and both inhalations and exhalations, we all need to both open and close at different points in our lives. We need to open ourselves to novelty in order to learn and grow, but we also need to be able to close ourselves (protect ourselves) to what is not good for us, as well as to close in order to metabolize and make sense of experience. People are far more likely to open, experiment, and explore when they feel safe; thus the need for the therapist to function as a secure base for them.

Good psychotherapy also involves a balance of comfort and challenge; that balance differs from patient to patient, and even with the same patient at different points in his or her life. The challenge I am referring to is not aggressive, but progressive—inviting the patient to explore and experiment, and communicating trust in the patient's capacities and possibilities. Some patients need stabilization (comfort), while others need de-stabilization (challenge), in order to restructure themselves and/or the emotions, cognitions, behaviors, or ways of relating that are maintaining their dissatisfaction and distress. The relative amount of comfort and challenge must be matched to each patient's developmental capacities and readiness—both in general (is the patient at a borderline level of personality organization or is he much more stable and grounded in his sense of self?) and within a given session (the patient's cycles of opening and closing within the therapy hour). If you are going to challenge him, it is important that the patient be able to regain his balance, center, and sense of self; thus teaching centering, meditation, and other attentional skills should usually be done before significant challenge.[6] Finally, good psychotherapy also often involves cycles of experiencing (experiential, affective work) and explaining (cognitive, analytic, understanding work).

Reflecting a dialectically balanced approach, nothing is more central to iPT than compassion and caring; at the same time, I emphasize homework—collaboratively designed experiments in living—as central to patients' change processes. Having procedural competence (i.e., knowing how to effectively implement exposure interventions, being able to bypass patients' defenses effectively and efficiently, etc.) and understanding the best available research are important, but they are not nearly as effective in the absence of compassion and care. As Frederickson (2013) emphasized, if you recognize that most patients' suffering is caused by their defenses, then interrupting and bypassing their defenses is an act of love and compassion.

Attention, Meditation, and Centering Skills

Attention may be the most fundamental of all psychological phenemona; not only does the quality and object of our attention largely determine the nature of our experience,[7] but most other phenomena—from one's emotional responses to one's physiology—are affected by what one places one's attention on and the quality of that attention (is it a deeply focused and single-pointed concentration or is one's mind wandering all over the place? Is it a nonjudgmental witnessing or is it highly critical of whatever arises?). As William James wrote, "The faculty of voluntarily bringing back a wandering attention, over and over again, is the very root of judgment, character, and will. No one is *compos sui* [master of himself] if he have it not. An education which should improve this faculty would be the education *par*

---

6 An exception to this is the manner in which ISTDP assesses the neurobiological discharge patterns of anxiety in the patient moment-to-moment; more on this later in this chapter. Thus, ISTDP therapists will exert pressure and challenge in the first session, but as soon as the patient's anxiety discharges into the smooth muscles (which means the anxiety level is too high), they will cease the challenge and regulate the patient's anxiety. As soon as the anxiety returns to the striated muscles, they will resume challenge. ISTDP requires a therapist that is highly attuned to patients' anxiety discharge patterns, among other dynamics.

7 "*My experience is what I agree to attend to*. Only those items which I *notice* shape my mind – without selective interest, experience is an utter chaos" (James, 1890, p. 402, emphasis in original).

excellence" (1892, p. 95). Thus, it is critical that patients develop skills in focusing their attention and "centering" themselves: "Skills in centering are essential to a sense of coherence, safety, and personal competence. Such skills become an important part of establishing and utilizing an internal 'base camp' from which patients can energize, orient, and organize their continuing efforts to develop" (Mahoney, 2003, p. 29).

The quality of one's attention has been highlighted in the growing research base documenting the effectiveness of mindfulness-based therapies (Brown, Marquis, & Guiffrida, 2013). It was originally believed that cognitive therapy was effective because patients changed the content of their thoughts, but that explanation is no longer tenable (Segal, Williams, & Teasdale, 2002). It is far more likely that what is most helpful is not changing the content of a patient's thoughts and beliefs, but rather the patient changing his *relationship* to these psychological phenomena, which requires attentional practice and skill. Because these skills are so important, I encourage my patients to engage in various forms of meditation—from secular forms to those that derive from their religious/spiritual tradition.

Additional Basic Principles of Change

Significant, enduring change rarely occurs in a linearly cumulative manner (Mahoney, 1991). Patients who are intentionally trying to change often repeatedly find themselves in old, maladaptive patterns; this frustrating reality is understandable when we recognize that old patterns offer familiarity and comfort, even when their consequences are painful or harmful. Patients attempting the ambitious project of transforming their sense of self and/or worldview are more likely to be successful if they incorporate—rather than reject or deny—their old sense of self and/or world into the newer, more complex system.

In addition, any significant change to a patient's core ordering processes will reverberate throughout the four quadrants, including their relationships, the latter influencing the patient's ability to maintain the new patterns and processes.[8] If the new processes are to emerge as consistent patterns, they need to be practiced regularly and consistently, which is one of the reasons I am a proponent of "homework" assignments—ways the patient can engage and embody the new self they are attempting to become. Thus, iPT integrates interior exploration (not just intrapsychic [UL] but interpsychic [LL]) with active experimenting with new ways of being (both what she does alone [UR] and how she behaves relationally [LR]).

---

8 Whenever feasible, encouraging other members of a patient's system to alter their behavior in a manner that will decrease their being "neurotic accomplices" (Wachtel, 1987) is an important Lower-Right and Lower-Left component of a patient's successful long-term change: "Active interventions often are critically important when the patient's interpersonal relationships are reinforcing any of his or her pathology. The influence of other people in the patient's life often is more powerful and pervasive than any amount of interpretation" (Gold & Stricker, 1993, pp. 328–329).

162 Treatment

How Integral Theory Informs Treatment Decisions

Different integral constructs—from patients' developmental levels and moment-to-moment states—inform iPT treatment decisions, but we will begin by exploring how the four quadrants impact treatment.

A Brief Tour of Conceptualizing and Intervening by Quadrant

The Upper-Left Quadrant: Experience, Self, Subjectivity

This is the quadrant that psychoanalytic and existential-humanistic psychotherapies have emphasized; it is fundamentally concerned with the patient's subjective experience of self. As such, integrally informed psychotherapists will inquire into any noteworthy patterns in the patient's self-experience (i.e., self-image, self-concept, self-esteem, self-efficacy; instability–stability; joy, zest, purpose, motivation; depression, sadness, emptiness; anxiety, "jitters"; cognitions [thoughts, beliefs, attitudes, expectations; recurrent mental imagery]) and political, religious, and/or spiritual beliefs and/or experiences. Among the many interventions that address this quadrant are distress-tolerance skills and emotion-regulation skills, catharsis, awareness or consciousness raising, structure (i.e., self, ego) building techniques, cultivating mindfulness and self-compassion, narrative reconstructions, guided imagery, free association/stream of consciousness, restructuring self-image, and defense work, including ISTDP's pressure and challenge.

The Upper-Right Quadrant: Behavior, Brain, Objectivity

This is the quadrant that behavioral and biopsychiatric therapies have emphasized; it is fundamentally concerned with how a patient's behavior, brain, and other externally observable dynamics and processes (anything that is measurable or capable of being captured by a video camera or other recording device; i.e., fMRI) impact a patient's condition. As such, integrally informed psychotherapists will inquire into any noteworthy patterns of patients' behavior (problematic behaviors are frequently the reason that patients seek therapy, and increases or decreases in specific behaviors are often a large part of what constitutes "successful outcome"), as well as patients' medical disorders, medications, and alcohol and/or drug use. Among the many interventions that address this quadrant are behavioral analyses, exposure therapies, behavioral rehearsals, self-management programs, relaxation training, cognitive restructuring,[9] and other cognitive techniques such as decatastrophizing, reattribution, diversion, and modifying maladaptive/dysfunctional assumptions and schemas. Other Upper-Right interventions include pharmacotherapy, repetitive Transcranial Magnetic Stimulation (rTMS), physical

---

9 This may seem like an Upper-Left intervention, but I explained in chapter 6 why it is more properly an Upper-Right intervention.

exercise, establishing proper sleep hygiene, and eating a healthy, balanced diet. Physical activity and bodily awareness are central to one's well-being; thus, encourage patients to be physically active, even if it is no more than walking.[10]

The Lower-Left Quadrant: Culture, Worldview, Intersubjectivity

This is the quadrant that diversity, multicultural, and relational psychodynamic psychotherapies have emphasized; it is fundamentally concerned with how patients' cultures, meaning-making systems, and relationships are implicated in their suffering. As such, integrally informed psychotherapists will inquire into patients' relationships with significant others, especially their spouse/partner, boss, friends, and family; patients' meaning-making systems; and patients' experience of ethnicity. This quadrant also includes the medium of the therapeutic relationship and how both the patient and therapist experience their intersubjectivity. Among the many interventions that address this quadrant are establishing a therapeutic relationship; attending to and mending ruptures in the therapeutic bond; basic attending skills and communicating empathy, genuineness, and positive regard; role playing; analysis and interpretation of resistance and transference; gender-role analyses; Socratic dialogue; the therapist's use of self-disclosure; the therapist's presence and use of authenticity in the here-and-now encounter; and helping the patient find stability in relationships.

The Lower-Right Quadrant: Social Systems, Environment, Interobjectivity

This is the quadrant that family systems therapists, social workers, and social justice advocates have emphasized; it is fundamentally concerned with how social systems (i.e., familial, economic, educational, and medical) often contribute to patients' distress: poor boundaries, triangulations, and indirect communication in families; poverty, poor schools, and inequitable access to medical care; as well as racism, sexism, classism, ageism, etc.[11] As such, integrally informed psychotherapists will inquire into a patient's socioeconomic status; the condition of the patient's neighborhood and home; environmental stressors and/or comforts; and analyses of interpersonal dynamics, including family history and dynamics. Among the many interventions that address this quadrant are basic session management skills,

---

10 If a patient cannot walk, due to a disability, they may be able to do some form of exercise, even if it is simply raising their arms and legs. However, contrary to some earlier research, graded exercise is often contraindicated with patients who suffer from Myalgic Encephalomyelitis, also known as Chronic Fatigue Syndrome (ME/CFS).
11 As one example, brain imaging studies have demonstrated that child abuse and neglect can cause permanent damage to both the neural functioning and structure of the developing brain: "Our brains are sculpted by our early experiences. Maltreatment is a chisel that shapes a brain to contend with strife, but at the cost of deep, enduring wounds" (Teicher, 2000, p. 64).

including role induction (regarding the roles of the patient and therapist); involving the patient's family or significant other in sessions; assertiveness and social skills training; genogram analysis, de-triangulation, and defining roles and boundaries within a family system; discussions of oppression, discrimination, and marginalization; social advocacy and "social liberation": working as a systemic change agent to promote more equitable social arrangements.

Shifting Among the Quadrants

Stylistic variations notwithstanding—in terms of the approaches in which therapists were initially trained and have thus acquired comfort and expertise—the iPT model holds that comprehensive change is unlikely to result from an overly narrow quadratic focus that unduly privileges an exclusively interior or exterior perspective. Thus, particular quadratic emphases usually shift throughout the course of therapy with a given patient. Rather than being a linear process proceeding in one direction, shifts in the quadratic focus of treatment may involve back-and-forth movement between interiors and exteriors, as well as between the individual and her contexts, with the need for a shift perhaps indicated by therapeutic "plateaus."

In general, iPT treatment decisions are shaped by an interaction of myriad patient, therapist, and treatment factors, including: developmental considerations; patients' affective states; patients' strengths and preferences; the nature and severity of the patient's problem(s); the therapist's preferred approach (as shaped by personal style and experience/expertise); and how the patient has responded to various treatment approaches or interventions. An iPT approach may be characterized as entailing attention and responsiveness to information from multiple sources (theory, objective data, intuition) and pertaining to different domains (quadrants, levels, states). Integrally informed psychotherapy is thus significantly idiographic and flexible in terms of its general approach and the specific interventions used.

Balance of Explicit Theory and Intuition/Procedural Knowledge

The therapists in the IPP study (Marquis & Elliot, 2015) conveyed a process of conceptualizing and intervening that is highly intuitive, more procedural than declarative, and more akin to clinical judgment than following prescribed steps. Indeed, there was a consensus among the therapists that, within a particular session, moment-to-moment decisions concerning interventions and responses were largely intuitive in nature rather than specifically dictated by the iPT model.

The notion that many integral therapists make many of their clinical decisions more intuitively than as a function of what the iPT literature specifies bears similarity to the tension Wachtel (1991) described when referring to theoretical integration at a conceptual level often not manifesting itself in moment-to-moment practice: "eclecticism in practice and integration in aspiration is an accurate description of what most of us in the integrative movement do much of the time" (p. 44). At the same time, even for therapists practicing a single-system approach, theory does not necessarily explicitly direct the clinical process:

In the psychoanalytic process itself, if the work is proceeding in a rich and vital way, broad underlying theoretical principles are almost invisible. The analyst, once past his earliest apprenticeship, does not retain his theory in mind for active, focused use as a lexicon of meanings. He does not continuously shift back and forth between his patient's communications and his theory, deciphering piece by piece as he goes along. He listens to the patient's account of his experience, and his attention is drawn now this way, now that. Certain themes stand out, certain pieces do not fit together. Gradually his thoughts about the patient crystallize ... Throughout this process, theoretical concepts as such may be missing from the analyst's thoughts. Nevertheless, they provide the invisible backdrop, the unseen framework, within which the analyst hears the patient's story. (Greenberg & Mitchell, 1983, p. 15)

As will be discussed in more detail subsequently, practicing "integrally" is really a sensibility, or an attitude that fundamentally keeps one open to numerous perspectives ("listening on many different channels") rather than explicitly dictating specific interventions. Although this process is more of a tacit, implicit, or procedural form of knowledge and decision-making than an explicit or declarative form, the iPT model does inform the therapy process. Some of the distinctive features and contributions of the iPT model include the four quadrants, the role of developmental dynamics, states and "state work," and Wilber's (2000b) thesis that awareness is the basic mechanism of therapeutic change.

The Prominence of States, the Nature of States, and "State Work"

As mentioned in chapter 3, perhaps the most intriguing finding from the IPP study is that the therapists reported attending more to their patients' moment-to-moment states (i.e., "state work") than to developmental or quadratic phenomena,[12] which is contrary to what the iPT literature has heretofore suggested. Recall that states may be conceptualized in multiple ways—in terms ranging from specific disorders (i.e., anxious or depressed states) to quadrants (i.e., neural states [UR], phenomenological states [UL], intersubjective/relational states [LL]) to specific developmental lines (i.e., affective states, cognitive states, spiritual states). Perhaps most relevant to the therapy they provided in the IPP study, however, are what are commonly referred to as affective states (Fosha, 2000) and self states (Wachtel, 2008).

In addition to having phenomenological (UL) and neurobiological (UR) dimensions, affective states reveal critical information regarding one's significant (attachment) relationships (LL; Fosha, 2000; Wachtel, 2008; Stolorow, Atwood, & Orange, 2002; Magnavita & Anchin, 2014). Consistent with attachment theory, one's

---

12 Of course, no state arises independently from developmental and quadratic phenomena; what I mean is that patients' affective states were the focus of clinical attention more than phenomena directly, immediately tied to developmental levels or quadrants.

experience of self, one's emotions, others, events, and their connection is state-dependent (Fosha, 2000). Of special importance are *core* affective states, which consist of affect that is undefended. Experienced viscerally with "oomph" (in other words, core affect is visceral and has a distinct "physical signature"), core affective states are inherently transformational:

> This visceral experience of core affect involves a state transformation (Beebe & Lachmann, 1994). In this altered state, deep therapeutic work can be accomplished as the patient gains access to deeper layers of unconscious material... vital sources of liveliness and energy... adaptive action tendencies intrinsic to the experience of core affect ... adaptive relational tendencies ... [and] a sense of being in touch with the essential or true self. (Fosha, 2000, p. 137)

In contrast to core affect, much (defended) emotional experience has an unclear "muddy" sense that does not constructively inform the choices one needs to make. What is stressed among affect-focused therapists, and consensually agreed upon by the therapists in the IPP study, is the necessity of *visceral experiencing*. Merely being cognitively aware of a conflict, emotion, or other issue is *not* sufficient; patients must feel those dynamics deep in their bodies—in their guts, hearts, faces, and sinews (Greenberg, 2008; Fosha, 2000). Precisely because core affective states are inherently transformational, a key clinical implication is to focus on bypassing all the ways that patients distort, block, or mute their affective experience (Fosha, 2000; Davanloo, 2005; Frederickson, 2013; Abbass, 2015). The closer a patient is to a core (i.e., undefended) state, the more likely therapy will proceed effectively, deeply, and quickly. Thus, whenever a patient is defended (not in a core state), one's therapeutic activities should, in general, be geared toward getting the patient in touch with a core state.

Depending on our current state, we may be functioning at, or near, our highest capacities, and thus feel safe, confident, and at ease with others; or we may be functioning at, or near, our "self-at-worst," and thus feel anxious, insecure, or otherwise uncomfortable with those same people. Of significance, these shifts from "self-at-best" to "self-at-worst" (Fosha, 2000, p. 125) occur within the same person who would from many integral perspectives (i.e., Wilber, 2000b; Cook-Greuter & Soulen, 2007) be characterized as inhabiting a single developmental level or center of gravity. The idea that we should respond to a patient based upon his center of gravity, rather than his current emotional state, is simply misguided:

> *Therapists intervene differentially with clients depending on their assessment of the in-session emotional state,* helping them accept and integrate certain emotions; to acknowledge some and bypass others; to regulate disruptive emotions; to express those that will enhance relationships; to contain and soothe painful emotions; and to explore and transform maladaptive emotions. (Greenberg, 2008, p. 51, italics added)

Although attending to patients' affective and defensive states appears to constitute the bulk of moment-to-moment therapeutic work (Schore, 2003; Fosha, 2000; Davanloo, 2000; Greenberg, 2002), this in no way minimizes the relevance of quadratic or developmental issues. In fact, the IPP study therapists unanimously agreed that a weakness of the extant iPT literature is that it currently has only a limited understanding of how the lower quadrants (both the intersubjective/cultural [LL] and the social/systemic [LR]) impact people's affective states.

Although it is impossible to describe all the ways state work may unfold,[13] it is essentially a process of helping patients, over the course of treatment, to become more fully aware of their multiple states, including aversive and previously dissociated states, and ultimately to regulate (and/or transform them) and integrate them. State work inevitably involves interpersonal as well as intrapsychic processes, in that relational dynamics may produce mutual resonance—what Stern (1985) refers to as "state sharing"—that allows a patient to experience and integrate states that would otherwise be defended against. Healthy state-related functioning also involves the capacity to consciously observe, understand, and regulate one's states; this entails an ability to tolerate the inevitable fluctuations in affective states as well as to proactively influence one's states, rather than merely being a passive victim of them.

Therapeutic Change Processes

In addition to the "human change processes" discussed near the beginning of this chapter, a number of other change processes are worthy of attention.

Amendments to Wilber's Thesis That Awareness Is the Basic Principle of Therapeutic Change

In his exposition of integral psychotherapy, Wilber (2000b) posited that awareness is the most basic and essential component of change in psychotherapy, and that common to many of the major theoretical approaches is the general principle that "*awareness in and of itself is curative*" (p. 99, italics in original):

> Every therapeutic school we have mentioned attempts, in its own way, to allow consciousness to encounter (or reencounter) facets of experience that were previously alienated, malformed, distorted, or ignored. [Awareness] is *curative* for a basic reason: *by experiencing these facets fully*, consciousness can genuinely acknowledge these elements and thereby let go of them: see them as an object, and thus differentiate from them, deembed from them, *transcend them*—and then integrate them into a more encompassing, compassionate embrace. (p. 99, italics in original)

---

13 Excellent resources regarding state work include Fosha (2000), Greenberg (2002), Abbass (2015), and Frederickson (2013).

168 Treatment

A core principle inherent in Wilber's thesis and in the literature that has given rise to iPT is that developmental change involves a process of "making subject object"; in other words, by bringing conscious awareness to that in which one was previously embedded (the many schemas, thoughts, feelings, values, and behaviors that were nonconsciously and reflexively enacted, and thus served as the "subject" driving mentation, emotion, and action), these phenomena become "objects" of attention and awareness, with the subject then becoming the more encompassing, observing self that can more objectively evaluate them and more consciously determine one's response. The therapists in the IPP study (Marquis & Elliot, 2015), like me, view Wilber's premise as conveying a vital but only partial truth.

When used as a generic term, "awareness" may commonly imply a largely cognitive/conceptual awareness, which is problematic because conceptual awareness, while important, is usually in-and-of-itself insufficient to produce enduring change. In order to be "inherently curative," awareness must be experiential—affective and visceral—in nature, and such transformative, experiential awareness is facilitated by interpersonal—rather than solely intrapsychic—processes. Although this perspective has tremendous support in various therapies (i.e., Fosha, 2000; Wachtel, 2008; Greenberg, 2008; Mahoney, 2003; Schore, 2003; Davanloo, 2000; Abbass, 2015; Frederickson, 2013), it has not garnered adequate attention in most of the iPT literature.

As mentioned in the preceding section on states, what appears to be transformative are core affective states (Fosha, 2000), and, by definition, the awareness that emerges in these states is emotional, visceral, and almost always arises within a relational context characterized by safety and empathic attunement. Although cognitive, conceptual insights often, if not usually, co-arise with such core states, such intellectual insight alone simply does not necessarily lead to transformation, and even Freud recognized and indeed emphasized this; "*emotional* insight is needed" (Wachtel, 2008, p. 223). Further underscoring the significance of Lower-Left quadrant dynamics in patients' transformations is the notion that "change is promoted most of all by *what actually happens between people*" (Wachtel, 2008, p. 223, original italics).

It is becoming increasingly clear that change processes in psychotherapy largely involve *procedural* learning. In other words, in contrast to *declarative* learning (learning an individual can explicitly discuss), patients frequently experience significant change—whether relational, emotional, or behavioral—that they nevertheless cannot articulate (i.e., they have acquired some new "know-how" that they are not able to declaratively describe).[14] For example, and of central significance in much psychotherapy, knowing "how to be with, or do things with, others"—"implicit relational knowing" (Wachtel, 2008, p. 241)—is largely procedural. A final strike against the notion that conceptual awareness is the curative agent is the

---

14 Mahoney shared this view: "much of what we teach in psychotherapy is neither explicit nor technical so much as it is an 'induction' of an experiential process" (2003, p. 68).

considerable evidence that insight often results from behavior change, rather than vice versa (Wachtel, 2008). On this point, Prochaska and Norcross wrote that "insight alone does not necessarily bring about behavior change" (2003, p. 534) and Mahoney emphasized that "Relative to action, insight is overrated" (2003, p. 148).

In response to views purportedly contradicting his position, Wilber might argue that his use of "awareness" implies more than cognitive or conceptual awareness. He stated that the process of contacting split-off, repressed, or otherwise denied aspects of self, and then "meeting them with awareness, and thus experiencing them fully, allows consciousness to differentiate (transcend) and integrate (include) their important voices in the overall flow of evolutionary unfolding" (2000b, p. 100). Wilber might argue that "experiencing them fully" involves not only mental but also bodily/visceral experience; however, Wilber did not explicitly state this. Thus, a key question is how "experiencing them fully" is interpreted and whether Wilber actually meant that awareness needs to be not only emotionally and viscerally experienced, but relationally as well. In short, the participants in the IPP study were all of the opinion that, in integral theory, the term "awareness" is not highly specified and seems to connote a largely conceptual, rational, cognitive form of awareness (Marquis & Elliot, 2015).

Even with expanded conceptions of awareness and the interpersonal processes by which it is facilitated, the notion of a central and universal curative factor does not do justice to the complexity of human change processes, which involve not only multiple quadrants and multiple dimensions of the human being, but a host of nonlinear dynamics (Thelen & Smith, 1994; Anchin, 2008; Magnavita & Anchin, 2014). Moreover, not all forms of therapy target awareness as a central therapeutic change process. For example, many effective behavioral treatments focus on explicit behavior change, rather than an increase in awareness per se. In fact,

> What many of the recent trends in psychoanalysis and in other realms of therapeutic practice point to, in essence, is that healing too may very largely go on unconsciously, that many of the processes that are mobilized in the course of a successful psychotherapeutic experience are likely never to be fully brought to consciousness. (Wachtel, 2008, p. 244)

Thus, contrary to much of the iPT literature, awareness—especially conceptual awareness—may not be necessary, let alone sufficient, for change and healing.

Awareness (Like Everything Else) Is an All-Quadrant Affair

A theory of change based principally on awareness is often predominantly localized in the UL quadrant, as it emphasizes intrapsychic processes as if largely independent of other quadratic phenomena, whereas in actuality the mind is fundamentally interconnected with the body (UR), relationships (LL), and systems (LR). For example, interpersonal neurobiology (Siegel, 2010; Schore, 2003) has demonstrated how the embodied experiential awareness described previously may entail an interaction of mind (UL), body (UR), interpersonal processes (LL), and neuroplastic changes in the brain (UR).

In summary, awareness—when construed more comprehensively as an embodied and experiential, rather than purely cognitive, phenomenon—is indeed important to therapeutic change. Furthermore, in a general sense, the cultivation of transformative awareness may be facilitated by the process of "making subject object" and the dual component processes of differentiation and integration. However, the process of facilitating such awareness is a multi-quadrant affair involving, at a minimum, interpersonal (LL), neurobiological (UR), and systemic (LR), in addition to phenomenological (UL), processes. For example, intersubjectively attuned therapists (LL) that provide a safe, empathic, validating environment (LR) will influence and potentially regulate their patients' neurophysiology (UR) and what they are viscerally experiencing (UL).

The Importance of Emotions

In my nearly 20 years of teaching psychology, counseling, and psychotherapy, I have encountered few topics that are more pervasively misunderstood than the nature of emotions and their significance to human health. Students—as well as many psychotherapists—frequently believe that emotions are primarily epiphenomenal (even if they don't use that term) problems that disrupt functioning and are best controlled rather than fully experienced, reflected upon, and communicated. Although I briefly touched upon the critical role that emotions serve in the previous discussion of affective states, they are so important that I will say a bit more about them here.[15]

My view—which reflects a consensus among affective neuroscientists (Damasio, 1999; LeDoux, 1996) and a broad range of affect-focused therapists (Fosha, 2000; Greenberg, 2002; Davanloo, 2000; Mahoney, 2003; Osborn et al., 2014; Smith, Lane, & Goldman, 2017)—is that emotions (used interchangeably here with affect; Fosha, 2000) are very much an All-Quadrant phenomenon: they are neurobiologically wired-in (UR); they are experienced subjectively (UL); they are fundamental sources of information and knowledge about one's environment (LR); and they are a deeply interpersonal and communicative aspect of human experience (LL). Because they are so fundamentally interpersonal, "The full experience of emotion depends on its expression ... *Expression* of affect deepens the *experience* of affect" (Fosha, 2000, p. 23). Richard Dawkins, Arthur Staats, and Steven Pinker have all emphasized the evolutionarily adaptive function of emotions—that emotional response mechanisms are what actually allow animals to learn. As Gregg Henriques puts it: "instead of coming equipped with a set of genetically preprogrammed lists

---

[15] I want to remind the reader of what I wrote in the preface: So that I do not have to continually make qualifications throughout this book, I want to emphasize that the integral psychotherapy that I am describing in this book is my personal and ever-evolving perspective; although it has been deeply influenced by Wilber and others, some of my views (in this case, the critical importance of emotions in psychotherapy and human health) are not necessarily shared by Wilber or all who identify as integral psychotherapists.

of commands of how to act, nature has built animals' emotional systems that assess whether the animal is effectively moving toward or away from its goals and shift the behavioral output accordingly" (2011, p. 66).

Emotion is also an important motivator and organizer of behavior and experience. The view that cognition and emotion are radically separate ways of knowing is not only overly simplistic, it is simply wrong (Pinker, 2009; Mahoney, 1991); emotions themselves inherently involve attentional, perceptual, and evaluative processes. As Mahoney pointed out:

> our arrogant left hemispheres would have us believe that our rationality has somehow transcended its own evolutionary heritage in the "lower" brains. While it is true that the limbic system is partially independent of the neocortex in its functioning, this apparent separation is misleading. Feeling is not exclusively limbic, and knowing is not exclusively neocortical. Besides the important interactions between these subbrains via the frontal and prefrontal areas, much, if not most, of our "higher" mental functioning is itself steeped in the patterns and preferences of our "feeling brains." This applies to all levels of that functioning—from base perception to abstract reasoning. (1991, p. 189)

It is important to note that just as thoughts can be accurate or inaccurate, emotions can likewise be "on target" or "off-base" (usually termed adaptive or maladaptive); more on this in a moment. Not only are emotions foundational to our construction of self (primary self-organizing processes; Guidano, 1987) and our sense of reality (Mahoney, 1991), emotional processing is central to decision-making and other meaning-making processes, as well as essential to optimal functioning and adaptation to changing environments. Emotion is central to human motivation and helps prepare us for rapid adaptive action. I want to be clear that I am not suggesting that all that patients need are catharses; recall that one of the important contrasts in iPT is experiencing (emotion) and explaining (consciously reflecting upon and understanding the experience).

Any emotion (from anger and shame to pride and joy) *can be adaptive or maladaptive*, as well as primary or secondary (Greenberg, 2002). What is most therapeutic is a deep awareness of primary adaptive emotions; these are one's fundamental, initial, and direct reactions to an event (i.e., feeling angry in response to an injustice or offense; feeling sad at a loss, etc.; Greenberg, 2002).[16] In contrast, secondary emotions are emotional responses to one's emotions or thoughts, rather than to the situation itself (i.e., feeling guilty about feeling envy or feeling angry about feeling fear; these are often *defenses* against specific emotions: shame as a cover for sadness, or sadness covering anger). Greenberg (2002) defines emotions as adaptive when they provide information (about a situation or the meaning of an

---

16 Although not identical to primary adaptive emotions, what Fosha (2000) termed "core affect" (discussed previously in the "states" section) is similar and is also deeply therapeutic.

event) and action tendencies that motivate constructive courses of action to take (i.e., anger about an injustice motivating the person to "right" the "wrong"; sadness about a loss motivating the person to grieve). In contrast, maladaptive emotions have the quality of "being stuck," "not leading anywhere," "going around in circles," occur repeatedly, don't change, and don't motivate constructive actions (i.e., shame of being worthless; anxiety of basic insecurity; anger at self for no apparent reason, anger or sadness that doesn't produce action, movement, or positive change). Although fear and anger may be unpleasant to experience, they signal danger/threat and offense/injustice respectively, and these are extremely important to be informed of. Similarly, although pride and joy may feel good, if one feels proud to have manipulated and taken advantage of others, or joy at others' suffering, these are maladaptive expressions of pride and joy. Thus, referring to emotions as "positive" or "negative" is not as accurate or informative as referring to them as "adaptive" or "maladaptive."

As I wrote with Mahoney:

> Emotions serve critical roles in directing attention, shaping perceptions, organizing memory, developing a healthy sense of selfhood, and motivating active engagement with the learning that life relentlessly requires. The most intense emotions are usually generated in (intersubjective) relationships with others ... the experience and regulation of emotions is learned in human relationships and is central to a coherent and valued sense of self. In contrast to many other perspectives on human experiencing, integral constructivism does not view emotions as either enemies or epiphenomena. Emotional experiences are the foundations of personal realities. (Mahoney & Marquis, 2002, pp. 802–803)

Patients' emotions (especially primary, adaptive emotions [Greenberg] or their core affect [Fosha]) *are rarely the problem; rather, not feeling them by defending against them* (whether with repression, projection, or with secondary or "cover" emotions [Davanloo]) *is deeply problematic*—both causing and maintaining their suffering.

A great deal of psychological disturbance derives from patients' defenses and their derivative poor emotional experiencing and processing;[17] in such cases, the person is deprived of: information, adaptive action tendencies, internal aliveness, and deep relating to others. Unfortunately, many, if not most, patients are so afraid of their feelings that they defend intensely against them and thus don't allow themselves to experience "core affect" (Fosha, 2000; Greenberg, 2008, 2006; McCullough & Kuhn, 2003; Osborn et al., 2014). Thus, anxiety and depression may not be mental disorders per se, but rather may be the consequences of chronically defending against one's feelings (Davanloo, 2000; Frederickson, 2013; Abbass,

---

17 In addition to emotion having the power to function as an attractor state, "all psychopathology seems to involve problems with emotional regulation and functions" (Magnavita, 2006, p. 888).

2015).[18] When people allow themselves to relax their defenses and to fully experience their emotions, they usually recognize that their feelings are not as dangerous as they feared.[19] Moreover, allowing one's self to experience previously disavowed emotions bestows a sense of mastery and competence and provides a wealth of previously unavailable material and meanings.

Working with Emotions in Psychotherapy

> Given the power and primacy of emotions in organizing and disorganizing our personal lives, it is important that therapists be familiar with more than theory and research on this topic ... In order to work constructively with the spectrum and intensity of human emotions, we must learn to appreciate their role in our lives and to experience them ... *An experiential familiarity with feelings is a must for [integral] constructive practice.* (Mahoney, 2003, p. 181, italics and brackets added)

It is critically important that therapists are not affect-phobic themselves, but rather are affectively competent—able both to feel deeply and to deal with the feelings that emerge within themselves and their patients (Fosha, 2000; Osborn et al., 2014; McCullough & Kuhn, 2003). Contrary to earlier cognitive views (i.e., Beck, 1976), "control of emotion ... is not always wise or adaptive, and overregulation of emotion or its avoidance, does not ensure health or happiness" (Greenberg, 2008, p. 49). "Feelings must not," Mahoney states, "be equated with problems. Emotions are not the problems; our estranged relationships with our emotionality (and that of our companions) are more fundamentally problematic than the emotions themselves" (1991, p. 177).

When people experience strong emotions, they are in the presence of a highly meaningful event (i.e., highly dangerous or potentially of great opportunity) or an

---

18 Although it is an empirical issue that I am not aware of being empirically investigated, ISTDP emphasizes that depression is not a feeling. Sadness is a feeling but depression usually involves other symptoms such as "feelings" of hopelessness and worthlessness as well as diminished self-esteem. I tend to agree with Frederickson (2013) that hopelessness and worthlessness are not feelings as much as they are *judgments*: one *concludes* that there is no hope or that one is worthless. Similarly, self-esteem is inherently an *evaluation* of one's worth. I am intrigued by this and would like to see well-designed empirical investigations of questions such as: "Do thoughts cause depression à la Beck or is depression the result of chronically defending against one's feelings (i.e., à la Freud—turning anger upon oneself rather than directing it toward the person who has offended, hurt, or betrayed the patient)?" At the same time, I also want to stress that these two etiological factors (maladaptive thoughts causing depression and chronic reliance upon defenses) are far from the only causes of depression, and there are likely many subtypes of depression, some of which are more biological or immunological in nature (see Müller, 2014, and Ingersoll & Marquis, 2014).

19 Most, but not all, affect-focused approaches emphasize that such work requires the patient to have emotion regulation skills and a reasonably intact sense of self (i.e., that they do not have the instability and fragility of self that characterizes those at psychotic or borderline levels of personality organization).

event that has triggered a core belief or schema. Personality theorists from Freud to Beck have emphasized that core schema are very rarely conscious. Of significance, "emotion often needs to be aroused to access the core (cognitive) structures generating it and ... the experience generated by these need to be further (cognitively) processed in therapy to promote change" (Greenberg, 2008, p. 51). At the same time, there are never any guarantees that emotional arousal and expression will necessarily lead to constructive change or development, but lasting, significant change virtually never occurs in the absence of strong emotion (Mahoney, 1991; Davanloo, 2005).[20]

I am often struck by how frequently psychotherapists merely talk *about* patients' emotions. I know this from personal discussions with therapists, participating in case discussions, and watching hundreds of professional videos of "expert" therapists. In contrast to talking about emotions, patients benefit in more significant and enduring ways by viscerally *experiencing* their emotions. Most patients need the safety of a secure therapeutic relationship to do this:

> When the therapist is perceived as an accepting, attuned, and affect-articulating presence, patients' emotional blocks diminish and they allow the disavowed parts of themselves to re-emerge for the renewed developmental opportunities that may be available to them ... An integral, constructive approach to psychotherapy involves an invitation to use the therapeutic relationship as a safe and secure base in and from which the patient, with the help of the therapist's sustained empathic attunement and inquiry, can learn to explore and experiment [with his or her emotional experiencing processes]. Precious little strengthens the bond between patient and therapist more effectively than the therapist's extending his inquiry into a) disruptions or perturbations of the self–self object bond or b) realms of experience that the patient perceives, even if tacitly, as threatening to the therapist. (Mahoney & Marquis, 2002, p. 805)

Emotion Regulation Skills

Although I am very intrigued with ISTDP (its "graded format" is designed to work in an emotionally intensive manner with patients that many consider "fragile" and enter therapy lacking emotion regulation skills) and am actively working to become as competent in its methods as I can, I advocate that a safe, supportive, validating, and empathic therapeutic relationship is essential—in part because the relationship itself can soothe the distress of patients who are under-regulated (Greenberg, 2002).[21] Emotion regulation skills that are helpful to teach patients

---

20 I have not directly addressed the "prime mover" issue because change can clearly occur by intervening into emotion, cognition, or behavior (Stricker, 1993).
21 "Internal security develops by feeling that one exists in the heart and mind of the other, and the security of being able to soothe the self develops by internalizing the soothing functions of the protective other" (Greenberg, 2006, p. 91).

include: deep, diaphragmatic breathing; identifying and labeling emotions; establishing a working distance (making the emotion an object of one's awareness and reflection); allowing and tolerating emotions; distraction; mindfulness; and developing empathy and compassion for self and others.

Working with Defenses and Resistance

It seems to me that many therapists avoid directly and persistently intervening to bypass patients' defenses, perhaps because they believe that if they challenge their patients too much, those patients might not be able to tolerate it or that it will damage the therapeutic relationship. Although these are valid concerns, I agree with Fosha that: "The danger of ineffectiveness and avoided action looms much larger than the damage from direct intervention" (2000, p. 2). Thus, this section will briefly address two approaches that I draw from in order to help patients experience the emotions that they chronically defend against. A fundamental premise of such work is that patients' feelings (especially their core affect or primary adaptive emotions) do not cause their suffering; rather, the defenses that distort or bury their feelings are what usually cause their suffering (Davanloo, 2005; Frederickson, 2013; Fosha, 2000). Because patients' defenses against their emotions are often a primary cause of their suffering, helping patients bypass their defenses—even if it is aversive or scary to them and might appear to be too challenging—so that they can access their core affect is actually an act of care and compassion.

Davanloo's Intensive Short-Term Dynamic Psychotherapy (ISTDP; 2005, 2000) and the many STDPs that were deeply influenced by it (Fosha's Accelerated Experiential Dynamic Psychotherapy [2000; AEDP]; Alpert's Accelerated Empathic Therapy [1991]) all focus on bypassing patients' defenses, but they do so in different ways. Because each of these approaches requires a full volume to adequately explain, I will here give a very brief overview of what I find most helpful about two of them: ISTDP and AEDP. Both ISTDP and AEDP rely heavily on Malan's (1979) triangle of conflict and triangle of persons.

The *triangle of conflict* (see Figure 7.1) is perhaps the primary conceptual tool that experiential psychodynamic therapists use to assess patients' moment-to-moment affective experience. In essence, when unconscious impulse-laden emotions reach a degree that they are about to be felt by the patient, anxiety emerges that triggers the patient's defenses, which pushes the emotion out of awareness.

The feeling is located at the bottom of the triangle to depict that it is the underlying "true" emotion, which is kept out of awareness by the patient's defenses: "It can be helpful to think of the feeling as *what* is avoided, the anxiety as *why* it is avoided, and the defense as *how* it is avoided" (Kuhn, 2014, pp. 322–323). Kuhn further emphasizes that feelings emerge at all three corners because anxiety itself is a feeling and any feeling can also be a defense (a secondary emotion) against the underlying "true" feeling.

Whereas the triangle of conflict represents an intrapsychic dynamic, the *triangle of persons* (see Figure 7.2) represents an interpersonal dynamic. In essence, dysfunctional relationship dynamics and aversive emotions that were originally

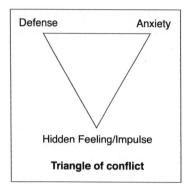 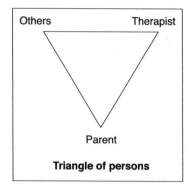

Figure 7.1 Malan's Triangle of Conflict

Figure 7.2 Malan's Triangle of Persons

generated in the past (with "genetic" figures—parents, siblings, caregivers) are re-experienced in current relationships (spouses, friends, children, co-workers), and those same dynamics also emerge with the therapist. Past relationships are placed at the bottom of the triangle because they are frequently "buried" and can often be discovered only by examining current relationships.

Intensive Short-Term Dynamic Psychotherapy

Davanloo created a deeply experiential psychodynamic approach that is brief, powerful, and efficient. Davanloo's most important contribution is his unique approach to *defense work*; he drastically shifted psychodynamic technique away from the goal of insight to a deeply visceral corrective emotional experience, with the aim of eliminating defenses completely. Davanloo greatly expanded the understanding of defenses beyond the major or "formal" defenses (repression, denial, projection, etc.) to include *tactical defenses* that diminish emotional closeness or contact with the therapist. Davanloo (2000) organized five groups of tactical defenses: equivocating, affective, relational, intellectual, and somatic/behavioral (Kuhn, 2014). The category of equivocating tactical defenses, as an example, includes the patient becoming vague, circumstantial, indecisive, or using cover words (saying he is "irritated" or "sad" rather than "angry") or indirect speech (qualifying his responses with "maybe" or "kind of") (Kuhn, 2014). Tactical defenses also include nonverbal behaviors such as avoiding eye contact or turning away from the therapist. Essential to his pioneering form of defense work are the noninterpretive techniques of challenge and pressure.

The major focus of ISTDP is the rapid removal of patients' defenses and resistance, which is accomplished by systematic "pressure" and "challenge" to defenses and resistance, and "head-on collision" with transference resistance: "Challenge is the key intervention in the whole technique, and it lies on a spectrum from relatively mild to exceedingly powerful, culminating in the head-on collision"

(Davanloo, 2005, p. 2632).[22] The relentless challenge to patients' defenses reflects ISTDP's view that the patient's defenses derive from a harsh superego's punitiveness toward the patient's self. As Fosha says: "Implicit in the technique of challenge and pressure is the belief that radical change is possible not only soon, but right here and now" (2000, p. 327). The patient's resistance must not only be challenged; the patient must recognize the resistance and the harm it causes him. Thus, the therapist *repeatedly* points out and underscores the high psychological costs of the patient's defenses and resistances (usually in the form of how they restrict the person's experience and intimacy) and, in the process, communicates intense disrespect for them. It is very important—especially with patients with ego-syntonic character defenses—that the therapist clearly differentiates the patient from his defenses, so that the patient does not feel disrespected as a person. "It is important to note that interpretation, which is central to psychoanalysis, has no place in this technique, and, further, it must be emphasized that the whole process contains a high level of affective response" (Davanloo, 2005, p. 2641). The major emphasis is on facilitating the patient's actual experience of feelings; cognitive responses are viewed primarily as resistance.

In addition to revising the psychoanalytic metapsychology of the unconscious, emphasizing the impact of all forms of trauma (as well as the intergenerational impact of trauma) on character development and psychopathology, ISTDP provides important principles that enable the therapist and patient to remain consistently focused on the crux of the patient's problem(s). Again, I can briefly touch upon only a few of these important contributions.

Three basic ISTDP principles are 1) when a patient expresses an emotion, encourage him to experience that emotion more deeply, 2) if the patient is too anxious, regulate his anxiety and then return to exploring his emotions, and 3) if the patient is defending, point out the defense and the ways it is harming him so he will be able to relinquish the defense and experience his emotion: "When patients respond with anxiety or defense, we do not follow these detours. Instead, we identify each detour and invite the patient to focus on his feeling. Maintaining a consistent focus on feeling is one of the most important skills for therapists to learn" (Frederickson, 2013, p. 5).

As most therapists know, when patients discuss their problems in general or vague terms, it is helpful to ask them about a specific instance of that problem. Frederickson stresses the importance of asking some questions in a specific way: "How do you feel toward X for doing Y?" The three-part structure of the question is useful because it allows the therapist to identify some emotions as defenses. In contrast, if a therapist asks "How do you feel about that?" the question is so vague

---

22 The interested reader is encouraged to consult Davanloo (2005, 2000). Although colleagues have told me that Davanloo does not consider the following works "pure" ISTDP, my students report that they find Frederickson (2013) and Abbass (2015) more inviting to read; I think both of the latter works are excellent and I highly recommend them. Kuhn (2014) is an ISTDP reference that thoroughly defines all the ISTDP terminology, such as "pressure," "challenge," and "head-on collision"; I highly recommend it as well.

that the patient can respond with "sad" or "anxious" and the therapist has no leverage with which to work with it. A question such as "What are your thoughts about that?" simply invites the defenses of rationalization and intellectualization. A question such as "What did you feel about what happened?" encourages the patient to detach from the present to consider the past. The way that these three questions are asked fails to elicit the patient's underlying emotion about the specific event. However, if you ask, for example, "How do you feel toward your husband for hitting you?" you now have a therapeutic leverage that the three previous questions did not provide. Based upon the universality of basic emotions (Eckman, 1984), the only primary, adaptive emotional response to being hit is anger; thus, if the patient says she feels sad, you can recognize her sadness as a defense against her anger, and point that out to her. "Confusing the stimulus with the feeling" (Frederickson, 2013, p. 52) is when the patient responds to that question with "I feel betrayed." In this instance, the husband betrayed her when he hit her; that betrayal (hitting her) is the stimulus to her feeling angry, but in this case the patient defends against her anger by confusing the stimulus with the feeling. Another example of this phenomenon: the therapist asks, "How do you feel toward your daughter for lying to you?" and the patient responds, "I feel disappointed." In this case, the therapist can respond, "Yes, she disappointed you when she lied to you. How do you feel toward her for disappointing you by lying to you?" "One of the most important points to remember is this: feelings do not hurt the patient; defenses hurt the patient. Feelings do not cause the patient's suffering; his defenses do" (Frederickson, 2013, p. 32).

While asking patients what they feel about various significant events, they will inevitably become anxious and consequently defensive (recall the triangle of conflict). Another key insight of Davanloo's (2005) was his noting three different discharge patterns of anxiety: striated muscle, smooth muscle, and cognitive and/or perceptual disturbance. If the patient's anxiety discharges into striated (voluntary) muscle (manifesting as fidgeting; sighing; jaw clenching; tension in the arms, shoulders, neck, legs, feet, etc.), the patient's anxiety is at a level that is manageable and the therapist should continue to explore the patient's emotions. If, however, the patient's anxiety discharges into either smooth muscle (bladder urgency; gastrointestinal issues such as nausea or diarrhea; migraine headache; bronchial symptoms such as asthma or difficulty breathing; feeling faint or dizzy; unable to sit up straight or walk due to lack of tension in striated muscles; etc.) or cognitive disruption or perceptual disturbance (momentary inability to think clearly; dissociation, drifting, confusion, losing track of thoughts, poor memory; blurry vision; ringing in the ears; falling asleep or exhibiting a freeze response; etc.), the patient's anxiety has exceeded his capacity to manage it; thus, the therapist should regulate the patient's anxiety until it returns to a manageable level (which is indicated by a return of anxiety in the striated muscles) (Frederickson, 2013; Kuhn, 2014).[23] This

---

23 Patients' anxiety can be regulated in a number of ways, both in-session and out of session. As "homework" practices, patients can be encouraged to practice deep diaphragmatic breathing, exercise, cultivate mindfulness and compassionate self-acceptance (for feeling the anxiety), and

moment-to-moment assessment of the patient's anxiety level ostensibly allows the therapist to relentlessly and forcefully confront and challenge her patients without exceeding a given patient's capacity to tolerate the challenge and the ensuing anxiety that derives from such challenge.

Many of my students and some of my colleagues are concerned that ISTDP therapists challenge their patients too much. However, if a patient's defenses are the primary cause of his suffering, maintaining a relentless focus to bypass his defenses is really an act of compassion, whereas allowing the patient to remain defended makes the therapist complicit in his suffering: "Never interrupt the patient's feelings, the outpouring of his inner life. Always interrupt defenses that block his inner life" (Frederickson, 2013, p. 17).

Accelerated Experiential Dynamic Psychotherapy

While studying with Davanloo, Diana Fosha learned about the therapeutic power of viscerally experiencing emotion. Like me, Fosha considers Davanloo's contributions to psychotherapy to be profound; however, she also thinks that the level of confrontation characteristic of ISTDP therapists requires a personality more common among trial attorneys than most psychotherapists. AEDP (Fosha, 2000) bears many theoretical similarities with ISTDP—such as the essential need for visceral experiencing and emphasizing the transformative impact of emotion as being intense and rapid rather than gradual and cumulative—but the therapeutic *approach* is virtually 180 degrees from that of ISTDP. Whereas ISTDP relentlessly challenges patients' defenses, AEDP seeks to provide an atmosphere of such safety that patients do not need to resort to defenses in the first place; this requires creating a relational field of empathic attunement, support, and safety that stems from Fosha's conceptual resonance with attachment theory. Whereas ISTDP is more of an intrapsychic approach, Fosha's approach is more interpersonal: "Who we are reflects the history of our relational bonds from infancy on. By synergistically linking emotion and attachment, the explosive transformational power of affect can be harnessed through a relational process and put to maximal lasting therapeutic use" (Fosha, 2000, p. 4). Without relational support

---

they can practice "establishing a working distance" (making the anxiety an object of one's awareness and reflection) (Greenberg, 2006). One thing is clear: "Ignoring anxiety ensures that it remains unregulated" (Frederickson, 2013, p. 59). Thus, in-session, therapists can help patients build their self-observing capacity, which involves facilitating their understanding of how a threatening feeling triggers their anxiety, which then triggers a defense (Kuhn, 2014). Also helpful—even if it seems counterintuitive—is asking patients to observe and describe the somatic sensations of their anxiety, as well as how it changes moment-to-moment (i.e., how their feelings of anxiety change after taking some deep breaths) (Kuhn, 2014). A safe, supportive, empathic, and validating environment is very helpful in regulating a patient's anxiety (Greenberg, 2006; Fosha, 2000). Finally, "The ability to regulate a patient's anxiety depends in large part on how well you, as a therapist, regulate your own ... To regulate others, you must be able to regulate yourself" (Frederickson, 2013, p. 89).

and regulation, emotion can become toxic and unbearable rather than transformational, which is why people resort to defenses in the first place. "The essence of the therapeutic presence in the affective model of change is being inside the patient's world as an other, and the patient's feeling it and knowing it" (Fosha, 2000, p. 29). Like other STDPs, AEDP demands an active therapist—one who skillfully counters patients' defensive emotionality while modeling emotional expression and processing.

In AEDP, the patient's anxiety is fundamentally viewed as a sign that he is not feeling safe; therefore, the AEDP therapist will try to provide a felt-sense of safety so that the patient does not need to resort to defensive strategies. When patients experience safety, their feelings of aloneness and anxiety diminish, thus allowing their previously defended-against-feelings to come to the fore. The presence of defenses or resistance signal that the patient feels a need to protect himself against a threat (even if that threat is unconsciously perceived); this feeling of danger may arise either from an intrapsychic emotion or the interpersonal threat of closeness with the therapist. Any core affects should be explored because of their inherently transformative nature; any defenses or maladaptive or secondary emotions should be bypassed so the patient can gain access to the adaptive emotions that are being distorted or covered by the defenses.

Consistent with attachment theory, Fosha maintains that anxiety derives from the nonavailability of the caregiver. In contrast, when a caregiver (or therapist) is emotionally available, what would otherwise be intolerable anxiety is kept at bay and the child (or patient) experiences the feeling of safety. There is nothing more paramount in AEDP than the patient's felt-sense of safety; as he feels increasingly safe, he will relinquish growth-inhibiting defenses and open himself to previously defended feelings and increased intimacy in interacting. I will close this section on AEDP with Fosha's own words:

> If there is no feeling of safety, anxiety, the mother of all psychopathology, takes hold ... Defenses arise to reestablish safety where the attachment relationship has failed to do so ... Their function is to exclude both intrapsychic and interpersonal affective experiences that threaten the integrity of the self and the viability of the attachment relationship ... The therapeutic implications of the attachment model are clear. The patient's feeling safe in the relationship with the therapist is essential: it reduces anxiety, precludes the need for relying on defenses, and supports the deep exploration of affective experience, which is the key to the profound transformation AEDP seeks to facilitate and work through. (Fosha, 2000, pp. 47–48)

Integrally Informed Psychotherapy or an "Integral Sensibility"

As mentioned earlier in this chapter, it may be more appropriate to term the type of work I am describing in this book "integrally informed psychotherapy" or as counseling with an "integral sensibility" rather than "integral psychotherapy" per se, the latter of which connotes a somewhat specific way to counsel.[24] In the IPP study (Marquis & Elliot, 2015), although the therapists began the study calling themselves "integral psychotherapists," by the end of the study they all preferred to refer to their work as being "integrally informed." Furthermore, the notion of an "integral sensibility" was unanimously endorsed by the therapists and, drawing upon the various denotations of the term sensibility, was characterized as an enhanced or expanded capacity for perception and responsiveness to clinical phenomena as guided by the heuristic tools and perspectives of integral metatheory. Existential psychotherapy (Yalom, 1980) and intersubjective psychoanalysis (Stolorow, Atwood, & Orange, 2002) have provided a precedent for just such a guiding attitude or orientation that can inform one's psychotherapeutic approach without mandating any specific set of practices or techniques. As with existential psychotherapy, there are no exact criteria with which to determine categorically what qualifies as integral psychotherapy, as you can have an integral sensibility and still approach therapy in many different ways. Variability in the specific approach notwithstanding, an integral sensibility entails certain "All-Quadrants, All-Levels" unifying principles, including developmental dynamics (with special attention to how they manifest moment-to-moment in patients' affective and self states) and quadratic dimensions of patients. An "All-Levels" orientation implies a responsiveness to developmental and well-being concerns across a spectrum ranging from the prepersonal to the "farther reaches of human nature." An "All-Quadrants" perspective calls for attention and responsiveness to the phenomenological, biological/behavioral, interpersonal/cultural, and societal/institutional factors involved with the person, her struggles and their resolution. Janet Lewis—one of the therapists in the IPP study—referred to her view in the following way: "that the way we're influenced by integral theory is that we've kind of got more ears, that we're listening on many different channels" (Marquis & Elliot, 2015, p. 20).

An integral sensibility or integrally informed psychotherapy does not necessarily entail interventions that are unique or specific to iPT; rather, integral metatheory guides the coherent coordination of a diverse array of interventions. As such, integrally informed psychotherapy will not always be explicitly discernible, and in any given session an integrally informed approach might not appear different than other theoretical approaches. For example, a particular session or series of iPT sessions might look the same as how a CBT therapist would counsel. Nevertheless, such apparently standard CBT work would have been decided based upon an integral conceptualization that CBT is what the patient needed.[25] Thus, an integral

---

24 Despite my agreeing and resonating with this point, I still prefer—primarily due to how it "comes off the tongue" or "reads"—to use the term "integral psychotherapy" or iPT than "integrally informed psychotherapy" or "counseling with an integral sensibility."
25 This is completely consistent with how Sechrest and Smith (1994) described integrated psychological psychotherapy: "There will not be any cognitive-behavior therapy, any psychodynamic therapy, any supportive therapy. But there will be cognitive-behavioral interventions for those aspects of problem complexes that seem amenable to those approaches, and there will be psychodynamic interventions for other aspects of problems" (cited in Magnavita, 2008, p. 286).

sensibility is more about the context than the content of interventions, and may be more outwardly recognizable as "integral" only when rendering explicit the "interiors" of the process—the rationale and cognitive maps underlying therapists' decision-making—and when tracing the therapeutic process over a broad segment of the therapy course.

The notion of an integral sensibility is also consistent with evidence-based practice (EBP), which the American Psychological Association defines as "the integration of the best available research with clinical expertise in the context of patient characteristics, culture, and preferences" (2005, p. 5). Rather than focus almost exclusively on "best research"—which in the past meant only clinical trial research—an integral sensibility allows therapists to begin with the patient and all of her developmental, quadratic, and other nondiagnostic variables, and use sound research (broadly defined to include not just random clinical trials but case study research and other study designs; Marquis, 2013), in tandem with their clinical expertise, to construct an idiographically tailored approach for each individual patient.

The Relative Importance of Core iPT Constructs in Practice

As noted previously, I now believe—in large measure due to the results of Marquis and Elliot (2015)—that working with affective, defensive, and other states constitutes the "lion's share" of psychotherapy; this was a clinically significant finding given that states have heretofore been ascribed less importance relative to other constructs in the extant iPT literature. As Baron Short—another of the IPP study therapists—said, referring to state work: "It's like the meat, it's the meat of the therapy." And still another of the IPP study therapists, Sarah Hubbard, summarized her viewpoint as follows:

> before this study started I would have put quadrants first, level (as in center of gravity) second, lines third, and states and types I don't know—a toss up for last place. And now from where I sit today ... I think I would put states first, and I would ... put level second ... I would put third quadrants ... and I would put types last and ... I would put lines fourth.

The experiences and observations of the therapists and researchers in the IPP study suggest the possibility that the practical importance of various integral concepts—as they have been written about to date—may not align neatly with what is required by clinical practice. It was further suggested that their relative importance may vary depending on the phase of treatment. For example, in the initial assessment phase, the four quadrants and developmental stage considerations may be most prominent, but most of the actual interventions throughout therapy involve attending to patients' states. At the same time, it is important to emphasize that quadratic and developmental dynamics may occupy center stage at any time throughout a course of therapy. For example, patients who present with psychotic, borderline, or less severe problems of living do require different interventions in general, and any number of quadratic variables may arise at any given time that may require being the focus of attention; for example: changes in mood or making a major life decision (i.e., to get married, change jobs, etc.) (UL); loss of a significant relationship or the death of a loved one (LL); the emergence of a severe medical problem (UR); or going through a custody dispute or losing one's home (LR).

Conclusion

I have attempted to provide core principles that guide my work as an integrally informed psychotherapist. Many of those principles—such as those in ISTDP—did not guide my work five years ago, and I suspect I will learn other principles in the future that I thus cannot write about now. Moreover, other integral therapists—from Ingersoll and Zeitler (2010) to Forman (2010) and Holden (2004)—would surely prioritize their guiding principles differently than I do. Nonetheless, I am confident that the principles I have presented here are sound, even though far from comprehensively exhaustive. On this point, I originally intended the title of this book to be *Toward an Integral Unifying Psychotherapy: Theory, Research, and Practice*—with the "toward" emphasizing that I recognize that although I am striving for it, I have not fully achieved a unifying approach to psychotherapy. Moreover, it is likely clear to the reader that I am more knowledgeable and competent in addressing Upper-Left and Lower-Left phenomena than I am in addressing neuroscientific (UR) and social-systemic (LR) phenomena. Trying to be truly comprehensive is a daunting task: "The challenge of a unified model of clinical science and psychotherapy puts a great deal of pressure on clinicians and clinical researchers to be conversant in the domains of systems from neurons to neighborhoods" (Magnavita, 2008, p. 287). Then again, many of the greatest things in life are challenging!

CHAPTER 8

An Integral Perspective on the Treatment of Anxiety Disorders

An Example of Integral Psychotherapy Treatment[1]

Introduction and a Caution about Empirically Supported Treatments

In chapter 6, I organized more than 200 interventions in an Integral Taxonomy of Therapeutic Interventions (ITTI) and also discussed ways to use it, the role of interventions in psychotherapy, suggestions regarding how to implement some of the interventions, and some cautions regarding the "tyranny of technique." In chapter 7, I provided a number of principles that guide my work as an integrally informed therapist. In this chapter, I will turn my attention to the treatment of anxiety disorders (to pick up where we left off in chapter 4). I will begin with some reminders regarding the limitations of "empirically supported treatments," address available treatments for anxiety quadrant-by-quadrant, and I will conclude with an illustrative case.

Treatments for anxiety disorders run quite a gamut, from pharmacological and behavioral to psychodynamic, cognitive, and existential, just to name a few. Several dozen meta-analytic reviews of treatments for anxiety disorders have been performed. Although many of these studies summarize a rather diverse array of disorders, the general conclusions are that psychotherapies demonstrate effectiveness compared to no treatment, control, or wait list comparison groups. Although this is a generalization, psychotherapeutic interventions also tend to have fewer dropouts and larger effect sizes than pharmacological interventions (Lambert & Ogles, 2004). However, to be a bit more specific, the results of meta-analytical research evaluating high-quality studies published in the 1990s emphasized that although the average patient who received "empirically supported treatments" for common disorders such as Major Depressive Disorder (MDD), Generalized Anxiety Disorder (GAD), and Panic Disorder improved substantially more—at the end of the study—than did the average control patient, still only

---

[1] This chapter is adapted/reprinted from Ingersoll, R. Elliot and Marquis, Andre (2014). *Understanding Psychopathology: An Integral Exploration*, 1st ed., pp. 266–313. Reprinted by permission of Pearson Education, Inc., New York.

about half of such patients showed such improvement, and all of those patients had passed numerous inclusion and exclusion criteria (Westen & Morrison, 2001). Thus, not only do issues of generalizability arise from such research; the data that are available suggest that, even among those who were substantially better at the end of treatment, the majority did not sustain their improvements at one- and two-year follow-ups, especially for disorders characterized by generalized affect states such as Major Depressive Disorder (MDD) and Generalized Anxiety Disorder (GAD) (Westen & Morrison, 2001). For these reasons, Westen and Morrison urge using terms such as "empirically supported" and "evidence-based" in more nuanced, qualified ways, being sure to acknowledge the limitations of time frames, sample selection, and the manner of reporting outcomes that can bias the conclusions one draws.

An important point in the previous paragraph is the distinction between treating a state (a temporary state of panic or anxiety) and treating a more chronic disorder such as GAD. For example, an emergency room visit can usually effectively remedy a given panic attack (state), but that is far from an effective treatment for a general disposition to be anxious with recurrent unexpected panic attacks (GAD or Panic Disorder). As the admirable research by Westen and Morrison (2001) makes clear, we do not currently know whether, or to what degree, the same interventions that have demonstrated efficacy in treating temporary states—such as depression and panic—are also effective in treating more chronic disorders, such as recurrent MDD and GAD. Studies that include long-term follow-up data are required to answer this question, and even when such claims are made in "empirically supported treatment" (EST) literature, the actual data to support such statements are difficult, if not impossible, to find (Westen & Morrison, 2001).

Across the 17 studies involving panic and the 5 studies involving GAD that Westen and Morrison (2001) examined, exclusion rates were 64% and 65%, respectively. What this means is that in an effort to isolate variables and create homogeneous groups—necessary components when trying to ascertain the cause and effect relationships that are the goal of experimental research designs—the researchers whose studies were examined by Westen and Morrison *excluded* people as participants in their studies if they were suicidal, had recently had previous psychotherapy, or had comorbid diagnoses such as major depression, substance abuse, or somatic disorders. Given that some of the exclusion criteria for these studies included depression and substance abuse/use disorders, which are *very common* among individuals with panic and GAD, this should lead you to seriously question the generalizability of such EST research. In short, we need to remain somewhat tentative with regard to claims regarding precisely how effective various treatments are for the average person who seeks help with any of the different anxiety disorders. Those who are interested in learning more about the limitations of EST research can consult Andrews (2000), Marquis and Douthit (2006), Slife, Wiggins, & Graham (2005), Wampold (1997), Westen and Morrison (2001), and Westen, Novotny, and Thompson-Brenner (2004).

Assessment

Careful, thorough, and ongoing assessment—of not just diagnostic criteria, but also of the whole person and her contexts—is critical because many of the specific objects/situations that patients are concerned with may represent merely the tip of the iceberg and/or may be symbolic of more significant fears/anxieties of which the person may be largely unaware. Also important is understanding each patient's capacity to tolerate a deeper exploration and experience of the anxiety and what it may represent or mean to him or her. Not only do anxiety and depression often co-occur in the same person—either at the same time or at different times—but a review of research on this topic suggests that having an anxiety disorder is perhaps the strongest single risk factor in the likelihood of developing depression (Hranov, 2007).

Although some researchers, theorists, and therapists consider anxiety and depression to be distinct disorders, the more common view today is that they are not only more closely related than the DSM-5 categorical classification system suggests (and the DSM-5 itself acknowledges this), they are likely overlapping syndromes with common neurobiological underpinnings and the amount of overlap is a function of whether they are described at symptom, syndrome, or diagnostic levels (Barlow, 2004; Hranov, 2007). The bottom line is that because many of the symptoms of anxiety overlap those of depression, it is not uncommon for some people with anxiety disorders (or a clinical presentation dominated by anxiety) to be erroneously diagnosed as depressed (Hranov, 2007; Ingersoll & Rak, 2006). At the same time, according to Beck and Emery (1985), people with GAD (compared to major depression) tend to have more positive views of themselves, more optimism for the future, and more positive memories of the past. Whereas depressed people tend to attribute their problems to global, structuralized deficits, anxious people more often criticize themselves for specific deficits and failure; an exception to this is that all of the social (evaluative) anxieties share a fear of being deemed inadequate or inferior (Beck & Emery, 1985). Also, because the *symptoms* of GAD and Panic Disorder can be produced by a host of medical conditions (such as hyper- and hypothyroidism, hypoglycemia, pheochromocytoma, hypercortisolism, chronic obstructive pulmonary disease, pulmonary embolus, aspirin intolerance, vestibular dysfunctions), a careful medical assessment by a physician is a critical component of an integral assessment (not to mention the DSM-5 category of Anxiety Disorder Due to Another Medical Condition). Finally, it is important to bear in mind the role that caffeine, cocaine, amphetamines, and other substances can play in producing anxiety symptoms, as can withdrawal from alcohol or other central nervous system (CNS) depressants (see the DSM-5 section on Substance/Medication-Induced Anxiety Disorder).

General (Integrative) Treatment Goals

Just as individuals are unique, so too are the goals of those who seek therapy with anxiety disorders. I value and prize diversity, individual choice, and healthy doses of nonconformity. Nonetheless, there does appear to be some general consensus that an integrative treatment of anxiety disorders (Wolfe, 2005) involves many of the following elements:

- reducing anxiety symptoms;
- helping patients increase their tolerance for anxiety and other painful affects;
- increasing the patient's sense of self-efficacy and agency;
- helping patients reduce their defensive exclusion of painful affects;
- restructuring patients' toxic self-representations;
- increasing awareness of, and modifying, how the patient defends against the pain of a wounded self;
- helping patients learn to more deeply engage authentically in their relationships such that they have more intimacy, which affords the psychological safety of a secure base.[2]

Another integrative approach to treating anxiety disorders is that of Gold (1993a). According to him, general goals of treatment with anxious patients involve:

- extensive assessment;
- symptom relief, cognitive and behavioral restructuring, and psychodynamic and interpersonal exploration;
- understanding and reconstructing the patient's early attachment experiences; more specifically, modifying pathogenic representations; internalizing adaptive, beneficial representations of self and others; and facilitating the patient's authentic, congruent self-experience.

General Approaches and Some Specific Interventions for Anxiety Disorders

In a nutshell, treating people with anxiety disorders involves helping them discover what they are *really* afraid of or concerned with, and to face those things (Barlow, 2004; Wachtel, 1977; Wolfe, 2005). Once one is aware of what the ultimate source of anxiety is, *exposure* to that source appears to be the key to effective treatment (Deacon & Abramowitz, 2004; Foa, Huppert, & Cahill, 2006; Richard & Lauterbach, 2006).[3] Another essential point is that virtually anything that helps a person

---

2 Barry Wolfe (2005) has developed one of the most integrative approaches to the treatment of anxiety. This list is from page 191 of his seminal *Understanding and Treating Anxiety Disorders: An Integrated Approach to Healing the Wounded Self.* For a more abbreviated overview of Wolfe's approach to understanding and treating anxiety disorders, consult Wolfe (2003).
3 Of course there are exceptions to this principle, as when a patient or her child is actually extremely ill and afraid of dying, or when someone is experiencing dire financial loss and is concerned about losing his home. In such cases, exposing them to death or facilitating their actually losing all their money and

develop a sense of control or self-efficacy, whether learning social skills or developing a sense of mastery with other coping responses, helps buffer the intensity of anxiety.

Upper-Right Quadrant Treatments

Behavioral

Behavioral interventions that appear helpful in treating anxiety disorders include modeling, behavioral skills training, assertiveness training (especially for anxiety disorders involving interpersonal interactions), and exposure treatments, the latter of which include both flooding and systematic desensitization. In essence, exposure treatments involve helping patients face what they are afraid of without retreating from it; the "without retreating from it" is referred to as "response prevention" and it is a critical component of exposure therapies because the typical response of avoiding the feared stimulus merely reinforces the activity of avoiding because such avoidance does in fact diminish one's anxiety, which is highly reinforcing. Because a variety of exposure methods have attained the status of "empirically supported treatments" (ESTs), I think it is important to reiterate that the EST movement has been critiqued by a range of scholars.

As previously mentioned, I have published a critique of the EST movement because I believe that aspects of the research protocols—such as common exclusion criteria, the diversity of dynamics that are subsumed under a single diagnostic category such as depression or anxiety, and so forth—produce results and conclusions that are often not generalizable to average "real-world" clinical settings (Marquis & Douthit, 2006). However, it is also important to point out that interventions involving exposure and the prevention of avoidant responses for some of the anxiety disorders appear to be exceptions to many of the methodological problems associated with EST lists; this is because they involve associations between specific stimuli or internalized representations of such stimuli and specific responses (whether behavioral, affective, or cognitive)—for example, panic symptoms, simple phobia, specific social phobia, PTSD following a single traumatic experience, and some obsessive-compulsive symptoms. However, disorders characterized by more generalized affect states (such as GAD and MDD) violate nearly all of the foundational assumptions underlying EST methodology. Thus, it is no coincidence that "empirically supported treatments" for the latter category of disorders rarely produce clinically significant improvement at one- and two-year follow-ups (Westen, Novotny, & Thompson-Brenner, 2004). It is noteworthy that all five of the disorders mentioned previously as examples of disorders that may be appropriately studied via EST protocols are anxiety disorders (or the

---

assets would not be indicated. Hopefully the reader recognizes that one must use clinical judgment with such principles; which is why they are general principles rather than hard-and-fast rules.

anxiety-related disorders or symptoms of PTSD and Obsessive-Compulsive Disorder [OCD]), and many of the change processes and specific interventions that are effective with them derive from behavioral approaches.

The single most important common element of behavioral approaches in the treatment of anxiety is that of *exposure*. Gold stresses two critical points regarding the tailoring of exposure interventions:

> First, the level of exposure must be gradual and tolerable for the patient (Wachtel, 1977). Sudden, severe jumps in the patient's anxiety will make new learning impossible ... Exposure ... must be graded to maximize the chance of success and to reinforce the development of tolerance of anxiety to a degree that exposure becomes reinforcing of the willingness to experience slightly greater levels of discomfort ... The second foundation of successful exposure is the formulation by the therapist of modes and experiences in which the meaning of the source of the anxiety can be identified and changed ... It is highly important therefore to help the patient to learn that his or her thoughts, feelings, desires, or behaviors did not and do not have the toxic and destructive potential with which they were associated. (Gold, 1993a, p. 298)

The prototypical graded exposure treatment is *systematic desensitization*, in which the therapist and the patient collaboratively develop a stimulus hierarchy: a list of anxiogenic stimuli, ranked from least anxiogenic to most anxiogenic. For example, a person with a snake phobia might list imagining snakes at a zoo, imagining encountering a snake on a nature walk, watching someone on TV handle a snake, seeing an actual snake at a distance, walking nearer to the snake, and actually holding a (nonpoisonous) snake. The therapist and patient then put aside the list while the patient learns to relax, usually some form of progressive relaxation. After the patient has learned how to reliably and consistently achieve a state of relaxation, the patient considers the least frightening stimulus from the list. The patient uses a subjective units of distress (SUDs) scale from 1 (low) to 10 (high) to report her level of anxiety. If the patient reports an SUD of 3 or more, the therapist guides her to relax; if she reports an SUD of 1 or 2, the therapist guides her to refocus on the anxiety-eliciting stimulus. With each repetition of this process, the patient remains more and more relaxed in the real or imagined presence of the conditioned stimulus, at which point the next stimulus on the hierarchy is encountered. Ultimately, the patient can focus on the previously most frightening stimulus and remain relaxed, reporting an SUD of 1 or 2. After this process is successfully applied, the person encountering the previously feared stimulus now elicits the conditioned response of relaxation rather than anxiety (Fall, Holden, & Marquis, 2010).[4]

---

4 Interestingly but not surprisingly, research has found that one of the key determinants of how successful exposure treatments are for a given person is the level of physiological arousal during the exposure interventions (Borkovec & Stiles, 1979; Mineka & Thomas, 1999).

One comment on the effectiveness of exposure-based treatments is worth noting, particularly because it comes from Barry Wolfe, who co-authored (with David Barlow) a classic NIMH report on the effectiveness of exposure treatments with phobias:

> the exposure-based behavioral therapy rarely cured the phobias. I was not seeing the rapid reduction or elimination of phobic symptoms in 60% to 70% of the cases I treated as I was led to expect by the research literature (Barlow & Wolfe, 1981). In my 25 years of experience with over 300 patients with anxiety disorder, I found that exposure therapy led to the rapid reduction of symptomatology in approximately 30% of the cases. (Wolfe, 2005, p. 5)

This is an excellent example of how therapy in real-world settings is often not as "neat and clean" as in random clinical trial (RCT) research, which is what is used to ascertain ESTs. While not diminishing the effectiveness (often times) of exposure methods, Wolfe's point highlights the need to tailor integrative treatment approaches for each individual.

Pharmacological

Although numerous psychotropic medications appear helpful in ameliorating the symptoms of anxiety, an integral psychotherapeutic approach not only integrates the many forms of treatment that are effective, it also considers it important to ponder why people are so anxious in our current culture, how we might be able to make our worlds safer places, and what might be the value of living constructively with anxiety. Although pervasive, the anxiety disorders, in general, are more responsive—at least in the short term—to psychotherapeutic interventions than many other mental disorders (Ingersoll & Rak, 2006; Westen & Morrison, 2001). Thus, while honoring each patient's needs and wishes, integral therapists are mindful to inform patients who primarily desire anxiolytics that although medications may be helpful in managing the distressing *symptoms* of anxiety, they may also mask some of the very signals that are alerting the individual to important dimensions of life (meaning, choices, etc.).

The use of psychotropic medications for anxiety is an interesting case: Not only are they perhaps the most commonly prescribed psychotropics, they are also prescribed predominantly by nonpsychiatrists (more than 80% of the time; Ingersoll & Rak, 2006). As we will soon see, several classes of psychotropics are used to treat anxiety: CNS depressants, SSRI antidepressants, benzodiazepines, and unique compounds such as buspirone (BuSpar).

All CNS depressants induce behavioral depression. Thus, their effects include not only relaxation and sleep, but relief from anxiety as well. However, if used excessively, they can also result in general anesthesia, coma, and death. The primary CNS depressants used to treat anxiety are barbiturates, which were created in the late 1800s and dominated the anti-anxiety market from the early 1900s to about 1960. However, barbiturates are not specifically anxiolytic; rather, their anxiety-reducing effects stem from their overall sedating effects, not unlike the effects of drinking a lot of alcohol. Because they have so many negative side effects—ranging from cognitive inhibition, sleepiness, behavioral depression, and ataxia (loss of muscle coordination) to physical and psychological tolerance and dependence, and overdose-related death—barbiturates are not widely used to treat anxiety these days. Quaaludes are another CNS depressant once used to treat anxiety but are no longer regularly used because they too induce tolerance and depression and were frequently overdosed.

Today, benzodiazepines are the prototypic anxiolytic medication and account for approximately 90% of all anxiolytic treatment (Ingersoll & Rak, 2006; Stahl, 2002). There are currently more than 40 benzodiazepines on the market, ranging from the older, more fat-soluble, longer mean half-life[5] 2-Keto compounds (Valium/diazepam, Klonopin/clonazepam, Librium/chlordiazepoxide, Centrax/prazepam, and Dalmane/flurazepam, etc.) to the newer 3-Hydroxy compounds (Restoril/temazepam, Ativan/lorazepam, Serax/oxazepam, and ProSom/Estazolam) to triazolo compounds (triazolam [marketed as Apo-Triazo, Halcion, Hypam, and Trilam], Xanax/Alprazolam, and Lendormin/brotizolam). Each of these three groups varies with regard to potency, duration of effect, and half-life. As mentioned in the neuroscience section of the etiology of anxiety disorders (in chapter 4), like other psychotropics, benzodiazepines do not act upon just anxiety; they also act as muscle relaxants, sedatives, intravenous anesthetics, and anticonvulsants.

It appears that benzodiazepines facilitate the binding of GABA via natural benzodiazepine receptors, inhibit synaptic action by facilitating conductance increases in chloride, and inhibit various stress-induced increases in norepinephrine, serotonin, and dopamine. Although benzodiazepines appear to reduce anxiety-related symptoms in approximately 75% of people, they are not without their side effects. First and foremost, although their potential for death by overdose is far less than that of the barbiturates, benzodiazepines are still lethal in overdose, particularly if massive quantities are taken with alcohol (Allen, 2010). Likewise, they can lead to physical tolerance, as well as physical and psychological dependence, although this is rare, especially among benzos with longer half-lives. If they are taken over only a short period of time or p.r.n. (i.e., infrequently, from the Latin *pro re nata*, meaning "as circumstances require"), then benzodiazepines tend not to induce tolerance to their therapeutic effects. Moreover, when rebound anxiety does occur during the withdrawal of benzodiazepine use, it usually lasts only two to three days (Ingersoll & Rak, 2006).[6]

---

5 Mean half-life refers to the time it takes for half of the dose to clear out of one's body. As a general principle, the shorter the half-life of a drug, the greater its potential for tolerance and addiction. However, tolerance and addiction are also more likely to occur with benzodiazepines that are more highly potent, taken in higher doses, or taken regularly for longer periods of time (i.e., for more than four weeks).
6 Rebound anxiety involves the anxiety one feels as a function of withdrawal symptoms (often feeling as or more anxious than one did prior to taking the medication).

Something of an "outlier" as an anxiolytic is buspirone (BuSpar), which was the first serotonergic drug to effectively treat anxiety symptoms.[7] Unlike the majority of anxiolytics, which seem to

> exert CNS depression by acting as GABA agonists, buspirone is actually a serotonin agonist and antagonist. Because serotonin is related to certain types of disinhibition of behavior and such disinhibition is also related to relief from anxiety, researchers have hypothesized since the 1980s that serotonin agonists may alleviate anxiety. (Barlow, 2004, p. 505)

Some of the advantages that buspirone has over benzodiazepines include the following: it is less likely to induce drowsiness and fatigue; it lacks hypnotic, muscle relaxant, and anticonvulsant properties; it does not impair cognitive or motor functioning; it has no synergistic effects with alcohol; it does not induce tolerance; and it has little potential for abuse and dependence (Barlow, 2004). Nonetheless, it does have side effects, which include gastrointestinal (GI) upset, dizziness, headache, and sometimes tension, restlessness, and nervousness.[8]

Two noradrenergic anxiolytics target the SNS symptoms of anxiety, such as increased heart rate, sweating, and trembling.[9] One of these is propranolol. By blocking beta-adrenergic receptors (thus referred to as a "beta-blocker"), it decreases SNS stimulation and thereby significantly reduces the *physical* symptoms associated with anxiety. However, propranolol does not affect the psychological symptoms of anxiety. Another noradrenergic anxiolytic that appears to reduce physical but not psychological dimensions of anxiety is clonidine.

Although it may seem confusing at first, clinicians have long known that many patients taking antidepressants also experience a reduction of anxiety. Recall from chapter 4 that many researchers and scholars believe that depression and anxiety may share more of a common basis than the DSM's categorical classification system suggests. At the same time, it is important to remember how idiosyncratic and unpredictable any given person's response may be to any treatment, whether psychological or pharmacological: not only have SSRIs apparently caused panic attacks in some people (Ingersoll & Rak, 2006), even progressive muscle relaxation can elicit anxiety in some patients (Mahoney, 2003).[10] Nonetheless, SSRIs also appear helpful in reducing anxiety symptoms in some people with anxiety disorders (Barlow, 2004; Ingersoll & Rak, 2006) and, far more often than not,

---

7 Interestingly, BuSpar is chemically less like an anxiolytic and more like a butyrophenone antipsychotic; it is classified as an azapirone (Barlow, 2004).
8 Another drug that affects the GABA system—that is prescribed off-label for different anxiety disorders—is gabapentin.
9 Noradrenergic refers to a compound that impacts noradrenaline, the latter of which is synonymous with norepinephrine.
10 The latter most likely occurs because they experience it as a loss of control.

progressive muscle relaxation is an excellent method with which to facilitate relaxation and a sense of calm.

Other Upper-Right-Quadrant Interventions

Other UR interventions that appear helpful in combating many anxiety symptoms include aerobic exercise and, perhaps more specifically, exercises involving balance, range of movement, and capacities to expand (Mahoney, 2003, p. 119). In one study (Broman-Fulks & Storey, 2008), 24 participants characterized as "high anxiety sensitivity" (Anxiety Sensitivity Index-Revised scores > 28) were randomly assigned to one of two groups, a no-exercise control group or the experimental group that completed six 20-minute aerobic exercise sessions. Even though aerobic exercise exposes individuals with high anxiety sensitivity to physiological cues that are very similar to those of anxiety, the aerobic exercise group had significantly less anxiety sensitivity after the exercise, whereas the control group's scores did not significantly change.

Many patients with anxiety problems breathe rapidly and from the chest. Teaching them to breathe slowly and deeply from the abdomen often helps diminish the intensity of their anxiety (Siegel, 2007). Both deep diaphragmatic breathing as well as mindful awareness of one's breathing have been found to be powerful components of anxiety reduction. Patients should not only be taught such breathwork; they should also be encouraged to *regularly* practice it both when they are anxious as well as when they are not, because the more one becomes proficient in using breathing to regulate anxiety, the more effective it is under conditions of anxiety and panic (Greenberg, 2008; Miller, Fletcher, & Kabat-Zinn, 1995; Wolfe, 2005).

Treatments Focusing on Interiors (Upper-Left and Lower-Left Quadrants)

Cognitive

In general, cognitive approaches posit that by ameliorating disturbances of information processing, core beliefs, and other cognitions, disturbances in anxious feelings and avoidant behaviors will diminish. Thus, cognitive therapists seek to minimize maladaptive thought processes such as catastrophic thinking, overgeneralizing, and exaggerating the magnitude of potential threats. Cognitive approaches also emphasize helping patients recognize earlier symptoms of anxiety and/or panic as well as helping them learn various coping strategies (e.g., decatastrophizing, questioning the evidence, distraction, thought stopping) to diminish or eliminate the anxiety and/or panic (Schoenfield & Morris, 2008).

How do cognitive therapists do this? First, patients are educated about cognitive distortions and other dimensions of faulty thinking. Another early goal is to increase each patient's self-awareness such that they recognize distorted, dysfunctional thinking *as it is occurring*; after all, it is only after a patient has developed the ability to identify her maladaptive cognitions that she can restructure those cognitions (see pp. 147–148 from chapter 6). Before patients will be able to consistently correct their faulty thinking on their own, therapists must help them do this many times in-session, and they do this largely through asking questions. Typical questions that Beck and Emery (1985) explore with their patients include:

- What is the evidence for or against this idea?
- What is the logic?
- Are you confusing a habit with a fact?
- Are you thinking in all-or-none terms?
- Are you taking selected examples out of context?
- Are you confusing a low probability with a high probability?
- Are you over-focusing on irrelevant factors? (pp. 196–198)

Cognitive therapists recognize the importance of a good therapeutic relationship. Thus, questions are not asked in mechanical, scripted ways. A good cognitive therapist is able to attend with warmth and empathy to each patient while also teaching cognitive principles and obtaining detailed information. Guidelines to follow when asking questions include:

- Resist the inclination to answer questions for the patient.
- Ask specific, direct, and concrete questions.
- Base each question on a rationale.
- Questions should be timed to foster rapport and problem solving.
- Avoid a series of rapid-fire questions.
- Use in-depth questioning.

Beck and Emery (1985) outlined three basic approaches that cognitive therapists take. They stated that

> Nearly all of the cognitive therapist's questions can be broken down to one of these questions: (1) "What's the evidence?" [analyze faulty logic, provide information, and help them learn to treat their thoughts, worries, and concerns as hypotheses to be tested] (2) "What's another way of looking at the situation?" [generate alternative interpretations of the situation; help the patient "decenter" by challenging the belief that he is the point around which all things revolve; and enlarge his perspective] and (3) "So what if it happens?" [decatastrophize and help them learn new coping skills] Some patients respond better to one approach than to another. Each patient, however, should develop skill in using all three approaches. (p. 201, brackets added)

Other cognitive interventions include:

- Understand the *idiosyncratic meanings* that the anxiety holds for the individual.
- Question/examine the evidence. However, this technique is much less effective with anxious than depressed patients because evidence that disconfirms the

Integral Treatment of Anxiety Disorders   195

depressed patient's view of a hopeless future powerfully negates the validity of such a view. In contrast, an anxious patient's worry and concern that he *may* lose his job is much more difficult to refute; after all, even if he retains his job, he can argue that it was merely because of the extra hours he worked, which resulted in more marital discord, and he is now anxious he will lose his marriage.

- Reattribute patients' anxiety to a host of factors, from genes (UR) and a hectic work schedule and financial worries (LR) to idiosyncratic patterns of thinking that exaggerate the person's psychological vulnerability (UL) and living within a culture in which racial, sexist, homophobic, and other threatening attitudes are present (LL).
- Develop alternatives. Help patients see that their panicky way of relating to their situation is merely one choice among others.
- Decatastrophize.
- Examine the fantasized consequences.
- Examine advantages versus disadvantages.
- Label the distortions.
- Develop replacement imagery.
- Use thought stopping.
- Use distraction.[11]

Beck prefers to employ behavioral strategies only *after* some cognitive groundwork is laid in which patients can integrate experiences that disconfirm their catastrophic expectations (Beck & Weishaar, 2008). Various imagery techniques can be used to help patients experience their patterns of anxiety in the therapist's presence, with the therapist asking them to share their worst- and best-imagined outcomes of the scenario. This can lead to both greater perspective on the situation as well as being a type of learning experience in itself (Beck & Weishaar, 2008). Some of the more commonly used behavioral interventions include:

- social skills training;
- assertiveness training;
- relaxation training;
- activity scheduling;
- bibliotherapy;
- shaping/graded task assignments;
- behavioral rehearsal/role playing;
- exposure (imaginal or in vivo).[12]

---

11 These and more cognitive interventions, as well as further descriptions of each, can be found in Freeman and Simon (1989).
12 These and more behavioral interventions, as well as further descriptions of each, can be found in Freeman and Simon (1989).

Psychodynamic/Attachment Theory

The more traditional psychodynamic approaches that have not developed radically beyond Freud's formulations aim, in general, to make the patient conscious of how anxiety stems from unconscious impulses to act out sexual and aggressive impulses. By analyzing dreams, transference, resistance to free association, slips of the tongue and *working through*,[13] patients learn more mature ways (usually via more mature defenses such as sublimation) of dealing with their impulses such that they are able to gratify some of them with minimal anxiety.

More contemporary dynamic approaches share a common emphasis on the interpersonal (LL)—in contrast to intrapsychic (UL)—aspects of both etiology and treatment: constructive change occurs not strictly from within a person, but primarily between people (Wachtel, 2008). More recent dynamic approaches also recognize the importance of "corrective emotional experiences," in contrast to primarily intellectual insight (recall chapter 7). What this means is that it is often not enough simply to correct faulty thinking (e.g., replacing "all social interactions will result in my being humiliated" with "some social interactions may be embarrassing but they are not the end of the world and, actually, I have enjoyed and benefited from some socializing"). Rather, it is often necessary to *experience* (physically and emotionally) social interactions that are positive (and developing social skills before embarking on this may be an important component to the success of such experiences). This may sound similar to some cognitive-behavioral therapy (CBT) approaches, and many psychodynamic theorists acknowledge this (Gold, 1993b; Wachtel, 2008). However, current dynamic approaches still emphasize the centrality of unconscious, conflictual, and defensive processes in most psychopathology. Thus, although CBT approaches appear more effective than dynamic ones in cases in which what is feared is clearly identifiable (as in specific phobias), when the primary concerns are not readily identifiable (as with GAD, Panic Disorder, Social Anxiety Disorders, etc.), effective treatment involves exploring the patient's internal and interpersonal worlds, understanding conflicts and defenses, and interpreting or bypassing those to gain an understanding of the ultimate source of the person's anxiety. These sources are often interpersonal in nature; after they have been discovered, the patient is repeatedly exposed to the anxiogenic situations (in person or imaginally). Wachtel points out that although most dynamic therapists do not use terminology such as "exposure" and "learning" (which are behavioral terms), those are, in fact, processes that Freud and many dynamic therapists facilitate (Wachtel, 1987, 2008).

A good example of how a change in theoretical understanding is connected to a change in treatment interventions—and also illuminating some of the reasons for the development of dynamic approaches—involves Freud's revising his

---

13 "Working through" is a gradual process of repeatedly processing insights into the patient's unconscious drives, wishes, and fantasies with a goal of helping him realize how his defenses against anxiety actually create many if not most of his symptoms (Wachtel, 2008).

understanding of anxiety. Originally, Freud posited that repression led to anxiety.[14] If repression is thought of as "not-knowing" (i.e., unconscious forgetting), then the "cure" is insight or "knowing." However, Freud (1926) revised his theory and stated that anxiety is not the consequence of repression; rather, anxiety results in the need to repress (the anxiety and the unconscious feeling that triggered the anxiety). Thus, if the source of pathology is anxiety/fear, then the "cure" is to become less afraid, which is accomplished, in large measure, by being exposed to what one fears and experientially learning (emotionally as well as intellectually) that one need not fear it (or at least not as much) (Wachtel, 1987, 2008).

Existential

Imagine a person seeking therapy to help with recurrent panic attacks, Social Anxiety Disorder, or some other anxiety disorder. Whereas most clinicians operating from a biomedical or cognitive-behavioral perspective will have as their priority the reduction of the anxiety symptoms, existential therapists tend to have rather different goals. Although they would agree with therapists of other theoretical orientations that panic attacks, excessive social anxiety, and so forth are not the essence of flourishing, existentialists view such anxiety as potentially communicating important information regarding problems, conflicts, or potentials that the person is not effectively dealing with.

> Though the existential therapist hopes to alleviate crippling levels of anxiety, he or she does not hope to eliminate anxiety. Life cannot be lived nor can death be faced without anxiety. Anxiety is guide as well as enemy and can point the way to authentic existence. The task of the therapist is to reduce anxiety to comfortable levels and then to use this existing anxiety to increase a patient's awareness and vitality. (Yalom, 1998, p. 249)

Effective work with a patient's existential anxiety recognizes the meaningful message in the anxiety and motivates the person to take the action needed to live more fully one's highest purposes, which can result in more authentic engagement with life (May, 1977). Because the primal dread of existential anxiety is usually displaced or camouflaged into secondary fears and anxieties, it is often necessary to work to discern what the underlying existential anxiety is: "Primary anxiety is always transformed into something less toxic for the individual; that is the function of the entire system of psychological defenses" (May, 1977, p. 196).[15] In the event

---

14 Prior to 1926, Freud had viewed anxiety primarily as a discharge phenomenon. It was a consequence of "repression and of the damming up of libidinal tension that repression brought about" (Wachtel, 2008, p. 197).
15 Integral psychotherapists view existentialism, like other perspectives, as "true but partial." Thus, although some integral therapists place a high premium on existential formulations, I do not believe that there are existential meanings in *all* anxiety conditions.

that what is primary for a given person is neurotic and not existential anxiety, then the work of the therapist is to help the patient recognize the exaggerated or unnecessary nature of his anxiety and to work through it, whether that is in a relatively analytic or cognitive-behavioral manner. Even though secondary manifestations of anxiety are not primary, they are nonetheless real and existential therapists begin treatment with what the patient presents as his concerns: "Thus in the treatment of many clients the existential paradigm of psychopathology does not call for a radical departure from traditional therapeutic strategies or techniques" (Yalom, 1980, p. 112). In addition to helping patients face and constructively use their existential anxiety, they also work to eradicate neurotic fears and anxieties: "Anxiety is more basic than fear. In psychotherapy, one of our aims is to help the patient confront anxiety as fully as possible, thus reducing anxiety to fears, which are then objective and can be dealt with" (May & Yalom, 1995, p. 264).

In an effort to help patients learn how to be, after Kierkegaard, "rightly anxious," existential therapists tend to confront patients' anxieties directly, sometimes even amplifying them. As Paul Tillich (1952) wrote in *The Courage to Be*, if we are not able to face and attend to the existential anxieties that derive from what is of ultimate concern in life to us, we will never realize what it is to be human—that which sets us apart from other animals. Thus, existential therapists may ask a patient "what keeps you from killing yourself?" Although this question may seem out of the ordinary, it can elicit what is most meaningful in life to that person—the "*why* to live for" in Nietzsche's dictum, which I paraphrase as "If you have a 'why' to live, you will find a 'how.'" Likewise, pondering how you would live if you knew you had only one month left to live can also reveal what is most important to you—what it is, precisely, that is most meaningful in your life. Consonant with Nietzsche's (1954) theory of eternal recurrence, if you would not like to live your life over and over again as you are currently living it, then change the way you are living.

Referring to the sickness of a variety of neuroses, including anxiety, Frankl (1985) wrote that the "cure is self-transcendence!" (p. 152). Frankl posited that we could become authentic human beings by exercising our freedom to create meaning in our lives in three fundamental ways: by doing good deeds or creative work, by loving others in such a way as to help them actualize their potentials, and by finding meaning in unavoidable suffering. In accord with Frankl's third way to create a meaningful life, the task of therapists is to help make "suffering that feels meaningless become meaningful" (Miller, 2004, p. 249).

Spiritual

From an integral perspective, when attempting to intervene with a patient's anxiety from a spiritual perspective, it is important to discern the relative *legitimacy* and *authenticity* of that person's relationship to his or her spirituality (recall the discussion of this from chapter 4). If patients' spirituality is primarily legitimate, intervening will largely involve working within their religious/spiritual system to help them make meaning of their anxieties and lives; this involves collaboratively discussing how the individuals can use their religious and/or spiritual beliefs to increase their feelings of safety and security (e.g., with devout Christians, the therapist can remind them that God's love and forgiveness is limitless and includes them). However, not all religious beliefs and practices are healthy for people, and some even contribute to their anxiety and should thus be explored, examined, and questioned. Excellent resources for distinguishing healthy and unhealthy aspects of some patients' understanding and practice of their spiritual tradition are Battista (1996) and Griffith (2010).

To the extent that the patient is open to actively cultivating the virtues within her spiritual tradition, a host of meditative and other disciplines appear helpful in diminishing anxiety, even if they do not eliminate it per se. For example, various meditative techniques that tend to be subsumed under the category of *mindfulness* have been empirically demonstrated to lessen anxiety symptoms (Linehan, 1993a; Miller, Fletcher, & Kabat-Zinn, 1995; Orsillo, Roemer, & Barlow, 2003). In essence, the practice of mindfulness involves cultivating "the awareness that emerges through paying attention on purpose, in the present moment, and nonjudgmentally to the unfolding of experience moment to moment" (Kabat-Zinn, 2003, p. 145). If future worries arise, direct one's attention back to the present with an accepting, nonjudgmental attention. This requires that patients allow themselves to open to their emotional experience, which many are afraid of. Thus, teaching patients centering, balancing, and self-regulating skills is often a necessary prerequisite. A key point here is that patients must *regularly and consistently* practice meditation in order to obtain maximum benefits (Orsillo & Roemer, 2011). On a related note, research has demonstrated that mindfulness-based interventions are more effective when performed by therapists who have their own daily meditative practice (Segal, Williams, & Teasdale, 2002).

Gratefulness is another spiritual virtue that can assist patients in reducing their anxieties. In my clinical experience, I have found that, with those patients with a religious or spiritual belief system, using a gratitude-related decatastrophizing intervention within their spiritual tradition makes decatastrophizing more powerful. For example, "you really want that promotion and feel like your world will collapse if you don't get it, but God will give you all you need. Therefore, cultivate gratitude for all that you currently have"; or for a Buddhist patient, "the self that you are worrying about is not your true nature. All of your worries will pass just as they are currently arising. Stay aware of the present moment and recognize and appreciate your Buddha-nature."

Wolfe's Integrative Approach

Wolfe (2003, 2005) outlined an integrative four-stage approach to anxiety disorders. First, the therapist must establish a therapeutic relationship with the patient. Second, the therapist teaches the patient a variety of techniques with which to lessen and regulate the anxiety. Such techniques include, but are not limited to, practicing being in the present moment (paying attention to bodily sensations rather than cognitive thoughts and worries); practicing deep, diaphragmatic breathing; and contradicting catastrophic thinking (this may involve examining the available evidence, self-affirmations, etc.). Third, the therapist elicits the patient's panicogenic and phobogenic conflicts. Fourth, the therapist must help the patient actually resolve the conflicts; this usually involves identifying the different elements of the conflict. The two-chair technique is helpful in understanding and magnifying the experience of the contrasting elements, with the therapist coaching the patient through various dialogues with the contrasting elements, and ultimately integrating the contrasting elements. Once this has occurred, a plan of action is created for the patient to implement what was learned.[16]

Although the various exposure therapies are highly effective in treating phobias over the short term (Westen & Morrison, 2001; Wolfe, 2003), longer-term effectiveness without relapse more often requires addressing the underlying dynamics of self-experience, one of which is a general tendency of anxiety-ridden people to have great difficulty, if they are able at all, *to fully experience painful affect*. This is part of the rationale for integrating behavioral approaches with more experiential-dynamic ones (Fosha, 2000; Greenberg, 2002, 2008; Wachtel, 1987; Wolfe, 2003).

As Wolfe has stressed, virtually all patients fear pain, especially emotional pain. Wolfe has repeatedly observed that when anxiety-ridden patients are finally able to allow themselves to fully experience the emotions they are afraid of, their anxiety usually diminishes:

> When such patients can maintain a strict attentional focus (without worrying, because worry often functions to avoid fully experiencing underlying fears) on what they fear, whether it be a specific external object or an internal sensation, they will contact the rage, humiliation, and despair that appear to be obscured by the anxiety. Often, but not always, patients will notice that experiencing these feelings is actually less painful than the anxiety. (Wolfe, 2003, p. 376)

Due to the importance of helping anxious patients deepen their affective experience, a primary component in an integral approach involves helping patients experience previously unbearable anxiety within the context of the secure base that the therapeutic relationship offers. This affords patients the opportunity to learn (*experientially, not just intellectually*) that allowing a fully felt exploration of the anxiety is not only tolerable but does not, in fact, result in the danger, abandonment, loss of control, or other consequences that were catastrophically feared. A primary function of secure attachment and the "secure base" it provides is to reduce anxiety, which diminishes the need to defensively exclude affective life. With such defensive exclusion in abeyance, "the transforming power of affect"

---

16 Although Wolfe (2003, 2005) described steps two and three in reverse order, he subsequently found that many patients need anxiety-management "tools" before they are willing to engage in the depth of work involved in eliciting panicogenic and phobogenic conflicts (personal communication, July 27, 2011).

(Fosha, 2000, p. 108) is released and the patient has an immediate, visceral experience of core, healing affect that runs directly counter to his expectations: of intense emotion decreasing rather than increasing anxiety.

Intervening from the Lower-Right Quadrant

Given that various systemic structures—from fast-paced, competitive work environments and an increasing sense of isolation from meaning-making communities to a host of inequitable social systems (economic, medical, educational, etc.)—appear to contribute to or trigger many people's anxieties, intervening at the systemic level can contribute to reductions of anxiety (Wachtel, 2017). Such systemic interventions may involve discussing the advantages and disadvantages of the patient reorganizing her daily patterns in order to experience fewer stressors (e.g., working fewer hours/day and/or fewer days/year; making time for relationships, hobbies, exercise, meditation, etc.). Although this might involve letting go of how much one can do or accomplish, and thus diminish one's income, it may lead to an increased quality of life. I recall counseling a woman in her late twenties whose presenting complaint was anxiety. As it turned out, she was a single mother of two children, who was not only working full-time, but also attending graduate school part-time and raising her children by herself. She reported being terribly stressed by financial concerns, worrying about being able to pay for school, and having enough quality time with her children. In this case and many others, it was most beneficial for me to act as a resource advocate for my patients—helping them access and utilize various social services that have a concrete effect on their social circumstances (e.g., grants and other forms of financial aid, public assistance services, grassroots community support groups, Head Start and other preschool programs, and encouraging people to utilize free public resources such as parks and other natural areas).

In addition to helping patients access support services that are already available, intervening from the Lower-Right quadrant may also involve advocating for structural changes within social systems and policies that contribute to patients' suffering. For example, I once counseled a gay man named Dave who had been monogamous with his life partner, Eric, for 30 years. Eric had recently been diagnosed with cancer when I began counseling Dave. Eric was self-employed and did not have health insurance and Dave was unable to place Eric on his insurance policy because its coverage extended only to partners in marriage. In the course of our sessions, Dave shared how this social injustice exacerbated an already anxiety-provoking situation. Thus, those who are able to change social systems and/or policies—like the one impacting Dave and Eric—such that they are more just and equitable will decrease the unnecessary suffering that so many people experience.

Summary and an Illustrative Case

Given that many anxious patients are snared within vicious circles, I posit that an optimal approach takes into account the synergistic aspects of at least the four quadrants. Thus, from an Upper-Right perspective, modifying overt behaviors and utilizing exposure therapies are essential; also helpful at times is the use of various psychotropic medications. From an Upper-Left perspective, promoting insight into deeper symbolic meanings of the feared situations and modifying maladaptive cognitions and catastrophic imagery are often critical. From a Lower-Right perspective, any number of various systems, from occupational and familial to economic and global politics, may be implicated in the patient's anxiety; working as an advocate for change of inequitable social systems is increasingly recognized as within the purview of counselors and other mental health professionals. From a Lower-Left perspective, it is imperative to pay attention to the specifics of the patient's significant relationships (and their capacities to function as secure bases for the patient) as well as the meaning-making systems they use (from implicit family of origin rules and messages to the central belief structures of their religious affiliations) to understand themselves and their lives. The following case illustrates many of the aforementioned dynamics.

Maria, a 25-year-old Mexican American, was a professional chef who had recently been invited to appear on a local TV show, but declined because she was too afraid that she would have a panic attack in front of the live audience that was part of the TV show. Being so disappointed at passing up such a big opportunity was what prompted her to seek professional help. Maria reported that she had worried about many things throughout her life, including worrying about having more panic attacks, and in particular that others would think she was crazy and that she would be humiliated to have a panic attack in public. Although she often had a drink or two with dinner, and would occasionally have three or four drinks at a party, it did not appear that substance use, or any medical condition, was responsible for her panic attacks.

Based upon her descriptions, it is likely that her father had Generalized Anxiety Disorder, although he was never diagnosed or treated for it. According to Maria, he worried "all the time" and avoided a career as a professional musician because he was too afraid to perform in front of live audiences. She further related that two of her three older siblings were excessive worriers. Thus, in addition to a likely genetic component to Maria's anxiety and panic, she may have learned from her father's and her siblings' modeling not only to worry, but to avoid those situations that caused her any anxiety.

As a child, Maria lived in a poor and crime-ridden part of town in an apartment with her parents and siblings. She reported that the apartment had exposed lead paint chipping away that she remembers was eventually repaired by the landlord during her early teen years. Her family shared their home with extended family members throughout much of her life and she would often share a room with various cousins, in addition to her sisters. Maria frequently overheard her parents discuss their worries about finances, the safety of the neighborhood, and of their extended family struggling in Mexico; hearing her parents so concerned about these social/environmental issues may have been a factor contributing to her not feeling that the world was one that she had much control over.

Maria and her siblings were the first of her family to be born in the United States, and she reported being frequently teased at school as being the child of "wetbacks." She ended up hating school, and frequently skipped school to help out at the restaurant at which her mother was a waitress (it was there that she became interested in cooking).

Although her declining the TV show was the first time that her anxiety had resulted in her actually avoiding a major event that she really wanted to participate in, it was not the first time that she had worried about being unable to ward off future panic attacks (she did not believe that she had control over her anxiety). She thus spent most of her time alone, with her one best friend, at the restaurant, or at home with her family. Her sense of herself was of someone who was weak, lacked emotional control, and had poor social skills. Deep down, she saw herself as incompetent, inadequate, and as something of a phony—"I don't know how I ever got to be head chef at the restaurant—I guess I'm just really lucky."

As for many Mexican Americans, Maria's family was extremely important to her, and her sense of self seemed very influenced by her family. She reported that her parents were loving and very involved in her life. She also said they had always been fairly controlling and overprotective, and were quite rigid in their rules and punishments. She realized that they did not encourage her to develop independence (she still lived at home when I counseled her). She expressed that she often felt a tension between making decisions about her life based on what was best for her family in contrast to what she wanted to do.

A crucial aspect of helping patients with anxiety disorders involves assisting them to become increasingly able to deepen their affective experience, and essential to this process is facilitating their experiencing previously unbearable anxiety in the presence of the therapist, with the patient using the therapeutic relationship as a "secure base." I agree with Wachtel (1977) and others (Barlow, 2004; Wolfe, 2005) that treating people with anxiety disorders is fundamentally a process of discovering what they are ultimately afraid of, and helping them face those things without the dreaded consequences occurring. I was less psychodynamic/attachment focused with Maria than was usual for me—partly because she reported feeling deeply loved by her parents and her best friend, and partly because she was insistent that she wanted her anxiety and panic symptoms to "go away as quickly as possible." Maria seemed to have a fairly secure attachment style, and related warmly and openly with me; thus, Maria and I formed a strong therapeutic relationship very quickly. To help her manage her anxiety and possible panic attacks, I referred her to a psychiatrist who prescribed her Lorazepam to be taken p.r.n. (UR). I encouraged her to use the Lorazepam only when she could not regulate her anxiety with the following strategies, which I instructed her in and she practiced in-session and at home: deep diaphragmatic breathing (UR), which she paired with her use of her rosary (which helped her become grounded; she was Catholic [LL]); cultivating mindfulness (nonjudgmental awareness that is focused on the present moment—more about sensing than thinking [UL]); and contradicting catastrophic thinking by examining the evidence that things would likely be catastrophic (UR/UL). Thus, we engaged a three-pronged approach that 1) tried to reduce her anxiety symptoms, 2) helped her increase her tolerance for anxiety, and 3) restructured her negative self-views with more positive, realistic ones. One of the ways we addressed the second task was by having her imagine a dreaded scenario occurring (such as having a panic attack on the TV show that she declined). As she would become anxious, she would practice her deep breathing but would also allow herself to more fully experience the anxiety than simply trying to minimize or avoid it. This gave her the emotional experience—not just the intellectual idea— not only that she could tolerate her anxiety, but that the catastrophes she feared were unlikely to occur (i.e., that she would be publicly humiliated and seen as incompetent). I also helped her see that she was socially quite skilled, and provided her with evidence that she was more capable and competent than she perceived herself to be (the third task). This eventually led her to feel more confident in her capacities to deal with her anxiety when it arose. The exposure work that we did together took the form of systematic desensitization, and her imagined scenarios all involved the TV show she had declined.

Cultural and social dimensions of Maria's struggles involved helping her recognize that although the racial taunting/bullying that she had experienced in school was utterly cruel and unjust, it had not occurred since her early teen years. She eventually found it helpful to acknowledge that although our society is not free from racism, she was not currently being overtly disadvantaged or oppressed because of her ethnicity. But that was a different matter than the economic hardships (LR) that her parents, and especially her extended family in Mexico, faced on a daily basis. Here, it was helpful to point out that although her family in Mexico truly lived in poverty, she was making a decent living as a chef, and there was no evidence that she could not continue to support herself while also sending some money to her extended family. Although such cognitive strategies are a far cry from ameliorating economic inequities among different social classes, it did seem to be one helpful component of managing her anxiety symptoms. The work I did with Maria emphasized the upper, individual quadrants, but we also addressed the lower quadrants—not only with respect to her culture (Mexican American, Catholic) and socioeconomic status, but also by using our therapeutic relationship as the foundation of our work together. When we ended our work together, Maria felt confident that if she were given another opportunity to be on a TV show, she would not hesitate to accept the offer. If you are interested in etiological factors and the treatment of Panic Disorder, Specific Phobia, Social Anxiety Disorder, Generalized Anxiety Disorder, and Obsessive-Compulsive Disorder, consult Ingersoll and Marquis (2014).

Conclusion

Hopefully this chapter has provided a glimpse of the breadth of treatment approaches and specific interventions that an integral psychotherapist uses when counseling patients with anxiety disorders, and how that manifested with a specific patient, Maria. A similarly broad array of integral intervention strategies applies to all mental disorders (see Ingersoll & Marquis, 2014). To return to anxiety disorders, a major theme that emerged from *Current Perspectives on the Anxiety Disorders: Implications for DSM-5 and Beyond* (McKay et al., 2009) was that a dimensional—rather than categorical—classification would vastly improve the diagnosis and treatment of anxiety disorders. Whereas categorical approaches assume that disorders arise from a relatively small number of causal factors, dimensional approaches assume that disorders result from the incremental effects of many factors. Dimensional approaches are much more consistent with current conceptualizations and research regarding the role of gene–environment interactions in psychiatric disorders (Taylor et al., 2009), all of which is consistent with an integral approach to unification in psychotherapy.

PART III
The Role of Research and Conclusion

CHAPTER 9

The Methodological Tower of Babel
Integral Methodological Pluralism in Psychotherapy Research[1]

This chapter considers various methodological issues pertinent to how psychotherapy—including a unified psychotherapeutic approach that is guided by a metatheory—can be systematically studied. The currently fragmented state of psychology and psychotherapy is briefly reviewed, and attempts at unification are suggested as a solution to this problem. The epistemological disparities of different research paradigms are examined, including the role that one's methodology plays in constraining the types of questions asked and thus the types of answers one is likely to find. Alternatives to empiricist-quantitative methodologies are considered, highlighting the need for methodological pluralism, and one specific form of this—integral methodological pluralism (IMP)—is outlined.

The Current State of Psychology and Psychotherapy: Fragmentation and the Need for Unification

Arthur Staats has been one of the most prominent critics of the dis-unification that characterizes the field of psychology, as well as arguably the most vocal proponent of the need for a unified psychology. As Staats has written:

> It is characteristic of the disunified science that almost no effort is made to establish relationships among [diverse phenomena] ... This is an essential feature of the faddishness that has been described, because no matter how much they pique our interest, isolated phenomena do not constitute subject matter for long-term study unless they are woven into a general fabric of expanding knowledge ... with the goal of establishing their relationships and the common underlying principles among them. (1991, p. 905)

---

[1] This chapter is adapted from Marquis, A. (2013). Methodological considerations of studying a unified approach to psychotherapy: Integral methodological pluralism. *Journal of Unified Psychotherapy and Clinical Science, 2* (1), 45–73.

Jack Anchin has similarly written eloquently on the need for unification in psychotherapy:

> unifying knowledge in any field of endeavor requires metatheory comprising a conceptual scaffolding that is sufficiently broad to encompass all of the specific knowledge domains distinctly pertinent to the field under consideration, that can serve as a coherent framework for systematically interrelating the essential knowledge elements within and among those domains. (2008, p. 325)

Although I want to cover some general epistemological issues first, let me say now that one of the primary purposes of this chapter is to demonstrate that the integral model provides a metatheoretical conceptual framework capable of weaving many disparate strands of knowledge together into a coherent, meaningful, and comprehensive fabric of knowledge.

Methodological Issues in Studying Unified Psychotherapies

Readers are likely aware that lists of "Empirically Supported Treatments" (ESTs) and "Best Practices" are created almost unilaterally by Random Clinical Trials (RCTs) that utilize experimental research designs, but there is also an extensive literature critiquing this convention (Andrews, 2000; Levant, 2004; Marquis & Douthit, 2006; Marquis, Douthit, & Elliot, 2011; Messer, 2001; Miller, 1998; Persons, 1991; Polkinghorne, 1999; Slife, 2004; Slife & Gantt, 1999; Slife, Wiggins, & Graham, 2005; Wampold, 1997; Westen & Morrison, 2001; Westen, Novotny, & Thompson-Brenner, 2004). Before proceeding with a brief critique of this methodological foreclosure, I want to stress that *we do not have to abandon the criterion of sound evidence to reject the narrow form of empiricism[2] that is currently threatening to monopolize—both ideologically and economically—psychotherapy research and practice.* I also want to point out that the hegemony with which narrow forms of science have been exerting control is reflected in phrases such as "*the* scientific method" rather than "*a* scientific method" or "scientific methods," which implies that there is only *one* method with which one can practice science, rather than many different logics of investigation that—although grounded in

---

2 Historically, empiricism was an epistemology that relied on *experience*—in contrast to abstract reason/logic or institutionalized religious authority. Originally, many forms of experience counted as valid evidence or data, ranging from externally observed phenomena to internal, subjective experience. William James (1978) outspokenly proposed a "radical empiricism" in which any consistently observed phenomenon—whether it was quantifiable or not—was considered valuable, legitimate data. If those data did not readily lend themselves to the methods of the natural sciences, then we would best advance our knowledge quest by devising novel methods, not by "acting out" our methodological "physics envy." Today's empiricism has been significantly narrowed: sensory experience (or data obtained via the extension of our senses, as with microscopes or telescopes) that can be "objectively" observed.

different philosophical assumptions and employing a variety of methods—nonetheless follow a scientific method that requires evidence for its theoretically formulated questions and hypotheses (Slife & Gantt, 1999; Marquis & Douthit, 2006). Before turning specifically to integral methodological pluralism (IMP), it is important, as backdrop, to address some epistemological disparities that have exerted a tremendous impact on the way psychotherapy research is funded, performed, and published.

Epistemological Disparities and the Need for a Pluralism of Methods

For approximately three decades, considerable debate has ensued regarding "mixed methods," "pluralistic," or "integrative" research, which Johnson and Onwuegbuzie (2004) define as *"the class of research where the researcher mixes or combines quantitative and qualitative research techniques, methods, approaches, concepts or language into a single study"* (p. 17, original italics). In contrast to integrative researchers, those favoring "empiricist-quantitative" approaches usually hierarchically prioritize "objective/behavioral" data, whereas those championing "hermeneutic-qualitative" approaches often overemphasize "subjective/phenomenological" and "intersubjective/hermeneutic" data (Esbjörn-Hargens, 2006). Kessel and Rosenfield (2008) highlighted some of the problematic aspects of hierarchical structures currently operating in and across disciplines, departments, and faculty lines (i.e., biomedical and other empirical/"objective" data are usually presumed to be more valid than social science data that are primarily phenomenological and/or interpretive in nature). Importantly, integral research includes both hierarchical and heterarchical components.[3]

Although it is beyond the scope of this chapter to address this issue in detail, integral metatheory differentiates between healthy and pathological forms of hierarchy (see Marquis, 2008), and there are some hierarchical developmental dynamics to which we should not be blind. For example, a researcher with the postformal cognitive capacity to view phenomena and dialectically consider data from multiple perspectives without unduly privileging one perspective or form of data over the others is (hierarchically) more cognitively developed and thus more competent to understand complex issues than a researcher who dogmatically/scientistically operates from only one perspective. At the same time, the heterarchical

---

[3] Integral metatheory uses the term *hierarchy* in its connotation (taken from the natural sciences, general systems theory, and structuralists such as Piaget) of involving developmental or evolutionary gradations of organization and wholeness, in which each subsequent stage or level of emergent capacities or structures is increasingly complex (i.e., from molecules to cells to organs to complex organisms). Whereas hierarchical organization involves the interaction of different developmental levels of complexity, heterarchical organization refers to the interaction or relating of entities or processes *within* a given level of developmental complexity: *"within* each level, heterarchy; *between* each level, hierarchy" (Wilber, 2000a, p. 28).

structure of the quadrants reminds us of the "central corollary [that] no discipline or perspective has permanent authorization over any others" (Kessel and Rosenfield, 2008, p. S232). In integral terms, consistently privileging one method or epistemology over another is called "quadrant absolutism." As I have previously written,

> to reduce the felt-experience of depression or anxiety (UL) to nothing but brain structures and neurotransmission (UR) is to subjugate lived experience to that which can be objectively observed and measured. Conversely, to disregard recent breakthroughs in neuroscience (UR) and explore only phenomenology (UL) would simply be the reverse form of "quadrant absolutism," in which one quadrant is consistently privileged, devaluing the important insights of the other three quadrants. Similar to intersubjective field theory, integral psychotherapy is a contextual perspective, and thus, experiential worlds (UL) and intersubjective cultural fields (LL), as well as observable behaviors and brain functions (UR) and social systems (LR) are viewed as "equiprimordial, mutually constituting one another in circular fashion" (Stolorow et al., 2002, p. 96). (Marquis, 2009, p. 17)

As Johnson and Turner (2003) point out, one of the fundamental principles of mixed method research is that it reduces the limits of each method (because the limits of one approach are complemented by the virtues of other approaches) while simultaneously maximizing the strength of each method (using each method to address its strong suit—i.e., traditional empiricism to quantitatively address observable behaviors and interactions, and hermeneutics to qualitatively disclose the meanings of those behaviors and interactions).[4] Although it is often asserted that empiricism is the superior epistemology because it is value-free or "neutral," that contention is untenable (Bartley, 1962; Polanyi, 1958; Polkinghorne, 1983), at least in matters pertaining to the social sciences. Detailed and sophisticated explications of this matter abound (Slife, 2004; Slife, Wiggins, & Graham, 2005; Wampold et al., 2005; Slife & Gantt, 1999; Bryceland & Stam, 2005). A simple version of the explanation states that a "value" signifies what matters—what we should attend to and what we can safely ignore. Although there are exceptions to this generalization,[5] the privileging of empiricism in psychology has more often than not resulted in psychologists directing most of their attention to constructs that are more readily quantified and externally observed than to important but interior processes and dynamics such as meanings, emotions, motivations, lived experience, spiritual experiences, and "what makes a life worth living."

---

4 It is precisely because each single method has both strengths and limitations that a very common phrase in integral literature is "true but partial."
5 For example, *Meditation and the Neuroscience of Consciousness* (Lutz, Dunne, & Davidson, 2007) and *The Framing of Decisions and the Psychology of Choice* (Tversky & Kahneman, 1981).

The Role of Research Questions and Research Methods

It is axiomatic that "methodology constrains both the kinds of questions that can be asked and the kinds of answers that can be provided" (Anchin, 2008, p. 337), and this should be emphasized to every clinician-in-training, researcher, and consumer of research. According to Staats, "There are various methods of research in psychology that produce observations that underlie divided positions, and *the methods themselves become the basis for division, opposition, and mutual ignorance,* even when related or complementary phenomena are involved" (1991, p. 906, italics added). At the heart of this issue is that the nature of our subject of inquiry (in this case, psychotherapy) should guide our choice of, and rationale for, our research methods. In contrast to this, traditional psychotherapy research tends to impose methodological foreclosure upon inquiry into the idiographic meanings of human suffering by insisting upon one narrow form of empiricism (the experimental design). Although I am a staunch advocate for the need for evidence, it can be argued that extreme objectivist declarations of empiricism's epistemological superiority—especially when it comes to psychotherapy and other human/social science research—are, at times, more of an ideological stance than a scientifically supported claim (Marquis & Douthit, 2006).[6]

The term "method*ology*" points not only to specific methods, but more importantly to the rationale or *underlying logic* justifying *why* a particular approach

---

[6] If I were a physicist, cosmologist, chemist, biologist, or other "hard" scientist, I doubt I would write about the limitations of empiricism. Unlike the "academic left" (Gross & Levitt, 1998), I have a deep appreciation and respect for the epistemological superiority of science over most other traditions - when it involves the domains studied by the natural and "hard" sciences. My critiques regarding the limitations of empiricism apply primarily to domains such as psychology, psychotherapy, and other social or "human sciences." As I have written elsewhere (Ingersoll & Marquis, 2014, p. 542):

> I consider myself—as did Michael Mahoney—a developmental or critical constructivist, in contrast to a radical constructivist or social constructionist. Although I believe that the latter—in their weak (moderate) forms—have some important insights that are relevant to counseling and psychotherapy, I concur with Gross and Levitt (1998) that in their strong (extreme) forms, cultural constructivism and social constructionism go too far in their declarations of science as just another discourse with no epistemological or ontological superiority to other knowledge claims. This is not to say that science cannot and does not at times devolve into scientism and fall prey to a host of errors . . . I stand behind my previously published critiques of the DSM, ESTs, and BPs but do *not* agree with social constructionists or cultural constructivists who suggest that science is nothing more than "a highly elaborated set of conventions brought forth by one particular culture (our own) in the circumstances of one particular period; thus it is not, as the standard view would have it, a body of knowledge and testable conjecture concerning the 'real' world" (Gross & Levitt, 1998, p. 45). This position states that the claims of science have no more validity about the nature of the external world than do the claims of other traditions (whether pre-modern religion or post-modern literary theory); it maintains that science is merely one discourse among many, with no privileged knowledge claims - never mind that it gave us understandings of gravity, thermodynamics, general relativity, the orbit of planets, atoms, the periodic table of elements, electricity, cells, microorganisms, germ theory, the laws of heredity, the structure of DNA, and evolution by natural selection.

or method is most appropriate for a specific investigative question. Essentially, a narrow form of empiricism and a methodological protocol borrowed from the natural sciences and medical drug research have resulted in a "culture of EST" that subverts in-depth intellectual discourse in the field of psychotherapy (Slife, Wiggins, & Graham, 2005; Wampold et al., 2005). A related point here is that key variables involved in successful outcomes that have tremendous empirical support from non-EST protocols—such as the therapeutic relationship (Norcross, 2011) or the personal qualities of the therapist (Beutler et al., 2004)—are notoriously ignored in EST research. Thus, approaches that emphasize dimensions of human experience that are either not readily observable or are difficult or impossible to manualize are excluded from being "empirically supported" by the values inherent in the method, not as a result of appropriately designed research consistently demonstrating their inferiority to cognitive behavioral therapies.

Despite my critiques, I am *not* advocating total abandonment of EST/RCT designs. In fact, I believe they are appropriate and useful when studying people whose problems involve well-circumscribed symptoms that are associated with specific stimuli, as in the case of specific phobias, some PTSD, and some obsessive-compulsive symptoms (Westen, Novotny, & Thompson-Brenner, 2004). However, for the majority of clinical conditions, I believe there are many viable alternatives that offer less violating methodologies vis-à-vis the question at hand. While I am a strong proponent of having some form of evidence or warrant for one's psychotherapy approach, I also think that it is particularly important to ask: "what constitutes valid evidence?" And here enter some of the deleterious effects of our field's notorious "philosophobia" (Mahoney, 2005, p. 338). A greater understanding of epistemology and more attention to the *process of inquiry* and appropriately matching a pluralism of methodologies to specific research questions—rather than "methodolatry" (idolatrous, absolutistic worship of a single method)—would serve our field well. As Miller emphasized, "the traditional experimental methods of validating clinical knowledge claims that we have taught our students for several generations are *necessarily and inevitably inadequate and incomplete*" (1998, p. 249, original italics).

As stated earlier, the nature of our subject of inquiry should guide our choice of methods, not vice versa. Thus, if all we are interested in are a person's observable behaviors or the activity of different brain regions, then a narrow form of empiricism is justifiable. If, on the other hand, interior dynamics such as self-esteem, meaning, or relationship satisfaction are our subject of study, then methods such as phenomenology or hermeneutics are more suited to the task.[7] Just because these

---

[7] At the same time, it is important to bear in mind that although empiricism cannot disclose phenomenological experience, interior dimensions can be studied in ways that are more objective or scientific, by which I technically mean "an outside view of interiors," which is a "zone 2" methodology (Wilber, 2006; this will be discussed in more depth subsequently); a good example of this is Shedler's (2010) overview of many meta-analyses of the efficacy of psychodynamic therapy, the latter of which is concerned largely with interior experiences and dynamics such as emotions, distressing thoughts

methods are qualitative and more "subjective" does not mean they are not also rigorous methods—*when performed properly*—that are capable of considerable degrees of reliability within communities competently trained to work with these forms of inquiry. In general, I would like to see an increased appreciation of the value of case-based research, naturalistic effectiveness studies, and a conception of clinical practice as a natural laboratory, or at least a more mutually informed relationship between experimental research scientists, clinical practitioners, and clinical subjects (Seligman, 1995; Edwards, Dattilio, & Bromley, 2004; Miller, 1998). I also recommend a shift away from psychotherapy research in which investigators prescribe specific step-by-step interventions to the study of more *empirically informed principles* of treatment. While I am certainly not suggesting a retreat from science, I am arguing that methodologically pluralistic approaches to psychotherapy research honor not only narrow forms of empiricism that have been adapted from the biomedical sciences, but evidence that is more broadly defined, including clinical practice, case formulation approaches, and hermeneutic and other interpretive forms of inquiry, as a *means* to our ultimate professional purpose: serving the well-being of those who seek psychotherapy.

Alternatives to Empiricist-Quantitative Methodologies

Many thoughtful alternatives to quantitative empiricism have been proposed. In fact, in addition to numerous volumes explicating what the most appropriate methodologies are for human/social science research (Giorgi, 1970; Polkinghorne, 1983; Hoyrup, 2000; Denzin & Lincoln, 2005), the *Journal of Clinical Psychology* devoted an entire issue to the topic of "How Can Research Discover How to Do Psychotherapy?" (1999, volume 55, issue 12). Other methodologies appropriate to investigating psychotherapy and providing evidence for different therapeutic approaches include but are not limited to: systematic analyses of case studies (Schneider, 1999; Edwards, Dattilio, & Bromley, 2004); naturalistic effectiveness studies (Seligman, 1995); intensive analyses of concrete-change performances (Greenberg, 1999); "discovery-oriented psychotherapy research" (Mahrer & Boulet,

---

and feelings, fantasy life, interpersonal relations, and so forth. The fact that CBTs are still vastly over-represented on lists of ESTs and "Best Practices"—compared to psychodynamic approaches—is of significant concern, especially when one considers that:

> Effect sizes for psychodynamic therapy are as large as those reported for other therapies that have been actively promoted as "empirically supported" and "evidence based." In addition, patients who receive psychodynamic therapy maintain therapeutic gains and appear to continue to improve after treatment ends ... The perception that psychodynamic approaches lack empirical support does not accord with available scientific evidence and may reflect selective dissemination of research findings. (Shedler, 2010, p. 98)

I and others have argued that this selective dissemination of research reflects the privilege granted to RCTs and other studies that follow experimental designs.

1999); hermeneutics and qualitative methods in general (Gadamer, 1989; Ricoeur, 1970); clinical/anecdotal research (Miller, 1998; Miller & Crabtree, 2005); case formulation approaches (Persons, 1991); and inquiries into how the qualities of therapists interact with qualities of patients to produce favorable or poor outcomes (Beutler & Clarkin, 1990).

Because all unified approaches to psychotherapy attempt to conceptualize and address multiple dimensions of patients and what will be the most effective course of treatment for them, it should be clear that the study of unified approaches to psychotherapy will need to follow some form of *methodological pluralism*. Before turning specifically to "integral methodological pluralism," I encourage complementing EST and other experimental research with some or all of the above methodologies. It is vitally important that we deeply ponder what it would mean to base our entire social science primarily, if not solely, upon externally observable phenomena. How would that render concepts such as meanings, values, compassion, and care? *We need not abandon scientific rigor to supplement empiricism with other methodologies!* Given the alternative methods of inquiry listed above, how might researchers choose which methods are most appropriate to the subject in question? Integral metatheory (Wilber, 2000a; Wilber, 2000b; Marquis, 2008) provides a comprehensive framework within which diverse methodologies complement and enrich, rather than contradict, one another, and this promotes a deeper understanding of the subject at hand.

Integral Methodological Pluralism

> We need many theory works that relate the different methods and their types of findings to one another, to show their complementarity, rather than using differences to disunify... The problem in this case is *how these separate areas of knowledge can be put together in a manner that enhances rather than discredits each* ... theories on each side should be valued for the extent to which they can incorporate and make heuristic the knowledge on both sides. (Staats, 1991, p. 906, italics added)

An integral approach to psychotherapy research calls for an integration of research methodologies—honoring the values and limits of each approach—and anticipates that a coherently organized pluralism of inquiries—an integral methodological pluralism (IMP)—will help advance our understanding of psychotherapy process and outcome far more than one narrowly defined form of empiricism. A key feature of the integral model is that it provides a conceptual scaffolding with which many of the parochial and acrimonious methodological debates can be transformed into mutually enriching dialogues, hopefully facilitating both humility in each camp's claims to total knowledge and a heightened curiosity about how other perspectives can enrich one's own perspective. Perhaps most importantly, *IMP prioritizes the research question*, and *then* determines the most appropriate research method(s) with which to address a particular research question, rather than

Integral Methodological Pluralism 217

prioritize a certain method, and subsequently inquire into only those questions that that method can appropriately address.

To elaborate, recall Figure 2.1 (p. 22, chapter 2), which displays different dimensions of patients and their suffering (experience, behavior, cultural worldview, social systems) as well as some prominent theorists (Freud and Rogers [UL], Skinner and Beck [UR], Stolorow et al. and Wachtel [LL], and Minuchin and Gottman [LR]). Not immediately evident in Figure 2.1 is that the perspective of each quadrant also corresponds to our major epistemological traditions. Reminiscent of the parable of the blind men arguing about what the elephant actually was, systematically integrating methodologies from these quadratic perspectives would mutually inform each perspective, as well as enrich the communicative exchange between researchers and clinicians. A simplified example of methodologies from each of the four quadrants appears in Figure 9.1.

Figure 9.1 reveals that *an* integral approach transcends dichotomous positions; I emphasize "an" (not "the") because there is not just one integral approach— integral metatheory is a broad framework capable of assimilating and accommodating tremendous diversity such that *how* one practices and researches in an

Upper-Left (UL): Interior-Individual: *Experience* General Epistemology: Phenomenology For example: Phenomenological analysis of patients' experiences of therapy (Rogers, Bugental, May) and patient self reports	Upper-Right (UR): Exterior-Individual: *Behavior* General Epistemology: Empiricism For example: Empirical investigations, from EST/RCT methodologies to other "objective" approaches such as neuroscience (Damasio, Siegel, LeDoux), applied behavioral analysis, and patient task/test performance
Lower-Left (LL): Interior-Collective: *Culture* General Epistemology: Hermeneutics For example: Interpretive inquiry (Ricoeur, Gadamer, Giorgi) including hermeneutic investigations of the intersubjectivity/in-betweenness/fit of patient and therapist (Stolorow et al.; Beutler & Clarkin) as well as information provided by the patient's friends, family members, co-workers, etc.	Lower-Right (LR): Exterior-Collective: *Systems* General Epistemology: Systemic/ecological analyses For example: Systemic analyses (including videotaped sessions) such as Greenberg's intensive observation, measurement, and analyses of concrete-change performances; as well as how patient and therapist engagement evolves; any other external analyses of systems such as environmental consequences that impact patient outcomes; and observations/evaluations by blind, unbiased, and trained "expert" observers

Figure 9.1 The Four Quadrants and Associated Epistemologies

"integrally informed" manner affords much idiographic nuance to each therapist or researcher as a function of one's prior training, personality, and other proclivities.[8] Integral metatheory suggests that no single perspective or methodology should be inherently privileged over others in all cases. Although a specific approach to inquiry may be more appropriate than another based upon a host of factors (i.e., quadrants, levels, lines, states, types, etc.), no single methodology consistently dominates within an integral paradigm. All of the available epistemologies—from traditional empirical methods to hermeneutics, phenomenology, and others—are components of IMP, which investigates its subject of inquiry with the methodologies of all four quadrants, and then triangulates/ "tetra-correlates" the data from those diverse methodologies to form a coherent understanding (Esbjörn-Hargens, 2006).

The Quadrants as Theoretical Bridges

IMP appears to offer the possibility of becoming what Staats (1991, 1999) referred to as a "bridging theory," in which disparate knowledge elements are coherently integrated into a more comprehensive, unified body of knowledge. Although the integral literature has yet to analyze in detail many of the differences between therapies that emphasize different quadratic perspectives (or the methodologies that likewise derive from different quadratic perspectives), the quadratic model does nonetheless appear to be a promising candidate to demonstrate how "discrepant theoretical perspectives can in fact be put together, thereby productively interrelating the knowledge encompassed by each" (Anchin, 2008, p. 316). Thus, even though integral metatheory may not yet constitute a true, formal bridging theory,[9] Staats also emphasized that:

> Once the nature of the task of constructing a grand theory is described, it becomes evident that a detailed treatment of all the elements of knowledge is not possible; there are too many... the task that results requires that the first grand, unified theories be frameworks, skeletons, and outlines, rather than complete (detailed) theories. (1991, p. 908)

---

8 If it seems confusing that thus far the word "integral" seems to have been used as designating a specific—i.e., Wilber's—metatheoretical approach, whereas in this sentence it seems that the word is being used in a more general adjectival sentence, this will be clarified in a few pages in the discussion of integral metatheory as "content-free." In short, although integral theorists posit the necessity of accounting for and integrating all four quadratic perspectives—whether in clinical practice or a program of research—precisely *how* one does that is left to the individual (recall p. 155 in chapter 7).

9 Some might argue that the quadratic model of integral metatheory is more of an "eclectic mixture" than a "true bridging theory" (Staats, 1991, p. 908), and at this point in time that may be true. Nonetheless, I do not see any reason why, with the continued work of many scholars and researchers, integral metatheory could not eventually develop into a fully fledged bridging theory.

Although the quadrants are currently primarily a skeletal framework, with only some surrounding flesh already developed, it does offer a coherent metatheoretical justification for how and why to reconcile not only the primary methodological differentiation—that between the empiricist-quantitative paradigm and the hermeneutic-qualitative paradigm (represented by the left and right quadrants)—but also the fundamental disparity between a focus on decontextualized individuals in contrast to contextualized systems (represented by the upper and lower quadrants). Moreover, it not only acknowledges that "personality, psychopathological phenomena, and psychotherapeutic processes and outcomes are investigated with widely varying methods of inquiry ... [it also] *values as equally legitimate and important the distinctly different 'ways of knowing'*" (Anchin, 2008, pp. 320–321, italics added) that the different methodologies afford. As Yanchar and Slife wrote, "all methods presumably come attuned to certain aspects of reality, while being blind to other aspects of reality ... Therefore, the value of methodological pluralism—indeed, the genuine strength of methodological pluralism—lies in its ability to provide such diverse profiles of psychological life and to join them into an integrated whole" (1997, p. 246).

As a unifying metatheory, IMP also "extends conceptual tendrils into other fields of study" (Anchin, 2008, p. 325). This interdisciplinary aspect of IMP—what Staats (1991) referred to as the "interfield" component of unification—is critical because it encourages a rich cross-fertilization of knowledge elements from different fields of knowledge. Along these lines, Esbjörn-Hargens stated that the integral model is

> *multidisciplinary* (e.g., helping to investigate ecological phenomena from multiple disciplines), *interdisciplinary* (e.g., helping to apply methods from political science to psychological investigation) and *transdisciplinary* (e.g., helping numerous disciplines and their methodologies interface through a content-free network). (2006, p. 82, original italics)

The "content-free" aspect of the integral model is a key feature because it "provides this unifying framework without the exclusionary processes that place constraints on the ontology of psychotherapy" (Anchin, 2008, p. 328).[10] A content-free framework denotes that although integral theorists posit the necessity of accounting for and integrating all four quadratic perspectives—whether in clinical practice or a program of research—precisely *how* one does that is left to the individual. For example, with regard to research, one can investigate the Upper-Right quadrant with applied behavioral analysis or neuroscience (Marquis &

---

10 Although Anchin wrote this with regard to the biopsychosocial systems framework, it is equally true of the integral model.

Douthit, 2006), just as one can clinically practice from the Upper-Left quadrant with a traditional psychoanalytic or person-centered approach (Marquis, 2009).

Dialectics Are Inherent to Quadratic Thinking

"In view of the singular manner in which it ontologically embraces and methodologically tackles opposition and contradiction, dialectical thinking constitutes an approach to inquiry and formulation strikingly suited to the formulation of unifying bridging theories" (Anchin, 2008, p. 319). The quadrants, in my view, are an epitome of such dialectical thinking—they explicitly emphasize the imperative need to consider conclusions and principles that derive from historically opposing perspectives.[11] Although dialectics have been described in numerous different ways, essential to them is the tension generated by simultaneously holding bipolarities in mind;[12] it is this tension that often generates novel insights that are unlikely to emerge without deeply considering the dynamic interplay of what appear to be contradictory or oppositional elements. As Anchin (2008) writes:

> The persistent core challenge confronting efforts at unification is coming to grips with a multiplicity of theoretical perspectives and the vast array of knowledge elements and modes of methodologically and clinically operating to which those perspectives collectively give rise. Nevertheless, once it is explicitly recognized that this *apparent* opposition between plurality and unity is in point of fact an overarching dialectic, the way is opened toward forging highly productive resolutions. (Anchin, 2008, p. 342; italics added)

In this vein, although the empiricist-quantitative and hermeneutic-qualitative paradigms derive from opposed foundational assumptions regarding what constitutes legitimate knowledge, it is crucial to consider that the different perspectives and their associated methodologies only *appear* contradictory, incompatible, or incommensurable; it is more appropriate to view them as complementary, deeply interconnected, and mutually enriching (Fay, 1996; Magnavita, 2008). In short, "both/and" thinking will advance and deepen our understandings of complex phenomena far more than "either/or" thinking. In my view, IMP offers a parsimonious theoretical justification for why and how to apply dialectics to a program of research, recognizing that each method/perspective, "being an integral part of the whole, contains distinctly valid elements of knowledge about the phenomenon or process under consideration. This type of conceptual analysis and

---

11 Unless you can take alternative, competing perspectives of your own position, you likely do not fully understand the position you espouse.
12 This type of dialectical thinking is a key feature of what Wilber terms the "vision-logic" stage of development, which bears similarity to Commons and Richards' (1984) four orders of "postformal" thinking: systematic, metasystematic, paradigmatic, and cross-paradigmatic thinking.

interactional investigation ... can deepen understanding of a phenomenon or process and offers the potentiality for formulating expanded, more encompassing conceptualizations" (Anchin, 2008, pp. 317–318).

Given that the focus of this chapter is on methodological issues that are relevant to studying psychotherapy, I want to suggest that the *very boundaries* (such as interior/qualitative and exterior/quantitative; individual and collective) *that divide therapists and researchers can also simultaneously connect them.* Strict empirical methods will never disclose the qualities of lived-experience or what makes a life worth living, just as phenomenology will never reveal the neurobiological underpinnings of our experience. Is it not becoming increasingly clear that our understanding of human nature, psychopathology, and change processes will be augmented by a metatheoretical scaffolding that honors the validity of different epistemologies, recognizes the limits of each, and provides a systematic way to organize them such that the different approaches synergistically complement, rather than contradict, one another? Simply consider the differences between radical behaviorism and classical psychoanalysis. Their divergent conclusions are a predictable outcome of polar assumptions. Skinner (1953) posited that the only data worth studying are externally observable behaviors and environmental contingencies, while Freud (1963) was primarily concerned not only with internal experience but also largely unconscious determinants of that experience. Skinner privileged looking at that which was externally observable; Freud privileged "looking" from within. It is not that one of them was right and the other wrong. They were both partially correct and both incomplete ("true but partial") because neither looked at the subject matter from more than one perspective (Marquis & Douthit, 2006).

Because phenomena as complex as human nature, suffering, and psychotherapy involve not only the dimension-perspectives of the four quadrants but also of levels, lines, types, and states, I argue that any approach that calls itself "empirically supported" or "evidence based" and proceeds to systematically exclude any of the major methodological systems (phenomenology, hermeneutics, empiricism, systems analyses, etc.) that appropriately elucidate pertinent dimensions of psychotherapy is dangerously narrow in scope. In fact, I suggest that this sort of hegemonic oversimplification (that characterizes the preponderance of experimental designs in psychotherapy research, as well as the biased dissemination of psychotherapy research that follows experimental designs) is largely what is responsible for the perceived incommensurability between research and practice that so many psychotherapists lament.

From the Four Quadrants to the Eight Zones

To add another level of complexity to this overview of IMP, *the domains of each of the four quadrants can also be viewed from the inside and the outside,* yielding "eight zones" and their associated perspectives, each of which has its own general research methodology (see Figure 9.2). Wilber has termed the sum total of those eight views "Integral Perspectivism," and the enactment of those eight methodologies

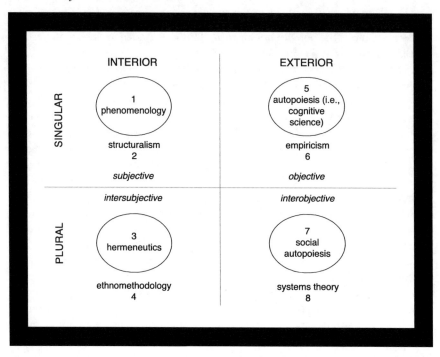

Figure 9.2. The Eight Zones and their Associated Methodologies. [13]

Adapted from Wilber (2006), pp. 36–37.

"Integral Methodological Pluralism" (Wilber, 2006, pp. 34–35). In case Figure 9.2 is not completely clear, I will attempt to explain it by speaking briefly about zones 1 and 2 and their associated methodologies. If we—as researchers—are interested primarily in inquiring into an aspect of an individual (for the sake of a simple example, in a micro/de-contextualized manner; therefore, one of the upper quadrants), our first choice of perspective and methodology involves whether we are going to inquire into interiors (attitudes, thoughts, feelings, motivations, fears; UL) or exteriors (behaviors, measurable brain activity, and other biomedically relevant processes that are measurable; UR). For the sake of this discussion, we will explore an individual's interiors.

To continue with the example, one of the things Figure 9.2 reveals is that we can actually study aspects of *any* of the four quadrants from either the *inside* (zones 1, 3, 5, 7—what is inside each of the four circles in Figure 9.2) or the *outside* (zones 2, 4, 6, 8). The disciplines of structuralism and phenomenology both inquire into the interiors of individuals—and are thus both UL paradigms—but they do so from different perspectives. Phenomenological approaches explore individual interiors

---

13 There are a number of critiques regarding the construct of social autopoiesis (see Mingers, 1992).

from *inside* the person's own perspective and thus the methods include practices such as introspection, phenomenological bracketing, and meditation; the data disclosed are felt-senses, images, impressions, intuitions, and other subjective experiences. However, the interior of individuals can also be studied from the *outside*— from a *more* objective or "scientific" perspective—and the general school of structuralism is a prime example of this perspective and methodology. Structural approaches, such as Piaget's (1977) work, explore internal processes—such as the mental structures or schemas with which a person perceives and construes self and world—but they "step back" and analyze and explain those internal processes as objectively as possible (as from the outside looking in). The stages (structures) of cognitive development that Piaget posited (or the stages/structures of any school of structuralism, from Kohlberg to Loevinger) will never present themselves to a person engaging in a phenomenological practice, even though their subjective experiences are governed or influenced, at least in part, by those very structures.[14] Thus, it is not so much that the data of either of those disciplines disconfirm or contradict the claims made by the other camp so much as they complement one another—precisely because they are looking at the same domain, an individual's interior, from different perspectives and with different methods. This point is evident in *The Structure of Scientific Revolutions*, in which Kuhn (1962) repeatedly emphasized that scientists working within different communities live in different worlds, referring to their perceiving and paying attention to different stimuli as a function of their discipline's paradigm. Fifteen years later, Kuhn further stated that "*members of different communities are presented with different data by the same stimuli*" (1977, p. 309; italics added).

An important point is that each of the eight methodological families in Figure 9.2 is an umbrella term that includes many distinct methods, each of which will disclose different data as a function of that method's perspective. For example, the umbrella of phenomenology includes but is not limited to introspection, Husserlian epoche/bracketing, and meditation; the umbrella of ethnomethodology includes but is not limited to ethnography, genealogy, archaeology, semiotics, and cultural studies (Esbjörn-Hargens, 2006). Wilber stressed that the eight perspectives and their associated methodologies are far from mere abstractions:

> We inhabit these eight spaces, these zones, these lifeworlds, as practical realities. Each of these zones is not just a perspective, but an action, an injunction, a concrete set of actions in a real world zone. Each injunction *brings forth* or discloses the phenomena that are apprehended through the various perspectives. It is not that perspectives come first and action or injunctions

---

14 Of course, to fully understand a person's interiors, we need to study not only zones 1 and 2, but also the other six zones. Collective dynamics—whether social systems (LR; zones 7 and 8) or cultural practices (LL; zones 3 and 4)—are profoundly influential in an individual's subjective experience, as are behaviors and neurobiological processes (UR; zones 5 and 6).

come later; they simultaneously co-arise (actually, tetra-arise). (2006, p. 34, parentheses and italics in original)

The above quote reveals the mutually constitutive nature of theories and their methods: not only do specific research methods derive from specific disciplines (or a specific theory within a discipline), *different research methods and their associated epistemologies actually yield different theories*. All of the available research traditions and their corresponding practices are crucial components of an IMP that attempts to address as many relevant variables as possible—in an effort to serve the diversity of our patients and their discontents.

In Staats' view, a truly unifying theory includes four key elements. It will begin as a broad, skeletal *framework* that will be "filled in" theoretically and empirically by many individuals. Given that there is a hierarchical structure to the different fields within psychology—which does *not* mean that any one level is more important or significant than any other (Staats, 1991, 1999)—such a unified theory will also need to be *interlevel* (or *multilevel*) and demonstrate how the different levels are interrelated. In addition to being interlevel, a unified psychology would also contain *interfield* dimensions; similar to how biology is bridged with chemistry, and chemistry with physics, psychology would be bridged with other fields of study, such as neurobiology, sociology, and so forth. Finally, *a proper unified theory would also unify with other unified theories*.

Integral metatheory has either already met, or has the potential to meet, all of Staats' elemental criteria. Regarding the first, it clearly provides a skeletal framework that can be mapped theoretically and empirically by a vast array of individuals. Relative to Staats' second element, integral metatheory's developmental model—briefly addressed in chapter 2 and more fully addressed in chapter 3—indeed affords multiple opportunities with which to connect and organize different subfields within psychology. For example, if you consider the behavior of a human being, it is a function of dynamics that also apply to animals of less developmental complexity (i.e., classical and operant conditioning, basic neurochemical processes) as well as more developmentally complex dynamics (the ability to abstract, capacities to serve others' needs rather than one's own immediate desires, deliberative processes that include a discontinuity between stimuli and one's responses, and some measure of exercising one's will—all of which provide the possibility that humans are not completely determined by forces external to themselves). With regard to the third element, the quadrants can be used not only to organize different aspects of psychotherapy, as demonstrated in Figure 2.1, but also to organize and link different fields. In this respect, it is important to note that different fields of study emphasize different quadratic perspectives (i.e., UR/physics; LR/ecology; LL/sociology; UL/art). The quadrants and the respective fields of study housed by each offer a systematic framework for studying, demonstrating, and understanding interfield relationships. Moreover, this framework for organizing phenomena studied by different fields corresponds with an essential component of integral metatheory's developmental model: specifically, the emergence of unique properties at each subsequent stage of developmental complexity (i.e.,

Integral Methodological Pluralism 225

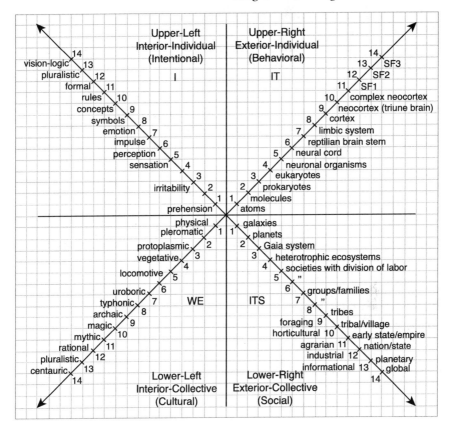

Figure 9.3 A quadratic view of the evolution of developmental complexity. From *The Fourth Turning*, by K. Wilber, 2014. Reprinted by arrangement with Shambhala Publications, Inc., Boston, MA.

physics studies the realm of matter; biology studies emergent properties of life; psychology studies emergent properties of mind, and so forth). Although an emergent domain (such as mind) is deeply interrelated with prior domains (such as matter and life), subsequent emergent complexity cannot be reduced to the prior levels (Margolis, 1986; Miller, 1978; Henriques, 2011). Wilber has demonstrated how phenomena in each of the four quadrants evolve through levels of increasing complexity (see Figure 9.3).

Finally, integral metatheory is fully capable of being integrated and unified with other unified theories. For example, Michael Mahoney and I wrote an article on "Integral Constructivism," in which we addressed the mutual resonance and convergence of his developmental constructivism (considered by many [i.e., Magnavita, 2008] to be a unified approach) with integral metatheory (Mahoney & Marquis, 2002), and numerous parallels and convergences between the integral model and both Magnavita's (2008) *component system model* and Henriques'

(2011) *new unified theory of psychology* have been drawn (Magnavita, Marquis, & Henriques, 2010).

Thus far, I have emphasized the quadratic aspects of IMP. However, no discussion of epistemological issues and their role in psychotherapy research would be complete without at least briefly touching upon how a researcher's developmental dynamics, her personality type, and her understanding and appreciation of different states of consciousness affect the type of research questions she is likely to consider important, the methods used to inquire into those issues, and the competence with which the data are analyzed. For example, the cognitive complexity of a researcher is critical to his expertise as a researcher. If you consider for a moment how many scholars have considered dialectical thinking (a capacity that emerges after formal operations) to be imperative to methodological pluralism and other issues pertinent to unification, it is immediately apparent that some researchers—although they may be talented within a narrow subfield and/or with one specific method—do not seem cognitively capable of dialectical thinking; they think in "either/or" terms rather than "both/and," and this places profound constraints upon what they are capable of considering and understanding. With regard to personality types, recall William James' (1978) description of tough- and tender-minded personalities. Whereas tough-minded people tend to be more empirical/fact-oriented, deterministic, and skeptical, tender-minded people tend to be more rational/principle-oriented, "free-willist," and dogmatic. It should not be too difficult to see how such different personality characteristics are likely to influence the type of data and methods a person will privilege in their research. However, such "type" issues interact with developmental dynamics; as a person develops more cognitive complexity, she is increasingly likely to recognize the strengths and limitations of each style, rather than manifest a more unidimensional, "pure" form of the personality style. Finally, if a researcher does not understand or appreciate the significance of altered states of consciousness (whether those of psychosis and dissociation or those achieved by advanced meditators or the greatest athletes, artists, musicians, poets, and so forth), factoring in the pertinent state(s) of consciousness as a critical variable in one's research will not be a priority, and thus the researcher is prone to systematic blind spots in his analyses and conclusions.

IMP Is Scalable

In order for a research project to be "fully integral," all eight zones and their associated methodologies would need to be implemented, a tall order indeed. However, an appealing aspect of IMP involves its *scalability*. In other words, provided that research accounts for the perspectives and methodologies that correspond to the four quadrants, the basic premise of IMP is accomplished (Wilber, 2006; Esbjörn-Hargens, 2006). The more resources one has (from financial funds and time to specific methodological and analytical skills), the more fully research could integrate methods from each of the eight zones, incorporate perspectives addressing the most relevant developmental *levels* and *lines*, as well as take into account different *types* of people and their *states* of consciousness.

Despite its brevity, it is hoped that this introduction to IMP has given the reader a sense of its potential as a unifying framework with which to study psychotherapy in more holistic, comprehensive, and coherent ways.

Conclusion

Even if we were not concerned about unification in psychotherapy, the volume and significance of the extant critiques of traditional psychotherapy research suffice to warrant major changes in the structure of such research. I further contend that a coherently organized methodological pluralism in psychotherapy research is an essential component of psychotherapy becoming increasingly unified, and suggest integral methodological pluralism (IMP) as a strong candidate for providing such a unified conceptual framework. Research recently published in the *Journal of Unified Psychotherapy and Clinical Science*—the Integral Psychotherapy in Practice study (Marquis & Elliot, 2015; Marquis et al., 2015)—is one small step in this direction, as well as an example of a "scaled down" version of IMP, in which a battery of quantitative and qualitative assessment instruments were administered to both patient-participants and therapist-participants, including pre-treatment, at regular intervals throughout treatment and post-treatment, and all sessions were videoed for analyses.

CHAPTER **10**

Conclusion[1]

If you have made it this far, we have covered quite a lot of ground together: human development; clinical assessment; the development of psychopathology; therapeutic treatment interventions, principles and change processes; and psychotherapy research. Thank you for your time and attention! In concluding this book, I want to reiterate a few things I stated earlier in the book. First, this represents my current views of what integral psychotherapy is. I am sure that what I write 10 and 20 years from now will include many additions and revisions to what I have written here. Second, in attempting to unify so many domains, I have likely failed to do justice to all of the details of various approaches and disciplines. You have likely made an assessment of how well I have managed this challenge; I hope the "forest" that I sketched here is sufficiently valuable to compensate for any individual "trees" that I may have oversimplified or not attended to enough. It is important to emphasize that iPT is an ongoing theoretical and applied endeavor that is currently in a relatively early stage of its development, and thus requires further development and refinement. While fairly in-depth understandings of individual quadrants and developmental levels have been achieved, less is known regarding the ways in which they interact and reciprocally influence each other, as well as specific clinical implications for many of those interactions.

I do not want to gloss over the difficulty of thoroughly implementing integrally informed psychotherapy or any other unified approach; it is not easy to become well-versed and competent in domains of systems that span "from neurons to neighborhoods" (Magnavita, 2008, p. 287). Not only must one master—or at least become competent in—processes across the spectrum of psychotherapeutic approaches; ideally, the many interactions, reverberations, and complications between the various quadratic, developmental, and state-related phenomena would be understood and appropriately attended to—a very tall order indeed. Fortunately, we need not burden ourselves with having to master all of this immediately;

---

1 Parts of this chapter are drawn from Marquis, A. & Elliot, A. (2015). Integral psychotherapy in practice part 2: Revisions to the metatheory of integral psychotherapy based on therapeutic practice. *Journal of Unified Psychotherapy and Clinical Science* 3 (1), 1–40.

unified psychotherapies—like psychotherapy integration in general—do not represent a specific school or orientation, but rather a continual *process* of exploration, understanding, and development. When one considers the complexity of implementing such a unified system of therapy, it seems more than warranted for integrally informed therapists to seek supervision from others who are practicing integrally informed psychotherapy—even if it is leaderless, or peer, supervision.

By their very nature and level of abstraction, metatheoretical approaches that strive to unify psychotherapy may appear to be removed to a certain degree from the concrete, the moment-to-moment, and the experiential. Nevertheless, the goals of the integral endeavor are ultimately practical ones aimed at enhancing the effectiveness of psychotherapy for as many patients as possible. A greater emphasis on affective states and other process issues—such as those discussed in chapters 3 and 7—may help make integral theory less structure-focused and more embodied, experiential, and applicable. As with any approach, while omissions and limitations are inevitable, it is hoped that integral psychotherapy will continue to develop and incorporate emerging research findings and additional theoretical perspectives. As I quoted in chapter 1, "any system guided by principles of unification is necessarily an evolving one, and by its very metatheoretical nature is equipped with both the scope and continuing capacity to incorporate new findings from clinical science" (Anchin & Magnavita, 2006, p. 28).

While discussing the role of theory with regard to basic principles of psychological change, Mahoney (1991) emphasized that the most important task is

> to choose a "conceptual base camp" from which to operate while one continues the explorations that constitute "The Work" of learning to comfort and to facilitate development. Such a base camp must, I believe, be pliable, portable, and itself capable of development, so that one's deep-felt commitments can be anchored in its abstractions while, simultaneously, one's unfinished lessons can be pursued within its moving expanse. (p. 266)

Given that we all have "unfinished lessons," one of the most important implications for practice (at least for integral psychotherapists) is to read far beyond the integral literature—including but not limited to relational, cultural, emotion-focused, social-systemic, and neurobiological literatures as well as the extant literature pertaining to integrative and unified approaches. Integralists, like everyone else, must remember that "there is always something more to be learned and that our own perspective is limited and therefore mistaken insofar as we take it to be the whole truth" (Stolorow, Atwood, & Orange, 2002, p. 111). Hence, even integral theory is "true but partial." Although a comprehensively unifying conceptual framework such as integral theory is important both epistemologically and practically, it does nothing to ensure any given individual's competence in the specific components that must fill that framework.

A core tenet of this book is that people are complex and multidimensional; they inhabit different developmental worlds and their suffering derives from a multitude of causes, ranging from their neurobiology, lack of positive reinforcement for adaptive behaviors, maladaptive cognitions, being emotionally under- or over-regulated, to the choices they make and a host of unhealthy familial and sociocultural dynamics and inequitable social arrangements. If this is true, then therapists need to conceptualize and practice in a manner that brings together such multidimensionality; the integral framework facilitates this.

By offering a parsimonious set of conceptual tools with which to integrate clinical information spanning myriad dimensions of human beings and their afflictions, an integral sensibility facilitates comprehensive, unified treatment. Nevertheless, it is impossible for any theory—even a metatheory—to actually account for *all* phenomena within a given domain or discipline. Overreach in attempts at explanation may itself become a limitation, rendering the approach excessively abstract and intellectual in the theoretically based yet ultimately applied realm of psychotherapy. Such overreach relates to one of the possible "shadows" of some integral adherents—something akin to a Cartesian quest for certainty that appears to function to defensively allay the feelings of uncertainty, ambiguity, and chaos that are so prominent in the practice of a comprehensively unified psychotherapy. In contrast, dynamic systems theorists (Thelen & Smith, 1994; Anchin, 2008; Mahoney, 1991) have posited that most psychological processes involve chaos, process, and emergence—which are not well conceived by binary logic and simple "either–ors." An excessive need for clarity and lack of ambiguity can potentially result in subtle reductionisms, such as privileging one or two quadrants over the others. To ward against our falling prey to such reductionisms, we can adopt a fallibilistic attitude and a devotion to dialogue with practitioners, theorists, and researchers from other perspectives, always remembering that our work

> requires an underlying tolerance of uncertainty and with it a radical, yet critical kind of openness that is conveyed over time in various ways including a readiness to soul-search, to negotiate, and to change ... some things are always left in the dark. One might say that one of the contexts of our actions is always *the context of ignorance of contexts*. And yet, act we must. (Hoffman, as cited in Moore, 1999, p. 122)

A potential drawback of having a conceptual framework capable of including and organizing such a vast array of knowledge is that it can erroneously convey to someone who identifies with it that he has a "theory of everything" when, in fact, all he has is a framework that might be devoid of the specific skills and knowledge needed to effectively practice, in this case, psychotherapy. In other words, just because a practitioner understands integral metatheory does not absolve him or her of the requisite work to understand the myriad theories, concepts, research findings, and skills that are subsumed within the quadrants, levels, states, lines, types, and so forth. In short, a comprehensive model does not guarantee or imply that the therapist is competent in the domains that are unified in that model.

We integral psychotherapists are further challenged to develop a deeper understanding of how intersubjective (LL) and macrosocial-systemic (LR) factors and dynamics are pertinent to therapy. We would do well to remember that psychological organization and experience involve configurations of states of consciousness that are a function of a person's developmental center of gravity, variables from all four quadrants, and other phenomena that are far more complex than the dynamics of a single stage of development. More inquiry is needed to determine how the multiple quadratic correlates of a given phenomenon are temporally, causally, or otherwise related. For example, our understanding is still limited with regard to how particular interpersonal dynamics (LL) within psychotherapy correspond with phenomenological states or events (UL) as well as neural and other physiological changes (UR), and how these therapeutic processes may be influenced by a host of systemic factors (LR) such as the institutional context in which psychotherapy takes place, as well as the sundry systems within which each person participates. Thus, a fundamental challenge for the continued development of iPT, not unlike the human beings with which it is concerned, is one of synthesis, integration, and unification.

Despite the difficulties, potential drawbacks, and challenges involved with iPT, it nonetheless provides an enhanced capacity to perceive and attend to phenomena spanning multiple dimensions and domains, and such attention to a wider range of data should engender more comprehensive, integrated, and unified treatment. At the very least, a metatheoretical approach such as integral psychotherapy should minimize the likelihood of conceptualizing and intervening in a reductionistic manner. As a deeply contextual and holistic approach, iPT also fosters a flexible and idiographic approach to serving the needs of each unique person.

An integral sensibility is not a distinct set of technical prescriptions, nor is it a specific clinical theory; rather, it is an attitude or perspective of being continuously open and sensitive to how a host of quadratic, developmental, and state-related dynamics interact and influence each patient's experience and behavior. Such an attitude not only broadens our conceptual horizons, it also reminds us to remain open to the evolution of our theoretical ideas rather than reify them into a static approach. I have offered one version of an integral approach to psychotherapy. I hope that this book stimulates dialogue and debate surrounding the merits and current limitations of this approach; even more so, I hope it helps therapists be more effective in reducing the suffering, and increasing the well-being, of those who seek our help.

Appendix
Integral Culture, Spirituality, and a Category Error[1]

> "Be sure your objective judgments are not for the most part concealed subjective ones." (the young Arthur Schopenhauer wrote this to his older self; cited in Yalom, 2005, p. 174)

Shortly after I returned from the 2015 Integral Theory Conference, I felt compelled to respond to one of the provocative panel debates that took place there. The title of the debate was "Integral culture has to abandon its spirituality to have a mainstream impact." For the motion were Sean Esbjörn-Hargens and Mark Fabionar; against the motion were Terry Patten and Dustin Dipema; Rob McNamara moderated the debate. It is important to note, as Sean did, that the issue is not about individuals abandoning their spirituality; the issue regards the role of spirituality in integral *culture*. The main point I want to make that was not mentioned in that panel is this: including spirituality as perhaps its central point is not what is keeping the integral movement from having mainstream impact; *what is most deleterious is its pervasively declaring specious conclusions about the ultimate nature of (external) reality based upon personal (internal) experience.* Before I unpack this point, I want to give a bit of context with regard to "where I'm coming from."

First, I am very confident that the vast majority of individual members within the integral community are not about to abandon their spirituality; that is precisely what has attracted almost every integralist to Wilber's writings and the integral community that emerged from and around his work. Second, let me emphasize that as someone who lived a deeply contemplative life for nearly ten years, and as a founding member of the Integral Institute, my worldview was *completely* consistent with that of Wilber for more than 15 years; thus, I am critiquing something that I have deeply resonated with and believed with all my heart and

---

[1] This section is adapted from Marquis, A. (in press). Integral culture, spirituality, and a category error. *Journal of Integral Theory and Practice, 10* (1). I am including this appendix because if someone Googles "Ken Wilber" they are likely to see aspects of his spirituality with which I disagree and from which I want to differentiate.

mind (i.e., this critique is not coming from an "outsider"). I have intensively practiced various forms of meditation, along with many other spiritual/self-transcending practices, and repeatedly experienced what Wilber (1995) termed psychic, subtle, causal, and non-dual states of consciousness. I now consider myself an atheist,[2] but an atheist who believes that virtues such as gratitude, love, compassion, and mindfulness are best described by the adjective "spiritual";[3] in this, I am in alignment with Sam Harris's (2014) *Waking Up: A Guide to Spirituality Without Religion* and Robert Solomon's (2002) *Spirituality for the Skeptic: The Thoughtful Love of Life*. Moreover, the bulk of my work continues to focus primarily on integral matters, especially the further development of integral psychotherapy; this reflects how much I still value the contributions Wilber has made with his AQAL model.

Integral culture does not need to cease emphasizing the importance of authentic spirituality with regard to many individual and systemically based problems. What I think we *do* need to abandon is the nearly ubiquitous tendency to make statements of fact about the external world (often rather grandiose statements about the ultimate nature of reality; Upper-Right quadrant) based upon one's internal, phenomenological (Upper-Left quadrant) experiences; when these spurious connections are made, they almost always involve spirituality. For example, someone has a *1st person, phenomenological experience* of "unity consciousness" or "sahaj Samadhi"—that the separate-self sense has completely dissolved and that one's ultimate identity as Spirit is non-dual (not separate from any arising phenomena); he or she then proceeds to make a *3rd person, objective statement* that the ultimate nature of reality is non-dual, that everything in the external world is a manifestation of, and derivative of, Spirit. Although the propositional truth of such a statement is possible, the felt profundity of one's phenomenological experience does not justify anything close to certainty in declaring such a statement. Wilber and much of the integral community make this fundamental mistake ubiquitously; it is pervasive throughout Wilber's writings and I heard it in many, if not most, of the presentations/panels I attended at all four of the Integral

---

2 Atheism is often contrasted with agnosticism, but both terms have different definitions. According to the first definition, atheism is "simply the absence of belief in the gods and agnosticism is simply lack of knowledge of some specified subject matter. The second definition takes atheism to mean the explicit denial of the existence of gods and agnosticism as the position of someone who, because the existence of gods is unknowable, suspends judgment regarding them" (Harvey, 2007, p. 35). I do not pretend to know with certainty that Spirit/God is not the source of everything; rather, I simply lack the belief that Spirit/God is the source of everything (thus, I adopt the first definition of atheism). However, the fact that one cannot disprove the existence of God does not support the view that God exists. One cannot prove that God does not exist because one cannot prove any negative claim; a classic example of this is Bertrand Russell's teapot. In this analogy, Russell asked us to imagine his claiming that a teapot is orbiting the Sun. How reasonable would it be for him to expect others to believe this claim because they cannot prove that a teapot is not orbiting the Sun? The teapot analogy demonstrates that the burden of proof rests with those making scientifically unfalsifiable claims, not with those who do not accept them.

3 See Harris (2014, p. 6).

Theory Conferences. This mistake is common among spiritual communities, but it is particularly ironic that people who adopt a theory (integral) whose central model is the four quadrants (and Wilber [2006] has clearly demonstrated how each quadrant, and each of the corresponding eight zones,[4] has its own methodology and thus its own validity claims) would so persistently make such a mistake. Referring to "the Big Three" (the UL, LL, and the two right-hand quadrants), Wilber stated: "*each of which has its own validity claim* and its own standards, and none of which can be reduced to the others" (1995, p. 145, italics in original), and then, referring to the specific validity claims of the UR and UL quadrants respectively: "*propositional truth* (referring to an objective state of affairs, or it) ... and *subjective truthfulness* (or sincerity, I) ... each of these validity claims ... can be exposed to its own different kinds of evidence ... and *checked* for their actual *validity*" (1995, p. 145, italics and parentheses in original). Despite these crucially important epistemological aspects of integral theory, it seems to me that Wilber and much of the integral community take their subjective experiences as evidence for (or, even worse, *proof* of) propositional statements about the universe; for example, "The [phenomenological] realization of the Nondual traditions is uncompromising: there is only Spirit, there is only God" (Wilber, 1997, p. 281, brackets added). This is fundamentally a zone confusion; we cannot use zone 1 methods (phenomenology/meditation) as verification of zone 8 realities (systems theory views of the external world) (refer to page 222 for a discussion of the eight zones).

I vehemently do not want individuals within the integral community to stop their spiritual practices, and I wish that the rest of the world would increasingly adopt what Wilber (1997) termed authentic spirituality; if much of the world did this, I think that individuals, as well as the cultures and systems in which they are embedded, would flourish more and suffer less. At the same time, I wish that the integral community would cease making the category error of making 3rd-person statements of fact about the nature of reality based upon their 1st-person experiences. Let me confess that there was at least a decade during which I, too, felt certain that I knew what the ultimate nature of reality was, and this derived from powerful 1st person, Upper-Left/zone 1, spiritual experiences while meditating, in *Darshan* with the spiritual teacher Adi Da, and experiences with psilocybin; I truly know—firsthand—how compelling such experiences can be. However, regardless of how persuasive those phenomenological experiences are, it is not intellectually or philosophically justifiable to argue (especially not with certainty) statements of fact about the external world (3rd-person propositions) on the basis of 1st-person experiences.

As Harris (2014) has pointed out, those who make connections between spirituality and science usually fall prey to one of two mistakes. Typical scientists often begin their project with an impoverished understanding of what authentic

---

4 The eight zones represent the inside and outside of each of the four quadrants; they were addressed in chapter 9.

spirituality[5] is (often confusing it with legitimate spirituality or considering only the latter). In contrast, most New Age proponents "idealize altered states of consciousness and draw specious connections between subjective experience and the spookier theories at the frontiers of physics" (Harris, 2014, p. 7–8).[6] Although the integral community has tremendous strengths and virtues that I do not see in typical New Agers, much, if not most, of the integral community does make unwarranted connections, if not with "the spookier theories at the frontiers of physics," at least between their subjective experiences in meditation and statements about the nature of the universe. Such statements likely reflect a type of wishful thinking that not only results in much integral literature losing credibility in the eyes of the mainstream, but also leads many integralists to minimize the importance of science, politics, economics, and other this-worldly enterprises.

When the questions being investigated are kept within the phenomenological domain of consciousness and other 1st-person (UL) experiences, then meditative and other contemplative practices may offer data that can be appropriately considered empirical (in the larger sense of William James' "radical empiricism");

---

5 Wilber (1997) distinguishes two aspects that any religion can provide: *authentic* (transformative) and *legitimate* (translative). Examples of *legitimate spirituality* include elaboration of one's belief system, such as reading literature or attending workshops related to one's beliefs, or conversion from one belief system to another within the same developmental level/stage. According to Wilber (1997), legitimate spirituality is the more commonly observed function of religion: to fortify the self. Through an *exoteric* system of beliefs and rituals, people are helped to understand and perhaps minimize the inherent suffering of life; thus, legitimate spirituality fosters feelings of security, comfort, consolation, protection, and fortification. Translative spirituality is said to be *legitimate* because it provides a certain sense of legitimacy to one's beliefs about the world and one's place therein.

An example of *authentic/transformative spirituality* involves someone who, after sustained contemplative practice, expands from the formal-operations stage of development into the vision-logic stage, and perhaps beyond. According to Wilber (1997), transformative spirituality constitutes a less commonly observed function of religion: *to deconstruct the self*. Rather than consoling, fortifying, or legitimizing the self, it involves *esoteric* practices to dismantle, transmute, transform, and liberate the self, ultimately (according to Wilber, 1997) from its illusion of separateness through a series of deaths and rebirths of the self into ever more inclusive developmental stages/levels, all of which constitutes the process of *authentic* spirituality. Authentic spirituality inquires into legitimate spirituality and concludes that the latter tends to entrench a person in their current stage of development and thus prolong, even if more comfortably, the illusion of separateness that is, ironically, the actual source of suffering.

From an integral perspective, both legitimate/translative and authentic/transformative functions of spirituality are vitally important. Equally important is distinguishing the two because of their different goals and processes. Readers interested in addressing spiritual issues in psychotherapy are referred to Marquis, Holden, and Warren (2001), Scotton, Chinen, and Battista (1996), and Griffith (2010).

6 It is relevant that Sam Harris has meditated for most of his life and has studied with a wide range of monks, yogis, lamas, and other contemplatives: "I spent two years on silent retreat myself (in increments of one week to three months), practicing various meditation techniques for twelve to eighteen hours a day" (Harris, 2014, p. 14).

however, as soon as questions about the external world arise, subjective experiences cease to be the most appropriate form of data to answer them:

> Although the insights we can have in meditation tell us nothing about the origins of the universe, they do confirm some well-established truths about the human mind: Our conventional sense of self is an illusion; positive emotions, such as compassion and patience, are teachable skills; and the way we think directly influences our experience of the world. (Harris, 2014, p. 8).[7]

Such insights into the illusory nature of the separate self that we call "I" are not incompatible with a rational, naturalized spirituality, and we do not need to resort to faith or anything metaphysical to develop the further reaches of consciousness, to cultivate loving and compassionate communities, or to honor the role of ritual and spirituality in individual and communal life. 1st-person contemplative practices can absolutely inform our understandings of consciousness and the nature of the mind, but they do not necessarily inform our understandings of the external world (*perhaps* they do, but more than likely they do not).

The development and state of our consciousness clearly affect the nature of our experience (UL) and that affects how we relate to one another and the world (LL, LR), all of which influence the quality of our lives. And, as Wilber (2000a) has repeatedly written, if our consciousness and identities expand beyond our individual, separate selves to include the rest of humanity and the world at large, our compassion and love will correspondingly expand to include them as well. This is not only well and good, it may be what our planet needs the most; but none of this requires our making statements of fact about the external world. Whereas a growing percentage of Americans identify as "spiritual but not religious" (Pew Forum on Religion in Public Life), I urge the integral community to be deeply, genuinely spiritual without claiming to know—beyond anything more than a hypothesis or conjecture—what the ultimate nature of reality is.

To repeat, what I am advocating is not a lessening of the centrality of spirituality in the world or the integral community. I am advocating that we cease making statements of fact on the basis of internal experiences (or from what is posited in religious texts written long before the advent of science), while still allowing transformations of consciousness to enhance the meaning in our lives and to better the world through magnified levels of compassion, mindfulness, gratitude, and love.

---

7 The idea that "the self is an illusion" is a central tenet of Buddhist psychology and refers to there not being an unchanging "thing" that is one's self or soul; rather, self is a process that is always in flux. Although we have the subjective experience of being a self, there is ample physiological and psychological evidence that the separate entity with which we identify does not actually exist in the manner in which we experience it (Hood, 2013).

References

Abbass, A. (2015). *Reaching through resistance: Advanced psychotherapy techniques*. Kansas City, MO: Seven Leaves Press.

Abramowitz, J. S., Storch, E. A., McKay, D., Taylor, S., & Asmundson, G. J. G. (2009). The obsessive-compulsive spectrum: A critical review. In D. McKay, J. S. Abramowitz, S. Taylor, & G. J. G. Asmundson (Eds.), *Current perspectives on the anxiety disorders: Implications for DSM-5 and beyond* (pp. 329–352). New York, NY: Springer Publishing Company.

Allen, D. M. (2006). Unified therapy with a patient with multiple cluster B personality traits. In G. Stricker & J. Gold (Eds.), *A Casebook of psychotherapy integration* (pp. 107–120). Washington, DC: American Psychological Association.

Allen, D. M. (2010). *How dysfunctional families spur mental disorders: A balanced approach to resolve problems and reconcile relationships*. Santa Barbara, CA: Praeger.

Alpert, M. (1991). Accelerated empathic therapy: A new short-term dynamic psychotherapy. *International Journal of Short-Term Psychotherapy, 7* (3), 133–156.

American Counseling Association. (2014). *Code of ethics of the ACA*. Alexandria, VA: Author.

American Psychiatric Association. (2000). *Diagnostic and statistical manual of mental disorders* (4th ed.). Washington, DC: American Psychiatric Association.

American Psychiatric Association. (2013). *Diagnostic and statistical manual of mental disorders* (5th ed.). Washington, DC: Author.

American Psychological Association. (2005). *Report of the 2005 presidential task force on evidence-based practice*. Washington, DC: Author.

American Psychological Association. (2010). *Ethical principles of psychologists and code of conduct*. Washington, DC: Author.

Anchin, J. C. (2005). Introduction to the special section on philosophy and psychotherapy integration and to the inaugural focus on moral philosophy. *Journal of Psychotherapy Integration, 15* (3), 284–298.

Anchin, J. C. (2008). Pursuing a unifying paradigm for psychotherapy: Tasks, dialectical considerations, and biopsychosocial systems metatheory. *Journal of Psychotherapy Integration, 18*, 310–349.

Anchin, J. C. & Magnavita, J. J. (2006). The nature of unified clinical science: Implications for psychotherapeutic theory, practice, training and research. *Psychotherapy Bulletin, 41* (3), 26–36.

Anchin, J. C. & Magnavita, J. J. (2008). Toward the unification of psychotherapy: An introduction to the journal symposium. *Journal of Psychotherapy Integration, 18*, 259–263.

Anchin, J. C., Magnavita, J. J., & Sobleman, S. A. (2012). Inaugural editorial statement. *Journal of Unified Psychotherapy and Clinical Science, 1* (1), iii–iv.

Anchin, J. C. & Pincus, A. L. (2010). Evidence-based interpersonal psychotherapy with personality disorders: Theory, components, and strategies. In Magnavita, J. J. (Ed.), *Evidence-based treatment of personality dysfunction: Principles, methods, and processes* (pp. 113–166). Washington, DC: American Psychological Association.

Andrews, G. (2000). A focus on empirically supported outcomes: A commentary on the search for empirically supported treatments. *Clinical Psychology: Science and Practice, 7*, 264–268.

Andrews, G., Charney, D. S., Sirovatka, P. J., & Regier, D. A. (Eds.). (2009). *Stress-induced and fear circuitry disorders: Advancing the research agenda for DSM-5*. Arlington, VA: American Psychiatric Association.

Ansbacher, H. L. & Ansbacher, R. R. (Eds.). (1956). *The individual psychology of Alfred Adler: A systematic presentation in selections from his writings*. New York, NY: Harper & Row.

Asay, T. P. & Lambert, M. J. (2003). The empirical case for the common factors in therapy: Quantitative findings. In M. A. Hubble, B. L. Duncan, & S. D. Miller (Eds.), *The heart and soul of change* (pp. 33–56). Washington, DC: American Psychological Association.

Asbury, K., Dunn, J. F., Pike, A., & Plomin, R. (2003). Nonshared environmental influences on individual differences in early behavioral development: A monozygotic twin differences study. *Child Development, 74*(3), 933–943.

Assagioli, R. (1988). *Transpersonal development: Dimensions beyond psychosynthesis*. San Francisco, CA: Aquarian.

Austin, J. H. (1999). *Zen and the brain*. Cambridge, MA: MIT Press.

Ballash, N., Leyfer, O., Buckley, A. F., & Woodruff-Borden, J. (2006). Parental control in the etiology of anxiety. *Clinical Child and Family Psychology Review, 9* (2), 113–133.

Barlow, D. H. (2004). *Anxiety and its disorders: The nature and treatment of anxiety and panic* (2nd ed.). New York, NY: Guilford Press.

Barlow, D. H. & Durand, V. M. (2002). *Abnormal psychology: An integrative approach*. Belmont, CA: Wadsworth.

Barlow, D. H. & Wolfe, B. E. (1981). Behavioral approaches to anxiety disorders: Reports on NIMH-SUNY, Albany Research Conference. *Journal of Consulting and Clinical Psychology, 49*, 191–215.

Bartley, W. W. (1962). *The retreat to commitment*. New York, NY: Alfred A. Knopf (reissued in 1984 by Open Court Press, LaSalle, IL).

Basch, M. F. (1988). *Understanding psychotherapy: The science behind the art*. New York, NY: Basic Books.

Battista, J. (1996). Offensive spirituality and spiritual defenses. In B. Scotton, A. Chinen, & J. Battista (Eds.), *Textbook of transpersonal psychiatry and psychology* (pp. 250–260). New York, NY: Basic Books.

Beatty, L. A. (2010). Drug abuse research: Addressing the needs of racial and ethnic minority populations. In L. Scheier (Ed.), *Handbook of drug use etiology: Theory, methods, and empirical findings* (pp. 325–340). Washington, DC: American Psychological Association.

Beck, A. T. (1976). *Cognitive therapy and the emotional disorders.* New York, NY: International Universities Press.

Beck, A. T. & Emery, G. (1985). *Anxiety disorders and phobias.* New York, NY: Basic Books.

Beck, A. T. & Weishaar, M. E. (2008). Cognitive therapy. In R. J. Corsini & D. Wedding (Eds.), *Current psychotherapies* (8th ed., pp. 263–294). Belmont, CA: Thomson.

Becker, E. (1973). *The Denial of Death.* New York, NY: Simon & Schuster.

Beebe, B. & Lachman, F. M. (1994). Representation and internalization in infancy: Three principles of salience. *Psychoanalytic Psychology, 11* (2), 127–165.

Beitman, B.C. (2003). Integration through fundamental similarities and useful differences among the schools. In J. C. Norcross & M. R. Goldfried (Eds.), *Handbook of psychotherapy integration* (pp. 202–230). New York, NY: Oxford University Press.

Beutler, L. E. (1995a). Issues in selecting an assessment battery. In L. E. Beutler & M. R. Berren (Eds.), *Integrative assessment of adult personality* (pp. 65–93). New York, NY: Guilford Press.

Beutler, L. E. (1995b). The clinical interview. In L. E. Beutler & M. R. Berren (Eds.), *Integrative assessment of adult personality* (pp. 94–120). New York, NY: Guilford Press.

Beutler, L. E. & Clarkin, J. F. (1990). *Systematic treatment selection: Toward targeted therapeutic interventions.* New York, NY: Brunner/Mazel.

Beutler, L. E., Malik, M., Alimohamed, S., Harwood, T. M., Talebi, H., Noble, S., & Wong, E. (2004). Therapist variables. In M. J. Lambert (Ed.), *Bergin and Garfield's handbook of psychotherapy and behavior change* (5th ed., pp. 227–306). New York, NY: Wiley.

Binswanger, L. (1958). The existential analysis school of thought. Translated by Ernest Angel. In R. May, E. Angel, & H. F. Ellenberger (Eds.), *Existence: A new dimension in psychiatry and psychology.* New York, NY: Basic Books.

Blasi, A. (1976). Concept of development in personality theory. In *Ego development: Conceptions and theories* (pp. 29–53). San Francisco, CA: Jossey-Bass.

Boer, F., Markus, M. T., Maingay, R., Lindhout, I. E., Borst, S. R., & Hoogendijk, T. H. G., (2002). Negative life events of anxiety disordered children: Bad fortune, vulnerability, or reporter bias? *Child Psychiatry and Human Development, 32,* 187–199.

Bogels, S. M. & Brechman-Toussaint, M. L. (2006). Family issues in child anxiety: Attachment, family functioning, parental rearing and beliefs. *Clinical Psychology Review, 26* (7), 834–856.

Boorstein, S. (1997). *Clinical studies in transpersonal psychotherapy.* Albany, NY: SUNY.

Borkovec, T. D. & Stiles, J. (1979). The contribution of relaxation and expectance to fear reduction via graded imaginal exposure to feared stimuli. *Behavior Research and Therapy, 17,* 529–540.

Bosquet, M. A. (2001). *An examination of the development of anxiety symptoms from a developmental psychopathology perspective.* Dissertation Abstracts International. Section B: The Sciences and Engineering. Vol 62 (5-B). Nov. 2001, p. 2514.

Bowlby, J. (1987). *The making and breaking of affectional bonds.* New York, NY: Tavistock Publications.

Bowlby, J. (1988). *A secure base: Parent–child attunement and healthy human development.* New York, NY: Basic Books.

Breggin, P. R. (1997). *Brain disabling treatments in psychiatry: Drugs, electroshock, and the role of the FDA.* New York, NY: Springer.

Broman-Fulks, J. J. & Storey, K. M. (2008). Evaluation of a brief aerobic exercise intervention for high anxiety sensitivity. *Anxiety, Stress, and Coping: An International Journal, 21* (2), 117–128.

Brooks-Harris, J. E. (2007). *Integrative multitheoretical therapy*. Boston, MA: Cengage Learning.

Brown, A., Marquis, A., & Guiffrida, D. A. (2013). Mindfulness-based interventions in counseling. *Journal of Counseling and Development, 91* (1), 96–104.

Bryceland, C. & Stam, H. J. (2005). Empirical validation and professional codes of ethics: Description or prescription? *Journal of Constructivist Psychology, 18*, 131–155.

Bugental, J. F. T. (1981). *The search for authenticity: An existential-analytic approach to psychotherapy*. New York, NY: Irvington.

Campbell, W. H. & Pohrbaugh, R. M. (2006). *The biopsychosocial formulation manual: A guide for mental health professionals*. New York, NY: Routledge.

Carere-Comes, T. (2001). Assimilative and accommodative integration: The basic dialectics. *Journal of Psychotherapy Integration, 11* (1), 105–116.

Carlsen, M. B. (1988). *Meaning-making: Therapeutic processes in adult development*. New York, NY: W. W. Norton.

Castonguay, L. G., Eubanks, C. F., Goldfried, M. R., Muran, J. C., & Lutz, W. (2015). Research on psychotherapy integration: Building on the past, looking to the future. *Psychotherapy Research, 25*, 365–382.

Chorpita, B. F. & Barlow, D. H. (1998). The development of anxiety: The role of control in the early environment. *Psychological Bulletin, 124* (1), 3–21.

Clarkin, J. F., Yeomans, F., & Kernberg, O. F. (2006). *Psychotherapy for borderline personality: Focusing on object relations*. New York, NY: Wiley.

Cohn, L. D. (1991). Sex differences in the course of personality development: A meta-analysis. *Psychological Bulletin, 109*, 252–266.

Commons, M. L. & Richards, F. A. (1984). A general model of stage theory. In M. L. Commons, F. A. Richards, & C. Armon (Eds.), *Beyond formal operations: Vol. 1. Late adolescent and adult cognitive development* (pp. 120–140). New York, NY: Praeger.

Cook-Greuter, S. (2000). Mature ego development: A gateway to ego transcendence? *Journal of Adult Development, 7*, 227–240.

Cook-Greuter, S. (2003). *Postautonomus ego development: A study of its nature and measurement*. Wayland, MA: Harthill USA.

Cook-Greuter, S. (n.d.) Ego-development: Nine levels of increasing embrace. White paper. Downloaded from www.cook-greuter.com Feb. 2, 2010.

Cook-Greuter, S. & Soulen, J. (2007). The developmental perspective in integral counseling. *Counseling and Values, 51*, 180–192.

Corey, G. (2001). *Theory and practice of counseling and psychotherapy* (6th ed.). Belmont, CA: Brooks Cole.

Corsini, R. J. & Wedding, D. (Eds.). (1995). *Current psychotherapies* (5th ed.). Itasca, IL: F. E. Peacock Publishers.

Damasio, A. (1999). *The feeling of what happens: Body and emotion in the making ofconsciousness*. New York, NY: Harcourt, Inc.

Davanloo, H. (2000). *Intensive Short-Term Dynamic Psychotherapy: Selected Papers of Habib Davanloo*. New York, NY: Wiley.

Davanloo, H. (2005). Intensive short-term dynamic psychotherapy. In B. J. Sadock & V. A. Sadock (Eds.), *Kaplan & Sadock's comprehensive textbook of psychiatry, Volume II* (pp. 2628–2652). New York, NY: Lippincott Williams & Wilkins.

Dawkins, R. (2015). *Brief candle in the dark: My life in science*. New York, NY: HarperCollins.

Deacon, B. J. & Abramowitz, J. S. (2004). Cognitive and behavioral treatments for anxiety disorders: A review of meta-analytic findings. *Journal of Clinical Psychology, 60*, 133–141.

Debiec, J. & Ledoux, F. E. (2009). The amygdala networks of fear: From animal models to human psychopathology. In D. McKay, J. S. Abramowitz, S. Taylor, & G. J. G. Asmundson (Eds.), *Current perspectives on the anxiety disorders: Implications for DSM-5 and beyond* (pp. 107–126). New York, NY: Springer Publishing Company.

Denzin, N. K. & Lincoln, Y. S. (Eds.). (2005). *The Sage handbook of qualitative research* (3rd ed.). Thousand Oaks, CA: Sage Publications.

Dienstbier, R. A. (1989). Arousal and physiological toughness: Implications for mental and physical health. *Psychological Review, 96*, 84–100.

Eckman, P. (1984). Facial expression of emotion: New findings, new questions. *Psychological Science, 3*, 34–38.

Eckstein, D., Baruth, L., & Mahrer, D. (1992). *An introduction to life-style assessment* (3rd ed.). Dubuque, IA: Kendall/Hunt.

Edwards, D. J. A., Dattilio, F. M., & Bromley, D. B. (2004). Developing evidence-based practice: The role of case-based research. *Professional Psychology: Research and Practice, 35*, 589–597.

Ellenberger, H. F. (1958). A clinical introduction to psychiatric phenomenology and existential analysis. In R. May, E. Angel, & H. F. Ellenberger (Eds.), *Existence: A new dimension in psychiatry and psychology* (pp. 92–126). New York, NY: Basic Books.

Engel, G. L. (1977). The need for a new medical model: A challenge for biomedicine. *Science, 196*, 129–136.

Engel, G. L. (1980). The clinical application of the biopsychosocial model. *American Journal of Psychiatry, 137*, 535–544.

Epstein, M. (1995). *Thoughts without a thinker: Psychotherapy from a Buddhist perspective*. New York, NY: Basic Books.

Erickson, M. H. & Rossi, E. L. (1981). *Experiencing hypnosis: Therapeutic approaches to altered states*. New York, NY: Irvington.

Erikson, E. H. (1963). *Childhood and society*. New York, NY: W. W. Norton.

Erikson, E. H. (1980). *Identity and the life cycle*. New York, NY: W. W. Norton.

Esbjörn-Hargens, S. (2006). Integral research: A multi-method approach to investigating phenomena. *Constructivism in the Human Sciences, 11* (1), 79–107.

Fall, K., Holden, J. M., & Marquis, A. (2004). *Theoretical models of counseling and Psychotherapy* (1st ed.). New York, NY: Routledge.

Fall, K., Holden, J. M., & Marquis, A. (2010). *Theoretical models of counseling and Psychotherapy* (2nd ed.). New York, NY: Routledge.

Fall, K., Holden, J. M., & Marquis, A. (2017). *Theoretical models of counseling and Psychotherapy* (3rd ed.). New York, NY: Routledge.

Fanous, A. H. & Kendler, K. S. (2005). Genetic heterogeneity, modifier genes and quantitative phenotypes in psychiatric illness: Searching for a framework. *Molecular Psychiatry, 10*, 6–13.

Farnsworth, J., Hess, J., & Lambert, M. J. (2001, April). *A review of outcome measurement practices in the Journal of Consulting and Clinical Psychology*. Paper presented at the annual meeting of the Rocky Mountain Psychological Association, Reno, NV.

Fay, B. (1996). *Contemporary philosophy of social science: A multicultural approach*. Cambridge, MA: Blackwell.

Feuerstein, G. (1997). *The Shambhala encyclopedia of yoga*. Boston: Shambhala.

Fisch, E. S. (2001). What is the endpoint of psychotherapy integration? A commentary. *Journal of Psychotherapy Integration, 11* (1), 117–122.

Flanagan, E. H. and Blashfield, R. K. (2002). Psychiatric classification through the lens of ethnobiology. In L. E. Beutler & M. L. Malik (Eds.), *Rethinking the DSM: A psychological perspective* (pp. 121–145). Washington, DC: American Psychological Association.

Foa, E. B., Huppert, J. D., & Cahill, S. P. (2006). Emotional processing theory: An update. In B. O. Rothbaum (Ed.), *Pathological anxiety: Emotional processing in etiology and treatment* (pp. 3–24). New York, NY: Guilford Press.

Forman, M. (2010). *A guide to Integral psychotherapy: Complexity, integration, and spirituality in practice*. Albany, NY: SUNY.

Fosha, D. (2000). *The transforming power of affect: A model for accelerated change*. New York: Basic Books.

Foucault, M. (1973). *The order of things*. New York, NY: Random House.

Frances, A. (2013). *Saving normal: An insider's revolt against out-of-control psychiatric diagnosis, DSM-5, Big Pharma, and the medicalization of ordinary life*. New York, NY: HarperCollins.

Frank, J. D. (1961). *Persuasion and healing*. Baltimore, MD: Johns Hopkins University Press.

Frank, J. D. (1982). Therapeutic components shared by all psychotherapies. In J. H. Harvey & M. M. Parks (Eds.), *The Master Lecture Series: Vol. 1, Psychotherapy research and behavior change* (pp. 73–122). Washington, DC: American Psychological Association.

Frankl, V. (1967). *Psychotherapy and existentialism: Selected papers on Logotherapy*. New York: Simon and Schuster.

Frankl, V. (1985). *Mans's search for meaning*. New York, NY: Washington Square Press.

Frederickson, J. (2013). *Co-creating change: Effective dynamic therapy techniques*. Kansas City, MO: Seven Leaves Press.

Freeman, A. & Simon, K. M. (1989). Cognitive therapy of anxiety. In A. Freeman, K. M. Simon, L. E. Beutler, & H. Arkowitz (Eds.), *Comprehensive handbook of cognitive therapy* (pp. 347–365). New York, NY: Plenum Press.

Freud, S. (1926/1959). *Inhibitions, symptoms, and anxiety*. Standard Edition, vol. 20, pp. 75–155. J. Strachey, trans. London: Hogarth Press.

Freud, S. (1963). *An outline of psychoanalysis*. New York, NY: W. W. Norton.

Fromm, E. (1941). *Escape from freedom*. New York, NY: Holt, Rinehart & Winston.

Fromm, E. (1956). *The art of loving*. New York, NY: Bantam Books.

Fromm, E. (1976). *To have or to be*. New York, NY: Harper & Row.

Gadamer, H. (1989). *Truth and method* (2nd ed.). New York, NY: The Crossroad Publishing Company.

Garfield, S. L. (2003). Eclectic psychotherapy: A common factors approach. In J. C. Norcross & M. R. Goldfried (Eds.), *Handbook of psychotherapy integration* (pp. 169–201). New York, NY, NY: Oxford University Press.

Garfield, S. L. (2006). *Therapies—Modern and popular: PsycCRITIQUES 2006*. Washington, DC: American Psychological Association.

Gergen, K. J. (1985). The social constructionist movement in modern psychology. *American Psychologist, 40* (3), 266–275.

Gilligan, C. (1982). *In a different voice: Psychological theory and women's development*. Cambridge, MA: Harvard University Press.

Giorgi, A. (1970). *Psychology as a human science: A phenomenologically based approach*. New York, NY: Harper & Row.

Glass, C. R., Arnkoff, D. B., & Rodriguez, B. F. (1998). An overview of directions in psychotherapy integration research. *Journal of Psychotherapy Integration, 8* (4), 187–209.

Glasser, W. (1990). *The basic concepts of reality therapy*. Canoga Park, CA: Institute of Reality Therapy.

Glosoff, H. L., Garcia, J., Herlihy, B., & Remley, T. P., Jr. (1999). Managed care: Ethical considerations for psychotherapists. *Psychotherapy and Values, 44* (1), 8–16.

Gold, J. R. (1980). *A retrospective study of the behavior therapy experience*. Unpublished doctoral dissertation, Adelphi University.

Gold, J. R. (1993a). An integrated approach to the treatment of anxiety disorders and phobias. In G. Stricker & J. R. Gold (Eds.), *Comprehensive handbook of psychotherapy integration* (pp. 293–302). New York, NY: Plenum.

Gold, J. R. (1993b). The therapeutic interaction in psychotherapy integration. In G. Stricker & J. R. Gold (Eds.), *Comprehensive handbook of psychotherapy integration* (pp. 525–532). New York, NY: Plenum.

Gold, J. R. & Stricker, G. (1993). Psychotherapy integration with character disorders. In G. Stricker & J. R. Gold (Eds.), *Comprehensive handbook of psychotherapy integration* (pp. 323–336). New York, NY: Plenum.

Goldfried, M. (2005). The history of psychotherapy integration. In J. C. Norcross & M. Goldfried (Eds.), *Handbook of Psychotherapy Integration* (pp. 46–93). Oxford: Oxford University Press.

Goleman, D. (1995). *Emotional intelligence*. New York, NY: Bantam Books.

Gray, J. A. (1985). Issues in the neuropsychology of anxiety. In A. H. Tuma & J. D. Maser (Eds.), *Anxiety and the anxiety disorders* (pp. 5–25). Hillsdale, NJ: Lawrence Erlbaum Associates.

Gray, J. A. & McNaughton, N. (1996). The neuropsychology of anxiety: Reprise. In D. A. Hope (Ed.), *Nebraska Symposium on Motivation: Vol. 43. Perspectives on anxiety, panic, and fear*. Lincoln, NE: University of Nebraska Press.

Greenberg, J.R. & Mitchell, S.A. (1983). *Object relations in psychoanalytic theory*. Cambridge, MA: Harvard University Press.

Greenberg, L. S. (1999). Ideal psychotherapy research: A study of significant change processes. *Journal of Clinical Psychology, 55*, 1467–1480.

Greenberg, L. S. (2002). *Emotion-focused therapy: Coaching clients to work through their feelings*. Washington, DC: American Psychological Association.

Greenberg, L. S. (2006). Emotion-focused therapy: A synopsis. *Journal of Contemporary Psychotherapy, 36*, 87–93.

Greenberg, L. S. (2008). Emotion and cognition in psychotherapy: The transforming power of affect. *Canadian Psychology, 49*, 49–59.

Greenberg, L. S. (2011). *Emotion-focused therapy*. Theories of psychotherapy series. Washington, DC: American Psychological Association.

Griffith, J. L. (2010). *Religion that heals, religion that harms: A guide for clinical practice*. New York, NY: Guilford Press.

Gross, P. R. & Levitt, N. (1998). *Higher superstition: The academic left and its quarrels with science*. Baltimore, MD: Johns Hopkins University Press.

Guidano, V. F. (1987). *Complexity of the self: A developmental approach to psychopathology and therapy*. New York, NY: Guilford Press.

Harper, L. V. (2005). Epigenetic inheritance and the intergenerational transfer of experience. *Psychological Bulletin, 131*, 340–360.

Harris, S. (2014). *Waking up: A guide to spirituality without religion*. New York, NY: Simon & Schuster.

Harvey, V. A. (2007). Agnosticism and atheism. In T. Flynn (Ed.), *The New Encyclopedia of Unbelief*. Amherst, NY: Prometheus Books.

Hauser, S. T., Powers, S. I., & Noam, G. G. (1991). Adolescents and their families: Paths of ego development. New York, NY: Free Press.

Henriques, G. (2011). *A new unified theory of psychology.* New York, NY: Springer.

Henriques, G. (2017). Character adaptation systems theory: A new big five for personality and psychotherapy. *Review of General Psychology, 21* (1), 9–22.

Henriques, G., Critchfield, K., Anchin, J., Shealy, C., Marquis, A., & Magnavita, J. (2015). *Unification: The Next Wave of Psychotherapy Integration?* Society for the Exploration of Psychotherapy Integration, June 19–21, Baltimore.

Herlihy, B. & Corey, G. (1996). *ACA ethical standards casebook.* Alexandria, VA: American Counseling Association.

Hettema, J. M., Annas, P., Neale, M. C., Kendler, K. S., & Fredrikson, M. (2003). A twin study of the genetics of fear conditioning. *Archives of General Psychiatry, 60,* 702–708.

Hettema, J. M., Prescott, C. A., Myers, J. M., Neale, M. C., & Kendler, K. S. (2005). The structure of genetic and environmental risk factors for anxiety disorders in men and women. *Archives of General Psychiatry, 62* (2), 182–189.

Hill, C. E. (1996). *Working with dreams in psychotherapy.* New York, NY: Guilford Press.

Hoffman, J. A. & Teyber, E. C. (1979). Some relationships between sibling age, spacing, and personality. *Merrill-Palmer Quarterly, 25,* 77–80.

Holden, J. M. (2004). Integral psychology: My spiritually based guiding metatheory of counseling. *Counseling and Values, 48* (3), 204–223.

Hollon, S. D. & Beck, A. T. (2004). Cognitive and cognitive behavioral therapies. In M. J. Lambert (Ed.), *Bergin and Garfield's handbook of psychotherapy and behavior change* (5th ed.). New York, NY: Wiley.

Hood, A. B. & Johnson, R. W. (1991). *Assessment in psychotherapy: A guide to the use of psychological assessment procedures.* Alexandria, VA: American Association for Psychotherapy and Development.

Hood, B. (2013). *The self illusion: How the social brain creates identity.* Oxford: Oxford University Press.

Horney, K. (1945). *Our inner conflicts.* New York, NY: W. W. Norton.

Hoyrup, J. (2000). *Human sciences: Reappraising the humanities through history and philosophy.* Albany, NY: SUNY.

Hranov, L. G. (2007). Comorbid anxiety and depression: Illumination of a controversy. *International Journal of Psychiatry in Clinical Practice, 11* (3), 171–189.

Hubble, M. A., Duncan, B. L., & Miller, S. D. (Eds.). (1999). *The heart and soul of change: What works in therapy.* Washington, DC: American Psychological Association.

Hudson, J. L. & Rapee, R. M. (2008). Family and social environments in the etiology and maintenance of anxiety disorders. In M. M. Antony & M. B. Stein (Eds.), *Oxford handbook of anxiety and related disorders* (pp. 173–189). New York, NY: Oxford University Press.

Hy, L. X. & Loevinger, J. (1996). *Measuring ego development.* Mahwah, NJ: Lawrence Erlbaum Associates.

Ingersoll, R. E. (2002). An integral approach for teaching and practicing diagnosis. *Journal of Transpersonal Psychology, 34,* 115–127.

Ingersoll, R. E. & Marquis, A. (2014). *Understanding psychopathology: An integral exploration.* Columbus, OH: Pearson.

Ingersoll, R. E. & Rak, C. F. (2006). *Psychopharmacology for helping professionals: An integral exploration.* Belmont, CA: Wadsworth.

Ingersoll, R. E. & Zeitler D. A. (2010). *Integral psychotherapy: Inside out/Outside in.* Albany, NY: SUNY.

Ivey, A. E. (1986). *Developmental therapy.* San Francisco, CA: Jossey-Bass.

James, W. (1890). *The principles of psychology.* New York, NY: Henry Holt & Co.
James, W. (1892). *Psychology: The briefer course.* New York, NY: Harper.
James, W. (1978). *Pragmatism and the meaning of truth.* Cambridge, MA: Harvard University Press.
Jang, K. L. & Shikishima, C. (2009). Behavioral genetics: Strategies for understanding the anxiety disorders. In D. McKay, J. S. Abramowitz, S. Taylor, & G. J. G. Asmundson (Eds.), *Current perspectives on the anxiety disorders: Implications for DSM-5 and beyond* (pp. 127–152). New York, NY: Springer Publishing Company.
Jensen, J. P., Bergin, A. E., & Greaves, D. W. (1990). The meaning of eclecticism: New survey and analysis of components. *Professional Psychology: Research and Practice, 21,* 124–130.
Johnson, R. B. & Onwuegbuzie, A. J. (2004). Mixed methods research: A research paradigm whose time has come. *Educational Researcher, 33* (7), 14–26.
Johnson, R. B. & Turner, L. A. (2003). Data collection strategies in mixed methods research. In A. Tashakkori and C. Tedllie (Eds.), *Handbook of Mixed Methods in Social and Behavioral Research* (pp. 197–319). Thousand Oaks, CA: Sage Publications.
Kabat-Zinn, J. (2003). Mindfulness-based interventions in context: Past, present, and future. *Clinical Psychology: Science and Practice, 10* (2), 144–156.
Kagan, J. (1997). Temperament and reactions to unfamiliarity. *Child Development, 68* (1), 139–143.
Karg, R. S. & Wiens, A. N. (1998). Improving diagnostic and clinical interviewing. In G. P. Koocher, J. C. Norcross, & S. S. Hill (Eds.), *Psychologist's desk reference* (pp. 11–14). New York, NY: Oxford University Press.
Keating, T. (1986). *Open mind, open heart: The contemplative dimension of the gospel.* Amity, NY: Amity House.
Kegan, R. (1982). *The evolving self: Problem and process in human development.* Cambridge, MA: Harvard University Press.
Kegan, R. (1994). *In over our heads: The mental demands of modern life.* Cambridge, MA: Harvard University Press.
Kegan, R. & Lahey, L. L. (2009). *Immunity to change: How to overcome it and unlock the potential in yourself and your organization.* Cambridge, MA: Harvard Business Review Press.
Kendler, K. S., Myers, J., & Prescott, C. A. (2002). The etiology of the phobias: An evaluation of the stress-diathesis model. *Archives of General Psychiatry, 59,* 242–248.
Kernberg, O. (1980). *Internal world and external reality: Object relations theory applied.* New York, NY: Jason Aronson.
Kessel, F. & Rosenfield, P. L. (2008). Toward transdisciplinary research: Historical and contemporary perspectives. *American Journal of Preventive Medicine, 35* (2), S225–S234.
Kierkegaard, S. (1954). *The sickness unto death.* W. Lowrie, trans. New York, NY: Doubleday & Co.
Kierkegaard, S. (1957). *The concept of dread.* W. Lowrie, trans. Princeton, NJ: Princeton University Press.
Kim-Cohen, J., Caspi, A., Moffitt, T. E., Harrington, H., Milne, B. J., & Poulton, R. (2003). Prior juvenile diagnoses in adults with mental disorder: Developmental follow-back of a prospective-longitudinal cohort. *Archives of General Psychiatry, 60,* 709–719.
Kindt, M. & Van Den Hout, M. (2001). Selective attention and anxiety: A perspective on developmental issues and the causal status. *Journal of Psychopathology and Behavioral Assessment, 23* (3), 193–202.
Knoblauch, F. W. (2008). Some disparate thoughts on the ideal of a unified psychotherapy. *Journal of Psychotherapy Integration, 18* (3), 301–309.

Kohlberg, L. (1969). Stage and sequence: The cognitive-developmental approach to socialization. In D. Goslin (Ed.), *Handbook of socialization theory and research* (pp. 347–380). Chicago, IL: Rand McNally.

Kohlberg, L. (1990). Which postformal levels are stages? In M. L. Commons, C. Armon, L. Kohlberg, F. A. Richards, T. A. Grotzer, & J. D. Sinnott, *Adult development: Models and methods in the study of adolescent and adult thought* (pp. 263–268). New York, NY: Praeger.

Kohut, H. (1977). *The restoration of the self.* New York, NY: International Universities Press.

Kohut, H. (1984). *How does analysis cure?* Chicago, IL: University of Chicago Press.

Kuhn, N. (2014). *Intensive short-term dynamic psychotherapy: A reference.* North Charleston, SC: Experient Publications.

Kuhn, T. S. (1962). *The structure of scientific revolutions.* Chicago, IL: The University of Chicago Press.

Kuhn, T. S. (1977). *The essential tension: Selected studies in scientific tradition and change.* Chicago, IL: The University of Chicago Press.

Lader, M. (1988). Beta-adrenergic antagonists in neuropsychiatry: An update. *Journal of Clinical Psychiatry, 49*, 213–223.

Lambert, M. J. (Ed.). (2004). *Bergin and Garfield's handbook of psychotherapy and behavior change* (5th ed.). New York, NY: Wiley.

Lambert, M. J. & Ogles, B. M. (2004). The efficacy and effectiveness of psychotherapy. In M. J. Lambert (Ed.), *Bergin and Garfield's handbook of psychotherapy and behavior change* (5th ed.). New York, NY: Wiley.

Lampropoulos, G. K. (2001). Bridging technical eclecticism and theoretical integration: Assimilative integration. *Journal of Psychotherapy Integration, 11* (1), 5–18.

Lang, P. J. (1994). The varieties of emotional experience: A meditation on James-Lange theory. *Psychological Review, 101* (2), 211–221.

Lanius, U. F., Paulsen, S. L., & Corrigan, F. M. (Eds.). (2014). *Neurobiology and treatment of traumatic dissociation: Towards an embodied self.* New York, NY: Springer.

Lazarus, A. A. (1995). Multimodal therapy. In R. J. Corsini & D. Wedding (Eds.), *Current psychotherapies* (5th ed., pp. 322–255). Itasca, IL: F. E. Peacock Publishers, Inc.

Lazarus, A. A. (2003). Multimodal therapy: Technical eclecticism with minimal integration. In J. C. Norcross & M. R. Goldfried (Eds.), *Handbook of psychotherapy integration* (pp. 231–263). New York, NY: Oxford University Press.

Lazarus, A. A. & Lazarus, C. N. (1991). *Multimodal life history inventory.* Champaign, IL: Research Press.

LeDoux, J. (1996). *The emotional brain: The mysterious underpinnings of emotional life.* New York: Touchstone.

Leonard, G. & Murphy, M. (1995). *The life we are given.* New York, NY: G. P. Putnam's Sons.

Levant, R. F. (2004). The empirically validated treatment movement: A practitioner/educator perspective. *Clinical Psychology: Science and Practice, 11*, 219–224.

Levitt, H. M., Neimeyer, R. A., & Williams, D. C. (2005). Rules versus principles in psychotherapy: Implications of the quest for universal guidelines in the movement for empirically supported treatments. *Journal of Contemporary Psychotherapy, 35* (1), 117–129.

Lewis, J. L. (2005). Forgiveness and psychotherapy: The prepersonal, personal, and transpersonal. *Journal of Transpersonal Psychology, 37* (2), 124–142.

Linehan, M. (1993a). *Cognitive-behavioral treatment of Borderline Personality Disorder.* New York: Guilford Press.

Linehan, M. (1993b). *Skills training manual for treating Borderline Personality Disorder.* New York: Guilford Press.
Loevinger, J. (1976). *Ego development.* San Francisco, CA: Jossey-Bass Publishers.
Loevinger, J. (1985). A revision of the Sentence Completion Test for ego development. *Journal of Personality and Social Psychology, 48,* 420–427.
Loevinger, J. (Ed) (1998). *Technical foundations for measuring ego development: The Washington University Sentence Completion Test.* Mahwah, NJ: Lawrence Erlbaum Associates.
Loevinger, J. & Wessler, R. (1970). *Measuring ego development.* San Francisco, CA: Jossey-Bass.
Lutz, A., Dunne, J. D., & Davidson, R. J. (2007). Meditation and the neuroscience of meditation: An introduction. In P. D. Zelazo, M. Moscovitch, & E. Thompson (Eds.), *The Cambridge Handbook of Consciousness* (pp. 497–549). Cambridge: Cambridge University Press.
Magnavita, J. J. (2006). In search of the unifying principles of psychotherapy: Conceptual, empirical, and clinical convergence. *American Psychologist, 61,* 882–892.
Magnavita, J. J. (2008). Towards unification of clinical science: The next wave in the evolution of psychotherapy? *Journal of Psychotherapy Integration, 18* (3), 264–291.
Magnavita, J. J. (2009) Psychodynamic family psychotherapy: Toward unified relational systematics. In J. H. Bray & M. Stanton (Eds.), *The Wiley-Blackwell Handbook of Family Psychology* (pp. 240–257). New York, NY: Wiley.
Magnavita, J. J. & Anchin, J. A. (2014). *Unifying psychotherapy: Principles, methods, and evidence from clinical science.* New York, NY: Springer.
Magnavita, J. J., Marquis, A., & Henriques, G. (2010). *The Unified Psychotherapy Project: Overview, Implications, and Challenges to Clinical Science.* Society for the Exploration of Psychotherapy Integration, May 28–30, Florence, Italy.
Mahler, M. S., Pine, F., & Bergman, A. (1975). *The psychological birth of the human infant: Symbiosis and individuation.* New York, NY: Basic Books.
Mahoney, M. J. (1991). *Human change processes: The scientific foundations of psychotherapy.* New York, NY: Basic Books.
Mahoney, M. J. (1993). Diversity and the dynamics of development in psychotherapy integration. *Journal of Psychotherapy Integration, 3* (1), 1–13.
Mahoney, M. J. (2000). Behaviorism, cognitivism, and constructivism: Reflections on persons and patterns in my intellectual development. In M. R. Goldfried (Ed.), *How therapists change: Personal and professional reflections* (pp. 183–200). Washington, DC: American Psychological Association.
Mahoney, M. J. (2003). *Constructive psychotherapy: A practical guide.* New York, NY: Guilford Press.
Mahoney, M. J. (2005). Suffering, philosophy, and psychotherapy. *Journal of Psychotherapy Integration, 15,* 337–352.
Mahoney, M. J. (2008). Power, politics, and psychotherapy: A constructive caution on unification. *Journal of Psychotherapy Integration, 18* (3), 367–376.
Mahoney, M. J. (personal communication) May 7, 2006.
Mahoney, M. J. & Marquis, A. (2002). Integral constructivism and dynamic systems in psychotherapy processes. *Psychoanalytic Inquiry, 22* (5), 794–813.
Mahrer, A. R. & Boulet, D. B. (1999). How to do discovery-oriented psychotherapy research. *Journal of Clinical Psychology, 55,* 1481–1493.
Malan, D. H. (1979). *Individual psychotherapy and the science of psychodynamics.* London: Butterworth.

Manners, J. & Durkin, K. (2001). A critical review of the validity of ego development theory and its measurement. *Journal of Personality Assessment, 77* (3), 542–567.

Margolis, J. (1986). *Pragmatism without foundations: Reconciling realism and relativism.* New York: Basil Blackwell.

Marquis, A. (2002). *Mental health professional's comparative evaluations of the Integral Intake, Life-Style Introductory Interview, and the Multimodal Life History Inventory.* Unpublished doctoral dissertation.

Marquis, A. (2007). What is integral theory? *Counseling and Values, 51* (3), 164–179.

Marquis, A. (2008). *The Integral Intake: A guide to comprehensive idiographic assessment in integral psychotherapy.* New York, NY: Routledge.

Marquis, A. (2009). An integral taxonomy of therapeutic interventions. *Journal of Integral Theory and Practice, 4* (2), 13–42.

Marquis, A. (2010). The Integral Intake: Results from phase one of the "Integral Psychotherapy in Practice" Study. *Journal of Integral Theory and Practice, 5* (3), 1–20.

Marquis, A. (2013). Methodological considerations of studying a unified approach to psychotherapy: Integral methodological pluralism. *Journal of Unified Psychotherapy and Clinical Science, 2* (1), 45–73.

Marquis, A. (in press). Integral culture, spirituality, and a category error. *Journal of Integral Theory and Practice, 10* (1).

Marquis, A. & Douthit, K. Z. (2006). The hegemony of "empirically supported treatment": Validating or violating? *Constructivism in the Human Sciences, 11* (2), 108–141.

Marquis, A., Douthit, K. Z., & Elliot, A. (2011). Best practices: A critical yet inclusive vision for the counseling profession. *Journal of Counseling and Development, 89* (4), 397–405.

Marquis, A. & Elliot, A. (2015). Integral Psychotherapy in Practice part 2: Revisions to the metatheory of integral psychotherapy based on therapeutic practice. *Journal of Unified Psychotherapy and Clinical Science, 3* (1), 1–40.

Marquis, A. & Holden, J. M. (2008). Mental health professionals' evaluations of the Integral Intake, a metatheory-based, idiographic intake instrument. *Journal of Mental Health Counseling, 30* (1), 67–94.

Marquis, A., Holden, J. M., & Warren, E. S. (2001). An integral psychology response to Daniel Helminiak's "Treating Spiritual Issues in Secular Psychotherapy." *Counseling and Values, 44* (3), 218–236.

Marquis, A., Short, B., Lewis, J., & Hubbard, S. (2015). Integral Psychotherapy in Practice part 3: Three case studies illustrating the differential use of integral metatheory in informing unified treatment. *Journal of Unified Psychotherapy and Clinical Science, 3* (1), 41–79.

Marquis, A., Tursi, M., & Hudson, D. (2010). Perceptions of counseling integration: A survey of counselor educators and supervisors. *Journal of Counselor Preparation and Supervision, 2* (1), 61–73.

Marquis, A. & Wilber, K. (2008). Unification beyond eclecticism and integration: Integral psychotherapy. *Journal of Psychotherapy Integration, 18* (3), 350–358.

Maslow, A. H. (1971). *The farther reaches of human nature.* New York, NY: Viking Press.

Masterson, J. (1981). *The narcissistic and borderline disorders.* New York, NY: Brunner/Mazel.

Maturana, H. R. & Varela, F. J. (1987). *The tree of knowledge: The biological roots of human understanding.* Boston, MA: Shambhala.

May, R. (1958). Contributions of existential psychotherapy. In R. May, E. Angel, & H. F. Ellenberger (Eds.), *Existence: A new dimension in psychiatry and psychology* (pp. 37–91). New York, NY: Basic Books.

May, R. (1977). *The meaning of anxiety.* New York, NY: W. W. Norton.

May, R. & Yalom, I. (1995). Existential psychotherapy. In R. J. Corsini & D. Wedding (Eds.), *Current psychotherapies* (5th ed., pp. 262–292). Itasca, IL: F. E. Peacock Publishers.

McCauley, J., Kern, D. E., Kolodner, K., Dill, L., Schroeder, A. F., DeChant, H. K., Ryden, J., Derogatis, L. R., & Bass, E. B. (1997). Clinical characteristics of women with a history of childhood abuse. *Journal of the American Medical Association, 277* (17), 1362–1368.

McCullough, L. & Kuhn, N. (2003). *Treating affect phobia: A manual for short-term dynamic psychotherapy.* New York, NY: Guilford Press.

McEwen, B. S. (1992). Paradoxical effects of adrenal steroids on the brain: Protection versus degeneration. *Biological Psychiatry, 31,* 177–199.

McKay, D., Abramowitz, J. S., Taylor, S., & Asmundson, G. J. G. (Eds.). (2009). *Current perspectives on the anxiety disorders: Implications for DSM-5 and beyond.* New York, NY: Springer Publishing Company.

McNaughton, N. & Gray, J. H. (2000). Anxiolytic action on the behavioral inhibition system implies multiple types of arousal contribute to anxiety. *Journal of Affective Disorders, 61,* 161–176.

McWilliams, N. (1994). *Psychoanalytic diagnosis: Understanding personality structure in the clinical process.* New York, NY: Guilford Press.

McWilliams, N. (2004). *Psychoanalytic psychotherapy: A practitioner's guide.* New York, NY: Guilford Press.

Messer, S. B. (2001). Empirically supported treatments: What is a nonbehaviorist to do? In B. Slife, R. Williams, & S. Barlow (Eds.), *Critical issues in psychotherapy: Translating new ideas into practice* (pp. 3–20). Thousand Oaks, CA: Sage Publications.

Messer, S.B. (2003). A critical examination of belief structures in integrative and eclectic psychotherapy. In J.C. Norcross & M.R. Goldfried (Eds.), *Handbook of psychotherapy integration* (pp. 130–168). New York, NY: Oxford University Press.

Messer, S. B. (2008). Unification in psychotherapy: A commentary. *Journal of Psychotherapy Integration, 18* (3), 363–366.

Middledorp, C. M., Cath, D. C., Van Dyck, R., & Boomsma, D. I. (2005). The co-morbidity of anxiety and depression in the perspective of genetic epidemiology: A review of twin and family studies. *Psychological Medicine, 35* (5), 61–624.

Miller, G. (1999). The development of the spiritual focus in psychotherapy and psychotherapist education. *Journal of Psychotherapy and Development, 77* (4), 498–501.

Miller, J. G. (1978). *Living systems.* New York, NY: McGraw-Hill.

Miller, J., Fletcher, K., & Kabat-Zinn, J. (1995). Three-year follow-up and clinical implications of a mindfulness-based stress reduction intervention in the treatment of anxiety disorders. *General Hospital Psychiatry, 17,* 192–200.

Miller, P. (2002). *Theories of developmental psychology.* New York, NY: Worth Publishers.

Miller, R. B. (1998). Epistemology and psychotherapy data: The unspeakable, unbearable, horrible truth. *Clinical Psychology: Science and Practice, 5,* 242–250.

Miller, R. B. (2004). *Facing human suffering: Psychology and psychotherapy as moral engagement.* Washington, DC: American Psychological Association.

Miller, W. L. & Crabtree, B. F. (2005). Clinical research. In N. K. Denzin & Y. S. Lincoln (Eds.), *The Sage handbook of qualitative research* (3rd ed., pp. 605–639). Thousand Oaks, CA: Sage Publications.

Millon, T. & Grossman, S. D. (2008). Psychotherapy unification. *Journal of Psychotherapy Integration, 18* (3), 359–372.

Mineka, S. (1985). Animal models of anxiety-based disorders: Their usefulness and limitation. In A. H. Tuma & J. D. Maser (Eds.), *Anxiety and the anxiety disorders* (pp. 199–244). Hillsdale, NJ: Erlbaum.

Mineka, S., Davidson, M., Cook, M., & Keir, R. (1984). Observational conditioning of snake fear in rhesus monkeys. *Journal of Abnormal Psychology, 93*, 355–372.

Mineka, S. & Thomas, C. (1999). Mechanisms of change in exposure therapy for anxiety disorders. In T. Dalgleish & M. Power (Eds.), *Handbook of cognition and emotion* (pp. 747–764). New York, NY: Wiley.

Mingers, J. (1992). The problems of social autopoiesis. *International Journal of General Systems, 21* (2), 229–236.

Moore, R. (1999). *The creation of reality in psychoanalysis: A view of the contributions of Donald Spence, Roy Schafer, Robert Stolorow, Irwin Z. Hoffman, and beyond*. Hillsdale, NJ: The Analytic Press.

Moreno, M., Lopez-Crespo, G., & Flores, P. (2007). Etiology of anxiety. In B. Helmut et al. (Eds.), *Antidepressants, antipsychotics, anxiolytics: From chemistry and pharmacology to clinical application* (Vol. 1 & 2) (pp. 667–783). Weinheim, Germany: Wiley.

Morgan, M. & LeDoux, J. E. (1995). Differential contribution of dorsal and ventral medial prefrontal cortex to the acquisition and extinction of conditioned fear. *Behavioral Neuroscience, 109*, 681–688.

Moyers, B. (1998). *The politics of addiction* (from the PBS series: *Close to Home*, DVD).

Müller, N. (2014). Immunology of major depression. *Neuroimmunomodulation, 21* (2–3), 123–130.

Muris, P. (2006). The pathogenesis of childhood anxiety disorders: Considerations from a developmental psychopathology perspective. *International Journal of Behavioral Development, 30* (1), 5–11.

Murphy, M. (1995). *The future of the body: Explorations into the further evolution of human nature*. Los Angeles, CA: Jeremy P. Tarcher, Inc.

Neiss, R. (1988). Reconceptualizing arousal: Psychobiological states in motor performance. *Psychological Bulletin, 103*, 345–366.

Neukrug, E. S. (Ed.) (2015). *The encyclopedia of theory in counseling and psychotherapy*. Thousand Oaks, CA: Sage Publications.

Nietzsche, F. (1954). *The portable Nietzsche*. W. Kaufmann, trans. New York, NY: The Viking Press.

Norcross, J.C. (1986). Eclectic psychotherapy: An introduction and overview. In J. C. Norcross (Ed.), *Handbook of eclectic psychotherapy* (pp. 3–24). New York, NY: Brunner/Mazel.

Norcross, J. C. (2005a). A primer of psychotherapy integration. In J. C. Norcross & M. R. Goldfried (Eds.), *Handbook of psychotherapy integration* (2nd ed.). Oxford: Oxford University Press.

Norcross, J. C. (2005b). The psychotherapist's own psychotherapy: Educating and developing psychologists. *American Psychologist, 60*, 840–850.

Norcross, J. C. (2011). *Psychotherapy relationships that work: Evidence-based responsiveness* (2nd ed.). Oxford: Oxford University Press.

Norcross, J. C. & Beutler, L. E. (2007). Integrative psychotherapies. In R. J. Corsini & D. Wedding (Eds.), *Current psychotherapies* (8th ed., pp. 481–511). Belmont, CA: Thomson.

Norcross, J. C., Karpiak, C. P., & Santoro, S. O. (2005). Clinical psychologists across the years: The division of clinical psychology from 1960 to 2003. *Journal of Clinical Psychology, 61*, 1467–1483.

Norcross, J. C. & Newman, C. F. (2003). Psychotherapy integration: Setting the context. In J. C. Norcross & M. R. Goldfried (Eds.), *Handbook of psychotherapy integration* (pp. 3–45). New York, NY: Oxford University Press.

Ohman, A. (1986). Face the beast and fear the face: Animal and social fears as prototypes for evolutionary analyses of emotion. *Psychophysiology, 23*, 123–145.

Orsillo, S. M. & Roemer, L. (2011). *The mindful way through anxiety: Break free from worry and reclaim your life.* New York, NY: Guilford Press.

Orsillo, S. M., Roemer, L., & Barlow, D. H. (2003). Integrating acceptance and mindfulness into existing cognitive-behavioral treatment for GAD: A case study. *Cognitive and Behavioral Practice, 10* (3), 222–230.

Osborn, K., Ulvenes, P., Wampold, B., & McCullough, L. (2014). Creating change through focusing on affect: Affect phobia therapy. In N. Thoma & D. McKay (Eds.), *Working with emotions in cognitive behavioral therapy: Techniques for clinical practice* (pp. 146–174). New York, NY: Guilford Press.

PDM Task Force (2006). *Psychodynamic diagnostic manual (PDM).* Silver Springs, MD: Alliance of Psychoanalytic Organizations.

Perls, F. (1959). *Gestalt therapy: Verbatim.* New York, NY: Bantam.

Perls, F., Hefferline, R., & Goodman, P. (1977). *Gestalt therapy: Excitement and growth in the human personality.* Goulsboro, ME: Gestalt Journal Press.

Persons, J. B. (1991). Psychotherapy outcome studies do not accurately represent current models of psychotherapy: A proposed remedy. *American Psychologist, 46*, 99–106.

Piaget, J. (1948). *Moral judgment of the child.* Glencoe: Free Press.

Piaget, J. (1977). *The essential Piaget.* H. E. Gruber & J. J. Voneche, eds. New York, NY: Basic Books.

Pine, D. S., Cohen, P., Gurley, D., Brook, J., & Ma, Y. (1998). The risk for early adulthood anxiety and depressive disorders in adolescents with anxiety and depressive disorders. *Archives of General Psychiatry, 55*, 56–64.

Pinker, S. (2009). *How the mind works.* New York, NY: W. W. Norton.

Pinker, S. (2011). *The better nature of our angels: Why violence has declined.* New York, NY: Viking Books.

Polanyi, M. (1958). *Personal knowledge: Towards a post-critical philosophy.* New York, NY: Harper & Row.

Polkinghorne, D. E. (1983). *Methodology for the human sciences: Systems of inquiry.* Albany, NY: SUNY.

Polkinghorne, D. E. (1999). Traditional research and psychotherapy practice. *Journal of Clinical Psychology, 55*, 1429–1440.

Porges, S. W. (2011). *The polyvagal theory: Neurophysiological foundations of emotions, attachment, communication, and self-regulation.* New York, NY: W. W. Norton.

Poulton, R., Pine, D. S., & Harrington, H. (2009). Continuity and etiology of anxiety disorders: Are they stable across the life course? In G. Andrews, D. S. Charney, P. J. Sirovatka, & D. A. Regier (Eds.), *Stress-induced and fear circuitry disorders: Advancing the research agenda for DSM-5* (pp. 105–124). Arlington, VA: American Psychiatric Publishing Inc.

Pressly, P.K. & Heesacker, M. (2001). The physical environment and counseling: A review of theory and research. *Journal of Counseling and Development, 79* (2), 148–160.

Prochaska, J. O. & Norcross, J. C. (2003). *Systems of psychotherapy: A transtheoretical analysis* (5th ed.). Pacific Grove, CA: Brooks Cole.

Rachman, S. J. (1979). The concept of required helpfulness. *Behaviour Research and Therapy, 17*, 279–293.

Rapee, R. M. & Bryant, R. A. (2009). Stress and psychosocial factors in onset of fear circuitry disorders. In G. Andrews, D. S. Charney, P. J. Sirovatka, & D. A. Regier (Eds.), *Stress-induced and fear circuitry disorders: Advancing the research agenda for DSM-5* (pp. 195–214). Arlington, VA: American Psychiatric Publishing Inc.

Rheingold, A. A., Herbert, J. D., & Franklin, M. E. (2003). Cognitive bias in adolescents with social anxiety disorder. *Cognitive Therapy and Research, 27* (6), 639–655.

Richard, D. & Lauterbach, D. (2006). *Handbook of exposure therapies.* New York, NY: Academic Press.

Ricoeur, P. (1970). *Freud and philosophy: An essay on interpretation.* New Haven, CT: Yale University Press.

Rogers, C. R. (1961). *On becoming a person: A therapist's view of psychotherapy.* Boston, MA: Houghton Mifflin.

Rogers, C. R. (1980). *A way of being.* Boston, MA: Houghton Mifflin.

Rogers, C. R. (1986). A client-centered/person-centered approach to therapy. In I. Kutash & A. Wolf (Eds.), *Psychotherapist's casebook* (pp. 197–208). San Francisco, CA: Jossey-Bass.

Rollins, J. (2005). A campaign for therapist well-ness. *Counseling Today*, October, 2005.

Rotter, J. B. (1975). Some problems and misconceptions related to the construct of internal versus external control of reinforcement. *Journal of Consulting and Clinical Psychology, 43* (1), 56–67.

Rowan, J. (1993). *Discover your subpersonalities: Our inner world and the people in it.* New York, NY: Routledge.

Rychlak, J. F. (1973). *Introduction to personality and psychotherapy: A theory construction approach.* Boston, MA: Houghton Mifflin.

Ryle, A. (1990). *Cognitive-analytic therapy: Active participation in change.* Chichester, UK: Wiley.

Sadler, J. Z. (2005). *Values and psychiatric diagnosis.* New York, NY: Oxford University Press.

Safran, J. D. (1998). *Widening the scope of cognitive therapy.* New York, NY: Jason Aronson.

Salovey, P., Brackett, M. A., & Mayer, J. D. (Eds.) (2004). *Emotional intelligence: Key readings on the Mayer and Salovey model.* Port Chester, NY: National Professional Resources.

Sartre, J. P. (1943/1993). *Being and nothingness: An essay on phenomenological ontology.* H. E. Barnes, trans. New York, NY: Washington Square Press.

Scher, C. D. & Stein, M. B. (2003). Developmental antecedents of anxiety sensitivity. *Journal of Anxiety Disorders, 17* (3), 253–269.

Schmidt, N. B., Zvolensky, M. J., & Maner, J. K. (2006). Anxiety sensitivity: Prospective prediction of panic attacks and Axis I pathology. *Journal of Psychiatric Research, 40* (8), 691–699.

Schneider, K. J. (1999). Multiple-case depth research: Bringing experience-near closer. *Journal of Clinical Psychology, 55*, 1531–1540.

Schneider, K. J. & May, R. (1995). *The psychology of existence: An integrative, clinical perspective.* New York, NY: McGraw-Hill, Inc.

Schoenfield, G. & Morris, R. J. (2008). Cognitive behavioral treatment for childhood anxiety disorders: Exemplary programs. In M. Matthew, J. E. Lochman, & R. Van Acker (Eds.), *Cognitive-behavioral interventions for emotional and behavioral disorders: School-based practice* (pp. 204–234). New York, NY: Guilford Press.

Schore, A. (2003). *Affect regulation and the repair of the self.* New York, NY: W. W. Norton.

Schwartz, J. M. & Begley, S. (2002). *The mind and the brain: Neuroplasticity and the power of mental force.* New York, NY: HarperCollins.

Scotton, B. W., Chinen, A. B., & Battista, J. R. (Eds.). (1996). *Textbook of transpersonal psychiatry and psychology.* New York, NY: Basic Books.

Sechrest, L. & Smith, B. (1994). Psychotherapy is the practice of psychology. *Journal of Psychotherapy Integration, 4*, 1–27.

Segal, Z. V., Williams, J. M. G., & Teasdale, J. D. (2002). *Mindfulness-based cognitive therapy for depression: A new approach to preventing relapse.* New York, NY: Guilford Press.

Seligman, M. E. P. (1971). Phobias and preparedness. *Behavior Therapy, 2,* 307–320.

Seligman, M. E. P. (1995). The effectiveness of psychotherapy: The *Consumer Reports* study. *American Psychologist, 50,* 965–974 (downloaded from Ovid web gateway, pp. 1–18).

Shapiro, F. (2001). *Eye movement desensitization and reprocessing: Basic principles, protocols and procedures.* New York, NY: Guilford Press.

Shedler, J. (2010). The efficacy of psychodynamic psychotherapy. *American Psychologist, 65* (2), 98–109.

Shertzer, B. & Linden, J. D. (1979). *Fundamentals of individual appraisal: Assessment techniques for psychotherapists.* Boston, MA: Houghton Mifflin.

Siegel, D. J. (2007). *The mindful brain: Reflection and attunement in the cultivation of well-being.* New York, NY: W. W. Norton.

Siegel, D. J. (2010). *The mindful therapist: A clinician's guide to mindsight and neural integration.* New York, NY: W. W. Norton.

Singer, J. A. (2005). *Personality and psychotherapy: Treating the whole person.* New York, NY: Guilford Press.

Skinner, B. F. (1953). *Science and human behavior.* New York, NY: Appleton-Century-Crofts.

Slife, B. D. (2004). Theoretical challenges to therapy practice and research: The constraints of naturalism. In M. J. Lambert (Ed.), *Bergin and Garfield's handbook of psychotherapy and behavior change* (5th ed., pp. 44–83). New York, NY: Wiley.

Slife, B. D. & Gantt, E. E. (1999). Methodological pluralism: A framework for psychotherapy research. *Journal of Clinical Psychology, 55,* 1453–1465.

Slife, B. D., Wiggins, B. J., & Graham, J. T. (2005). Avoiding an EST monopoly: Toward a pluralism of philosophies and methods. *Journal of Contemporary Psychotherapy, 35,* 83–97.

Sloan, R. B., Staples, F. R., Cristol, A. H., Yorkston, N. J., & Whipple, K. (1975). *Psychotherapy vs. behavior therapy.* Cambridge, MA: Harvard University Press.

Smith, J. S., Lane, R., & Goldman, R. (2017). *Are we there yet? Seeking theoretical onvergence.* Presentation at the 33rd Annual Society for the Exploration of Psychotherapy Integration conference, Denver, Colorado.

Sollod, R. N. (1993). Integrating spiritual healing approaches and techniques into psychotherapy. In G. Stricker & J. R. Gold (Eds.), *Comprehensive handbook of psychotherapy integration* (pp. 237–248). New York, NY: Plenum.

Solomon, R. (2002). *Spirituality for the skeptic: The thoughtful love of life.* Oxford: Oxford University Press.

Sroufe, L. A. (1990). Considering the normal and abnormal together: The essence of developmental psychopathology. *Development and Psychopathology, 2,* 335–347.

Staats, A. W. (1991). Unified positivism and unification psychology: Fad or new field? *American Psychologist, 46,* 899–912.

Staats, A. W. (1999). Unifying psychology requires a new infrastructure, theory, method, and a research agenda. *Review of General Psychology, 3,* 3–13.

Stahl, S. M. (2002). Don't ask, don't tell, but benzodiazepines are still the leading treatments for anxiety disorder. *Journal of Clinical Psychiatry, 63,* 756–757.

Steindl-Rast, D. (1984). *Gratefulness, the heart of prayer: An approach to life in fullness.* New York, NY: Paulist Press.

Stern, D. N. (1985). *The interpersonal world of the infant: A view from psychoanalysis and developmental psychology.* New York: Basic Books.

Stolorow, R. D., Atwood, G. E., & Orange, D. M. (2002). *Worlds of experience: Interweaving philosophical and clinical dimensions.* New York, NY: Basic Books.

Stolorow, R. D., Brandchaft, B., & Atwood, G. E. (1987). *Psychoanalytic treatment: An intersubjective approach.* Hillsdale, NJ: The Analytic Press.

Stricker, G. (1993). The current status of psychotherapy integration. In G. Stricker & J. R. Gold (Eds.), *Comprehensive handbook of psychotherapy integration* (pp. 533–545). New York, NY: Plenum.

Stricker, G. & Gold, J. R. (1996). Psychotherapy integration: An assimilative, psychodynamic approach. *Clinical psychology: Science and practice, 3,* 47–58.

Stricker, G. & Gold, J. R. (2011). Integrative approaches to psychotherapy. In S. B. Messer & A. S. Gurman (Eds.), *Essential psychotherapies: Theory and practice* (pp. 426–459). New York, NY: Guilford Press.

Sue, D. W., Arredondo, P., & McDavis, R. J. (1992). Multicultural psychotherapy competencies and standards: A call to the profession. *Journal of Psychotherapy and Development, 70* (4), 477–486.

Sullivan, H. S. (1953). *The interpersonal theory of psychiatry.* New York, NY: W. W. Norton.

Taylor, S., Asmundson, G. J. G., Abramowitz, J. S., & McKay, D. (2009). Classification of anxiety disorders for DSM-5 and ICD-11: Issues, proposals, and controversies. In D. McKay, J. S. Abramowitz, S. Taylor, & G. J. G. Asmundson (Eds.), *Current perspectives on the anxiety disorders: Implications for DSM-5 and beyond* (pp. 481–512). New York, NY: Springer.

Taylor, S., Jang, K. L., Stewart, S. H., & Stein, M. B. (2008). Etiology of the dimensions of anxiety sensitivity: A behavioral-genetic analysis. *Journal of Anxiety Disorders, 22* (5), 899–914.

Teicher, M. H. (2000). Wounds that time won't heal: The neurobiology of child abuse. *Cerebrum, 2* (4), 50–67.

Thelen, E. & Smith, L. B. (1994). *A dynamic systems approach to the development of cognition and action.* Cambridge, MA: MIT Press.

Tillich, P. (1952). *The courage to be.* New Haven, CT: Yale University Press.

Tversky, A. & Kahneman, D. (1981). The framing of decisions and the psychology of choice. *Science, 211* (4481), pp. 453–458.

Van Audenhove, C. & Vertommen, H. (2000). A negotiation approach to intake and treatment choice. *Journal of Psychotherapy Integration, 10* (3), 287–299.

Van Brakel, A. M. L., Muris, P., Bögels, S. M., & Thomassen, C. (2006). A multifactorial model for the etiology of anxiety in non-clinical adolescents: Main and interactive effects of behavioural inhibition, attachment and parental rearing. *Journal of Child and Family Studies, 15,* 569–579.

van der Kolk, B., McFarlane, A., & Weisaeth, L. (Eds.). (1996). *Traumatic stress: The effects of overwhelming experience on the mind, body, and society.* New York, NY: Guilford Press.

Visser, F. (2003). *Ken Wilber: Thought as passion.* Albany, NY: SUNY.

Wachtel, P. L. (1977). *Psychoanalysis and behaviorism: Toward an integration.* New York, NY: Basic Books.

Wachtel, P. L. (1982). Vicious circles: The self and the rhetoric of emerging and unfolding. *Contemporary Psychoanalysis,* 18 (2), 259–273.

Wachtel, P. L. (1987). *Action and insight.* New York, NY: Basic Books.

Wachtel, P. L. (1991). Towards a more seamless integration. *Journal of Psychotherapy Integration, 1,* 32–41.

Wachtel, P. L. (1993). *Therapeutic communication: Knowing what to say when.* New York: Guilford Press.

Wachtel. P. L. (2008). *Relational theory and the practice of psychotherapy*. New York, NY: Guilford Press.

Wachtel. P. L. (2017). *The poverty of affluence: A psychological portrait of the American way of life* (reissue ed.). New York, NY: Rebel Reads.

Wachtel. P. L & Greenberg. L. (2010). *Psychodynamic and experiential perspectives: Convergences and divergences in the reading of a videotape*. Presentation at the 26th Annual Society for the Exploration of Psychotherapy Integration conference, Florence, Italy.

Walsh, R. (1999). *Essential spirituality: The 7 central practices to awaken heart and mind*. New York, NY: Wiley.

Walsh, R. & Vaughan, F. (Eds.). (1993). *Paths beyond ego: The transpersonal vision*. Los Angeles, CA: Jeremy P. Tarcher.

Walsh, R., & Vaughan, F. (1994). The worldview of Ken Wilber. *Journal of Humanistic Psychology, 34* (2), 6–21.

Wampold, B. E. (1997). Methodological problems in identifying efficacious psychotherapies. *Psychotherapy Research, 7,* 21–43.

Wampold, B. E. (2001). *The great psychotherapy debate: Models, methods, and findings*. Mahwah, NJ: Lawrence Erlbaum Associates.

Wampold, B. E., Lichtenberg, J. W., & Waehler, C. A. (2005). A broader perspective: Counseling psychology's emphasis on evidence. *Journal of Contemporary Psychology, 35,* 27–38.

Wang, J. L. (2006). Perceived work stress, imbalance between work and family/personal lives and mental disorders. *Social Psychiatry and Psychiatric Epidemiology, 41* (7), 541–548.

Warren, S. L., Huston, L., Egeland, B., & Sroufe, L. A. (1997). Child and adolescent anxiety disorders and early attachment. *Journal of the American Academy of Child and Adolescent Psychiatry, 36,* 637–644.

Wedding, D. & Corsini, R. J. (2010). *Case studies in psychotherapy* (6th ed.). Pacific Grove, CA: Brooks Cole.

Weems, C. F. & Costa, N. M. (2005). Developmental differences in the expression of childhood anxiety symptoms and fears. *Journal of the American Academy of Child and Adolescent Psychiatry, 44* (7), 656–663.

Welwood, J. (2000). *Toward a psychology of awakening: Buddhism, psychotherapy, and the path of personal and spiritual transformation*. Boston, MA: Shambhala.

Werner, H. (1940). *Comparative psychology of mental development*. New York, NY: International Universities Press, Inc.

Westen, D. & Morrison, K. (2001). A multidimensional met-analysis of treatments for depression, panic, and generalized anxiety disorder: An empirical examination of the status of empirically supported therapies. *Journal of Consulting and Clinical Psychology, 69,* 875–899 (downloaded from Ovid web gateway, pp. 1–36).

Westen, D., Novotny, C. M., & Thompson-Brenner, H. (2004). The empirical status of empirically supported psychotherapies: Assumptions, findings, and reporting in controlled clinical trials. *Psychological Bulletin, 130,* 631–663 (downloaded from Ovid web gateway, pp. 1–65).

Whiteside, S. P. & Ollendick, T. H. (2009). Developmental perspectives on anxiety classification. In D. McKay, J. S. Abramowitz, S. Taylor, & G. J. G. Asmundson (Eds.), *Current perspectives on the anxiety disorders: Implications for DSM-5 and beyond* (pp. 303–328). New York, NY: Springer Publishing Company.

Widiger, T. A. & Clark, L. A. (2000). Toward DSM-5 and the classification of psychopathology. *Psychological Bulletin, 126,* 946–963.

Wilber, K. (1980). *The atman project: A transpersonal view of human development.* Wheaton, IL: Quest Books.

Wilber, K. (1983). *Eye to eye: The quest for the new paradigm.* Boston, MA: Shambhala.

Wilber, K. (1995). *Sex, ecology, spirituality: The spirit of evolution.* Boston, MA: Shambhala.

Wilber, K. (1997). *The eye of spirit.* Boston, MA: Shambala.

Wilber, K. (1999). *The collected works, Volume 4. Integral psychology, transformations of consciousness, selected essays.* Boston, MA: Shambhala.

Wilber, K. (2000a). *The collected works, Volume 6. Sex, ecology, sprirituality.* Boston, MA: Shambhala.

Wilber, K. (2000b). *Integral psychology: Consciousness, spirit, psychology, therapy.* Boston, MA: Shambhala.

Wilber, K. (2000c). *The collected works, Volume 7. A brief history of everything, the eye of spirit.* Boston, MA: Shambhala.

Wilber, K. (2006). *Integral spirituality: A startling new role for religion in the modern and postmodern world.* Boston, MA: Integral Books.

Wilber, K. (2014). *The fourth turning: Imagining the evolution of an integral Buddhism.* Boston, MA: Shambhala.

Wilber, K., Patten, T., Leonard, A., & Morelli, M. (2008). *Integral life practice: A 21st-century blueprint for physical health, emotional balance, mental clarity, and spiritual awakening.* Boston, MA: Integral Books.

Wolfe, B. E. (2001). A message to assimilative integrationists: It's time to become accommodative integrationists: A commentary. *Journal of Psychotherapy Integration, 11* (1), 123–131.

Wolfe, B. E. (2003). Integrative psychotherapy of the anxiety disorders. In J. C. Norcross & M. R. Goldfried (Eds.), *Handbook of psychotherapy integration* (pp. 373–401). New York, NY: Oxford University Press.

Wolfe, B. E. (2005). *Understanding and treating anxiety disorders: An integrative approach to healing the wounded self.* Washington, D. C.: American Psychological Association.

Wolfe, B. E. (2008). Toward a unified conceptual framework of psychotherapy. *Journal of Psychotherapy Integration, 18* (3), 292–300.

Yalom, I. D. (1980). *Existential psychotherapy.* New York, NY: Basic Books.

Yalom, I. D. (1998). *The Yalom reader.* New York, NY: Basic Books.

Yalom, I. D. (2002). *The gift of therapy: An open letter to a new generation of therapists and their patients.* New York, NY: HarperCollins.

Yalom, I. D. (2005). *The Schopenhauer cure.* New York, NY: HarperCollins.

Yalom, I. D. (2009). *Staring at the sun: Overcoming the terror of death.* San Francisco, CA: Jossey-Bass.

Yalom, I. D. (2015). *Creatures of a day.* New York, NY: Basic Books.

Yanchar, S. C. & Slife, B. D. (1997). Pursuing unity in a fragmented psychology: Problems and prospects. *Review of General Psychology, 1*, 235–255.

Yehuda, R. (2009). Role of neurochemical and neuroendocrine markers of fear in classification of anxiety disorders. In G. Andrews, D. S. Charney, P. J. Sirovatka, & D. A. Regier (Eds.), *Stress-induced and fear circuitry disorders: Advancing the research agenda for DSM-5* (pp. 255–264). Arlington, VA: American Psychiatric Publishing Inc.

Young, J. E., Klosko, J. S., & Weishaar, M. E. (2006). *Schema therapy: A practitioner's guide.* New York, NY: Guilford Press.

Zillman, E. A. & Spiers, M. V. (2001). *Principles of neuropsychology.* Belmont, CA: Wadsworth.

Index

Abbass, A. 31, 32, 65, 129, 166–168, 172, 177
Accelerated Experiential Dynamic Psychotherapy 88, 105, 175, 179–180; *see also* Fosha, D.
advocacy 132–134, 138, 165
affect *see* emotion
agency xiii, 32, 33, 35, 44–45, 188
altered states of consciousness *see* states
Anchin, J. i, xi–xvi, xx, xxiv–xxvi, 3, 7–11, 13–14, 21, 23–24, 30, 32, 45, 109–110, 123, 150, 156, 165, 169, 210, 213, 218–221, 229–230
anxiety: discharge patterns 160n6, 178; regulation of 128–129, 160n6, 177–178, 193, 199
anxiety disorders: etiology of 74–106; treatment of 184–205
AQAL (All-Quadrants, All-Levels) ii, xii, xiv, xxvi, 20–25, 28, 36, 130, 141–142, 145, 152, 154, 233
assessment: as a process 111–112; interviews 113–114; need for holistic 109–110; need for integral 114–115; of anxiety 187; quadratic 115–118, 121–125
attunement xiv, 87, 111–112, 134–135, 143, 159, 168, 174, 179

awareness xiv, xxiii, 40, 47, 49–51, 53, 56, 58–59, 61, 65n15, 79, 90–91, 112, 128, 134–135, 137, 147, 149, 152–153, 158, 162–163, 175, 187, 193, 197, 199, 203; as therapeutic change process 165, 167–171

Beck, A. 22, 36, 76, 84, 138, 150, 156, 173–174, 186, 194–195, 216
behavioral views xix, xxiii–xxiv, 13–14, 20–24, 31–33, 79, 83–84, 88–89, 117, 135–136, 143, 147–148, 151, 156, 162, 169, 171, 187–190, 195–196, 200, 202, 212, 214, 217, 219, 221, 230
biological views xx–xxii, xxiv, 10, 13, 19, 27, 75–78, 80, 84, 96, 98, 103–105, 123n7, 165, 170, 173n18, 181, 186, 221, 225, 230
Brooks-Harris, J. xi, 7–8

change processes xiv–xv, 32–35; 39–40, 44, 65n14, 70, 133, 144, 147–148, 157–161, 169–170, 174, 196, 221, 231
cognitive restructuring 11, 134, 136, 147, 151, 156, 162, 187, 195
cognitive views xix–xx, xxiv, 13, 22, 31–32, 36, 41n3, 59, 67, 75, 84–86, 89, 94, 145–147, 150–151, 160–162, 166, 168–171, 173–174, 187, 193–199, 202, 214, 230

communion xiii, 44–45
consciousness 21–22, 26n7, 28, 30, 35, 41n2, 50, 57, 67–68, 70–71, 73, 134–136, 167, 169, 233, 235–236; *see also* states
constructivism xv, 7, 20, 32, 36n14, 157, 225; different types 213n6, 225
content free 13, 15, 67–68, 156, 218n8, 219

Davanloo, H. 31–32, 65, 76n4, 116n2, 128–129, 133, 158n5, 166–168, 169, 172, 174–179
defenses xiv, xxiii, 14, 31, 60, 83, 88, 90, 127–128, 133, 146, 158–160, 162, 171–173, 175–180, 196–197
developmental dynamics xiv, xxii, 10, 25–29, 32–37, 39–43, 73, 93–95, 99, 119, 145, 155, 159, 161, 165–169, 181–182, 211, 226–227; general principles of 44–45, integral principles of 46–51; and the environment 54–56; in anxiety disorders 101–104; *see also* self; *see also* ego development; *see also* stages; *see also* spectrum of development; *see also* states
dialectics xiii, xv, 9–11, 16, 24, 26, 32, 34, 40, 45, 56, 71, 153n7, 158n5, 160, 211, 220, 226
discharge patterns of anxiety *see* anxiety
diversity xi, xiv, xix, xx, 9, 13–14, 17, 23, 36, 39, 42, 44, 52, 57, 67, 69, 70, 82, 110, 114–115, 117–118, 132, 156, 163, 186, 188, 217, 224
dynamics of stage models 70

ego development xxii, 26, 28–29, 40–41, 51–52, 54, 58, 64, 102
eight zones xxiv, 47, 141, 221–222, 226, 234
emergence xxi, 3, 9, 26, 48, 58, 69, 71–72, 137, 183, 224, 230
Emotion Focused Therapy 36 *see also* Greenberg, L.
emotion regulation skills 135, 162, 166–167, 173n19, 174–175
emotion xv, 14, 28, 32–34, 36, 40, 47, 53, 65, 71, 77, 80–82, 87, 91, 95–97, 116n2, 117–121, 123, 125, 128, 133, 136, 146, 151–152, 158–160, 166, 168–170, 196–197, 199–201, 212, 214n7, 229–230, 236; importance of 170–173; working with emotions 173–180
empirically supported treatments (ESTs) xii, 10, 36, 129, 184–185, 188, 210, 214–215, 221

epigenetics 98, 99n21
epistemological issues *see* methodological issues
etiology of anxiety disorders: attachment theory xxiii, 86–88, 165, 179–180, 196; behaviorism 3–4, 13, 36, 76, 83–84, 221; cognitive views 84–86; developmental dynamics 101–104; evolutionary and genetic views 76–79; existential views 90–94; family and social systems 95–101; neuroscience 79–83; physiology 79; psychodynamic views 87–90; Wolfe's integrative view 94–95
evidence-based practice xvi, 132, 143, 182, 185
evolutionary views xxii, 71, 76, 76n5, 78–79, 99n22, 170–171
existential views xix, xixn1, 20, 26, 31, 41n3, 56, 59–60, 90–94, 100–101, 148, 156, 162, 181, 197–198
explicit knowledge 165–166, 169

flatland 110, 127, 129
Fosha, D. xxii, 30–32, 36, 41, 61–62, 65–66, 74, 76n4, 86, 88, 105, 112, 158, 165–168, 170–173, 175, 177, 179–180, 200–201
four quadrants *see* quadrants
Frederickson, J. 31–32, 65, 112, 128n11, 129, 158, 160, 166–168, 172, 173n18, 175, 177–179
Freud, S. 22, 74, 90, 168, 173n18, 174, 196–197, 217, 221

Greenberg, L. 30, 32, 36, 65, 88, 156, 165–168, 170–174, 193, 200, 215, 217

Henriques, G. xi, xx, xxiv–xxv, 7–8, 10–12, 13n8, 36, 170, 225–226
heterarchy 211n3
hierarchy 44, 51, 57, 67, 72, 189, 211, 224
holism (holistic) xiii, xx, xxiv, 9, 16–17, 19, 24, 27, 36, 44, 51, 56, 109, 132, 231
holons 21n2, 44–45, 72
human change processes *see* change processes
humanistic views xix, 12, 20, 31, 60, 110, 120, 125, 127, 156, 162

integral: as a sensibility 180–182; constructs in practice 182–183
Integral Intake xxiii, 109–111, 113–121, 125–130; research on 118–129

Index   259

integral methodological pluralism *see* methodological issues
Integral Psychotherapy in Practice (IPP) study 61, 63–64, 119–120, 130, 164–169, 181–182
integrally-informed xxi, 15, 127, 146, 155–157, 162–165, 180–184, 218, 229
integration: eclecticism 3–7, 119, 131–132, 164; common factors 4–6, 132, 143; theoretical integration 4, 6, 132, 164; assimilative integration 4, 6, 32; metatheoretical integration xii, xv–xvi, xx–xxi, 7, 9–10, 12–14, 17, 20–21, 31–32, 36, 114, 118, 155–156, 210, 218n8, 221, 229, 231
interventions xiii, xiv, xxii–xxiii, 3–6, 8–9, 11, 14–17, 19, 25, 30, 35–36, 39, 43, 64, 66, 73, 100, 106, 111–112, 114, 130–166, 175–176, 181–182, 184–185, 187–205, 215; by quadrant 162–164; role and meaning of 142–145; taxonomy of 131–140, 145–147
Intensive Short-Term Dynamic Psychotherapy 176–179
Intuition 30, 144, 164, 223

Kegan, R. 25, 27, 29, 34, 40, 44–46, 48, 51, 54–55, 67, 69–70, 95n18, 137, 143–144, 153–154, 157

levels xii–xiv, xxii, 8–12, 20, 25, 26n7, 27–31, 35, 40–45, 50–52, 56–64, 66, 68–70, 72, 102, 131, 133–142, 151–152, 156–157, 160, 162, 166, 173n19, 181–182, 211n3, 224–227; *see also* stages
lines xxii, 28, 31, 46, 57, 64, 67–68, 72–73, 119, 145–146, 157, 182, 221
Loevinger, J. xxii, 27–29, 40, 51–54, 64, 67, 70, 102, 223
logic of stage models 70, 72

Magnavita, J. xi, xx, xxiv–xxvi, 3, 7–11, 13–14, 19, 23–24, 29n9, 32, 109–110, 165, 169, 172n17, 181n25, 183, 220, 225–226, 228–229
Mahoney, M. xii, xxiii, xxv, 7, 9–13, 16–17, 25, 27–28, 32–33, 36n14, 39–41, 44, 46, 50, 54, 56, 60, 62, 67, 72, 79, 95n18, 111–113, 118n3, 132, 135, 137, 139–140, 142, 144–145, 147–148, 152, 154–155, 157–159, 161, 168–174, 192–193, 213n6, 214, 225, 229–230

meditation 27–28, 55, 58, 94, 134–135, 139, 142, 144, 146–152, 160–161, 199, 201, 223, 226, 233–236
methodological issues 209–211, 221; alternative methods 215–216; integral methodological pluralism 216–227; methodological pluralism 211–212; role of research questions and methods 213–215
mindfulness xv, 31, 134–135, 139, 147, 161–162, 175, 178n23, 195, 199, 205, 233, 236

neuroscience xix, xxi–xxii, xxiv, 7, 9–10, 19, 25, 27, 63n12, 75–76, 79–84, 89–90, 96, 102, 104–105, 166, 170, 183, 191, 212, 217, 219, 221, 223n14, 224, 229–230

parenting styles xxiii, 86, 97, 105
patient (use of term in contrast to "client") xixn1
principles *see* treatment principles; *see also* states and state work
procedural knowledge xxiii, 164–165, 168
psychotherapy integration *see* integration

quadrants xii–xiv, xxi–xxiv, 10–11, 20–25, 27–28, 31, 35, 37, 50, 62–64, 65n14, 73–76, 84, 86, 97, 115–116, 119–120, 122–124, 130–142, 146, 149–151, 155, 157, 161–165, 167–170, 181–182, 184, 188, 193, 201–204, 212, 217–222, 224–226, 228, 230–231, 233–234

research *see* methodological issues
resistance 33, 116n2, 133, 137, 145, 158, 163, 175–180
Rogers, C. 22, 30, 46, 60, 110, 144, 217

self 20, 22, 26–34, 41, 46–55, 58–59, 65, 70, 88–89, 92–95, 102, 105, 116, 121–122, 124n8, 133–138, 142, 146–148, 151, 153, 157–162, 166, 168–174, 187, 233, 235n5, 236; distal 47–48; proximate 47–48, 50–51
self-system *see* self
smooth muscle *see* anxiety
social justice 13, 111, 134, 138, 163
spectrum of development, pathology, and treatment 40, 58–60; critique of 60–64
spirit (as not necessarily religious) xiv, xxi, 27, 33, 151, 154, 232–236

spirituality xii, xiv, xix–xxi, 17, 19, 22, 27–28, 33, 58, 92–94, 99, 110–111, 114–115, 117–118, 123, 124n8, 134–139, 142, 149, 151–152, 161–162, 198–199, 212; authentic 93–94, 234–235, 235n5; legitimate 93–94, 198, 235n5; category error within integral culture 232–236

stage theories of development 27–29, 40, 44–45, 52–58, 61, 64, 67–70, 72–73

stages xiii, xxii, 25–30, 40–58, 61, 64, 66–73, 93–94, 102–103, 114, 145, 156, 182, 211n3, 223–224 *see also* levels

stage models *see* logic of stage models; *see* dynamics of stage models

state work 64–66; 145, 165, 167, 182

states: xv, xxii–xxiii, 8, 20, 26n7, 27–32, 40, 41n2, 49, 57, 61, 64–66, 73, 95, 119, 134, 135–136, 152, 155, 157, 164–170, 181–182, 185, 188, 226–227, 229–231; altered states of consciousness 30, 41n2, 115, 150, 166, 226, 235

striated muscle *see* anxiety

suprapersonal 26n7, 27, 41, 148; *see also* transpersonal

taxonomy of therapeutic interventions *see* interventions

technique, tyranny of 152–153

tetramesh 150

theory of psychotherapy 16n10, 19, 40, 58n7, 67, 109, 118

theory of the person 27, 40, 46, 58n7, 67

transformation 33, 36–37, 43, 58, 93–94, 156, 166, 168, 180, 236

translation 57–58, 156

transpersonal 41, 41n2, 94, 148–149; *see also* suprapersonal

trauma xxiii, 10–11, 31n12, 76n4, 81, 87–88, 96, 99, 103, 105, 126, 135, 142, 177, 188

treatment of anxiety disorders: behavioral 188–190; cognitive 193–195; existential 197–198; general goals and approaches 186–188; illustrative case 201–204; pharmacological 190–193; psychodynamic/attachment theory 196–197; spiritual 198–199; systemic 201; Wolfe's integrative approach 199–201;

treatment principles: 140–149, 155–183; balance of explicit and implicit knowledge 164–165; *see also* anxiety disorders, treatment of; *see also* treatment of anxiety disorders

treatments by quadrant: 134–138; upper-right 162–163; upper-left 162; lower-left 163; lower-right 163–164; *see also* treatment of anxiety disorders

triangle of conflict 128, 175–176, 178

triangle of persons 128, 175–176

types xiii, xxii, 11, 20, 28–31, 35–37, 40, 45, 54–55, 57–58, 61, 68, 72–73, 102, 113, 115–116, 119, 123, 126, 129, 145, 157, 182, 226–227

unification xi–xii, xiv–xvi, xx–xxii, 4, 7–20, 24, 36–37, 40, 154–157, 181, 183, 205, 209–210, 216, 218–220, 224–231

Unified Psychotherapy Project 9

Wachtel, P. 4, 6, 22, 23n4, 31–32, 36–37, 44, 46, 54, 61–63, 65, 72n18, 88–89, 112, 161n8, 164–165, 168–169, 187, 189, 196–197, 200–201, 203, 217

Wilber, K. xii, xx–xxiii, xxvi, 11, 15, 16n10, 19–21, 23, 25–29, 31, 35–37, 40–41, 44–51, 54, 56–61, 64, 66–68, 70–72, 79, 93–94, 110, 124n8, 129, 133, 145–147, 150–151, 165–170, 211n3, 214n7, 216, 218n8, 220n12, 221–223, 225–226, 232–236

Wolfe, B. xx, xxii–xxiii, xxvi, 4n4, 6–7, 16, 74, 76n4, 84, 87–89, 94–95, 187, 190, 193, 199–200, 203

Yalom, I. xxii, 30–31, 60, 74, 90–92, 94, 112, 135, 138–140, 142–144, 149, 153, 155, 158n4, 181, 197–198, 232

zones *see* eight zones